D0207705

WESTERN

PLACES,

AMERICAN

MYTHS

Wilbur S. Shepperson Series
in History and Humanities

WESTERN PLACES, AMERICAN MYTHS

How We Think About the West

GARY J. HAUSLADEN

Editor

University of Nevada Press

Reno & Las Vegas

Wilbur S. Shepperson Series in History and Humanities
Series Editor: Jerome E. Edwards

This book was funded in part by a grant from the Charles Redd Center
for Western Studies at Brigham Young University.

University of Nevada Press, Reno, Nevada 89557 USA
Copyright © 2003 by University of Nevada Press
All rights reserved
Manufactured in the United States of America

Design by Omega Clay

Library of Congress Cataloging-in-Publication Data
Western places, American myths : how we think about the West / Gary J.
Hausladen, editor.
   p.   cm.—(Wilbur S. Shepperson series in history and humanities)
Includes bibliographical references and index.
 isbn 0-87417-531-3 (hardcover : alk. paper)
   1. West (U.S.)—Historical geography. 2. Frontier and pioneer life—
West (U.S.) 3. West (U.S.)—Ethnic relations. 4. Ethnology—West (U.S.)
5. West (U.S.)—Description and travel. 6. Regionalism—West (U.S.)
I. Hausladen, Gary, 1946– II. Series. Wilbur S. Shepperson series in
history and humanities (Unnumbered)
F590.6 .w47 2003
978—dc21   2002015360

The paper used in this book meets the requirements of American
National Standard for Information Sciences—Permanence of Paper for
Printed Library Materials, ANSI Z39.48-1984. Binding materials were
selected for strength and durability.

First Printing

12 11 10 09 08 07 06 05 04 03   5 4 3 2 1

Winner of the Wilbur S. Shepperson Humanities Book Award for 2002
This book is the recipient of the Wilbur S. Shepperson Humanities Book
Award, which is given annually in his memory by the Nevada Humanities Committee and the University of Nevada Press. One of Nevada's
most distinguished historians, Wilbur S. Shepperson was a founding
member and long-time supporter of both organizations.

Dedicated to

Marilyn Elise,

Lynn, and

Linda Lou

Contents

Illustrations

Acknowledgments

The provocation for an anthology on the American West by a group
of geographers, launched with a little help from friends in art and history
(each of whom, of course, is a closet geographer), originated in the class-
rooms of the University of Nevada, Reno, during a speaker series on Western
geographies in the spring of 1999. The enthusiasm of contributors, col-
leagues, students, and the general public alike attested to an insatiable demand for things Western and confirmed that a spatial perspective would play
well to a diverse and attentive audience. Thanks to the hundreds of avid Westerners who participated in the series. And special thanks to Paul Starrs and
Bill Wyckoff, with whom I collaborated on putting the series together.
Throughout the project they have continued to offer sage advice, for which I
am deeply grateful.

The making of any book accrues a great number of debts. For an anthology, the list of debtees is multiplied severalfold. First and foremost, of course,
are the authors, all of whom met deadlines, responded expeditiously, and
produced useful and interesting insights into aspects of the American West.
Other than offering guidelines and providing continuity, I have tried to do as
little editing as possible as I saw these essays for the first time and realized
that the art of editing is to ask really good writers to contribute and then let
them do what they do best.

From the beginning we had the support and commitment of the University of Nevada Press and especially its director, Ron Latimer, who attended
several lectures in the series and was convinced of the appeal of the project
from the first evening when Bill Wyckoff presented his overview of historical
geographers and the American West. All the folks at the Press have worked
hard to facilitate the process and made my life as editor a great deal easier.

We were fortunate that the review process served as a positive influence in
the evolution of the book. Three anonymous outside reviewers offered con-

structive and detailed comments and suggestions, which have made the book all that much better. It certainly helped that these three were enthusiastic in their overall support for the project.

One of the great joys of exploring topics historical is working with archivists, especially those who are the keepers of our photographic history. For this anthology several authors acknowledge the valuable contributions made by these folks. Here mentioned are the archives they represent. Special thanks to the Academy of Motion Picture Arts and Sciences, the British Film Institute, the Colorado Historical Society, the Denver Public Library, the Los Angeles Public Library, the Montana Historical Society, the National Park Service Archive, and the Nevada Historical Society.

Of course, the person whose support mattered most is my wife, Marilyn Elise. She could be my most supportive cheerleader and my most constructive critic, often at the same time.

WESTERN

PLACES,

AMERICAN

MYTHS

Introduction

GARY J. HAUSLADEN

But not just the West of geography. It was also the West of the mind, of the spirit, a concept that for generations had reassured Americans of a future.
—ROBERT ATHEARN

Western Places, American Myths is a body of essays bound by setting, its ligaments the American West. How fitting it is that a geographical region, no matter how loosely or ambiguously defined and understood, ties together a range of essays from across disciplines; the regional tradition is a most resilient thread. The power and importance of the American West, ambiguous or not, cannot be overstated. Not just a real geographical region, the West is a mythic concept that repeatedly transcends simple historical-geographical description. For Americans, the West is part of our psyche, an essential part of who we are as a people.

Within the book's title, *Western Places, American Myths,* are three apparent dichotomies that actually distill the essence of many a Western study. The first is the West as a separate, exceptional region as opposed to the West as an inherent part of a national culture. A second juxtaposes the historical, or "real," West against the mythic West. Finally, there is the West as region versus the West as process. In practice, these are anything but entire dichotomies; rather, they constitute complementary parts of the same whole.

Exceptional versus National

However defined, there are identifiable traits that distinguish the Trans-Mississippi West from the eastern regions of the country. A quick survey of thematic maps reveals obvious differences. A topographic map shows vast basins, deserts, and major mountain ranges not found in the East; a rainfall map displays the greater aridity of the interior regions west of the 98th meridian; a population density map highlights the great distances between major urban centers; a federal lands map displays the large proportions of Western land under federal control; and the simplest kind of political map underscores the much larger sizes of Western states and counties compared to all but a handful of their distant eastern neighbors. Cartographic support abounds for identifying the American West as a separate and exceptional region.

Although regions are nearly sacred constructs for geographers, the viability of the region as a discrete unit of scholarly study has been belabored about the head and shoulders by Western historians in recent years. Because questions of race, ethnicity, gender, and class have proliferated in late-twentieth-century historical inquiry, it is at times argued that the concepts of "regional" or "sectional" division are in danger of obsolescence.[1] Although each term refers to a large geographical area that comprises some part of the greater union, "region" tends to elicit positive connotations, whereas "section" carries a negative connotation; if diverse regions provide the strength of a federation, competing sections aim for separation and autonomy from other sections. The origins of this distinction can be traced back to the Constitutional Convention and *The Federalist* papers that helped mold the U.S. federal republic in the late eighteenth century.[2]

> Regions unite . . . sections divide. Regions can both complement and compliment one another; sections can only compete. Regions have their roots in a warm and hearty connection between distinctive people and distinctive places; sections have their roots in political and economic struggles for dominance.[3]

The most debated regional boundaries are those of the West, famed as the site of a westward-rolling Euro-American migration throughout the continent's written history. About the West's latter-day borders there is even less agreement. To the rescue on a white horse rides Patricia Nelson Limerick, for whom the region "permitted an unexpected approach to the seemingly intractable divisions of history, a way to find, quite literally, common ground in seemingly detached and separate narratives."[4] Interestingly, geographers D. W. Meinig[5] and William Wyckoff and Lary Dilsaver[6] have also devoted time to suggesting and documenting the "West" as a setting of multiple regions. The 1996 argument of four noted historians in *All Over the Map*[7] is that regionalism has become increasingly important during a period of nationalization and globalization and that, as a result, the region maintains an important place in historical and geographical inquiry and scholarship.[8]

At the same time, however, that the West celebrates its individual and regional identity, it is woven intricately into the fabric of the U.S. political economy. Patterns of highways, railroads, and air routes attest to interconnectedness. Although certain elements of sectionalism are maintained, ours is clearly a national culture, dominated by trends pioneered in major cities north, south, east, and west. And some would argue that the context for understanding the American Western frontiering experience goes even beyond the national scale. Recent critiques attacking the exceptionalist nature of the frontiering experience offer a dependency, or a world systems, framework for examining the frontier experience as one part "of larger processes in the expansion and development of capitalism."[9] In fact, William Robbins writes that the conquest of the West and the development of the United States are understandable only within the context of the globalization of capital. Western expansion was not in isolation, as something exceptional or unique: "Success and failure in the American West, after all, were components of larger processes in the expansion and development of capitalism."[10] In *Creating Colorado,* William Wyckoff adds a geographer's perspective, contending that the expansion of the global economy is a necessary context for understanding the growth and development of Colorado and, by extension, of the entire American West.[11] As complement to the historians' emphasis on global patterns, Wyckoff highlights "the impacts of capitalism in varied regional settings."[12]

This is quite a departure from the classic interpretation of the Western frontiering experience as something exceptional, as a process that produced a unique American nation in the process. The identification of the West as the explainer of American development began over one hundred years ago with the Bureau of Census 1890 report on "the closing of the frontier" and the subsequent frontier thesis of Frederick Jackson Turner, which initiated a deepening scholarly fascination with the West and the region's impact, real or imagined, on national character. As historian Gerald Nash notes:

> [The frontiering experience] molded the distinctive character of Americans, shaping traits such as individualism, hard work, and self-reliance; it was the major determinant of the democratic character of their political institutions; and it provided American cultural life with unique characteristics. Such, in brief, was the message conveyed by Turner.[13]

At the same time that historian Turner was setting the agenda for the scholarly pursuit of Western history, showman Buffalo Bill Cody was popularizing, and profiting by, the unique role of the Western experience in his Wild West extravaganza (always he was careful not to refer to his re-creation of frontiering experiences as a "show"). While the Turner frontier thesis became dogma to a small but increasing number of academic scholars, Buffalo

Bill offered his images of conquering the American West to thousands of avid fans at each and every show for nearly four decades in both America and Europe. Although they differed in approach and audience, and although their interpretations of the frontiering experience were often contradictory, both Turner and Cody came to the same conclusion: The frontier was gone, and, in the process, pioneers had created a new and distinctive nation. The impact of these two men on scholarly research and popular culture, respectively, cannot be overestimated. In many ways, Buffalo Bill's impact may have been the more effective and longer lasting. A century later, Turner's thesis has been roundly discredited by new histories of the American West, which putatively promote the importance of ethnicity, gender, and class. Even the term *frontier* has come under considerable scrutiny by contemporary historians. Richard White's revisionist Western history text, *"It's Your Misfortune and None of My Own,"*[14] includes no index entry for *frontier* and pointedly never uses the word in over six hundred pages. The influence of Buffalo Bill, however, and, to a lesser extent, Frederick Jackson Turner, on the general public seems to have carried the day. In fact, there stands the ultimate test of survivability in the twenty-first century: Surfing the Web uncovers numerous Web sites devoted to Buffalo Bill and a plethora of others devoted to the Turner frontier thesis. Add to this mountain of evidence the voice of at least one scholar, Patricia Nelson Limerick, who reminds us of how little attention the American public invests in such scholarly debates:

> It is perfectly evident that the public has a very clear understanding of the word "frontier," and that understanding has no relation at all to the definitional struggling of contemporary historians.[15]

Nor is it just in the United States that the general public has any clear picture of the frontier and the importance of the frontiering experience on the national psyche. In Russian Siberia, the Australian outback, the Amazonian uplands, or the South African veldt are found comparative experiences—and a literature returning to Turner's heroic figures.[16] It is safe to say that the basic premise of the Turner thesis—that a frontier experience has a powerful influence over the society involved—has led to studies of frontiering experiences in different cultural contexts.

For us, the century-old debate over the salience of this thesis has produced ardent defenders, evangelical opponents, and a major revisionist approach to the whole history of the American West. How valid and useful the thesis was can be argued, but there is no arguing one pivotal and salient point: Conquering and taming the American West are an important part of our geographical history and an essential element in the view of ourselves as a nation. As D. W. Meinig reminds us:

> Americans never ceased to speak of the frontier and the American West never
> lost its romance . . . it became enshrouded in myth and symbol and was accorded a special importance in the development of the American nation and of
> the character of the American people.[17]

We may quibble about pettifogging academic details of the exceptional American West and its national reach, but we can't grasp the details because, ultimately, the big picture is right, and we want any ghost on the screen to go away.

Historical versus Mythic West

Whether Western regionalism is discussed for its production of a distinctive regional identity, or whether the issue is the frontiering experience in the West as it has contributed to the development of the U.S. political economy and culture, there is a second juxtaposition focused on the relationship between the mythic and the real West. The damning criticism of Turner and his followers is that they mythologized a Western experience that never unfolded as Turner had theorized. Most criticisms of Turner emphasize what he leaves out or at the very least marginalizes: Native Americans, Hispanic—later Mexican—settlers, women and children, Asians, blacks, land speculators, cities, and corporations. To be fair, Turner's acolytes, especially Ray Allen Billington,[18] so set Turner's arguments in stone that they seemed almost a cartoon.

Attacks launched on the exceptionalist nature of Western expansion reach to the heart of the "real" West and the mythic West debate. It can seem a moot point, not to diminish the importance of understanding what actually happened and how our Western experience actually unfolded. But where it comes down to the importance of the distinct Western narratives in the American story, the real and the mythic feed off each other, revealing a drama simple and complex, historic and modern. As Dydia DeLyser suggests:

> One cannot truly create so simple a dichotomy between the "real" or historic
> West and the mythic West. That would imply that the two can be readily separated, whereas, in fact, they have been in many ways mutually constitutive.[19]

No region is more associated with the concept of myth than is the American West. A brief glance at some of the more important books on the region speaks to this association—Henry Nash Smith's *Virgin Land: The American West as Symbol and Myth*, Robert Athearn's *The Mythic West in Twentieth-Cen-*

tury America, Chris Bruce's *Myth of the West,* and Richard Slotkin's *Gunfighter Nation: The Myth of the Frontier in Twentieth-Century America,* to name a few. Richard Slotkin perhaps best captures the spirit of the myth and its role in the evolution of American society in *Gunfighter Nation,* thought by many to be the quintessential explanation of the mythic West.

> The Myth of the Frontier is our oldest and most characteristic myth, expressed in a body of literature, folklore, ritual, historiography and polemics produced over a period of three centuries.[20]

Region versus Process

There is a final apparent dichotomy: the tension between the West as region and the West as process, an especially intriguing dichotomy for historians on a sound geographical footing and for geographers themselves. For the geographer, the concept of a region carries with it, as John Agnew and James Duncan suggest, the connotation of dynamic processes.[21] Geographers see regions as larger-scale places, comprised of three components: location, locale, and sense of place. Location is the spatial extent, the geographical area under consideration; locale is the settings in which social relations are constituted, where interactions between individuals and society and between society and the environment occur in continuing cycles; and sense of place suggests the structure of feelings that individuals have for a place or region based on their participation in social relations. This is not the venue to launch into a discourse on a geographical approach to the concept of region; suffice it to say, for the geographer, region is about process, a continuous reinvention and redefining of place,[22] akin in many ways to concepts first presented by D. W. Meinig in 1978 concerning "the continuous shaping of America."[23]

For many Western scholars in sister disciplines, however, we find the tension between region and process taking on two different aspects. For some, *region* refers simply to the geographical area under consideration (location), and *process* refers to the social interactions that take place within the region (locale). For others, the dichotomy between region and process addresses the need for two different kinds of historiography. The nineteenth-century West is about frontier history, whereas the twentieth-century West is about regional history. These more commonly accepted treatments of the dichotomy deserve a few words.

Most critiques of Frederick Jackson Turner, whether pro or con, put him firmly in the camp of seeing the West as process as much as place, and this process is specifically identified with the frontier experience (frontiering). Although such an interpretation is commonly accepted, it discredits the entire collection of Turner's scholarship. In his later writings Turner acknowledged that the history of the West in the twentieth century demanded a new kind of history, as Richard Etulain has characterized as the difference between a "to-the-West" and an "in-the-West" approach, or, put another way, in a frontier-ing versus a regional historiography.[24] Turner "viewed the frontier as both place and process,"[25] but proponents and opponents alike ensured that the process part of the formula would gain ascendancy and structure Western historiography well into the twentieth century.

It was not until the 1930s that Walter Prescott Webb explicitly examined the history of the West as both a region and as a process; however, at the same time that he broadened the horizons of Western historiography to include both region and process, he promulgated the myth of the West as free terri-tory to be had for the taking, as an assault on nature rather than on men. In the finest tradition of Frederick Jackson Turner's frontier thesis, Webb confirmed the conquest of the American West as the process that produced individualism and democracy and provided freedom from our European an-tecedents.[26] Later historians also took up the banner of a nineteenth–twen-tieth-century split, eventually leading to the New Western historians. William Cronon's approach viewed the frontier as process (nineteenth century), the West as region (twentieth century), and Patricia Limerick contended that the nineteenth century was about process, the twentieth century about place.[27]

But possibly, the key statement for geographers and historians alike was of-fered by D. W. Meinig in 1972, when he systematically defined the many Wests as both regions and processes. According to this approach, it is not that the nineteenth century is about the frontier, and the twentieth century is about the region. Rather, the evolution of the American West is a continuous process, and the delimitation of the region and the understanding of the varied compo-nents of the process change over time, especially as we have moved from a sin-gular perspective, based on the thesis of Frederick Jackson Turner, to multiple perspectives that take into account the complexity of processes at work on the frontier. It is not that the complexity emerges after 1890—it was always there; it is that our appreciation for the complexity emerges, especially after 1960.

Demarcating the West

For scholars across disciplines, the concept of the American West elicits im-ages that highlight the great diversity of this region over space and time. To refer to this region as "the West" seems ludicrous; it would be more correct to say that there are many "Wests of the imagination." The concept of the American West is firmly and forever planted, never mind that each one of us has a slightly different definition of what the region encompasses or how it is demarcated. Just how different these demarcations could be is underscored by Walter Nugent's survey of Western historians, journalists, and writers, who had a particularly difficult time agreeing upon the eastern boundary of the American West.[28] Interestingly, there is a region included in all of the surveys that Nugent identifies as "the unambiguous West" (Map 0.1).[29] William Wyckoff and Lary Dilsaver grappled with this problem in the "Introduction" to *The Mountainous West,* in which, after an exhaustive discussion of various delineations of the American West, they conclude that "the West is indeed an aggregate of distinctive subregions."[30] Three decades of demarcating the West by major scholars in geography and history only underscore the ambiguous boundaries of the American West.

D. W. Meinig first brought the concept of many Wests to the forefront of American geography in 1972.[31] His West consisted of the eleven Western states of Montana, Wyoming, Colorado, New Mexico, Idaho, Nevada, Utah, Arizona, Washington, Oregon, and California (Map 0.2). He was one of few who included the three Pacific Coast states in their entirety and who based the region on whole state units.[32] In 1986 *The Mythic West in Twentieth-Century America* presented us with "Robert Athearn's West," which included the western Dakotas, Nebraska, Kansas, Oklahoma, and Texas; all of Montana, Idaho, Wyoming, Nevada, Utah, Colorado, Arizona, and New Mexico (Map 0.3).[33] Completely left out were the three Pacific Coast states.

Most recently, 1997 brought additional Wests. First, *Many Wests,* edited by David Wrobel and Michael Steiner, uses state-based units as well, beginning with the Dakotas, Nebraska, Kansas, Oklahoma, and Texas, all states west of these, Alaska and Hawaii, as well as British Columbia and northern Mexico (Map 0.4).[34] And the New Western historians have given us the *Atlas of the New West,* in which the "New West" is defined as extreme western Texas, western Montana, Wyoming, Colorado, and New Mexico; all of Idaho, Nevada, Utah, and Arizona; and eastern Washington, Oregon, and California, thus excluding 70 percent of California and most of Oregon and Washington (Map 0.5)![35] Keep in mind that some authors, such as Frank and Deborah Popper, have argued that the West in the late twentieth century was expanding rapidly—eastward—as counties in the western Plains depopulated as agriculture there died off and ground went to conservation banks of returned grassland in federal hands.[36]

Difficult as the West is to define and demarcate, its importance is undiminished. One may argue that the reasons why the West maintains its hold

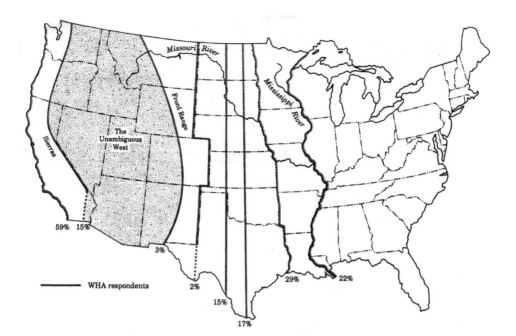

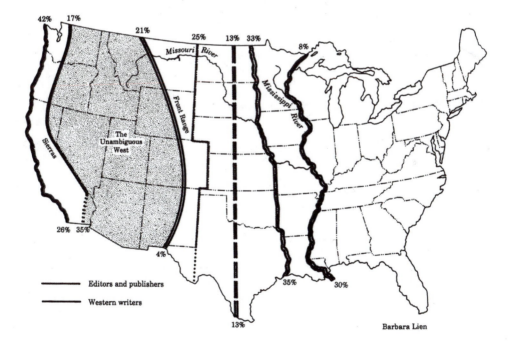

MAP 0.1. From Walter Nugent, "Where Is the American West? Report on a Survey," *Montana: The Magazine of Western History* 42 (summer 1992): 6. Courtesy Montana Historical Society.

A

B

MAP 0.2. From D. W. Meinig, "American Wests: Preface to a Geographical Introduction," *Annals of the Association of American Geographers* 62 (June 1972): 171. Courtesy Association of American Geographers.

on Americans has changed over the last century; originally the Western experience was seen as part of the process of nationalization; now it is cast more often as a response to the homogenizing forces of nationalization and globalization.

The Chapters

There are common themes that lend themselves well to the three parts of this book: continuity and change, enduring regional voices, and the West as visionary place. In Part 1, "Continuity and Change," four chapters address

MAP 0.3. From Robert Athearn, *The Mythic West in Twentieth-Century America* (Lawrence: University Press of Kansas, 1986): facing page 1. Courtesy University Press of Kansas.

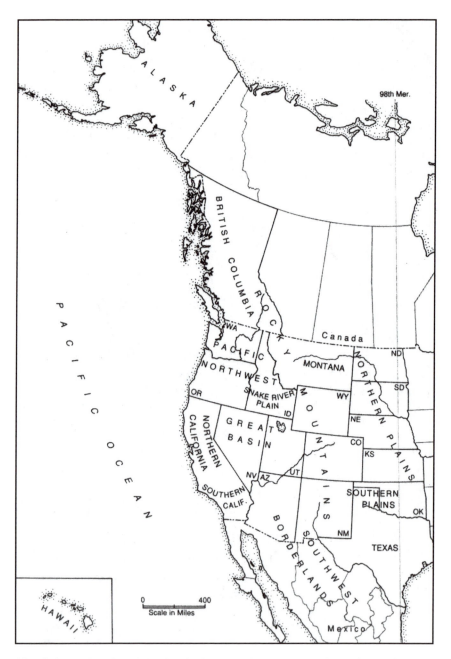

MAP 0.4. From David Wrobel and Michael Steiner, eds., *Many Wests: Place, Culture and Regional Identity* (Lawrence: University Press of Kansas, 1997): facing page 1. Courtesy University Press of Kansas.

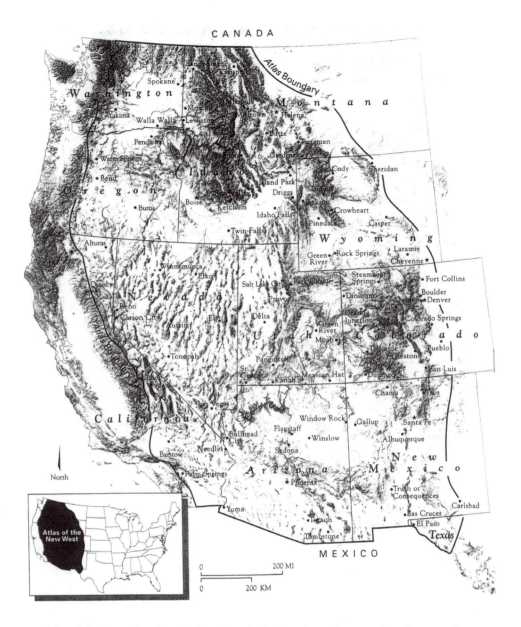

MAP 0.5. From *Atlas of the New West: Portrait of a Changing Region*, gen. ed. William E. Riebsame, director of cartography James J. Robb. Copyright 1997 by the Regents of the University of Colorado, a Body Corporate on behalf of the Center for the American West. Used by permission of W. W. Norton Co., Inc.

themes that are generic to the entire region. Bill Wyckoff begins the discussion with an overview chapter that examines the relationship between the American West as a region and historical geography as a field of study. The American West is not just where scholars have carried out historical and geographical research; more importantly, Western research themes laid the groundwork for many research themes for the entire discipline. As a bonus, the chapter provides a comprehensive and exhaustive bibliography of work on the American West done primarily by historical geographers. The next two chapters address signature and iconic elements in American Western diversity—the ranch and land tenure. Can anything be more Western than ranching? Paul Starrs presents ranching as much more than simply an economic activity for Westerners. The ranching landscape, in addition to being the most extensive regional use of private lands, is an "element of life" in the American West. Jack Wright then argues that land tenure has evolved in direct response to the geographic character of Western places. He focuses on land trusts and open space programs in comparative perspective to reveal how cultural differences in the region have profoundly affected the conservation landscape. The national park system was born in the West, and Lary Dilsaver discusses how the system has evolved as a key component of the region, even though national parks were originally selected on the basis of their "national significance."

In Part 2, "Enduring Regional Voices," the essays depart from the more traditional white Euro-American male interpretations of Western expansion to examine other perspectives, namely those of women, Mormons, Mexican Americans, and Native Americans. The grouping of these "voices" in a separate section is not intended to further marginalize approaches and peoples that were too long ignored; rather, it is intended to highlight the importance and necessity of these kinds of approaches. Richard Jackson reexamines the Mormon culture region, focusing on how it has changed in recent decades. Terry Haverluk reveals how continued Mexican immigration into the entire region, not just the five traditional southwestern states, has led to Hispanic culture becoming increasingly mainstream in the American West. Akim Reinhardt tackles the Native American perspective by examining different myths as they have sculpted Native American perceptions of place and space. Within the context of conquering the frontier, Karen Morin relates how women's travel journals in the late nineteenth century reveal much about overlapping imperialisms of Britain and the United States. Although these chapters deal specifically with what Patricia Limerick refers to as formerly "invisible voices," issues of ethnicity and gender are dealt with in a number of chapters in parts 1 and 3 as well. Bill Wyckoff, Jack Wright, Gary Hausladen, and Paul Starrs all focus on these kinds of issues in their chapters. In addition, Peter Goin's essay in photographs abounds in images related to Native American cultures.

Part 3, "The West as Visionary Place," takes a more humanistic approach to the West as culture region. Drawing from diverse media, various images are explored as they contribute to our understanding of how we think about the American West. Pauliina Raento reminds us that gambling, referred to in polite society as "gaming," is the logical, if not most romantic, extension of the Western experience. Essentially a frontier activity, gaming has become the legal basis for the economy of one Western state, Nevada, and the economic foundation of Las Vegas, the most mythic, if not mystical, of all American cities. There are many celebrations of spirit sites throughout the American West. Peter Goin provides a pictorial sharing the sense of wonder that these places provoke. Dydia DeLyser examines the role of Western ghost towns as a contemporary means for trying to recapture our Western past. How do these re-creational venues promulgate the stereotypical mythology of our Western heritage? Much like literature and film, ghost towns offer images of how it was and/or how we believe it should have been. Nowhere is the blending of the historic and the mythic more pronounced than in such settings. Gary Hausladen brings the collection to a close by arguing that in this century cinema has been a powerful medium for creating myths and projecting the American West to the rest of the country and the world. Key western movies are used to examine the role of setting in dealing with issues of settlement and utopianism, as well as empire and territorial expansion.

The twelve essays reflect the eclectic nature of Western scholarship, examining diverse topics, some historical, some contemporary, from diverse, sometimes conflicting perspectives, with widely divergent scope and voices. What ties them together, however, is not just the West as region but also the possibilities for the kinds of topics the West has to offer geographers, historians, and photographers, not to mention other physical and social scientists. They cry out for the compelling nature of this part of America, which has always held a special fascination for scholars and laypeople alike. These essays bring together geography, history, popular culture, and a comprehensive view of the region, and they bridge the humanities and social sciences. They argue for how Western places should be viewed.

These essays represent examples of what is being done and what needs to be done in dealing with this most enigmatic of places. We will never fully get to know the West in all its historical and geographical manifestations. We need, however, to never stop trying. In reality and in myth, the American West remains an important part of our history and culture. The more we discover about our Western past and present, the more we understand who we are as a people and a nation.

Notes

1. Patricia Nelson Limerick, "Region and Reason," in *All Over the Map: Rethinking American Regions,* eds. Edward Ayers, Patricia Nelson Limerick, Stephen Nissenbaum, and Peter Onuf (Baltimore: Johns Hopkins University Press, 1996), 84.

2. For on overview on the origins of sectionalism, see Peter Onuf, "Federalism, Republicanism, and the Origins of American Sectionalism," in *All Over the Map,* Ayers et al., 11–37.

3. Limerick, "Region and Reason," 83.

4. Ibid., 95.

5. D. W. Meinig, "American Wests: Preface to a Geographical Introduction," *Annals of the Association of American Geographers* 62 (June 1972): 159–184.

6. William Wyckoff and Lary Dilsaver, eds., *The Mountainous West: Explorations in Historical Geography* (Lincoln: University of Nebraska Press, 1995).

7. Edward Ayers, Patricia Nelson Limerick, Stephen Nissenbaum, and Peter Onuf, *All Over the Map: Rethinking American Regions* (Baltimore: Johns Hopkins University Press, 1996).

8. Additional sources on regionalism are discussed in Paul Starrs, "The Importance of Places, or, a Sense of Where You Are," *Spectrum* 67 (summer 1994): 5–17; and Paul Starrs, "Region, Reveries, and Reverence," *Yearbook of the Association of Pacific Coast Geographers* 61 (1999): 193–207.

9. William Robbins, *Colony and Empire: The Capitalist Transformation of the American West* (Lawrence: University Press of Kansas, 1994), 13–14.

10. Robbins, *Colony and Empire,* 14.

11. William Wyckoff, *Creating Colorado: The Making of a Western American Landscape, 1860–1940* (New Haven: Yale University Press, 1999), 3–4, 13–14.

12. Wyckoff, *Creating Colorado,* 13.

13. Gerald Nash, *Creating the West* (Albuquerque: University of New Mexico Press, 1991), 3.

14. Richard White, *"It's Your Misfortune and None of My Own": A New History of the American West* (Norman: University of Oklahoma Press, 1991).

15. Patricia Nelson Limerick, "The Adventures of the Frontier in the Twentieth Century," in *The Frontier in American Culture,* ed. James Grossman (Berkeley: University of California Press, 1994), 79.

16. Examples of comparative frontier studies include Fred Alexander, *Moving Frontiers: An American Theme and Its Application to Australian History* (Melbourne: Melbourne University Press, 1947); H. C. Allen, *Bush and Backwoods: A Comparison of the Frontier in Australia and*

the United States (East Lansing: Michigan State University Press, 1959); Mark Bassin, "Turner, Solov'ev, and the 'Frontier Hypothesis': The Nationalist Signification of Open Spaces," *Journal of Modern History* 65 (September 1993): 473–502; David Breen, "The Turner Thesis and the Canadian West: A Closer Look at the Ranching Frontier," in *Essays on Western History: In Honour of Lewis Gwynne Thomas,* ed. Lewis Thomas (Edmonton: University of Alberta Press, 1976), 147–156; A. L. Burt, "If Turner Had Looked at Canada, Australia and New Zealand When He Wrote about the West," in *The Frontier in Perspective,* eds. Walker Wyman and Clifton Kroeber (Madison: University of Wisconsin Press, 1957), 59–77; Anthony Christopher, "Southern Africa and the United States: A Comparison of Pastoral Frontiers," *Journal of the West* 20 (January 1981): 52–60; Michael Cross, ed., *The Frontier Thesis and the Canadas: The Debate on the Impact of the Canadian Environment* (Toronto: Copp Clark, 1970); Dietrich Gerhard, "The Frontier in Comparative Perspective," *Comparative Studies in Society and History* 1 (1959): 205–229; John Greenway, *The Last Frontier: A Study of Cultural Imperatives in the Last Frontiers of America and Australia* (Melbourne: Lothian Publishing, 1972); Cole Harris and Leonard Guelke, "Land and Society in Early Canada and South Africa," *Journal of Historical Geography* 3 (1977): 135–153; Gary Hausladen and William Wyckoff, eds., "Special Issue on Settling the Russian Frontier: With Comparisons to North America," *Soviet Geography* 30 (March 1989); Marvin Mikesell, "Comparative Studies in Frontier History," *Annals of the Association of American Geographers* 50 (March 1960): 62–74; David Miller and Jerome Steffen in *The Frontier: Comparative Studies* (Norman: University of Oklahoma Press, 1977); William Norton, "A Comparative Analysis of Frontier Settlement in the Cape Province, South Africa and Southern Ontario, Canada," *South African Geographer* 12 (1984): 43–55; William Savage and Stephen Thompson, eds., *The Frontier: Comparative Studies,* vol. 2 (Norman: University of Oklahoma Press, 1980); Jerome Steffen, *Comparative Frontiers: A Proposal for Studying the American West* (Norman: University of Oklahoma Press, 1980); Leonard Thompson and Howard Lamar, "The North American and Southern African Frontier," in *The Frontier in History: North America and Southern Africa Compared,* eds. Howard Lamar and Leonard Thompson (New Haven: Yale University Press, 1981), 14–40; and Walker Wyman and Clifton Kroeber, eds., *The Frontier in Perspective* (Madison: University of Wisconsin Press, 1957).

17. D. W. Meinig, *The Shaping of America: A Geographical Perspective on 500 Years of History: Transcontinental America, 1850–1915,* vol. 3 (New Haven: Yale University Press, 1998), 31.

18. See, for example, Ray Allen Billington, *America's Frontier Heritage* (Albuquerque: University of New Mexico Press, 1966); *Frederick Jackson Turner: Historian, Scholar, Teacher* (New York: Oxford University Press, 1973); and *Land of Savagery, Land of Promise: The European Image of the American Frontier* (New York: Norton, 1981).

19. Dydia DeLyser, "Authenticity on the Ground: Engaging the Past in a California Ghost Town," *Annals of the Association of American Geographers* 89 (December 1999): 609.

20. Richard Slotkin, *Gunfighter Nation: The Myth of the Frontier in Twentieth-Century America* (New York: Athenaeum, 1992), 10.

21. John Agnew and James Duncan, "Introduction," in *The Power of Place: Bringing Together Geographical and Sociological Imaginations,* eds. John Agnew and James Duncan (Boston: Unwin Hyman, 1989), 2.

22. In *Creating Colorado,* William Wyckoff offers a slightly different interpretation, using a framework that focuses on location, place, and landscape.

23. D. W. Meinig, "The Continuous Shaping of America: A Prospectus for Geographers and Historians," *American Historical Review* 83 (December 1978): 1186–1205.

24. Richard W. Etulain, "Prologue: the Twentieth-Century West," in *The Twentieth-Century West: Historical Interpretations,* eds. Gerald Nash and Richard Etulain (Albuquerque: University of New Mexico Press, 1989), 2–4.

25. Etulain, "Prologue," 2.

26. Walter Prescott Webb, *The Great Frontier* (Boston: Houghton Mifflin, 1951), 3–6.

27. For a geographical discussion of the approaches of the four architects of the New Western history, see Gerry Kearns, "The Virtuous Circle of Facts and Values in the New Western History," *Annals of the Association of American Geographers* 88 (September 1998): 377–409.

28. Walter Nugent, "Where Is the American West? Report on a Survey," *Montana: The Magazine of Western History* 42 (summer 1992): 2–23.

29. Nugent, "Where Is the American West?" 6.

30. Wyckoff and Dilsaver, eds., *The Mountainous West,* 5–7.

31. D. W. Meinig, "American Wests: Preface to a Geographical Introduction," *Annals of the AAG* (June 1972): 159–184.

32. Meinig, "American Wests," 171.

33. Robert Athearn, *The Mythic West in Twentieth-Century America* (Lawrence: University Press of Kansas, 1986), facing p. 1. The epigraph to this introduction is drawn from page 10 of Athearn's book.

34. David Wrobel and Michael Steiner, eds., *Many Wests: Place, Culture and Regional Identity* (Lawrence: University Press of Kansas, 1997), facing p. 1.

35. Center of the American West, *Atlas of the New West* (New York: Norton, 1997), 50.

36. Robert Lang, Deborah Popper, and Frank Popper, "Is There Still a Frontier? The 1890 Census and the Modern American West," *Journal of Rural Studies* 13 (October 1997): 377–386; and Lang, Popper, and Popper, "'Progress of the Nation': The Settlement History of the Enduring American Frontier," *Western Historical Quarterly* 26 (fall 1995): 289–307.

PART 1
CONTINUITY AND CHANGE

[The West] is a powerful symbol within the national mythology, but as soon as we attempt to connect symbol with substance, to assess the relationships between the West as a place in the imagination and the West as a piece of the American continent, we are confronted with great variation from place to place.

—D.W. MEINIG

1 | Understanding Western Places

The Historical Geographer's View

WILLIAM WYCKOFF

Historical geographers have long been wedded to the American West. Their wanderings have taken them to the Great Basin, Mormon country, the Southwest, varied California settings, and Montana's Big Sky. As historical geographers, they have probed how places have changed over time and how the people and environments of the West have intermingled in diverse ways. This essay explores why that marriage of discipline and locality is significant. First, we can see how the larger discipline of historical geography has been shaped by research in the American West. In other words, geographers working in the West have changed their larger academic field because of what they found in the region. Second, we can discover why the historical geographer's point of view is valuable in understanding the West as a distinctive American region. The questions they pose are essential, not only to a larger academic audience, but also to Westerners themselves.

The first part of this essay offers a quick sketch of the early courtship between the American West and the budding field of historical geography, including a sense of how those tentative initial encounters shaped the larger academic discipline. The second part of the essay outlines six themes within modern historical geography that provide valuable ways to comprehend the region. The themes remind us how the historical geographer's view, when applied to the West, allows us to see its varied localities in fresh and penetrating ways. Their work also suggests that these scholars were powerfully drawn to the West because the region offered a special sense of place and an evolving landscape that was as attractive as it was enigmatic.

Initial Encounters

Historical geography's early academic roots were not in the West. Scholars who have searched for the birth of the profession point to the first decade of the twentieth century and to academic efforts by geographers in the East.[1] In 1903 two important books appeared that assessed America's larger historical evolution in the context of its varied environmental settings. Indeed, both Ellen Churchill Semple's *American History and Its Geographic Conditions* and Albert Perry Brigham's *Geographic Influences in American History* offer a strong dose of environmental determinism in their historical geographical treatments of national evolution.[2] Neither author puts a great deal of emphasis upon the West, other than to argue how its climate and resources determined patterns of economic development and cultural temperament within the region.

As the field matured, however, three pioneering geographers came upon the scene and were destined to change things. Their fascination with the West initiated an ongoing conversation between historical geographers and that larger American region. Between 1925 and 1935, the three protagonists, none native to the region, were Edmund Gilbert, Ralph Brown, and Isaiah Bowman. These men honed the tools of modern historical geography in the West, exploring the region in detail, either through the archive or in the field. Their efforts initially wed place and profession in a way that set the stage for later twentieth-century research. Each in his own way, these three academic pioneers suggested how the West could be freshly understood from the historical geographer's view.

In far-off Great Britain, history and then geography student Edmund Gilbert was intrigued by the West.[3] His interests focused on the early exploration and mapping of the region as well as on its distinctive regional character. By the late 1920s, Gilbert landed a position as Lecturer in Human Geography at Reading University and succeeded in publishing several pieces of research on the American West. Gilbert's shorter publications, based primarily on explorer accounts and maps of the region, included work on pioneer trails and animal life.[4] His primary contribution came in 1933 with a book entitled *The Exploration of Western America, 1800–1850: An Historical Geography.*[5] Although still tinged with some of the environmental determinism of Semple and Brigham, Gilbert also displayed a detailed knowledge of primary documents. In particular, the book's final chapter, "The Representation of Western America on Maps," demonstrates an early and budding interest in how earlier explorers and settlers perceived the environment and geography of the region.

Whereas Gilbert's later career focused more on the British Isles, his larger interests in regional geography and in reconstructing changing place perceptions over time were clearly forged in his early archival forays into the West.

While Gilbert was pondering Western maps from distant Britain, young Ralph Brown was leaving the Midwest headed for Colorado.[6] Brown received his doctorate in geography from the University of Wisconsin in 1925 and then took a teaching position at the University of Colorado. Brown soon became immersed in his Western surroundings. He traveled widely in the region and published several articles on Colorado's human geography, as well as additional work on New Mexico and Montana.[7] Brown's work included important historical dimensions, and it also displayed his willingness to combine the rewards of field reconnaissance with thorough archival work. His article on Monte Vista, Colorado, for example, offered a style of settlement geography combining historical narrative, land use maps, and photographs of cultural landscapes.[8] By bringing his expertise in historical research methods to the study of past geographies, Brown pointed the way not only for his own career but also for the new subfield of historical geography.

Brown left Colorado for Minnesota in 1929. Indeed, much of his later work was reoriented to eastern North America. Still, his enduring continental study, *Historical Geography of the United States,* revealed interpretations of the West that extensively utilized government documents and dozens of primary resources.[9] From the National Archives to the Henry E. Huntington Research Library in California, Brown reconstructed the exploration, mapping, and settlement of the West. His interests centered on topics such as transportation, economic development, and environmental perception. He included maps of the region, many historical illustrations, and a comprehensive coverage that still reads well over a half-century later. The book's meticulous coverage of the West's varied subregions demonstrates that Brown continued to be drawn to the region long after he left Colorado.

Isaiah Bowman's Western ramblings were also significant. Educated at Harvard, Bowman ventured to South America, where he participated in several pioneering expeditions in the Andes.[10] By the mid-1920s, however, Bowman's geographical interests shifted to the more global challenges of pioneer settlement in marginal lands. *The Pioneer Fringe,* published by the American Geographical Society in 1931, was a broadly comparative assessment of frontier settings that ranged from North America and Australia to Mongolia and Siberia.[11] Bowman made an extensive trip to the American West in 1930 as part of his ambitious research efforts. His detailed field-oriented descriptions of eastern Oregon and central Montana appeared in the 1931 volume. He included reconstructions of settlement history, land use, and economic evolution, and he explicitly compared the "pioneer" conditions in these Western regions to similar settings elsewhere in the world.

Bowman's seminal article in the *Geographical Review* on the "Jordan Country" of central Montana also appeared in 1931.[12] The article focused on the persisting frontier conditions in one of the most sparsely settled parts of Montana (Figure 1.1). It proved to be a meticulous and enduring case study of settlement geography in the marginal West, an approach revisited explicitly later by John Alwin and more generally echoed in the work of historical geographers such as Robert Sauder and Marshall Bowen.[13] Bowman's strong field orientation, his attention to the evolving cultural landscape, and his focus on comparative aspects of frontier settlement all contributed to the development of later work in historical geography.

Berkeley and Beyond

Historical geography in the West also flowered from native roots. Berkeley's new geography department in California established traditions in cultural and historical studies that benefited greatly from the university's location within the West. Indeed, the region proved to be fertile ground for many

FIG. 1.1. Sparsely settled eastern Montana attracted the interest of geographer Isaiah Bowman as he searched the West for marginal agricultural landscapes in the 1930s. Courtesy Montana Historical Society, Helena, Montana.

Berkeley scholars, and their fieldwork and case studies shaped the larger evolution of academic geography. Carl Sauer, a midwesterner by birth, came to Berkeley in the early 1920s.[14] Although much of his own research centered on Latin America and eastern North America, Sauer inspired a generation of cultural and historical geography students who often focused on the American West. Sauer Ph.D.'s included Joseph Spencer, who wandered southern Utah's Mormon country as he assembled his dissertation on the region's historical settlement geography.[15] Leslie Hewes also grounded his work in the West, concentrating on the evolution of the agricultural economy of the central Great Plains.[16] Jan Broek, although only a visitor from Europe, also profited from his Berkeley connections as he explored the changing landscapes of California's Santa Clara Valley.[17] Perhaps most importantly, James Parsons graduated with a Berkeley Ph.D. in 1948, contributed numerous pieces of research on California and the West, and remained in the region to further define the Berkeley tradition in cultural and historical geography.[18] Each of these students reflected Sauer's passion for interpreting the past through human-environment interactions and through penetrating, eclectic reconstructions of the cultural landscape.

Indeed, one Berkeley-inspired milestone reflecting these inclinations was the 1959 publication of a special issue of the *Annals of the Association of American Geographers* (AAG) that focused on southern California's historical geography and evolving cultural landscape.[19] The issue was edited by William L. Thomas and shaped with the help of Parsons. It reflected the same strong Berkeley orientation evident in *Man's Role in Changing the Face of the Earth*, also edited by Thomas and published in 1956. The papers appearing in the *Annals* were originally presented at a national AAG conference in Santa Monica (1958) and were designed to be regional case studies that explored some of the broad, globally defined human-environment themes addressed in the earlier volume. In typical Berkeley fashion, the California issue featured a sweeping overview of the region's changing cultural landscape, from prehistoric times to the mid-twentieth century. Major contributors included Berkeley notables such as George Carter, Homer Aschmann, Hallock Raup, and Edward Price.

Meanwhile, the Berkeley links produced more creative offspring in the field, notably from a group of "third generation" scholars who focused considerable talent and energy upon the West. In particular, Andrew Clark and James Parsons, both Sauer students, became dominant academic figures in their own right and trained their own collections of doctoral students. Clark, based at the University of Wisconsin after 1951, emphasized meticulous regional studies, a healthy skepticism of many conventional historical interpretations, mappable processes of geographical change through time, and a penchant for detailed archival work.[20] Clark's students shared such proclivities. James Gibson's study of Russians in the West, D. Aidan McQuillan's dissection of ethnic settlements on the Great Plains, and Cole Harris's powerful synthesis of settlement and colonization in British Columbia exemplify the ongoing connections between the Berkeley tradition and historical geography in the West.[21]

Several of Parsons' students also focused their energies on the West.[22] Unlike the Clark tradition, the Parsonian penchant for encountering the landscape and for assessing human-environment interrelationships remained a prominent predilection among his progeny. Echoing Parsons' own eclectic fascination for the evolution of the Western landscape, Paul Starrs has examined diverse topics, including the evolution of ranching in the West, agriculture in California (with Parsons), as well as the implications of recent movements of Californians into nearby Nevada and Utah (with John B. Wright).[23] John B. Wright, another Parsons student, has explored the West's diverse traditions of land preservation and development and pondered the historical and contemporary dimensions of varied environmental issues throughout the region.[24] Wright's narrative style, always personal and passionate, suggests his willingness to go beyond academic debates and to plunge into the important and very particular policy implications of many resource-related issues within the region. Bret Wallach reflects a similar interest in contemporary regional settings within the West but also places such assessments into their larger historical contexts.[25]

John Brinckerhoff Jackson, another scholar of the Western cultural landscape, also had close ties to the Berkeley tradition.[26] Although not an academic geographer, Jackson played a pivotal role in cultivating an appreciation of the American cultural landscape. His *Landscape* magazine, begun in 1951, featured many short pieces on the West and displayed a fresh, penetrating view of the region's vernacular landscape. Although centered on the contemporary visible scene, Jackson's forays into the landscape always contained a strong historical dimension that paralleled the bent of historical and cultural geographers, particularly those of the Berkeley tradition. Jackson's travels brought him to Berkeley in 1956, where he met Sauer and other Berkeley geographers. Thereafter, Jackson frequently participated in Berkeley seminars and offered his own course in landscape architecture. His later career featured continued close relations with many historical and cultural geographers as well as an ongoing fascination with the American West, particularly his beloved New Mexico.[27]

Meinig's Mark

D. W. Meinig, although not trained at Berkeley, added another presence to historical geography in the West after 1950. A native of the eastern Washington Palouse, Meinig had an affection for Western American geography that began with a childhood fascination with maps and travel.[28] College years took him to Georgetown University and to the University of Washington, where he received a doctorate in geography in 1954. During the 1950s, Meinig published various studies that focused on the West, including material on agricultural and transportation geography.[29] His penchant for comparative geographical research also made use of Western examples, and it suggested his early interest in global and continental processes of colonization and imperialism.[30]

Although Meinig taught at the University of Utah until 1959, he contributed his most important studies of the West after he left the region. While at Syracuse University, Meinig produced several important works on the historical geography of the West between 1965 and 1971. *The Great Columbia Plain: A Historical Geography, 1805–1910*, an outgrowth of his doctoral dissertation, appeared in 1968.[31] The detailed historical geography of his home region of eastern Washington displayed his intimate knowledge of that locality seasoned with an enthusiasm for the archives and a unique skill for narrating, in both words and maps, how places changed through time. Studies of Texas, the Southwest, and the Mormon culture region secured Meinig's reputation as the West's leading cultural and historical geographer of the period (Figure 1.2).[32] In particular, his "Core-Domain-Sphere" model of the Mormon presence in the West and of Texas influence in the Southwest became cited as a useful generic framework in understanding the evolution of culture regions elsewhere.[33]

Meinig's 1972 article, entitled "American Wests: Preface to a Geographical Interpretation," advertised his intent to write a book about the entire region.[34] Indeed, Meinig completed research across much of the West during the period in anticipation of producing a synthesis on the West. Although his plans for a Western book were later folded into an even more ambitious writing project, the shorter article advanced ideas that shaped the larger profession. First, Meinig argued that historical geographers needed to conceptualize the West as a series of distinctive societies and subregions and that assertions

Fɪɢ. 1.2. Central Utah's Mormon country has fascinated generations of historical geographers. This quiet scene in rural Piute County has been shaped by almost 150 years of Mormon settlement. Photo by author.

about the West's regional unity were sometimes more apparent than real. Second, Meinig offered a generic four-stage model that placed each one of these major regional societies (Mormon country, the Hispanic Southwest, southern California, and so forth) into a larger evolutionary context. His schematic view of changing patterns of circulation, population, culture, and political areas again exemplified his interest in taking the West's particular characteristics and placing them in a broader context.

Ultimately, Meinig's vision of historical geography transcended even the boundaries of his internally complex West. In his "American Wests" article, he tellingly suggests that "if this is indeed a useful generic model for the study of colonization and nation-building, the entire scheme could well be applied to the entire nation."[35] Meinig's perspective shifted soon thereafter, and, like Brown before him, he refocused his interests on the continental scale. In many ways, themes and topics planned for the Western book, particularly his emphasis on spatial systems, were folded into his *Shaping of America* series, beginning in 1986.[36] Indeed, portions of Meinig's earlier research on the

West reappear in the third volume of the series as he considers the nation's spatial expansion in the last half of the nineteenth century.[37] Just as importantly, his earlier Western historical geographies allowed him to hone his skills, build his thematic arsenal, and develop the methods and narrative style to explore the larger issues he faced in his later continental-scale work.

Six Themes

Since 1970, historical geographers have grown even more plentiful in the West. The larger subdiscipline also has grown, along with a flowering of parallel interests in fields such as Western American history and environmental studies. The remainder of this essay identifies six broad contemporary research themes within historical geography that remain intimately intertwined with the American West and shaped by ongoing research within the region. A sampling of recent work within the field suggests some of the ways in which the West can be better understood from the historical geographers' viewpoint and how historical geographers have produced a distinctive research agenda that complements the work of Western American historians.

Human-Land Relationships

Historical geographers continue to use the West to explore human-land relationships. The reasons are obvious. The West's extraordinary ecological diversity offers a rich laboratory to study human adaptations in varied localities and to assess how people have refashioned the region's natural environments. In addition, the post–1970 environmental movement increased interest in many resource-related issues within the West. Further, historical geographers have benefited from close intellectual ties with Western American historians. In the tradition of Walter Prescott Webb and James Malin, historical geographers have been intrigued with how Westerners coped with the many challenges of the West's fragile and marginal environments.[38] The budding perspective of environmental history has also built intellectual connections between historical geography and the work of historians such as Richard White, Donald Worster, Roderick Nash, and Dan Flores.[39]

A growing historical geography literature exemplifies the interest in human-land relationships across the West. The splendid *Atlas of the New West*, a joint effort by historians and geographers, highlights many historical and contemporary dimensions of life within the region.[40] John Hudson, David Wishart, Bradley Baltensperger, and Frank and Deborah Popper have assessed how diverse peoples have adjusted to the challenges of settling the Great Plains.[41] Similarly, Marshall Bowen, James Wescoat, Victor Konrad,

Jeanne Kay, Paul Starrs, and Robert Sauder have reconstructed patterns of human settlement in marginal mountain and valley settings across the interior West.[42] Elsewhere, Lary Dilsaver and William Preston have examined the changing human landscape of California; William Bowen and James Gibson have explored Oregon's agricultural frontiers, and James Shortridge has probed the challenges of farming in Alaska.[43] Close ties between the West's evolving biogeography and historical geography are also suggested in studies by Conrad Bahre, William Wyckoff and Katherine Hansen, Thomas Veblen and Diane Lorenz, and Thomas Vale.[44] Similarly, cultural agents of geomorphic change in the West are investigated by William Denevan, Yi-Fu Tuan, William Graf, and Randall Rohe.[45] In addition, the broader environmental impacts of Western extractive industries such as mining and lumbering have received increased attention from Rohe as well as from Richard Francaviglia and Michael Williams (Figure 1.3).[46]

FIG. 1.3. Central City, Colorado, illustrates the enduring theme of human-induced environmental change in the West. This view, taken during the 1860s, shows a mining town that is growing as rapidly as nearby slopes are being deforested. Courtesy Denver Public Library, Western History Collection.

Some historical geographers have focused upon the complex interrelationships between the Western environment, the history of settlement, and federal government management policies. Large portions of the region are directly controlled by the Bureau of Land Management, the U.S. Forest Service, the National Park Service, and other federal agencies. Historical geographers have assessed how these institutions have altered the West's environment and shaped the ongoing encounter of Westerners with their regional setting. For example, Richard Jackson has examined the evolving tensions between Western residents and federal management institutions in mountainous portions of the West.[47] Graf explores similar issues in his study of the origins of the Sagebrush Rebellion within the intermountain West.[48]

The special natural and human environments of Western national parks have attracted growing numbers of historical geographers. Thomas and Geraldine Vale have documented the pace and scope of landscape change within Yosemite National Park as well as revisited John Muir's assessments of the region.[49] Stanford Demars also uses Yosemite to explore the evolution of Western tourism.[50] Elsewhere in California, historical geographers have examined the complex land management stories of places such as Sequoia and Kings Canyon National Parks and Muir Woods National Monument.[51] In the Western interior, Barbara Morehouse has delved into the ecological and institutional evolution of Grand Canyon National Park.[52] To the north, Judith Meyer has looked at the enduring interplay of nature and culture in Yellowstone, and Dilsaver and Wyckoff have retraced the ongoing tensions between development and preservation in Glacier National Park.[53]

The Making of the Cultural Landscape

A more eclectic group of historical geographers continues to explore the broad cultural landscape theme within the West. Building on the Berkeley tradition and the influence of notables such as Sauer and Jackson, these historical geographers have produced a variety of topical and regional studies that focus on important attributes of the visual scene. Their studies suggest ways in which the region's diverse landscape signatures can tell us a great deal about the West's historical evolution and modern character. In addition, these studies have enlivened larger theoretical discussions within the discipline concerning the role of the landscape concept in the practice of historical geography.

Varied elements within the visual scene have been explored and suggest the possibilities of using the landscape theme as an important interpretive tool within the region (Figure 1.4). For example, a growing number of historical geographers have focused upon the architecture of the rural West's folk landscape, a visual legacy on the land that is fast disappearing in the early twenty-first century.[54] Their studies assess the varied ways in which the West's built fabric represents both traditional and innovative impulses within the region. In addition, Francaviglia has reconstructed elements of Western mining landscapes and used these elements to pose more general theoretical questions about how we should preserve the past.[55] More broadly, Martyn Bowden and Paul Starrs vividly display how Western values associated with cowboys and cattle grazing are intimately tied to elements of the region's ranching landscape.[56] The Vales's evocative reconnaissance of U.S. Highway 89 within the interior West is also a highly visual exploration of the cultural landscapes they encountered along the route.[57] In addition, the ordinary visible scenes they describe are used to make broader regional interpretations about the West's cultural, economic, and historical character. Works of regional historical geography have often employed a strong visual component, as well. Historical and modern photographs, for example, become integral components of regional historical geographies undertaken by Meinig in eastern Washington, Harris in British Columbia, and Wyckoff in Colorado.[58]

Environmental Perception and Place Images

Related to their interests in landscape, historical geographers also have been fascinated with how people have perceived and imagined the West as a place and region, and their work has increasingly intersected with Western American historians drawn to similar topics.[59] Indeed, the West is fertile ground for the study of how past peoples assessed their surroundings, and such work has contributed key conceptual frameworks and case studies to the larger literature on environmental perception. The region's environmental diversity, the variety of human responses to its setting, the accessibility of maps, explorers' accounts, and settlement narratives, and the special cultural values placed upon many Western landscapes have all contributed to the link between the West and the environmental perception theme. Well-developed, indeed extraordinary, traditions of boosterism and mythmaking within the West have also contributed to the interest in regional images (Figure 1.5). Indeed, many have followed in Gilbert's footsteps.

Various Western localities offer opportunities for studying changing environmental perceptions and place images. The vast, challenging, and often enigmatic environment of the Great Plains provides a setting for assessing environmental perception within that region (Figure 1.6). Studies by Martyn Bowden, Malcolm Lewis, John Allen, Brian Blouet, Merlin Lawson, and

Fɪɢ. 1.4. The cultural landscapes of the West can change overnight. This 1879 view of booming Leadville, Colorado, captures a glimpse of instant urbanization. In the distance, earlier pioneer cabins in the middle of bustling Harrison Avenue have yet to be removed. Courtesy Colorado Historical Society, #F3030.

Fɪɢ. 1.5. Mythmaking in the West has attracted historical geographers interested in the evolution of regional place images. Railroads and civic boosters created varied stereotypes of Western scenery and economic opportunities. These idealized landscapes are from the Southwest. Brochures from the author's collection.

James Shortridge, for example, examine changing perceptions of the Great Plains as seen through the eyes of earlier travelers, cartographers, settlers, and writers.[60] Historical geographers also peruse a similar array of sources in the mountain West.[61] Perceptions of varied parts of California have caught the attention of Paul Starrs, Robert Sauder, Kenneth Thompson, John Leighly, and James Vance, whereas John Allen focuses on early geographical images of the Pacific Northwest.[62] In addition, Allen's recently edited three-volume collection, *North American Exploration,* offers an extraordinary synthesis of the role of early mapmakers and explorers in shaping images of both the U.S. and Canadian West.[63] Valerie Fifer's study of Western tourism also explores how railroad companies and guidebook authors shape regional images of destinations such as Colorado and California.[64]

Western artists and writers have created distinctive place images, and some historical geographers have used their work to define the West's re-

FIG. 1.6. Environmental perceptions of the Great Plains continue to be shaped by the same sky, grass, and distance that have always defined the region's landscape. This sparsely settled ranching country is located in eastern Colorado south of La Junta. Photo by author.

gional identity. The rich possibilities of this line of research are suggested by Kevin Blake's exploration of novelist Zane Grey's regional imagery and by Allen's reconnaissance of landscape paintings of the Rocky Mountains.[65] Similarly, Ronald Rees has assessed how Canadian prairie landscape paintings reflected changing environmental images of the region, and Wyckoff and Shortridge have examined how novels and popular literature shaped regional images of the Great Plains.[66] Research by Dydia DeLyser on the ghost town of Bodie and by Francaviglia on the popularization of Western images suggests how settings in the West can be used to pose broader theoretical questions dealing with how the past is perceived, repackaged, and reconstructed in the present.[67]

Western historical geographers have also looked at place perceptions and imagery shaped by gender (Figure 1.7). In particular, women often experienced Western life and travel very differently than did men. Women typically found themselves in social and spatial settings different than those of their male counterparts.[68] In addition, elite women had perceptions of the West very different than those of poorer, less advantaged women. Paralleling the women's history movement in the West, a growing geographical literature has assessed these diverse, gender-related experiences by reconstructing female perception of the region and by placing these images in the context of the region's environmental and cultural diversity. For example, Vera Norwood and Janice Monk examine the varied experiences of women in the Southwest, whereas Karen Morin and Jeanne Kay Guelke explore the interplay between place and Mormon women in the West.[69] Morin also suggests that female travel narratives can offer valuable insights into how elite women embodied certain cultural characteristics of their time as they journeyed through the region.[70]

Cultural Diversity in the West

The West's cultural diversity—both yesterday and today—has increasingly taken center stage in recent interpretations of the region. The New Western historians correctly emphasize the region's unique mix of peoples who have shaped the West's history.[71] Native Americans, Hispanics, blacks, and varied Asian groups, for example, are being recognized for their own contributions to Western history as well as for their complex connections with varied Euro-American populations. These fresh, often dramatic cultural juxtapositions encountered within the West, the recency and friction of the contacts, and their often bold spatial expression upon regional, rural, and urban settings have all drawn historical geographers into the West, as well. The West offers

FIG. 1.7. Young women performed a myriad of duties on Western farms, and their life experiences often differed sharply from those of their male counterparts. These youthful shockers are wheat farming in southwest Montana's Gallatin Valley early in the twentieth century. Courtesy Montana Historical Society, Helena, Montana.

varied examples at different scales in which historical geographers have tested notions of assimilation, ethnic persistence, and culturally defined patterns of landscape evolution.

Not surprisingly, Native American experiences within the West have received increased attention from several historical geographers. Karl Butzer as well as Thomas Ross and Tyrel Moore have offered continental-scale assessments that reconstruct Native American geographies and ecological adaptations.[72] There are also local and regional syntheses of Native Americans in the West, detailing traditional settlement patterns as well as the consequences of European contact. For example, David Wishart has effectively pondered evolving Native American patterns on the Central Plains and how the arrival of Euro-Americans destroyed traditional lifeways within the region.[73] Stephen Jett, Martha Henderson, and Jerry McDonald have examined many elements of the Apache and Navajo settlement landscape in the Southwest; Elliot Mc-

Intire has offered additional perspective on the Hopi; and David Hornbeck and William Preston have reconstructed precontact Indian patterns within California.[74] Harris's analysis of Native American and Euro-American contacts within colonial British Columbia offers additional models for further study elsewhere in the American West.[75]

The tools of the historical geographer have also been utilized to explore the role of immigrant populations in the American West. Such assessments have focused upon mapping the evolution of ethnic settlements, reconstructing patterns of cultural change over time, and examining signatures of ethnicity on the landscape (Figure 1.8). Both Meinig and Hornbeck as well as Richard Nostrand and Alvar Carlson have studied enduring Hispanic cultural influences in the Southwest, including Hispanic impacts on the region's settlement system and cultural landscape.[76] Charles Gritzner has contributed additional work on the folk Hispanic landscape, whereas Daniel Arreola, James Curtis, and Brian Godfrey have focused on more urban expressions of Hispanic culture in the Southwest and California.[77] Terry Jordan also has offered an invaluable regional synthesis on the varied origins of the West's cattle ranching cultures.[78]

FIG. 1.8. Cultural diversity often reveals itself across the West, in both rural and urban settings. This quiet signature of Hispanic influence is found along the Pecos River, just outside of the village of Puerto de Luna, New Mexico. Photo by author.

Other settings of ethnicity in the West are also receiving increasing attention from historical geographers. European ethnic settlement on the Great Plains has been penetratingly assessed by Bradley Baltensperger, D. Aidan McQuillan, John Lehr, and Jeffrey Morski.[79] Rohe has examined the impact of immigrant Chinese miners on the West, and Susan Hardwick and Daniel Arreola have profiled local patterns of Chinese settlement in northern California.[80] The Mormons' unique cultural imprint within the intermountain West has generated its own historical geography literature. Mormon settlement, place perceptions, environmental impacts, and landscape signatures have been explored by varied Western historical geographers. Prominent contributors include Meinig, Kay, Francaviglia, and Jackson, as well as Lowell Bennion and Gary Peters.[81] Both the study of the Sacramento Valley by Susan Hardwick and Donald Holtgrieve and William Wyckoff's regional treatment of Colorado discuss how diverse ethnic groups shaped cultural geographies in those localities.[82] At the national level, Michael Conzen and James Allen and Eugene Turner have also offered invaluable syntheses on the geography of ethnicity in America.[83]

Changing Urban Geographies

Both Western American historians and historical geographers have been increasingly drawn to the region's cities. City planning historian John Reps has reconstructed many elements of the urban landscape in the American West, and his approach parallels that of many historical geographers with interests in historical cartography, urban planning, and the cultural landscape.[84] In addition, Western American historians Richard White, John Findlay, and Carl Abbott have offered syntheses of the West emphasizing the pivotal role played by cities in the evolution of the region's economy.[85] Other studies of Western American cities by nongeographers also suggest the links to geographical themes. Reyner Banham and Mike Davis have produced vivid analyses of the cultural landscapes of Los Angeles, whereas Kathleen Underwood, Mary Murphy, and Stephen Leonard and Thomas Noel offer other outstanding examples of Western urban studies focused upon many elements of social geography and community identity.[86]

Western American cities are also garnering growing attention among historical geographers themselves (Figure 1.9). These scholars bring varied methodologies and research interests to the topic. For example, Meinig's study of Spokane places that Western city in the larger regional context he introduced earlier in his academic career.[87] Gunther Barth and William Wyckoff link the evolution of Western cities to the larger structure of American capitalism.[88]

Fig. 1.9. Historical geographers are increasingly drawn to the cities of the West. This postcard view of busy Broadway in early-twentieth-century Los Angeles reveals a landscape that was destined to transform the very definition of the American urban experience. Postcard from the author's collection.

Elsewhere, geographers such as Arthur Krim, Barbara Rubin, Allen Scott, and Edward Soja offer fresh interpretations of ever-changing Los Angeles, whereas Elizabeth Burns, Brian Godfrey, Neil Shumsky, Larry Springer, and Terrence Young explore different dimensions of San Francisco's complex social and urban evolution.[89] Susan Hardwick, Dennis Dingemans, and Robin Datel have also examined the urban evolution and multiethnic character of Sacramento.[90] In the Southwest, Arreola and Curtis investigate the region's evolving urban landscape, strongly linking land use patterns and cultural geographies to the persisting ethnic signatures of the Borderlands.[91] Wyckoff's regional studies of Colorado contain extensive treatment of intraurban historical geography, and Larry Ford's broader work on American cities utilizes an abundance of useful examples from the American West.[92]

This growing literature suggests that Western American cities have their own urban story to tell and that it differs markedly from the story of cities of eastern North America. Western urban places often grew under very different historical circumstances than did cities in the East, and their evolving neighborhoods, land use patterns, and landscapes are quite distinctive from those of their eastern counterparts. Indeed, one can argue that over the past half-century Western cities have increasingly become a model for national urban trends. Historical geographers working in the urban West are thus contributing not only to our understanding of regional character but also to our larger appreciation for the evolution of the American city in the context of an increasingly globalized economy.

West as Periphery: Geographies of Colonialism

The role of the West as an economic and political periphery permeates much of the research in the New Western history, and it resonates with similar approaches in Western historical geography. New Western historians such as William Robbins, Patricia Nelson Limerick, Richard White, and Donald Worster suggest how American capitalism and geopolitical inequalities have manifested themselves across the West.[93] Building on older perspectives offered by Bernard De Voto, Walter Prescott Webb, and K. Ross Toole, these historians suggest that the West is a splendid setting to explore the unfolding consequences of economic and political imperialism.[94]

Historical geographers are well positioned to test the validity of such core-periphery relationships, evaluate how they play out in particular places on the Western landscape, and document how such flows of economic and political influence change through time among shifting global, national, and regional centers of power (Figure 1.10). How *has* the West functioned as a periphery, as a vast resource-rich hinterland on the colonial edge of continental and global networks of political power and economic influence? Meinig addressed these precise questions in his earlier model of the West's evolution, and the exploration continues as an even more explicit theme in his recent assessment of the West's varied subregions in his multivolume *Shaping of America* series.[95]

As Robbins and Worster argue, the forces of capitalism have played out differently around the West.[96] Many areas remain on the economic margin, some localities temporarily benefit from readily harvested natural resources,

FIG. 1.10. The smelter stack above Anaconda, Montana, symbolized the formative, sometimes coercive power of corporate America in creating the West. This 1923 view illustrates how the Industrial Age transformed lives and landscapes across much of the peripheral West. Courtesy Montana Historical Society, Helena, Montana.

FIG. 1.11. Stable Western communities are few and far between. Historical geographers are trained to explore what values and institutions have held communities together and torn others apart. This is the Manville Community Church in eastern Wyoming. Photo by author.

and other places, particularly the West's growing cities, successfully compete in an increasingly globally oriented, amenity-driven economy. A number of examples suggest that historical geographers are well equipped to assess the geographical details of that story in varied Western settings. Barth's description of Denver and San Francisco as "instant cities" reminds us of both the dynamism and shortcomings of urban capitalism within the West.[97] Vance has also demonstrated the importance of the railroad in shaping the evolution of capitalism in the West, whereas Cathy Kindquist has explored the role of Rocky Mountain road-building in transforming the culture and economy of the mining camp.[98] Within the Pacific Northwest, Gibson has assessed European and American commercial trade networks, and these studies nicely illustrate the early imposition of capitalism into the region.[99] Also at the regional scale, Harris and Wyckoff directly examine the diverse impacts of capitalism on British Columbia and Colorado, respectively.[100] In agrarian California, Don Mitchell also demonstrates how economic inequalities did not prevent laborers from shaping the social geography of the Golden State in enduring ways.[101]

FIG. 1.12. Always an unfinished landscape, the West remains a region very much in formation. This 1970s view shows suburban Denver in the making along Interstate 25, south of downtown. Courtesy Colorado Historical Society, Colorado Highway Department boxed collection, #F33995.

Historical Geographers and the West

Sprouting from its early twentieth-century roots, the field of historical geography has blossomed within the West, particularly over the past forty years. The sampling of themes in this essay suggests that the discipline is well positioned to illuminate the West in refreshing and insightful ways. The ability of the historical geographer to wed environment and place as well as to link locality, region, and nation with the global setting allows for an exploration of many topics that should be of great interest to both academics and Westerners themselves. The West's regional complexity and the rapidity of its economic and cultural evolution have also made it a fascinating laboratory to assess more general models and methodologies within historical geography. Clearly, it has been a productive, increasingly eclectic marriage of discipline and locality.

Still, there is a great deal that remains undone. Historical geographers, for example, have never studied large portions of the Western interior and produced definitive regional assessments. The regional impacts of capitalism, urbanization, the information revolution, and globalization in the West have only begun to be assembled. Much more work also can be done on the West's vast public lands and how their evolution has been molded by a very different set of variables than those molding the Midwest and East. The accelerating changes of the twentieth-century West also remain only thinly probed by historical geographers. How have its environmental and cultural geographies been altered, and what values and institutions have held communities together (Figure 1.11)? Simply put, Western historical geographers still have many stories to tell about how Western places have changed through time. Indeed, one of the West's special fascinations is that it remains a region still very much in the making (Figure 1.12). To paraphrase the Western writer Wallace Stegner, we have yet to produce a body of scholarship to match the scenery, to somehow capture the face of Western landscapes at once ephemeral and everlasting, to record and comprehend human signatures only recently etched upon a vast and fragile land. That is a tall order for historical geographers, but in the end, it remains the primary reason why we still go west.

Notes

1. Michael Conzen, "The Historical Impulse in Geographical Writing about the United States 1850–1990," in *A Scholar's Guide to Geographical Writing on the American and Canadian Past,* eds. Michael Conzen, Thomas Rumney, and Graeme Wynn (Chicago: University of Chicago Press, 1993), 3–90.

2. Albert Perry Brigham, *Geographic Influences in American History* (Boston: Ginn, 1903); Ellen Churchill Semple, *American History and Its Geographic Conditions* (New York: Houghton Mifflin, 1903).

3. Guy Robinson and John Patten, "Edmund W. Gilbert and the Development of Historical Geography," *Journal of Historical Geography* 6 (1980): 409–419.

4. E. W. Gilbert, "South Pass: A Study in the Historical Geography of the United States," *Scottish Geographical Magazine* 45 (1929): 144–154; Gilbert, "Animal Life and the Exploration of Western America," *Scottish Geographical Magazine* 47 (1931): 19–28.

5. E. W. Gilbert, *The Exploration of Western America, 1800–1850: An Historical Geography* (New York: Cambridge University Press, 1933).

6. Stanley Dodge, "Ralph Hall Brown, 1898–1948," *Annals of the Association of American Geographers* 38 (1948): 305–309.

7. A sampling of Brown's Western American work includes Ralph Brown, "Trans-Montane Routes of Colorado," *Economic Geography* 7 (1931): 422–425; Ralph Brown, "Irrigation in a Dry-Farming Region: The Greenfields Division of the Sun River Project, Montana," *Geographical Review* 24 (1934): 596–604; Ralph Brown, "A Southwestern Oasis: The Roswell Region, New Mexico," *Geographical Review* 26 (1936): 610–619.

8. Ralph Brown, "Monte Vista: Sixty Years of a Colorado Community," *Geographical Review* 18 (1928): 567–578.

9. Ralph Brown, *Historical Geography of the United States* (New York: Harcourt, Brace, 1948).

10. Gladys Wrigley, "Isaiah Bowman," *Geographical Review* 41 (1951): 7–65.

11. Isaiah Bowman, *The Pioneer Fringe* (New York: American Geographical Society, 1931).

12. Isaiah Bowman, "Jordan Country," *Geographical Review* 21 (1931): 22–55.

13. John Alwin, "Jordan Country: A Golden Anniversary Look," *Annals of the Association of American Geographers* 71 (1981): 479–498; Robert Sauder, *The Lost Frontier: Water Diversion in the Growth and Destruction of Owens Valley Agriculture* (Tucson: University of Arizona Press, 1994); Marshall Bowen, "A Backward Step: From Irrigation to Dry Farming in the Nevada Desert," *Agricultural History* 63 (1989): 231–242; Marshall Bowen, *Utah People in the Nevada Desert* (Logan: Utah State University Press, 1994).

14. Conzen, "Historical Impulse in Geographical Writing," 25–33.

15. Joseph E. Spencer, "The Middle Virgin River Valley, Utah: A Study in Culture Growth and Change" (Ph.D. diss., University of California–Berkeley, 1936); Joseph Spencer, "Development of Agricultural Villages of Southern Utah," *Agricultural History* 14 (1940): 181–189.

16. Leslie Hewes, "Geography of the Cherokee Country of Oklahoma" (Ph.D. diss., University of California–Berkeley, 1940); Leslie Hewes, *The Suitcase Farming Frontier: A Study in the Historical Geography of the Central Great Plains* (Lincoln: University of Nebraska Press, 1973).

17. Jan Broek, *The Santa Clara Valley, California: A Study in Landscape Change* (Utrecht, Netherlands: A. Oosthek's Uitgevers-Mij, 1932).

18. James J. Parsons' Western American contributions include "The Uniqueness of California," *American Quarterly* 7 (1955): 45–55; "A Geographer Looks at the San Joaquin Valley," *Geographical Review* 76 (1986): 371–389; "Hillside Letters in the Western Landscape," *Landscape* 30, no. 1 (1988): 15–23; "Quartzsite, Arizona: A Woodstock for RV'ers," *Focus* 42, no. 3 (1992): 1–3. His larger geographical contributions are ably assessed in Marie Price and Paul F. Starrs, "In Memoriam: James J. Parsons," *Ubique* 17, no. 2 (October 1997): 8–10.

19. William L. Thomas Jr., ed., "Man, Time, and Space in Southern California," *Annals of the Association of American Geographers* 49, no. 3 (pt. 2) (1959).

20. Clark's career is reviewed in Conzen, "Historical Impulse in Geographical Writing," 56–66, and in D. W. Meinig, "Prologue: Andrew Hill Clark, Historical Geographer," in *European Settlement and Development in North America: Essays on Geographical Change in Honour and Memory of Andrew Hill Clark*, ed. James R. Gibson (Toronto: University of Toronto Press, 1978), 3–26.

21. James R. Gibson, *Imperial Russia in Frontier America* (New York: Oxford University Press, 1976); D. Aidan McQuillan, *Prevailing over Time: Ethnic Adjustments on the Kansas Prairies, 1875–1925* (Lincoln: University of Nebraska Press, 1990); R. Cole Harris, *The Resettlement of British Columbia: Essays on Colonialism and Geographical Change* (Vancouver: University of British Columbia Press, 1997).

22. Price and Starrs, "In Memoriam."

23. Paul F. Starrs, *Let the Cowboy Ride: Cattle Ranching in the American West* (Baltimore: Johns Hopkins University Press, 1998); Paul F. Starrs and James J. Parsons, "The San Joaquin Valley: Agricultural Cornucopia," *Focus* 38, no. 1 (1988): 7–11; Paul F. Starrs and John B. Wright, "Great Basin Growth and the Withering of California's Pacific Idyll," *Geographical Review* 85 (1995): 417–435.

24. John B. Wright, *Rocky Mountain Divide: Selling and Saving the West* (Austin: University of Texas Press, 1993); John B. Wright, *Montana Ghost Dance: Essays on Land and Life* (Austin: University of Texas Press, 1998).

25. Bret Wallach, "The West Side Oil Fields of California," *Geographical Review* 70 (1980): 50–59; Bret Wallach, "Sheep Ranching in Wyoming's Dry Corner," *Geographical Review* 71 (1981): 51–63; Bret Wallach, "The Telltale Southern Plains," in *Many Wests: Place, Culture, and Regional Identity*, eds. David Wrobel and Michael Steiner (Lawrence: University Press of Kansas, 1997), 141–155.

26. For perspective on J. B. Jackson and his impact upon geography, see D. W. Meinig, "Reading the Landscape: An Appreciation of W. G. Hoskins and J. B. Jackson," in *The Interpretation of Ordinary Landscapes: Geographical Essays*, ed. D. W. Meinig (New York: Oxford University Press, 1979), 195–244; Conzen, "Historical Impulse in Geographical Writing," 54–56; Paul Groth, "J. B. Jackson and Geography," *Geographical Review* 88 (1998): iii–vi; John Brinckerhoff Jackson and H. L. Horowitz, eds., *Landscape in Sight: Looking at America* (New Haven: Yale University Press, 1997).

27. For a sampling of Jackson's Western American work, see John Brinckerhoff Jackson, "High Plains Country: A Sketch of the Geography, Physical and Human, of Union County, New Mexico," *Landscape* 3, no. 3 (1954): 11–22; John Brinckerhoff Jackson, "The House in the Vernacular Landscape" in *The Making of the American Landscape,* ed. Michael Conzen (Boston: Unwin Hyman, 1990), 355–369; John Brinckerhoff Jackson, *A Sense of Place, a Sense of Time* (New Haven: Yale University Press, 1994), 11–67.

28. D. W. Meinig, "A Life of Learning," Charles Homer Haskins Lecture, American Council of Learned Societies (ACLS), *ACLS Occasional Paper* 19 (1992): 1–20.

29. For example, see D. W. Meinig, "Wheat Sacks out to Sea: The Early Export Trade from the Walla Walla Country," *Pacific Northwest Quarterly* 45 (1954): 13–18; D. W. Meinig, "The Growth of Agricultural Regions in the Far West, 1850–1910," *Journal of Geography* 54 (1955): 211–232; D. W. Meinig, "Isaac Stevens: Practical Geographer of the Pacific Northwest," *Geographical Review* 45 (1955): 542–558.

30. Examples of comparative work grew from his research experiences in Australia. See D. W. Meinig, "Colonization of Wheatlands: Some Australian and American Comparisons," *Australian Geographer* 7 (1959): 205–213; D. W. Meinig, "A Comparative Historical Geography of Two Railnets: Columbia Basin and South Australia," *Annals of the Association of American Geographers* 52 (1962): 394–413. Meinig's ongoing interests in processes of colonization and imperialism in the West can be traced in D. W. Meinig, "Strategies of Empire," *Culturefront: A Magazine of the Humanities* 2, no. 2 (summer 1993): 12–18; D. W. Meinig, "The Mormon Nation and the American Empire," Tanner Lecture, *Journal of Mormon History* 22 (1996): 33–51.

31. D. W. Meinig, *The Great Columbia Plain: A Historical Geography, 1805–1910* (Seattle: University of Washington Press, 1968).

32. D. W. Meinig, *Imperial Texas: An Interpretive Essay in Cultural Geography* (Austin: University of Texas Press, 1969); D. W. Meinig, *Southwest: Three Peoples in Geographical Change, 1600–1970* (New York: Oxford University Press, 1971); D. W. Meinig, "The Mormon Culture Region: Strategies and Patterns in the Geography of the American West, 1847–1964," *Annals of the Association of American Geographers* 55 (1965): 191–220.

33. Wilbur Zelinsky, *The Cultural Geography of the United States: A Revised Edition* (Englewood Cliffs, N.J.: Prentice Hall, 1992); Wilbur Zelinsky, "The Pennsylvania Town: An Overdue Geographical Account," *Geographical Review* 67 (1977): 127–147.

34. D. W. Meinig, "American Wests: Preface to a Geographical Interpretation," *Annals of the Association of American Geographers* 62 (1972): 159–184.

35. Ibid., 83.

36. D. W. Meinig, *The Shaping of America: A Geographical Perspective on 500 Years of History,* vol. 1, *Atlantic America, 1491–1800* (New Haven: Yale University Press, 1986); D. W. Meinig, *The Shaping of America: A Geographical Perspective on 500 Years of History,* vol. 2, *Continental America, 1800–1867* (New Haven: Yale University Press, 1993); D. W. Meinig, *The Shaping of America: A Geographical Perspective on 500 Years of History,* vol. 3, *Transcontinental America, 1850–1915* (New Haven: Yale University Press, 1998).

37. Meinig, *Transcontinental America*, 31–183.

38. Walter Prescott Webb, *The Great Plains* (Boston: Ginn, 1931); James Malin, *Winter Wheat in the Golden Belt of Kansas* (Lawrence: University Press of Kansas, 1944).

39. Richard White, *Land Use, Environment, and Social Change: The Shaping of Island County, Washington* (Seattle: University of Washington Press, 1980); Richard White, "American Environmental History: The Development of a New Historical Field," *Pacific Historical Review* 54 (1985): 297–335; Donald Worster, *Rivers of Empire: Water, Aridity, and the Growth of the American West* (New York: Oxford University Press, 1985); Donald Worster, "New West, True West: Interpreting the Region's History," *Western Historical Quarterly* 18 (1987): 141–156; Roderick Nash, *Wilderness and the American Mind* (New Haven: Yale University Press, 1982); Dan L. Flores, "Agriculture, Mountain Ecology, and the Land Ethic: Phases of the Environmental History of Utah," in *Working the Range: Essays on the History of Western Land Management and the Environment*, ed. John R. Wunder (Westport, Conn.: Greenwood Press, 1985), 157–186; Dan L. Flores, "The Rocky Mountain West: Fragile Space, Diverse Place," *Montana: Magazine of Western History* 45, no. 1 (winter 1995): 46–56; Dan L. Flores, "Place: An Argument for Bioregional History," *Environmental History Review* 18 (winter 1984): 1–18; Dan L. Flores, *Horizontal Yellow: Nature and History in the Near Southwest* (Albuquerque: University of New Mexico Press, 1999).

40. William E. Riebsame, ed., *Atlas of the New West: Portrait of a Changing Region* (New York: Norton, 1997).

41. John C. Hudson, *Plains Country Towns* (Minneapolis: University of Minnesota Press, 1985); John C. Hudson, "Settlement of the American Grassland," in *The Making of the American Landscape*, ed. Michael Conzen (Boston: Unwin Hyman, 1990), 169–185; John C. Hudson, "The Geographer's Great Plains," in *Occasional Publications in Geography, Kansas State University* (Manhattan: Department of Geography, Kansas State University, 1996); David J. Wishart, "Settling the Great Plains, 1850–1930," in *North America: The Historical Geography of a Changing Continent*, eds. Robert D. Mitchell and Paul A. Groves (Totowa, N.J.: Rowman and Littlefield, 1987), 255–278; Bradley H. Baltensperger, "Agricultural Adjustment to Great Plains Drought, 1870–1990," in *The Great Plains: Environment and Culture*, eds. Brian W. Blouet and Frederick C. Luebke (Lincoln: University of Nebraska Press, 1979), 43–60; Bradley H. Baltensperger, "Farm Consolidation in the Northern and Central States of the Great Plains," *Great Plains Quarterly* 7 (1987): 256–265; Deborah E. Popper and Frank J. Popper, "The Great Plains: From Dust to Dust," *Planning* 53 (December 1987): 12.

42. Marshall Bowen, "The Heritage of an Empty Land: Independence Valley, Nevada," *Journal of Cultural Geography* 6, no. 2 (1986): 67–79; Marshall Bowen, "A Backward Step"; Marshall Bowen, *Utah People*; Marshall Bowen, "Crops, Critters, and Calamity: The Failure of Dry Farming in Utah's Escalante Desert, 1913–1918," *Agricultural History* 73 (1999): 1–26; James L. Wescoat, "Challenging the Desert," in *The Making of the American Landscape*, ed. Michael Conzen (Boston: Unwin Hyman, 1990), 186–203; Victor Konrad, "Homesteading the Pryor Mountains of Montana," in *The Mountainous West: Explorations in Historical Geography*, eds. William Wyckoff and Lary M. Dilsaver (Lincoln: University of Nebraska Press, 1995), 194–223; Jeanne Kay, "Mormons and Mountains," in *The Mountainous West*, 368–395; Starrs, *Let the Cowboy Ride*; Sauder, *Lost Frontier*.

43. William L. Preston, *Vanishing Landscape: Land and Life in the Tulare Lake Basin* (Berkeley: University of California Press, 1981); Lary M. Dilsaver, "After the Gold Rush," *Geographical Review* 75 (1985): 1–18; William A. Bowen, *The Willamette Valley: Migration and Settlement on the Oregon Frontier* (Seattle: University of Washington Press, 1978); James R. Gibson, *Farming the Frontier: The Agricultural Opening of the Oregon Country, 1786–1846* (Vancouver: University of British Columbia Press, 1985); James R. Shortridge, "The Evaluation of the Agricultural Potential of Alaska, 1867–1897," *Pacific Northwest Quarterly* 68 (1977): 88–98; James R. Shortridge, "The Alaskan Agricultural Empire: An American Agrarian Vision, 1898–1929," *Pacific Northwest Quarterly* 69 (1978): 145–158.

44. Conrad J. Bahre, *A Legacy of Change: Historic Human Impact on Vegetation of the Arizona Borderlands* (Tucson: University of Arizona Press, 1991); William Wyckoff and Katherine Hansen, "Environmental Change in the Northern Rockies: Settlement and Livestock Grazing in Southwestern Montana, 1860–1995," in *Northwest Lands, Northwest Peoples: Readings in Environmental History*, eds. Dale Goble and Paul Hirt (Seattle: University of Washington Press, 1999), 336–361; Thomas T. Veblen and Diane C. Lorenz, *The Colorado Front Range: A Century of Ecological Change* (Salt Lake City: University of Utah Press, 1990); Thomas R. Vale, "Forest Changes in the Warner Mountains, California," *Annals of the Association of American Geographers* 67 (1977): 28–45; Thomas R. Vale, "Mountains and Moisture in the West," in *The Mountainous West: Explorations in Historical Geography*, eds. William Wyckoff and Lary M. Dilsaver (Lincoln: University of Nebraska Press, 1995), 141–166.

45. William M. Denevan, "Livestock Numbers in Nineteenth Century New Mexico and the Problem of Gullying in the Southwest," *Annals of the Association of American Geographers* 57 (1967): 691–703; Yi-Fu Tuan, "New Mexican Gullies: A Critical Review and Some Recent Observations," *Annals of the Association of American Geographers* 56 (1966): 573–597; William L. Graf, "Mining and Channel Response," *Annals of the Association of American Geographers* 69 (1979): 262–275; Randall E. Rohe, "Man as Geomorphic Agent: Hydraulic Mining in the American West," *Pacific Historian* 27 (1983): 5–16.

46. Randall E. Rohe, "Man and the Land: Mining's Impact in the Far West," *Arizona and the West* 28 (winter 1986): 299–338; Richard V. Francaviglia, *Hard Places: Reading the Landscape of America's Historic Mining Districts* (Iowa City: University of Iowa Press, 1991); Michael Williams, "The Last Lumber Frontier?" in *The Mountainous West: Explorations in Historical Geography*, eds. William Wyckoff and Lary M. Dilsaver (Lincoln: University of Nebraska Press, 1995), 224–250.

47. Richard H. Jackson, "Federal Lands in the Mountainous West," in *The Mountainous West: Explorations in Historical Geography*, eds. William Wyckoff and Lary M. Dilsaver (Lincoln: University of Nebraska Press, 1995), 253–278.

48. William L. Graf, *Wilderness Preservation and the Sagebrush Rebellions* (Savage, Md.: Rowman and Littlefield, 1990).

49. Thomas R. Vale and Geraldine R. Vale, *Time and the Tuolumne Landscape: Continuity and Change in the Yosemite High Country* (Salt Lake City: University of Utah Press, 1994); Thomas R. Vale and Geraldine R. Vale, *Walking with Muir across Yosemite* (Madison: University of Wisconsin Press, 1998).

50. Stanford E. Demars, *The Tourist in Yosemite: 1855–1985* (Salt Lake City: University of Utah Press, 1991).

51. Lary M. Dilsaver and William Tweed, *Challenge of the Big Trees: A Resource History of Sequoia and Kings Canyon National Parks* (Three Rivers, Calif.: Sequoia Natural History Association, 1990); Lary M. Dilsaver, "Resource Conflict in the High Sierra," in *The Mountainous West: Explorations in Historical Geography,* eds. William Wyckoff and Lary M. Dilsaver (Lincoln: University of Nebraska Press, 1995), 281–302; Lary M. Dilsaver, "Preservation Choices at Muir Woods," *Geographical Review* 84 (1994): 290–305.

52. Barbara J. Morehouse, *A Place Called Grand Canyon: Contested Geographies* (Tucson: University of Arizona Press, 1996).

53. Judith L. Meyer, *The Spirit of Yellowstone: The Cultural Evolution of a National Park* (Lanham, Md.: Rowman and Littlefield, 1996); Lary M. Dilsaver and William Wyckoff, "Agency Culture, Cumulative Causation and Development in Glacier National Park, Montana," *Journal of Historical Geography* 25 (1999): 75–92.

54. An excellent assessment of folk architecture in the mountain West is offered by Terry G. Jordan, Jon T. Kilpinen, and Charles F. Gritzner, *The Mountain West: Interpreting the Folk Landscape* (Baltimore: Johns Hopkins University Press, 1997). Additional case studies are offered by Victor Konrad, "Homesteading the Pryor Mountains"; Allen Noble, "Pioneer Settlement on the Plains: Sod Dugouts and Sod Houses," *Pioneer America Society Transactions* 4 (1981): 1–19; Randall E. Rohe, "The Geography and Material Culture of the Western Mining Town," *Material Culture* 16 (1984): 99–120.

55. Francaviglia, *Hard Places.*

56. Martyn J. Bowden, "Creating Cowboy Country," *Geographical Magazine* 52, no. 10 (1980): 693–701; Starrs, *Let the Cowboy Ride.*

57. Thomas R. Vale and Geraldine R. Vale, *Western Images, Western Landscapes: Travels along U.S. 89* (Tucson: University of Arizona Press, 1989).

58. Meinig, *Great Columbia Plain;* Cole Harris, *Resettlement of British Columbia;* William Wyckoff, *Creating Colorado: The Making of a Western American Landscape, 1860–1940* (New Haven: Yale University Press, 1999).

59. For examples of parallel works by western American historians, see Peter B. Hales, *William Henry Jackson and the Transformation of the American Landscape* (Philadelphia: Temple University Press, 1988); Anne Farrar Hyde, *An American Vision: Far Western Landscape and National Culture, 1820–1920* (New York: New York University Press, 1990); William H. Goetzmann, *Looking at the Land of Promise: Pioneer Images of the Pacific Northwest* (Pullman: Washington State University Press, 1988); Katherine G. Morrissey, *Mental Territories: Mapping the Inland Empire* (Ithaca, N.Y.: Cornell University Press, 1997); Nash, *Wilderness and the American Mind;* Carlos A. Schwantes, *So Incredibly Idaho! Seven Landscapes That Define the Gem State* (Moscow: University of Idaho Press, 1996); Henry Nash Smith, *Virgin Land: The American West as Symbol and Myth* (New York: Vintage Books, 1950).

60. A sampling of their work would include Martyn J. Bowden, "The Great American Desert in the American Mind: The Historiography of a Geographical Notion," in *Geographies*

of the Mind: Essays in Historical Geosophy in Honor of John Kirtland Wright, eds. David Lowenthal and Martyn J. Bowden (New York: Oxford University Press, 1976), 119–148; Mal-
com G. Lewis, "Regional Ideas and Reality in the Cis–Rocky Mountain West," *Transactions
of the Institute of British Geographers* 38 (1966): 135–150; Malcolm G. Lewis, "The Great
Plains Region and Its Image of Flatness," *Journal of the West* 6, no. 1 (1967): 11–26; John L.
Allen, "Patterns of Promise: Mapping the Plains and Prairies, 1800–1860," *Great Plains
Quarterly* 4 (1984): 5–28; John L. Allen, "The Garden-Desert Continuum: Competing Views
of the Great Plains in the Nineteenth Century," *Great Plains Quarterly* 5 (1985): 207–220;
Brian W. Blouet and Merlin P. Lawson, eds., *Images of the Plains: The Role of Human Nature
in Settlement* (Lincoln: University of Nebraska Press, 1975); James R. Shortridge, "The Expectations of Others: Struggles toward a Sense of Place in the Northern Plains," in *Many
Wests: Place, Culture, and Regional Identity,* eds. David Wrobel and Michael Steiner (Lawrence: University Press of Kansas, 1997), 114–135.

61. John L. Allen, *Passage through the Garden: Lewis and Clark and the Image of the Northwest*
(Urbana: University of Illinois Press, 1975); John L. Allen, "Maps and the Mountain Men:
The Cartography of the Rocky Mountain Fur Trade," in *The Mountainous West: Explorations
in Historical Geography,* eds. William Wyckoff and Lary M. Dilsaver (Lincoln: University of
Nebraska Press, 1995), 63–91; Richard H. Jackson, "Myth and Reality, Environmental Perception of the Mormons, 1840–1865: An Historical Geosophy" (Ph.D. diss., Clark University, 1970); Richard H. Jackson, "The Mormon Experience: The Plains as Sinai, the Great
Salt Lake as the Dead Sea, and the Great Basin as Desert-cum-Promised Land," *Journal of
Historical Geography* 18 (1992): 41–58; Jeanne Kay and Craig Brown, "Mormon Beliefs
about Land and Natural Resources, 1847–1877," *Journal of Historical Geography* 11 (1985):
253–267; Martin Mitchell, "Gentile Impressions of Salt Lake City, Utah, 1849–1870," *Geographical Review* 87 (1997): 334–352; Starrs, *Let the Cowboy Ride;* William Wyckoff and Lary
M. Dilsaver, "Promotional Imagery of Glacier National Park," *Geographical Review* 87
(1997): 1–26; William Wyckoff and Chantelle Nash, "Geographical Images of the American
West: The View from *Harper's Monthly,* 1850–1900," *Journal of the West* 33, no. 3 (July 1994):
10–21.

62. Examples of California image and perception studies include Kenneth Thompson,
"Negative Perceptions of Early California," *California Geographer* 18 (1978): 1–15; Kenneth
Thompson, "Insalubrious California: Perception and Reality," *Annals of the Association of
American Geographers* 59 (1969): 50–64; Paul F. Starrs, "The Navel of California and Other
Oranges: Images of California and the Orange Crate," *California Geographer* 28 (1988):
1–41; John B. Leighly, "John Muir's Image of the West," *Annals of the Association of Ameri-
can Geographers* 48 (1958): 309–318; James E. Vance Jr., "California and the Search for the
Ideal," *Annals of the Association of American Geographers* 62 (1972): 185–210; Robert A.
Sauder, "Sod Land versus Sagebrush: Early Land Appraisal and Pioneer Settlement in an
Arid Intermontane Frontier," *Journal of Historical Geography* 15 (1989): 402–419; John L.
Allen, "The Geographical Images of the American Northwest, 1673–1806: An Historical
Geography" (Ph.D. diss., Clark University, 1969).

63. John L. Allen, ed., *North American Exploration* (Lincoln: University of Nebraska Press,
1997). Individual titles are vol. 1, *A New World Disclosed;* vol. 2, *A Continent Defined;* and vol.
3, *A Continent Comprehended.*

64. Valerie J. Fifer, *American Progress* (Chester, Penn.: Globe Pequot Press, 1988).

65. Kevin Blake, "Zane Grey and Images of the American West," *Geographical Review* 85 (1995): 202–216; John L. Allen, "Horizons of the Sublime: The Invention of the Romantic West," *Journal of Historical Geography* 18 (1992): 27–40.

66. Ronald Rees, "Images of the Prairie: Landscape Painting and Perception in the Western Interior of Canada," *Canadian Geographer* 20 (1976): 259–278; William Wyckoff, "The Garden and the Desert in the Imaginative Literature of the Great Plains," *Proceedings of the Middle States Division, Association of American Geographers* 12 (1978): 94–97; Shortridge, "The Expectations of Others."

67. Dydia DeLyser, "Authenticity on the Ground: Engaging the Past in a California Ghost Town," *Annals of the Association of American Geographers* 99 (1999): 602–632; Richard Francaviglia, "Walt Disney's Frontierland as an Allegorical Map of the American West," *Western Historical Quarterly* 30 (1999): 155–182; Richard Francaviglia, David Narrett, and Bruce Narramore, eds., *Essays on the Changing Images of the Southwest* (College Station: Texas A & M University Press, 1994).

68. Jeanne Kay, "Landscapes of Women and Men: Rethinking the Regional Historical Geography of the United States," *Journal of Historical Geography* 17 (1991): 435–452.

69. Vera Norwood and Janice Monk, eds., *The Desert Is No Lady* (New Haven: Yale University Press, 1987); Karen M. Morin and Jeanne Kay Guelke, "Strategies of Representation, Relationship, and Resistance: British Women Travelers and Mormon Plural Wives, ca. 1870–1890," *Annals of the Association of American Geographers* 88 (1998): 436–462; Kay, "Mormons and Mountains."

70. Karen M. Morin, "Trains through the Plains: The Great Plains Landscapes of Victorian Women Travelers," *Great Plains Quarterly* 18 (1998): 235–256; Karen M. Morin, "Peak Practices: Englishwomen's 'Heroic' Adventures in the Nineteenth-Century American West," *Annals of the Association of American Geographers* 89 (1999): 489–514.

71. Patricia Nelson Limerick, *The Legacy of Conquest: The Unbroken Past of the American West* (New York: Norton, 1987); White, *New History.*

72. Karl Butzer, "The Indian Legacy in the American Landscape," in *The Making of the American Landscape,* ed. Michael Conzen (Boston: Unwin Hyman, 1990), 27–50; Thomas E. Ross and Tyrel G. Moore, eds., *A Cultural Geography of North American Indians* (Boulder, Colo.: Westview Press, 1987).

73. David J. Wishart, *The Fur Trade of the American West, 1807–1840: A Geographical Synthesis* (Lincoln: University of Nebraska Press, 1979); David J. Wishart, *An Unspeakable Sadness: The Dispossession of the Nebraska Indians* (Lincoln: University of Nebraska Press, 1995).

74. Stephen C. Jett, "The Origins of Navajo Settlement Patterns," *Annals of the Association of American Geographers* 68 (1978): 351–362; Stephen C. Jett and Virginia E. Spencer, *Navajo Architecture: Forms, History, Distributions* (Tucson: University of Arizona Press, 1981); Stephen C. Jett, "The Navajo in the American Southwest," in *To Build in a New Land: Ethnic Landscapes in North America,* ed. Allen Noble (Baltimore: Johns Hopkins University Press, 1992), 331–344; Martha L. Henderson, "Settlement Patterns on the Mescalero Apache Res-

ervation since 1883," *Geographical Review* 80 (1990): 226–238; Martha L. Henderson, "American Indian Reservations: Controlling Separate Space, Creating Separate Environments," in *The American Environment: Interpretations of Past Geographies,* eds. Lary M. Dilsaver and Craig E. Colten (Lanham, Md.: Rowman and Littlefield, 1992), 115–134; Jerry N. McDonald, "La Jicarilla," *Journal of Cultural Geography* 2, no. 2 (1982): 40–57; Elliot G. McIntire, "Changing Patterns of Hopi Indian Settlement," *Annals of the Association of American Geographers* 61 (1971): 510–521; David J. Hornbeck Jr., "The California Indian before European Contact," *Journal of Cultural Geography* 2, no. 2 (1982): 23–39; Preston, *Vanishing Landscape.*

75. Harris, *Resettlement of British Columbia.*

76. Meinig, *Southwest;* Meinig, *Transcontinental America,* 36–69, 113–133; Richard L. Nostrand, *The Hispano Homeland* (Norman: University of Oklahoma Press, 1992); Alvar W. Carlson, *The Spanish-American Homeland: Four Centuries in New Mexico's Rio Arriba* (Baltimore: Johns Hopkins University Press, 1990); Alvar W. Carlson, "Spanish Americans in New Mexico's Rio Arriba," in *To Build in a New Land: Ethnic Landscapes in North America,* ed. Allen Noble (Baltimore: Johns Hopkins University Press, 1992), 345–61; David J. Hornbeck Jr., "Spanish Legacy in the Borderlands," in *The Making of the American Landscape,* ed. Michael Conzen (Boston: Unwin Hyman, 1990), 51–62.

77. Charles F. Gritzner, "Log Housing in New Mexico," *Pioneer America* 3, no. 2 (1971): 54–62; Charles F. Gritzner, "Hispano Gristmills in New Mexico," *Annals of the Association of American Geographers* 64 (1974): 514–524; Daniel D. Arreola, "Mexican American Housetypes," *Geographical Review* 78 (1988): 299–315; Daniel D. Arreola, "Border-City Idée Fixe," *Geographical Review* 86 (1996): 356–369; Daniel D. Arreola and James R. Curtis, "Zonas De Tolerencia on the Northern Mexican Border," *Geographical Review* 81 (1991): 333–346; Daniel D. Arreola and James R. Curtis, *The Mexican Border Cities: Landscape Anatomy and Place Personality* (Tucson: University of Arizona Press, 1993); Brian J. Godfrey, *Neighborhoods in Transition: The Making of San Francisco's Ethnic and Nonconformist Communities* (Berkeley: University of California Publications in Geography, no. 27, 1988).

78. Terry G. Jordan, *North American Cattle-Ranching Frontiers: Origins, Diffusion, and Differentiation* (Albuquerque: University of New Mexico Press, 1993).

79. Bradley H. Baltensperger, "Agricultural Change among Nebraska Immigrants, 1880–1900," in *Ethnicity on the Great Plains,* ed. Frederick C. Luebke (Lincoln: University of Nebraska Press, 1980), 170–189; Bradley H. Baltensperger, "Agricultural Change among Great Plains Russian Germans," *Annals of the Association of American Geographers* 73 (1983): 75–88; D. Aidan McQuillan, "Farm Size and Work Ethic: Measuring the Success of Immigrant Farmers on the American Grasslands, 1875–1925," *Journal of Historical Geography* 4 (1978): 57–76; D. Aidan McQuillan, "The Mobility of Immigrants and Americans: A Comparison of Farmers on the Kansas Frontier," *Agricultural History* 53 (1979): 576–596; D. Aidan McQuillan, *Prevailing over Time;* John C. Lehr, "Ukrainians in Western Canada," in *To Build in a New Land: Ethnic Landscapes in North America,* ed. Allen Noble (Baltimore: Johns Hopkins University Press, 1992), 309–330; John C. Lehr and Jeffrey Picknicki Morski, "Global Patterns and Family Matters: Life History and the Ukrainian Pioneers Diaspora," *Journal of Historical Geography* 25 (1999): 349–366.

80. Randall E. Rohe, "After the Gold Rush: Chinese Mining in the Far West, 1850–1890," *Montana: Magazine of Western History* 32, no. 1 (1982): 2–19; Susan W. Hardwick, *Chinese Settlement in Butte County, California: 1860–1920* (San Francisco: R and E Associates, 1976); Daniel D. Arreola, "The Chinese Role in Creating the Early Cultural Landscape of the Sacramento–San Joaquin Delta," *California Geographer* 15 (1975): 1–15.

81. Meinig, "Mormon Culture Region"; Lowell C. Bennion and Gary B. Peters, *Sanpete Scenes: A Guide to Utah's Heart* (Eureka, Utah: Basin/Plateau Press, 1987); Kay, "Mormons and Mountains"; Richard V. Francaviglia, *The Mormon Landscape* (New York: AMS Press, 1979); Richard H. Jackson, ed., *The Mormon Role in the Settlement of the West* (Provo, Utah: Brigham Young University Press, 1978); Richard H. Jackson, "Religion and Landscape in the Mormon Cultural Region," in *Dimensions of Human Geography: Essays on Some Familiar and Neglected Themes* (Chicago: University of Chicago, Department of Geography, Research Paper no. 186, 1978), 100–127; Jackson, "Myth and Reality"; Jackson, "The Mormon Experience."

82. Susan W. Hardwick and Donald G. Holtgrieve, *Valley for Dreams: Life and Landscape in the Sacramento Valley* (Lanham, Md.: Rowman and Littlefield, 1996); Wyckoff, *Creating Colorado*.

83. Michael Conzen, "Ethnicity on the Land," in *The Making of the American Landscape* (Boston: Unwin Hyman, 1990), 221–248; James Allen and Eugene Turner, *We the People: An Atlas of America's Ethnic Diversity* (New York: Macmillan, 1987).

84. John W. Reps, *Cities of the American West: A History of Frontier Urban Planning* (Princeton, N.J.: Princeton University Press, 1979).

85. Richard White, *New History*, 459–612; John M. Findlay, *Magic Lands: Western Cityscapes and American Culture after 1940* (Berkeley: University of California Press, 1992); Carl Abbott, *The Metropolitan Frontier: Cities in the Modern American West* (Tucson: University of Arizona Press, 1993).

86. Reyner Banham, *Los Angeles: The Architecture of Four Ecologies* (Harmondsworth, U.K.: Penguin, 1971); Mike Davis, *City of Quartz: Excavating the Future of Los Angeles* (New York: Vintage Books, 1992); Mike Davis, *Ecology of Fear: Los Angeles and the Imagination of Disaster* (New York: Vintage Books, 1999); Kathleen Underwood, *Town Building on the Colorado Frontier* (Albuquerque: University of New Mexico Press, 1987); Mary Murphy, *Mining Cultures: Men, Women, and Leisure in Butte, 1914–41* (Urbana: University of Illinois Press, 1997); Stephen J. Leonard and Thomas J. Noel, *Denver: Mining Camp to Metropolis* (Niwot: University Press of Colorado, 1990).

87. D. W. Meinig, "Spokane and the Inland Empire: Historical Geographic Systems and a Sense of Place," in *Spokane and the Inland Empire: An Interior Pacific Northwest Anthology*, ed. David H. Stratton (Pullman: Washington State University Press, 1991), 1–31.

88. Gunther Barth, *Instant Cities: Urbanization and the Rise of San Francisco and Denver* (New York: Oxford University Press, 1975); William Wyckoff, "Incorporation as a Factor in Formation of an Urban System," *Geographical Review* 77 (1987): 279–292; William Wyckoff, "Revising the Meyer Model: Denver and the National Urban System, 1859–1879," *Urban Geography* 9 (1988): 1–18; William Wyckoff, "Central Place Theory and the Location of

Services in Colorado in 1899," *Social Science Journal* 26 (1989): 383–398; William Wyckoff, "Postindustrial Butte," *Geographical Review* 85 (1995): 478–496.

89. Arthur Krim, "Los Angeles and the Anti-Tradition of the Suburban City," *Journal of Historical Geography* 18 (1992): 121–138; Barbara Rubin, "A Chronology of Architecture in Los Angeles," *Annals of the Association of American Geographers* 67 (1977): 521–537; Allen J. Scott and Edward W. Soja, eds., *The City: Los Angeles and Urban Theory at the End of the Twentieth Century* (Berkeley: University of California Press, 1998); Elizabeth K. Burns, "Subdivision Activity on the San Francisco Peninsula, 1860–1970," *Yearbook of the Association of Pacific Coast Geographers* 39 (1977): 17–32; Elizabeth K. Burns, "The Enduring Affluent Suburb," *Landscape* 24, no. 1 (1980): 33–41; Godfrey, *Neighborhoods in Transition;* Brian Godfrey, "Urban Development and Redevelopment in San Francisco," *Geographical Review* 87 (1997): 309–333; Neil Shumsky and Larry Springer, "San Francisco's Zone of Prostitution, 1880–1934," *Journal of Historical Geography* 7 (1981): 71–89; Terrence Young, "Modern Urban Parks," *Geographical Review* 85 (1995): 535–551.

90. Susan W. Hardwick, "A Geographical Interpretation of Ethnic Settlement in an Urban Landscape: Russians in Sacramento," *California Geographer* 19 (1979): 87–104; Susan W. Hardwick, "Suburban Commercial Development in the Shadow of Downtown Sacramento," *Yearbook of the Association of Pacific Coast Geographers* 49 (1987): 51–63; Dennis Dingemans and Robin Datel, "Urban Multiethnicity," *Geographical Review* 85 (1995): 458–477.

91. Arreola and Curtis, *Mexican Border Cities.*

92. William Wyckoff, "Denver's Aging Commercial Strip," *Geographical Review* 82 (1992): 282–294; Wyckoff, *Creating Colorado;* Larry R. Ford, "The Visions of the Builders: The Historical Evolution of the San Diego Cityscape," in *San Diego: An Introduction to the Region,* ed. Philip Pryde (Dubuque, Iowa: Kendall-Hunt, 1992), 185–203; Larry R. Ford, *Cities and Buildings: Skyscrapers, Skid Rows, and Suburbs* (Baltimore: Johns Hopkins University Press, 1994).

93. William G. Robbins, *Colony and Empire: The Capitalist Transformation of the American West* (Lawrence: University Press of Kansas, 1994); William G. Robbins, "In Pursuit of Historical Explanation: Capitalism as a Conceptual Tool for Knowing the American West," *Western Historical Quarterly* 30 (1999): 277–293; Limerick, *Legacy of Conquest;* White, *New History;* Worster, *Rivers of Empire.*

94. Bernard De Voto, "The West: A Plundered Province," *Atlantic* 169 (August 1934): 255–264; Walter Prescott Webb, *The Great Frontier* (Boston: Houghton Mifflin, 1952); K. Ross Toole, *Twentieth-Century Montana: A State of Extremes* (Norman: University of Oklahoma Press, 1972).

95. Meinig, "American Wests"; Meinig, *Transcontinental America.*

96. Robbins, *Colony and Empire;* Worster, *Rivers of Empire.*

97. Barth, *Instant Cities.*

98. James E. Vance Jr., *The North American Railroad: Its Origin, Evolution, and Geography* (Baltimore: Johns Hopkins University Press, 1995); Cathy E. Kindquist, *Stony Pass* (Silver-

ton, Colo.: San Juan County Book Company, 1987); Cathy E. Kindquist, "Communication in the High Country," in *The Mountainous West: Explorations in Historical Geography*, eds. William Wyckoff and Lary M. Dilsaver (Lincoln: University of Nebraska Press, 1995), 114–137.

99. James R. Gibson, *The Lifeline of the Oregon Country: The Fraser-Columbia Brigade System, 1811–47* (Vancouver: University of British Columbia Press, 1998); James R. Gibson, *Otter Skins, Boston Ships, and China Goods: The Maritime Fur Trade of the Northwest Coast, 1785–1841* (Montreal: McGill-Queen's University Press, 1999).

100. Harris, *Resettlement of British Columbia;* Wyckoff, *Creating Colorado.*

101. Don Mitchell, *The Lie of the Land: Migrant Workers and the California Landscape* (Minneapolis: University of Minnesota Press, 1996).

2 | An Inescapable Range,
or the Ranch as Everywhere

PAUL F. STARRS

   Imperfect though the human eye may be, it's plain enough that what you see is what you get. Children learn early in life to trust their eyes, making sense of what they see. The human brain, hardwired to detect difference, welcomes a big picture, seizing upon the dissimilar. And so to recognize that ranch landscapes are everywhere, yet are almost undetectable, requires the acceptance of a landscape (one or many) vested with a subtlety both aggressive and primordial. Indistinct except to the schooled observer, rangeland's variations nevertheless drape the land (Figure 2.1). Long vistas and small departures—a single cow dotting a sagebrush sea—are shapes that barely register across a monotony of semblance. If seeing is believing, then to apprehend is to be well on the way to understanding. Do that math successfully, and the ranch lies nearly everywhere in the American West.
   Estimates classify upward of one-third of the United States as rangeland—extensive, vegetated in shrubs or grass, but not in crops and unforested. Even forestland, though, and wide desert, or deep wetland is grazed. Something more than 70 percent of the West has long been browsed by big herbivores, which in the Pleistocene included animals now all but unimaginable: giant bison, enormous elk, and sagebrush-eating behemoths dotted hither and yon. But for some thirty decades, extending back to Spanish and Mexican times, this realm has been what writer Wallace Stegner dubbed "ranch country." The term was more aesthetic than economic because in its extensive Western form, typical of so much of pastoralism elsewhere about the world, ranching requires many an acre for few domesticated animals (generally cattle but sometimes sheep or goats). Cows have their own cagey relationship to

the world about them. Packed with a cheerful evasiveness, ranch country cows, through the American West, are today still less seldom seen than people (Figure 2.2).

Across a big terrain, twelve hundred miles east to west by easily a thousand miles south to north, human company in the West is a real rarity, especially after Interstates are bypassed in favor of those side roads formed of packed gravel, dirt, or asphalt, and variously fractured, cratered, and relict. The scope is captured by Western road books, and in a simple comparison, it's evident that William Least-Heat Moon's *Blue Highways* stands at a vast spiritual standoff from Larry McMurtry's *Roads: Driving America's Great Highways*. Least-Heat Moon's is a 1982 paean to obscure back roads, but McMurtry has word-processed a self-satisfied millennium-year ode bragging on his own eight-lane Interstate peregrinations. The tension between byway and highway is all-Western, spaced across better than a billion acres of land. Whether someone's traverse is by the small forgotten roads or on the big routes routinely traveled at eighty-plus miles per hour, there are places where the company is slim and you shall not want for space. It is over that mile after mile of evident nothingness that the ranch dominates, if owlish and a bit obscured.

A minimal human presence is seen through this broad terrain, and the animals that unapologetically graze the range have galvanized antilivestock ideologues. Cow haters such as Luddite gadfly Jeremy Rifkin, poster bad boy Richard Symanski, or the writers Lynn Jacobs and George Wuerthner decry ranching as a self-evident abuse of nature, as an investiture of way too much land in the hands of far too few good people, as a Brobdingnagian gluttonous bovine impedance to biodiversity. To put it simply, for ranching dissenters, the lowing of livestock, the trappings of transhumance, and assuredly a cowhand's call each are held to cheapen what would otherwise presumably be a human-free experience of perfectly pristine nature. The rest of the world, though, tends to see the matter rather a bit differently: Ranching represents a valued closeness of people to nature that is all too seldom now achieved. Such distancing from the land comes at a cost to the human spirit and intellect (Figure 2.3).[1]

More practiced philosophers who have been about the block grasp the significance of the human presence—or the formidable import of its absence.[2] Across the West, cattle and cowhands commingle in an economy that has been precarious ever since its inception. In places, the vestiges of ranching are about all the culture there is. They are also about all there is ever likely to be. To wish humans were simply not a presence on the land is frivolous. It is more productive to think about how land, and its people, should be used and

Fɪɢ. 2.1. White cow on sage. The perspective of Americans toward their environment can very much be determined by reactions to this image—some see a corruption of nature, the rest see something altogether interesting. The moral calculus is complex; the initial reaction, much quicker. Photo by author, July 1989, Jiggs, Nevada.

Fɪɢ. 2.2. ɪʟ Ranch, fifteen miles from Tuscarora, Nevada. The size of the mailbox is a complex bit of mathematics: Roughly, it reflects the number of hands working at a ranch, speaks to the distance of the ranch house from the nearest local road where a mail truck might pass by, or speaks to the relative infrequency of visits to town. In any event, the mailbox of the ɪʟ Ranch is in part a tribute to its great distance from any sizeable town—in its case, Elko (Tuscarora doesn't count). Photo by author, 1998.

Fɪɢ. 2.3. The ranch space is rarely orderly or notably neat. It is instead, as here in the Carroll Canyon Ranch, west of Austin, Nevada, heavily colonized by clutter and messiness. That is the way of the ranch—although all the space is known and even to some extent allocated. Photo by author, 1993.

managed and in this to see that livestock ranching, although subject to local abuse, is at least ideologically a big-stakes player in Western well-being and cultural sustenance.

Natural landscapes of the American West are defined by a prevailing aridity and, equally, by great strands of mountains that temper and flavor the prevailing dryness.[3] But the Western cultural landscapes—those noticed, anyway—are lately those of cities and a fat, blasé sprawl. That makes the populous citified West what it is now. There is also a boundary: Pretty much everyplace where cities aren't there are ranches; ranching is what happens (for good or bad) almost everyplace else (Figure 2.4). Nucleated city societies, often chunky ones, contrast with vast interstices dotted by minor towns and still smaller communities and ranches. These antipodal qualities—"the West as City" and "the West as the Rest"—should hardly surprise anyone; they are the twinned ciphers that kept the West dramatic and confusing to everyone, from the bemused nineteenth-century U.S. Congress to the fresh-scrubbed dot-commed New Western migrants of the twenty-first century. It can be said, with no exaggeration, that the ranch is a natural feature in the American West. This essay examines what that means.

The Ranch

Ranches in the West make use of a marginal space, which might be called ranching's realm. Its hero and amanuensis was the curious but memorable landscape historian and cultural geographer, J. B. Jackson—Brinck to his ac-

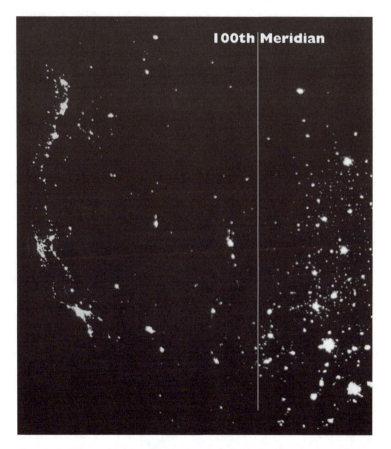

FIG. 2.4. Where the West begins is never difficult to ascertain, at least not in the traditional histories that set the 100th (or 98th) meridian as the divide between humid East and arid West. But in this view of the western United States at night, a slightly different test becomes usable. The West is where lights become clumped, the nodes more intense, as befits an oasis civilization, and the interstitial space, where black indicates no town large enough to make a lasting impression on satellite optics (about twenty thousand people), is in evidence. AVHRR image, 1992.

quaintances. For almost twenty years Brinck Jackson was the publisher and editor of *Landscape* magazine and fascinated by the folklore, function, and the intellectual meaning—what followers of the French *Annales* school called the *mentalitée*—of the everyday landscape. He wrote at great length (six books) about what he sometimes called the "vernacular landscape," which he valued far more than the juried and weighted, high-culture and haughty-concept creations of the United States' social and architectural arbiters. Jackson liked the gritty and the commonplace; it spoke to him. Strikingly, he never dealt too much or all that explicitly with the landscape of the Western ranch, although he cheerfully described himself as a rancher to those he met in his home territory of northern New Mexico. For him were instead other topics: roads, porches, hot springs, town grid plans, and the House Trailer People whom he contemplated in his memorable "Four Corners Country."[4]

We may well consider, though, what Jackson touched upon only in passing—what a lifeway, practice, and land use such as ranching mean to the American scene (Figure 2.5). Many a Western ranch involves an array of lands used. At one level are valley-floor natural meadows, irrigated pasture, fields dry or fallowed. Beyond that, in a widening gyre, is the adjoining Bureau of Land Management acreage, a vast majority of the public lands in the West. And ascending—literally so, in height—is USDA-Forest Service acreage in the distant background and uplands. The roster of kinds of lands, and forms of ownership, is at least hierarchical, and probably something closer to Byzantine. That is why transhumance is so important because it puts cattle or sheep or other livestock to work, transporting themselves with paced efficiency from one place or elevation to another—and when done skillfully has them gaining weight all the way up and back down. The level of skill encapsulated in the ability to herd animals that are as a matter of course quite cantankerous or at least willful, along twenty or thirty miles of difficult terrain, reflects more than a casual acquaintance with the land in between: It's an odyssey. Little wonder that there was such fascination, and a truly rude rapport, between the 1960s "back to the landers" and the West's rough-hewn ranch hands. In thinking of ranching and its practitioners, it would be difficult not to return to the wonderfully sardonic short story by Bobbie Louise Hawkins, entitled "Curtis Stuck His Boot up in the Air." The storyette ends with Bobbie-as-narrator hauling out the heavy artillery, a rhetorical Big Bertha, which she turns into a cannonade at her brother: "Curtis," she says, "every hippy in the world wants to be a cowboy."[5] Few truer words are writ.

And yet there is something else happening in ranching today. The ranch society has become iconographic, so symbolic that the details of its realities

Fig. 2.5. This 1954 view of the Bar 99 Ranch reflects all the elements of the ranch it-self after its first eighty years of existence. The pasturelands, some irrigated, some now dry, are at the lower edge of the photograph; the hay meadows are not cropped, in the standard sense of cutting into the soil, but have grass that is windrowed and put up. The dry fields, the Bureau of Land Management fall and winter range, and the U.S. Forest Service land in the upper elevations—the canyons at back—are each in-gredients of an intricate mix. Photograph from Bar 99 ranch house; courtesy Frank Smith, Fish Lake Valley, Nevada.

are all but lost. When I worked at the Bar 99 Ranch, in western Nevada, in the 1980s, it was a place full of life. It boasted a bevy of Mexican ranch hands, a somewhat bemused part-owner ("I'm not sure why, but this is the happen-ingest place I've ever lived!"), ranch buildings dating back to the early 1870s, and a whipcord economy of hay raising, cattle movements to the White Mountains and Silver Peak range, and fervid function. Now, not even the sign survives, and the cottonwoods—always an indication of whether a ranch is in good repair or not—are splintered ragged, in studious uncare.

A ranch fills many a function: historical reservoir, diversifier of landscape, avatar of conspicuous display, cultural arbiter, sustainer of open space, agri-cultural reservoir. None of these is transcendently good—but the collective effect is to remind us that the ranch has more significance than its relatively paltry contribution to the overall Western economy might suggest. What ranching does well involves a low-intensity agriculture that produces a presence on the earth, food and fiber (a livestock industry mantra), and the significant roots of community. A ranch is never entirely good or wholly bad; it can be managed in many ways. To dismiss all ranchers and ranching as "bad" is on the same sophomoric intellectual footing as declaring all cars evil because they sometimes hurt people.

Everywhere

The landscape of ranching, were that there was any single one such, would constitute a most intricate mixture of space and place. Ranch space is, of course, an essential component of the American West, that one-third of the North American continent that is in effect defined by a sizeable void where night lights illumine not. The dark space is ranching, the territory in between. Ranching's realm is really, then, definable as being where most people are absent. But belonging to ranching is also a supremely ideological landscape, formed by aspiration and the desire to own and control.[6] A census of ranchers would turn up pretty paltry counts. For all that, their voices resound. Although ranchers tend to number few and be far between, they have an unmistakable significance and vociferousness, which goes some way toward explaining why the ranch is perennially and somewhat perniciously under assault.

People and place make the ranch, and with it a landscape both speculative and real. The frontal attack on ranching is like an assault on middle-class values: a lead pipe cinch to garner attention. Verifiably genuine, ranch landscapes are a territory of the imagination. But just as nomads have been out of style in the chronicles of world history through the ages, a people and a nature apart, so would ranches and livestock and their cowhand employees turn out to be beyond the pale in America's own imagery. The ranch was pointedly not a feature in such a canonical image as the painting of "American progress" that came to us from John Gast (1872) and others (Figure 2.6). Nationally condoned uses for the opening lands of the American West didn't include ranching. Sodbusting and farming, throwing out Native Americans, stretching telegraph wires and railroad tracks, bringing in miners and settler wagons were the uses more readily approved in the epic vision of westward-moving progress. The symbol of the West would today be less the ranch and more the subdivision; in the forming American West, cities did (and do) make up 60–98 percent of the residents.

Where it appeared, and if it registered, the ranch has amounted to a long detour on a longer road, usually oiled or constructed of hard-packed dirt.

Long were the sight lines. And so why have the landscapes of ranching proved elusive, little attended to; why is the ranch—as a functioning environment—so glanced o'er and forgotten? There's a story. This question is not posed to be difficult. But recall that the demotion—or the simpler failure to appear—of the ranch in most landscape, architectural, and even geographical studies is a supremely ideological fact.[7] For all that, the ranch is unmistakably extant. At the very least, we know the ranching world for its laborers, variously cowhands or buckaroos, who have long been, in the timeless words of bard and author Kinky Friedman, "America's most precious gift to the children of the world."[8] The folklorist J. Frank Dobie would note, hardly without bemusement, that "the cowboy became the best-known occupational type that America has given the world." But the ranch itself is less unknown than

FIG. 2.6. The 1873 painting by George Crofutt (after a painting the year before executed by John Gast) showing "American Progress" remains the archetypal image of Americans ("Progress" is she of the flowing robes) moving westward across the continent. Yet strikingly, for all the telegraph wires, the buffalo and Native Americans being pushed aside, the miners and farmers scraping the earth, there is nothing in this painting to suggest the significance of ranching.

unstudied. In fact, we see ranch property, ranch real estate, all the time—but its form and extent register not.[9]

If ranch labor is astoundingly and atypically familiar, the place, or setting, is something else. Although a ranch is dependent upon extensive space, it, too, has its own place, hardly well recorded at all. The ranch is a slice of promise, an evocative way of life, a body of practice; it is an economy (if a poor one) and a community (a powerful one). Verifiably genuine, ranch landscapes are also a territory of the imagination. The ranch is defined by a number of features, but especially by the marginality of its site and situation; by the overwhelming mythos, which even ranchers themselves buy into with cheerful glee; by the manipulation of image—especially, these days, by nonranchers. Finally, ranching has its own decisive, highly effective community, something that sociologists and experts in "community studies" have truly done damn all to help define.

Legal scholars such as Carol Rose and Robert Ellickson instantly acknowledge the astounding efficiency of the ranching community's avoidance of transaction cost in dealing with potential legal problems their own way: informally, and within the family of ranchers.[10] That this makes good sense is obvious enough—informal settling of disputes keeps many a lawyer at bay—but it also reflects how ranchers have dealt with one another, and with even outside disputes, for generations—and worldwide. Often on the outs with the powers that be, routinely suspected of fast action because they have accumulated relatively large holdings of both land and the far more liquid commodity of livestock, ranchers relish their distance from the madding crowd. They know they have it better, and their ethos of satisfaction is so pervasive that nonranchers have voted with fat wallets through the last 150 years or so, buying up ranches of their own: Look at Clint Eastwood, Tom McGuane, Harrison Ford, David Letterman, Ted and Jane (Turner and Fonda, together or separately). They are purchasing a ready-made right to be set apart from the society at large, and in buying something so big, have acquired their right to be "just folks," real rustics. The mix may seem a strange one, but the econo-mytho-mathematics is unavoidable.

Ranching can lay claim to singular and recognizable landscapes. Much of North America west of the 100th meridian is not wilderness but instead home to over sixty thousand extraordinarily dispersed livestock ranches (Figure 2.7). Ranches are rarely treated as discrete landscape elements; they are perhaps too spread out, too difficult to enter by unfamiliar roads, too removed—in the physical setting of ranches themselves—from a highly urbanized mainstream society in the early twenty-first-century West. It is also true

Fig. 2.7. To refer to someplace as a "home ranch" is to draw on a deep meaning of Western practice. The home ranch is the base of operation for a ranch that has many parts, by definition dispersed around various and sundry parts, and often those additional line camps or secondary or tertiary operations are at sites of former ranches that went under and have since been accumulated into one continuing operation. But the "home ranch" is also, as J. P. S. Brown notes, part of Western mythos: It is the core of the outfit, the heart of the matter. It evokes even more than it implies. Photo by author, 1984.

that ranch proprietors do not always offer an easy ethnographic encounter for the landscape-scale researcher.

For all the qualities of the West as an oasis civilization, ranching—whether in Sonora, Baja, and Chihuahua, British Columbia, or in the New West of the United States—is the most extensive regional use of public and private lands. Discussions of conservation easements, land trusts, and the importance of sustaining agricultural society today are evermore turning back to ranching and the rancher as a paramount figure (Figure 2.8). Much of the private land around Western cities has, historically, been grazed; a good bit of it is privately controlled, and that is land at what John Fraser Hart has called the "perimetropolitan bow wave," where urban fringe meets current—but soon to be former—rangeland.[11] Ranch land is what is being developed, its vistas and isolation prized and paid for by everyone from media giants to the earnest aspiring smallholders who become ranchette owners, heading for a slice of space with enough room for a doublewide pad, a petite adobe abode, or the pretentious and proverbial suburban "starter castle." It is difficult to argue against a public covetousness, but the ecological effect of slicing up once-intact habitat into tiny parcels is anything but reassuring. How to prevent that? The question, for being a good one, is anything but easily answered.

FIG. 2.8. "Entering Public Lands," broadcasts the sign from southern Utah, and this is country that has, in the last decade, become even more of a flashpoint over public land use than Nevada, titular home of the Sagebrush Rebellion. With great and known natural splendors, and a strong and unified Mormon culture, chunks of the Colorado Plateau country of Utah have been put into national monument status by presidential decree; this illustrates, yet again, the disparities among culture, politics, preservation, and different degrees of use. Photo by author, near Paria, Utah, 1987.

Fig. 2.9. There is a casual yet conscious order to the ranchyard that escapes too many experts in the culture of ranching; only Blanton Owen, Rusty Marshall, and Margie Purser have really captured its function with any accuracy. The ranchyard is a microcosm of ranching's realm, in general; some parts intensively used, other parts left alone, still other parts safeguarded for the future or for conservation. The mix is always an enticing one, although the order and function are often known only to the rancher (Oasis Ranch, Fish Lake Valley, Nevada). Photo by author, 1989.

Although the geographical extent of the landscapes of ranching is evident, ranching's import as a lifeway remains a conundrum, or at least a big hole, to most landscape historians, architects, environmental historians, and cultural geographers. They find ranch landscapes outré and difficult to access. Howard Wight Marshall, in his American Folklife Center work in Paradise Valley, Nevada, remains one exception. But there are few others—Brinck Jackson, Frank Popper, Blanton Owen, Simon Evans, Terry G. Jordan, and Richard Slatta are among them—who have actually grappled with the ranch landscape. Even the formidable Marshall invested much more intellectual weight and credit in the dressed stone ranch house or the broken-gable barn than in the controlled chaos of the ranch main yard or the elusive qualities of the line camp or public range (Figure 2.9).[12]

Architects and material culturists who cherish order warm slowly, if ever, to the inchoate chaos of ranching reality. Folklorists, usually a flexible lot, have only recently begun to grapple with the enormous divide that exists between written stories, sanitized for our narrative protection and for a smoother read, and the cascading confusions and contradictions that are the hallmark of a genuine story, as it is actually being told. A transcribed rendering of any good tale-telling session would be laced with fourteen interruptions, six trips to tend tureens on the stove, the importunate demands of several telephone calls, and pauses while three corks are prised forth.[13] Ranching and its landscapes aren't neat; they are all too human, another reminder of how right J. B. Jackson was.

The ranch realm is simple at first glance, at second appearance hugely complex, at third look a moveable feast. An aerial view of a ranch in western Nevada, which has passed through multiple ownership changes since it was created in the late nineteenth century, is significant. In one view it includes every perspective on the property needed for ranch country to function, from core deeded acreage to the multiple tiers of federally owned, and often privately used, land that about half the West's ranchers who keep more than 120 head of cattle rely on for at least some of their yearly grazing.

Practice

As functioning metaphor, livestock ranching is about quotidian life, where the real smothers the imaginary. Especially involved is a celebration of distinctive labor and the ranch hand's purpose. It is, indeed, one of the very few careers where the workaday is worshipped. And yet the labor can be suffocating. A solid labor-landscape theory might argue that ranching is romanticized precisely to trap workers into doing willingly the onerous; Eleanor Marx Aveling (Karl's daughter) once tried to organize the cowhands of Texas, to sparse avail.[14]

A ranch is of little moment without the cow and cowhand. But the cow, alone, is hardly interesting except as villain. A friend of mine, once a cowhand in Big Smoky Valley, Nevada, and, now Reed College professor emeritus, Owen Ulph, has remarked on the formidable contest. "If, indeed, the cow outfit serves any metaphysical purpose, it is as an enormous stage for the presentation of an unending play in which a creature of unrestricted autonomy sits on the back of a creature of feverish volatility and together they struggle to subjugate a creature whose chief characteristic is perverse intractability," he writes. And "so uncanny," he continues, "is the intuition of the cow that it can almost always sense what the rider wants, and do the opposite. The cow's flaw is that it is so addicted to this course of action that a shrewd hand can turn the animal's perversity against itself."[15] The confrontation is elemental, educational, and perpetually a part of pastoralism. The contact, the cycle of husbandry and healthy chaos, remains something that those who work with animals can cherish.

At a less allusive level, ranching is about almost everywhere. According to the United Nations Development Program, International Union for the Conservation of Nature, Conservation International, and assorted U.S. government definitions, any place not forest is, technically, rangeland. Rangeland is, in part, not cropland and not forestland, a contrast evident from above, in an image of the U.S.-Canadian boundary. Here stands an institutional fault line where dry-farmed land—once grassland—was plowed open in Montana but in Alberta and Saskatchewan remains unbroken rangeland. Farming is, by contrast, an intensive land use, even in its "no-till" or "minimum till" variants, a far more invasive use of the earth than grazing, which spreads the effects of mouth and hoof to a larger dominion. The aggression involved in cropping, however geometrically precise and attractive from the air, is nonetheless an ongoing problem that no small number of experts has commented on. Cures to cropping are less easy than those to overgrazing, which generally involve more intensive observation and a regular moving of animals and an entire avoidance of grazing in the most sensitive areas that must be protected from the tractive power of herbivore hooves. Canada picked certainly the less destructive course; south of the border is a landscape of low rent and hard effect.

Going transboundary is nothing unusual in the ranching realm. Its voice in literature includes Gertrude Stein, who noted with her typical surgical precision, "After all, anybody is as their land and air is." That is not, incidentally, a simple answer—Stein's *Geographical History of America* remains one of a very few great knowing documents in American literature.[16] More contrasts inhere: There is, on the one hand, the sweeping, but for that hardly inelegant, remark of historian Paul Wallace Gates, writing of the greed that motivated the thronging crowds that descended upon the North American continent in a search for the ownable:

> The lust for land attracted to America an ever increasing stream of immigrants which relentlessly flowed over the face of the country, seeking out every nook and cranny which might be made a source of wealth and income. As time passed the ownership map changed; it never was in stasis as in old world countries, division and engrossment were continually in operation.[17]

To have a landscape of ranching so much defined by the presence of absence is a dilemma: When what we're asked to think about is what isn't there, how are we, as historians of landscape and cultural geographers, supposed to cope? When I think of quandaries involving the definition of what isn't there,

there are only a few who have jousted, it seems to me, with these kinds of
questions about character and place—Charles Olson, in *Call Me Ishmael,* his
panegyric on the meaning of the Pacific Ocean in *Moby Dick,* or Patricia Limerick, in her analysis of the efficacy of the frontier, or there is the oft-
whomped Frederick Jackson Turner (who was, after all, writing about "character," if rather in the aggregate), or, of course, J. B. Jackson in "Optimo City,"
American Space, "The Accessible Landscape," or our old friend, "Chihuahua;
As We Might Have Been."[18]

Little wonder, then, that the literature of ranching is so bound up with that
essential Western theme, as viable in a novel or a short story (think of O.
Henry's *Heart of the West*) as in any thinly disguised roman-à-clef. Ranching,
ultimately, is alluring because its theme—its essential practice—is community and possibility and exposure to failure.[19] Nearly any contact of modern-day human with nature exposes knowledge that we have lost through the
years. There are other skills gained, no doubt, in our postgraduate training as
urban warriors, but the basic context of preindustrial society was rooted in
skills of observation that are ever more deeply eroded, if not washed to the
distant sea.

The community of the Western range includes ranch hands, formidable in
mythology, who are a ranch's employees (Figure 2.10). Day-to-day ranch hand
life includes the trappings of domestication, human practices, animal ethol-
ogy (behavior), and the tensions betwixt. The ranch workers are involved in
the occupation and physical settlement of the land, with a distinct and novel
material culture. They tend the physical features, and the physiognomy, of the
ranch. Generally left to the owner are the difficult relations of public lands
and private lands, made manifest in a contest between rancher and government. There are the imponderables of economy, and those of image: Some
see the rancher as a perfected feature on the land; others see the rancher and
rangeland as a gross intrusion on the earth.

Ranching is a great adaptive strategy to dry land. There's more to grazing
and ranching than that. The rancher's use of land has a distinct meaning, involving elaborate and self-conscious values that have little to do with a functional response to the environment. Ranching is truly a culture, pluralistic,
gender-diverse, multiracial, evolving through time. John Wesley Powell argued
in 1878 for ranching as the mainstay for a sustainable Western society, basing
his advocacy upon traverses through northern New Mexico, Utah, and other
parts of the arid West. Donald Worster echoed that note more recently, re-
marking that irrigation and an extensive raising of livestock are the two remarkable and distinctive innovations in the history of the United States and

FIG. 2.10. The classic figure of the American West could be a miner, a robber baron, a farmwife, a merchant, a farmworker. No figure is more recognizable, though, than the cowhand. Geoff Pope, the ranch manager at Deep Springs Ranch, is especially picturesque but also true to the spirit and substance of the persona. Photo by author, Deep Springs Lake, April 1984.

Canada. Ironically, and not accidentally, irrigation and ranching are each derived primarily from Hispanic roots; little wonder that a recent Worster writing project was completion of a new biography of John Wesley Powell, following upon the no less memorable effort by Wallace Stegner, that yielded *Beyond the Hundredth Meridian, the Second Opening of the West.*[20]

Age-old roots extending back to Iberian and North African experience along the Mediterranean fringe provided a huge assortment of built and work-related traits that today constitute the modern ranch. Basic contrasts were formed, as the geographer Terry Jordan has noted, between black-Caribbean-Anglo and even Scottish traits in cowboy country and those of Spanish and Mexican California. Over slow time, however, there has been a coalescence, even if significant differences remain in the buckaroo and cowboy strains.

Ranches are constituted of parts: the corrals, the line camps, the distinctly fenced pastures, the windmills and water supplies. All were discerned and allotted under the watchful eyes of Western surveyors, who intervened to draw ghostly, but for that no less real, lines that took ranching from an open-access good to legally codified "property." The roads and trails form an elaborate infrastructure (Figure 2.11). Its fundamental nature is the *range*—a loan word from the Spanish *ranchear,* which is itself taken from the Frankish and meant originally to "travel through" or despoil. The word *ranger* glides down to us from the same precedent, and the notion of an open range on this continent dates back not just to Spanish inroads, it also created the roaming cattle tender. Consider, along those lines, that the hero of the first splashy bestseller in Western literature was, unsurprisingly, the Virginian; "When you call me that, *smile.*"[21] The roots of the West in the East include a paradoxical and laconic personal style that is all-cowboy—and the syntax and spare commentary are probably a tradition hailing from the hollers of western Virginia and the uncertain Elizabethan argot of the Appalachian Mountains. Certainly, the cowhand's dialectical roots are as much Scots and Irish as Castilian, Basque, or Italian—after the type was recognized and propagated, the cowboy could be from most anywhere.

FIG. 2.11. The Western ranch does not exist solely as big buildings or main ranch headquarters. Absolutely essential are the secondary and tertiary facilities, including the line camps, the distant waterholes and loading chutes, and, especially, the isolated holding corrals, where animals can be gathered and retained until they can be trucked or herded off, as in this image from Lida Flat, western Nevada. Photo by author, February 1984.

Fig. 2.12. If a prime water right is among the most important of all possible assets of a Western ranch, not far behind would be its haystack, as with this wall of prime alfalfa hay in Fish Lake Valley, Nevada. The water source is the White Mountains in the background, a fourteen-thousand-foot-high sponge that holds and absorbs winter precipitation and yields it with geological relentlessness and constancy through the spring and summer months, when little rain otherwise falls on the valley floor. But that does make impoundment of the water into reservoirs and its planned release onto thirsty fields viable. Photo by author, June 1989.

There is also a more domesticated and local ranching scene. The ranch house, through its patron, parodist, and disseminator, Howard May, became iconic in the American West and imitated everywhere, for better or worse. For much of the world, the Ponderosa and Southfork, from television's *Dallas,* remain the ranches that are known. Bunkhouses are self-explanatory; so, too, is the main yard, the tree-lined approach, the fields, the shop, the haystack (Figure 2.12), the main gate or ceremonial entry.

The culture of celebration is another matter, less clear-cut and certainly shaped more by other, outside influences, especially those of birth and synergy. Keep in mind that the ranch landscape is a kind of extreme, wherever it appears. That earlier phrase from Paul Gates, warning of land tenure and the practices of engrossment, reaches to the core of American ideology, a primal (Victor Hanson says "Preclassical Greek") ethos that the large landholding is largesse.[22] The desire to acquire, catalogue, and conspire after land was, after all, perhaps the most distinctive trait of nineteenth-century Americans; it laced them together like turbid teens at a "twister" party. The sign of the speculative development is as recognizable an element in the twenty-first century as it was in 1885—in fact, because the "engrossment" can now be broken into smaller parcels, at neat profit, the change is all the more evident (Figures 2.13, 2.14, 2.15 triptych).

Landscape architect Reyner Banham has warned about the perils of a wholly contrarian debate in which something is *all* wrong or *all* okay.[23] Ranches as we see them today are a kind of relict landscape, and those that have survived to now have, we may reckon, a kind of Darwinian adaptability. Rangeland has gone from an open-access resource to a mix of private and public holdings to being, at the millennium, the deepest repository of unurbanized—literally, conserved—land in many parts of the West. U.S. Supreme Court Justice Sandra Day O'Connor, in *Lazy B,* her memoir of growing up on Arizona's largest public-lands ranch, writes "The world will not be a better place if ranching ceases on the public lands of this nation. . . . The best way to preserve these vast acreages of public lands in the Southwest necessarily calls for responsible use of those lands by people who care about both those lands and their own survival."[24]

There are dissenters. I take Banham's warning seriously. Barry Goldwater, with his cheerful embrace of extremism in the defense of liberty being no vice, is recently gone from the scene, and yet ranching opponents like Jeremy Rifkin are not (Figure 2.16). A proposal for wholesale landscape extirpation would presumably earn some comment from our more lucid historic preservationists—but perhaps not. Proranching entities are not reliably better; many of them seem bent instead upon preserving the option to subdivide, which propounds other, grimmer realities. Aside from working ranches,

FIGS. 2.13, 2.14, 2.15. The gatepost is a signal statement of ranch identity; often the gatepost lies miles away from the ranch itself, and the elusive "presentation of self" of the ranch is wrapped up in those pillars. But they are also signals of aspiration. The Ruby Dome Ranch, a ranchette community near Lamoille and Elko, Nevada, is not a finished product, but the first reach toward the public is the fancy name. The Rancho Co$ta Plente is in a lighter vein, outside Pocatello, Idaho, and the white fence—as much as the moniker—suggests what the owners want to be. The Montana Land Reliance's "cows not condos" is a rejoinder to each of the other images—but one of at best local success. Photos by author.

some of which thrive, my favorites are organizations such as MALT, the Marin Agricultural Land Trust, which in hyperwealthy Marin County, California, has put together a vast coalition that maintains the agricultural landscape of West Marin as a stunningly diverse and intriguing place.

Elsewhere I have argued that the American West is becoming something else, and its vernacular, which constitutes whatever is occurring at the moment, is amply worthy of a fourth and fifth look. As the sundry authors of the *Atlas of the New West* claim, we are losing landscapes of breadth and depth.[25] The ranch landscape, the galactic city, and the national park amount to signature and iconic elements in western North American diversity. They are all about different kinds of possession; they are about the definition and establishment of distinct property regimes. But they are also about landscapes and those who direct them.

The question is this: Why ought we to care about ranching's landscapes? From them, what can we learn? Much, I'd argue. We learn about the processes of change and evolution on the American scene—how land taken is re-

Fig. 2.16. Not everyone likes cows, and this sign near Mono Lake, California, makes its point with precision. There are at least a dozen volumes by cow loathers, and each has passion, although by no means all can be taken seriously. The evolving West will continue to see offsetting forces—for and against public land use, for and against resource development (on any scale), for and against a human presence in rural lands. The choices are clear enough; the paths of possible action, less so. Photo by author.

distributed, and how this seemingly small change affects the natural, urban, rural, and ecological world in complex ways. Study of the ranch reveals a landscape of labor and diverse productivity and how labor, ownership, and absentee forces such as the federal government influence the local. The ranch offers an education in difference, especially of ethnicity and race, but also of men from women. Ranching teaches us about internal function: about the Practice of Parts, about the Calendrical Cycle, about how the rural can improve upon the urban. The ranch remains, at least at this juncture, an archive of material culture—and an intricate built world little known or lauded. In any world of ranches, it is difficult not to be fascinated by linkages, especially urban and rural: How many wives work in town to keep the ranch afloat?

Bernard De Voto singled out a notable theme in Western geography and history when he wrote of the West as a "Plundered Province" in 1939. He was not inclined to pull punches, so he also routinely later lambasted the excesses of the stockmen and women of the 1930s and 1940s, for their attempts to seize control, if not actual ownership, of the public domain. He fretted about the West's cooption to the hands of a few. He singled out allodial tenure—private, fee-simple, broad in extent—as a kind of Western impossibility, as Joe Jorgensen, Carol Rose, and Robert Ellickson have each, from different fields, pointed out.[26] But De Voto was no less concerned about community in the West—and that's slippery as stream trout, something never easily defined or grasped. A healthy and vibrant community has been the subject of hundreds of Western films, the unspoken theme behind a thousand novels, the topic of a hundred thousand photographs snapped by interested observers and travelers to the West. When seen it is knowable. And the society that ranching helps sustain—paid for with property taxes, feedstore bills, and brand inspection fees, secured by real property and even more real worries and pleasures—is a big element in the sustenance of Western culture. Geographically, it may well be the biggest part of the West, leastways in area occupied.

Finally, ranching teaches us about two things. It teaches us much about our blinkered vision of preservation, about options that deserve to be kept open. And, at last, ranching ought to help us ask questions about self-image, about hating ourselves. Why dismiss ranching, besides its awkwardness as a subject of study? These are two questions much bound up with the geography of the West, but also with its history, its folklore, its sociology and economy. The questions that emerge are as much about environment and about a philosophy of land use and stewardship as they are about biodiversity or positive externalities. In fact, the balance sheets of any ranch in the West include a huge deferred income to the proprietors, income they have given up because ranch owners prefer to live someplace that they believe in and that they also believe offers them a better life and a chance to lead the life pursuing the good.

In considering these parting questions, think back to Brinck Jackson, in some of his distinctive essays on the borderlands, the commons as an institution, in his discussions of the Plains. J. B. Jackson was at one point a rancher himself, and he knew well ranch byways and practice; he was himself a kind of remittance man—like the second and third sons of the European gentry who "went west" to attempt their fortunes. Still, Jackson seldom wrote on the ranch landscape as a feature of the American West, although his essay on "Chihuahua; As We Might Have Been" gestated themes that are clear enough in their implications. Why J. B. Jackson chose not to write more of ranches and ranching is itself an interesting question. The ranch is among the most enduring elements of the life of the West, with widespread influences on the American *genres de vie*.

Who can explain why "ranching" is so vilified? The answer isn't a simple one. There is no good reason to write off this practice that dominates, still, today, early in the twenty-first century, the use of the lands of the West. Some dislike ranching for the same reason that Las Vegas or Disneyland or Salt Lake City or the small town of the Midwest is loathed. These are, by jings, who we are. Brinck Jackson approved; maybe he was on to something. Ranching remains: everywhere, preservationist, adaptive/improvised, historical, and a solution. As Jackson wrote, late in life:

> The city was not always so exclusive, so determined to defend its boundaries. In earlier times the landscape, rural as well as urban, always contained a variety of spaces and structures which the public, no matter how humble, could occupy and use on a strictly temporary basis. The origin of these common spaces and the right to use them is obscure but their effect on the social order was good. They brought classes together and allowed people to work together and come together without competitiveness and suspicion. The tradition of common spaces and structures directly contradicts [Robert] Ardrey's theory that the basic spatial division is one of defensible private territories. But it is also at variance with the theory proposed by [Robert] Sack: that territoriality is a means of establishing control over people and things.
>
> The nineteenth century helped do away with most of these customary rights and spaces, but our own century has seen the beginning of their return. A social historian could establish within a decade or two when a reaction against autonomy set in, and also greater accessibility—accessibility not only to work and the public realm but accessibility from the street to the house.[27]

Why, then, the ranch? The answer, from a geographical point of view, is simple enough: Because it fits as well as a leather loafer or cloth romeo, tried and trod by a hundred generations of experience. How will the ranch survive—and perhaps thrive—into this new millennium? That remains to be seen. The challenges are many and unforgiving. Whenever vigilance wanes—or cupidity conquers—there is always someone waiting to knock at the door, muttering a mantra of cash in the escrow account, promising an easy buyout. That has turned more than a few landholders around. Some few, though, have gone to the other side and have instead put land in conservation easements, sold off development rights, attempting to preserve, however they can, a landscape that they like. They believe their children, or other generations hence, should not be unreasonably and excessively tempted to sell a cow outfit to the knacker, as if a ranch were an old nag, waiting to be rendered into glue. That end, of sitting aside and bearing witness to what geographer James J. Parsons once called "slicing up the open space," is unfitting.[28] Surely something better can be managed than that kind of ugly end for the most undramatic, but extensive and perhaps even stirring, use of land in the western half of the United States. The ranch, everywhere perhaps.

Notes

1. This is a comment echoed by Stephen Trimble, as by Stegner and others. See also the book by Gary Paul Nabhan and Trimble, *The Geography of Childhood: Why Children Need Wild Places* (Boston: Beacon Press, 1994). I reviewed it in *Annals of the Association of American Geographers* 85, no. 1 (March 1995): 228–229.

2. The argument about whether humans are "natural" or not has never excited geographers much; the answer is "of course, they are." And the human role in environmental change is, indeed, sometimes exaggerated; Karl W. Butzer has discussed some of this in an intriguing review, "The Human Role in Environmental History," a review of Redman, *Human Impact on Ancient Environments* (1999), published in *Science* 287 (31 March 2000): 2427–2428.

3. The nature of the mountainous West is treated, with summit intelligence and great geographical wit, by William Wyckoff and Lary Dilsaver, "Defining the Mountainous West," in *The Mountainous West: Explorations in Historical Geography*, eds. William Wyckoff and Lary Dilsaver (Lincoln: University of Nebraska Press, 1995), 1–60. They suggest five crucial traits of the mountainous West (they prefer that term to the "arid West"): barriers to travel and settlement, islands of moisture, zones of concentrated resources, area of governmental control, and visions of the mountainous West as a restorative sanctuary. Better to read their entire text than this summary; the volume, and especially this essay, is rich.

4. The reference is to J. B. Jackson, *American Space: The Centennial Years 1865–1876* (New York: Norton, 1972), and to Paul F. Starrs, *Let the Cowboy Ride: Cattle Ranching in the American West* (Baltimore: Johns Hopkins University Press, 1998).

5. Bobbie Louise Hawkins, "Curtis Stuck His Foot . . . ," in *Back to Texas* (Berkeley, Calif.: Bear Hug Books, dist. by Serendipity Books, 1977), 111.

> Curtis stuck his foot up in the air at me.
> "You don't see that kind of boot where you come from, do you?"
> He had a right to be proud. It was a handsome boot.
> "Sure I do. If somebody can afford 'em."
> "Naw, I mean, you don't see those boots with pointed toes and heels like that. Those people where you live, they wear . . . the kind of boots they wear has square toes and a strap across here."
> "Not all of them," I said. Then I decided to get him. "Curtis," I said, "There isn't a hippy in the world that doesn't want to be a cowboy."
> His face blushed fiery red. He could just about stand it.

6. Thomas M. Power, *Lost Landscapes and Failed Economies: The Search for a Value of Place* (Washington, D.C.: Island Press, 1996).

7. Blanton Owen, Rusty Marshall, Margie Purser, Terry Jordan, and others would fit this tintype.

8. The quotation is from Kinky Friedman, "God's Own Cowboys," *New York Times* (national ed.) 140 (1991): A11.

9. J. Frank Dobie, *Guide to Life and Literature of the Southwest*, rev. ed. (Dallas: Southern Methodist University Press, 1942, 1952), 89.

10. These two authors are among the more thoughtful proponents of land tenure studies, which often look at how distinctive legal regimes are created and sustained in the United States. Rose's arguments are presented in *Property and Persuasion* (Boulder, Colo.: Westview Press, 1993); and Ellickson's work in a variety of articles, and still more in *Order without Law: How Neighbors Settle Disputes* (Cambridge: Harvard University Press, 1991). Their shared argument is a concern with property law and its formation; they depart where it comes to the societal implications. Ellickson, in particular, has made a special point of examining the ranching world and its avoidance of transaction costs (following upon Coase's Nobel Prize–winning work) as reason enough for ranchers to try to settle disputes from within their community instead of having to go to outside parties.

11. John Fraser Hart is among the most careful and apt commentators on changing uses of American land. His book, *The Land That Feeds Us* (New York: Norton, 1991), has deserved status as a classic; his essay, "The Perimetropolitan Bow Wave," is among the few that makes real sense in looking at late-twentieth-century change in the American urban fringe landscape (*Geographical Review* 81, no. 1: 35–51).

12. The comment by Frank Popper appears in "Commentary: Zen Public-Land Policy," *American Land Forum Magazine* 7, no. 4 (fall 1986): 11–13. On the distinctions in law and practice across borders, consult Simon M. Evans, "The Origin of Ranching in Western Canada: American Diffusion or Victorian Transplant?" *Great Plains Quarterly* 3, no. 2 (1983): 79–91. The most significant ranching studies across scale include Richard Slatta, *Cowboys of the Americas* (New Haven: Yale University Press, 1990); and Terry G. Jordan, *North Amer-*

ican Cattle-Ranching Frontiers: Origins, Diffusion, and Differentiation (Albuquerque: University of New Mexico Press, 1993).

13. Alessandro Falassi, *Folklore by the Fireside: Text and Context of the Tuscan Veglia* (Austin: University of Texas Press, 1980).

14. This striking chapter, organizing cowhands into laboring cohorts, was attempted by both Big Bill Haywood (of World War I fame) and Karl Marx's daughter, Eleanor Marx Aveling. Both accounts are in the out-of-print *Looking Far West: The Search for the American West in History, Myth, and Literature,* eds. Frank Bergon and Zeese Papanikolas (New York: New American Library, 1978). The excerpts are entitled "Cowboy Proletarians" (Eleanor Marx Aveling and her husband, Edward Aveling), 390–392; and "Big Bill Organizes the Bronc Busters," 396–397.

15. Owen Ulph, *The Fiddleback: Lore of the Linecamp* (Salt Lake City, Utah: Dream Garden Press, 1981), 52–53.

16. Gertrude Stein, *The Geographical History of America; or, The Relationship of Human Nature to the Human Mind* (New York: Vintage, 1973).

17. Paul Wallace Gates, "The Land System of the United States in the Nineteenth Century" in *Proceedings of the First Congress of Historians from Mexico and the United States* (Monterrey, Nuevo Leon, Mexico, 4–9 September 1949; Mexico City: Editorial Cultura, 1950), 222–255.

18. Charles Olson, *Call Me Ishmael: A Study of Melville* (San Francisco: City Lights, 1948); Patricia Nelson Limerick, *Something in the Soil: Legacies and Reckonings in the New West* (New York: Norton, 2000), a suitable followup to her earlier opus, *The Legacy of Conquest: The Unbroken Past of the American West* (New York: Norton, 1987).

19. O. Henry (William S. Porter), *Heart of the West* (Garden City, N.Y.: Doubleday, 1911).

20. Donald Worster, *A River Running West: The Life of John Wesley Powell* (New York: Oxford University Press, 2000); the original is John Wesley Powell, G. K. Gilbert, C. E. Dutton, A. H. Thompson, and Willis J. Drummond, *Report on the Lands of the Arid Region of the United States, with a More Detailed Account of the Lands of Utah* (Washington, D.C.: Government Printing Office, 1879). The Stegner volume is, of course, *Beyond the Hundredth Meridian: John Wesley Powell and the Second Opening of the West* (1953; reprint, Lincoln: University of Nebraska Press, 1982).

21. Owen Wister, *The Virginian: A Horseman of the Plains* (1902; reprint, New York: New American Library, 1979).

22. Victor Davis Hanson, *The Other Greeks: The Family Farm and the Agrarian Roots of Western Civilization* (New York: Free Press, 1995).

23. Reyner Banham, "Having It All: Partisan Greed and Possession of the Desert," in *Old Southwest, New Southwest: Essays on a Region and Its Literature,* ed. Judy Nolte Lensink (Tucson, Ariz.: Tucson Public Library, 1987), 155–163.

24. Sandra Day O'Connor and H. Alan Day, *Lazy B: Growing Up on a Cattle Ranch in the American Southwest* (New York: Random House, 2002), 311.

25. Although I remain a fan of the idea of the *Atlas of the New West,* I have noted some of its problems in "Review of *Atlas of the New West,*" *Cartographic Perspectives* 30 (spring 1998): 65–68; and again in *Yearbook of the Association of Pacific Coast Geographers* 59 (1997): 144–149. To take a more judicious path, start with a look of your own and consult William Riebsame and James J. Robb, *Atlas of the New West: Portrait of a Changing Region,* essays by Patricia Nelson Limerick and Charles Wilkinson, photographs by Peter Goin (New York: Norton, 1997).

26. Bernard De Voto in 1934 wrote "The West: A Plundered Province" for *Harper's Monthly Magazine* 169: 355–364, although in the previous several years he had established *Harper's* as a paragon of defense of public land policy. From the distinguished anthropologist Joe Jorgensen emerged a brilliant essay examining the contrasting—and incommensurable— views of different southwestern groups: "Land Is Cultural, So Is a Commodity: The Locus of Differences among Indians, Cowboys, Sod-Busters, and Environmentalists," *Journal of Ethnic Studies* 12, no. 3 (1984): 1–21. This cross-disciplinary view was echoed by Carol Rose in a groundbreaking essay on boundaries, "The Comedy of the Commons: Custom, Commerce, and Inherently Public Property" *University of Chicago Law Review* 53, no. 4 (1986): 711–781, and later by Robert C. Ellickson, *Order without Law: How Neighbors Settle Disputes* (Cambridge: Harvard University Press, 1991). Interestingly, he had published on dispute resolution, in a California ranching context, the same year that Rose published her essay in his "Of Coase and Cattle: Dispute Resolution among Neighbors in Shasta County [California]," *Stanford Law Review* 38 (1986): 623–687.

27. John Brinckerhoff Jackson, "The Accessible Landscape," *Whole Earth Review* 58 (1988): 9.

28. The comment is by James J. Parsons, "Slicing Up the Open Space: Subdivisions without Homes in Northern California," *Erdkunde* 26, no. 1 (1972): 13–17; yet Parsons was more right about the dangers of subdivisions than in some of his speculations about the effects of livestock. Recent research by Jeremy Maestas, Rick Knight, and Wendell Gilgert documents biodiversity in plants and animals on rangeland, on subdivided land, and on protected land (such as parkland acreage where livestock grazing is excluded). Their data show that the highest biodiversity of native species, and highest diversity overall, is on rangeland. Although overgrazing can clearly be a problem, if the goal is diverse nature, grazed land may be just the thing. See Jeremy D. Maestas, Richard L. Knight, and Wendell C. Gilgert, "Biodiversity and Land-Use Change in the American Mountain West," *Geographical Review* 90, no. 3 (2001): 509–524.

3 | Land Tenure

The Spatial Musculature of the American West

JOHN B. WRIGHT

The morphology of landscape is part accident, part assertion, and always contested. When conflicting visions of land ownership and use collide, invigorating stress becomes enraging strain, and the outcome is typically tabulated as winners and losers. However, in the American West this robustly Darwinian process rarely results in the extinction of land claims, and places are best seen as shifting stages where the exercise of power and resistance to it vie for dominance. The matter of land tenure will always form the spatial musculature of this fractious region, but its geographic configuration is dynamic.

Land

The impress of the West's initial claimers, be they Indians or Europeans, remains vital in the landscape.[1] But this is rarely a monolithic, indelible stamp. Zelinsky's "Doctrine of First Effective Settlement" argues that an initial group's viable adaptation to a landscape will inevitably be absorbed and applied by succeeding cultures.[2] This doctrine assumes that land tenure patterns, once established and profitable, are at most amended and not erased. At its core is the assumption of maintained power. Evidence from the American West suggests both persistence through marshaled force and widespread, ideologically diverse opposition to it—often with a goal of reestablishing a former real or imagined tenure structure. Complainants abound, be they radical left or right, environmentalist or extractor, Indian, Hispano, Mormon, or Anglo. Turner's "frontier" may be over, but the matter of whose land it is and what the land should best be used for is far from decided.[3] For good or ill,

Limerick's "unbroken history" prevails, and the West remains a panorama of discord and dissent.[4]

Before Western land tenure conflicts can be explored, some basic reminders must first be offered about geographic myths, the assembly and disposal of land, and resulting regional patterns. For some, the American West and the rest of the United States are a manifest revelation of God's mercantile intention, for others a stark reminder of conquest, oppression, and destructive exploitation. A diversity of geographic thought stalks our world.

Myth

Myths are things that never were but always are. The Americas are a myth-ridden place where untruths and the search for meaning bind together like paralleling strands of a rope.[5]

In the West, the strands continue to tighten like a noose.

Two dominant myths about the Americas at the time of European contact—that the land was largely unoccupied and that the land was ecologically pristine—have proven to be stunningly false. Denevan, drawing on work ranging from Woodrow Borah to George Lovell, speculates that 54 million indigenous people resided in the Americas in the marker year of 1492.[6] North America contained four million with a sizeable population in the Southwest (125,000). A heavily peopled landscape was at once inconvenient and auspicious for Europeans seeking wealth and souls through the sword and cross. The immense demographic losses from disease, famine, and war between 1492 and 1650 may have created the impression of "emptiness," but in no fashion can the land ever be dismissed as unclaimed. The persistence of this myth still plays out in land tenure disputes between Indian nations and the U.S. government.[7]

The Edenic myth of an environmental paradise in the Americas also collapses from the simplest of things, a declarative recital of land alteration at the time of contact: the Pleistocene extinctions of megafauna,[8] widespread forest clearing, grassland creation and maintenance by fire, the construction of agricultural fields, terraces, ridges, and mounds,[9] the vast irrigation systems of the Aztec, Hohokam, and Inca,[10] immense cities, causeways, and thousands of miles of roads.[11] The survival of this myth can largely be blamed on vivid mass-culture representations in movies such as *1492—The Conquest of Paradise* and by the uninformed or disingenuous statements of environmentalists (and some Indians) falling back on selective portrayals of Indians as pacifist "ecologists."[12]

Myths arise whenever needed. During the homesteading era, untested farmers prayed that plowing the soil or planting trees would bring civilizing rain to a stubbornly arid landscape.[13] During the neohomesteading residential boom of the late twentieth century, amenity migrants to the Rockies would prefer that warmth follows the Mercedes. Misperceptions, abetted by real estate agents and other growth-promoting "boomers," continue to lure the unprepared into the West from former utopian enclaves in California now gone overgrown and feral.[14] Myths collapse upon entry, and migrants often flee after discovering that much of the West really *is* much different than expected.[15] It is revealed to be a dualistic region—one that is colder and hotter than rumored; environmentally ransacked and conserved; disappointingly urban and relentlessly rural; safer but not crime-free; safer but not absent earthquakes, fires, and floods; cheaper to live in but bereft of meaningful wages; a place for a fresh start but one where locals belittle new arrivals; and ultimately, the West is unmasked as a frustratingly real terrain where your problems do not abate from the gentle whispering of horse healers or the wetting of a trout fly line.

But the most powerful myth of the postmodern West is that its land-mad past has been reprieved to quaint panoramas, fiction, art, movies, affected fashion, cowboy pop music, and retro log architecture. The visceral disputes over land and life in each Western state come as a complete shock to newcomers. No one told them that the geographic rules hadn't been nailed down. It has been this way from the beginning, throughout the assembly and disposal of the land base we call the United States of America.

Assembly

The main period of land acquisition by the U.S. government spanned the years of 1789–1867. Spreading out from the core of thirteen colonies in the East, an American westering urge became an unstoppable juggernaut of manifest destiny that stalled briefly at the Pacific Rim, only to reemerge in Hawaii. During this explosive expansion, half-meant treaties with Indian nations, cessions, purchases, annexations, and hardball treaties with Mexico and Britain were used to absorb 2.3 billion acres in a broad swath of resource-rich temperate zone terrain.[16] Thomas Jefferson was an egalitarian transcontinental thinker and a slave owner. America was spawned from these Jeffersonian fraternal twins of expansive optimism and exclusive arrogance. The country's present global economic and military dominance rose from the resulting land base and tradition of righteous aggression, as did persistent land tenure conflicts in the West.

The American process of land assembly was little concerned with the niceties of law or ethics. Of the 800 treaties entered into with Indian nations, 430 were never ratified by Congress, and significant provisions of the remaining 370 ratified treaties were broken.[17] Regarding Mexico, it was a weak state and could not sustain its claims, so fight. Use the Mormon settlement of Utah as a weapon of war. Stare down the English in the Pacific Northwest. Chase away, kill, or intimidate anyone who complained. The intention was brutally elegant—take more land. America was born of conquest and the raw, unadorned application of force. Taking land was simply the nineteenth-century way of state building. Racial bigotry and the recitation of geographic and cultural myths were used to rationalize the capturing of what was manifestly "American." There would be winners and losers. We would be the winners. There was little chance it would emerge any other way.

Map 3.1 and Table 3.1 display the pattern of land claiming and the costs involved. America came cheap—an average cost of thirteen cents per acre.[18] This would become the single most lucrative real estate takeover in history. Over the years, the disposal of much of these lands would bring in sufficient revenues and taxes to build budget surpluses, implement an awakening industrial society, and eventually transform America into a globalizing colossus.

Disposal

The United States came of age as a real estate broker. The laws and acts passed by Congress were centered on a ferocious set of ideas—fill the land with people, farm the soils, graze the grasses, extract the metals, cut the forests, dam the rivers, and prevail against rank nature.[19] Transform chaos into cosmos whatever it took. Build America. Succeed. Get rich. Then get richer. The noble idea of making land and prosperity available to all classes (a clear response to the "King's Woods mentality" of the still-much-hated English) quickly morphed into base corruption and crude laissez-faire rationales for breaking laws while breaking land.

The myth of a pristine and durable (or at least a limitless) West excused all abuses. If you failed here you could pull up stakes and try again there. If you violated a law, that was forgivable, everyone else was doing it. Western settlement came from this absence of law and order. Worse, it often occurred with little concern for justice. Once again, this was simply the nineteenth-century way.

A listing of selected methods of land and resource disposal displays the range of ways the captured land was more or less given away. The essential dualism of the West is revealed in the intentions and outcomes of each piece of legislation.

General Land Office (1812)—real estate brokerage
General Preemption Act (1841)—squatter's rights
Homestead Act (1862)—160 acres free
Railroad grants—giveaways of vast corridors/checkerboards
Mining Law (1872)—mineral giveaway
Timber Culture Act (1873)—160 acres free
Desert Land Act (1877)—640 acres/$1.25 per acre
Timber Cutting/Timber and Stone Acts (1878)—timber and land giveaways
Reclamation Act (1902)—water subsidies
Enlarged Homestead Act (1909)—320 acres free
Stock Raising Homestead Act (1916)—640 acres/$1.25 per acre
Taylor Grazing Act (1934)—grazing subsidies
Bureau of Land Management (1946)—grazing subsidies
Farmer's Home Administration (1950)—farmland subdivision loans
Subdivision Regulations (2000)—de facto homestead acts

Various homesteading bills both provided precious opportunity to a burgeoning population and preordained the failure of most farmers in an arid
province.[20] Plowing brought on by the 1862 Homestead Act brought no rain.
Various railroad grants extended trade but railroaded naive land-hungry folk
into sure-lose gambles. The 1872 Mining Law said if you find minerals anywhere on federal land feel free to mine them. This law is still in force, creating fiscal, social, and ecological upheaval throughout the region. The Timber
Culture Act of 1873 was endorsed by Bernard Fernow, the first president of
the Society of American Foresters. He promised that trees would bring rain.
Of course, they did not. The Desert Land Act of 1877 tempted farmers out
onto often unirrigable land and forced them to lie by saying they had applied
water in order to keep it. The Bureau of Reclamation dammed rivers and
created agricultural districts in arid lands. Many of these acres are now urbanized and out of production. Forest reserves were formed to stop timber
poaching only to devolve into a National Forest system run as a timber company, thus creating the present crisis of confidence. As late as 1909, the Enlarged Homestead Act lured mostly urban dwellers into 640-acre wheat
farms that boomed during the high prices and moist storms of World War I
and failed when peace and aridity returned. The Taylor Grazing Act of 1934
leased away unhomesteaded land for pennies, a practice continued since the
formation of the Bureau of Land Management (BLM) in 1946 from the
merger of the General Land Office and the Grazing Service. The BLM remains
one of the most controversial agencies in the West, taking hits from both the

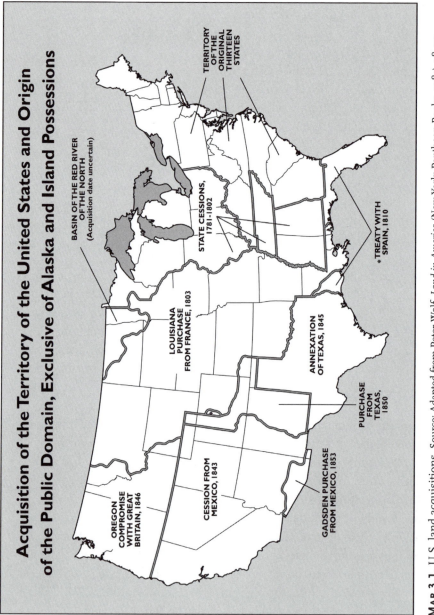

Acquisition of the Territory of the United States and Origin of the Public Domain, Exclusive of Alaska and Island Possessions

BASIN OF THE RED RIVER
OF THE NORTH
(Acquisition date uncertain)

TERRITORY
OF THE
ORIGINAL
THIRTEEN
STATES

STATE CESSIONS,
1781-1802

LOUISIANA
PURCHASE
FROM FRANCE, 1803

*TREATY WITH
SPAIN, 1810

OREGON
COMPROMISE
WITH GREAT
BRITAIN, 1846

CESSION FROM
MEXICO, 1843

ANNEXATION
OF TEXAS, 1845

PURCHASE
FROM
TEXAS,
1850

GADSDEN PURCHASE
FROM MEXICO, 1853

MAP 3.1. U.S. land acquisitions. Source: Adapted from Peter Wolf, *Land in America* (New York: Pantheon Books, 1981), 38–39.

Table 3.1 Acreage and Costs of Acquisitions

Date	Acquisitions	Area (in thousands of acres)			Cost (in thousands of dollars)	Price per acre($)
		Total	Land Only	Inland Water		
1781–1802	State cessions	236,826	233,416	3,410 (10%)	6,200	.11
1789–1850	Indian treaties	45,000	—	— (19%)	90,000	0.20
1803	Louisiana Purchase	529,912	523,446	6,465 (23%)	23,214	0.04
1819	Cession from Spain (Florida)	46,145	43,343	2,802 (2%)	6,674	0.14
	Red River Purchase	29,602	29,067	535 (1%)	—	—
1846	Oregon Compromise	183,386	180,644	2,742 (8%)	—	—
1848	Mexican Cession	338,681	334,479	4,202 (15%)	16,295	0.05
1850	Purchase from Texas	78,927	78,843	84 (3%)	15,496	0.20
1853	Gadsden Purchase	18,989	18,962	27 (1%)	10,000	0.53
1867	Alaska Purchase	375,304	362,516	12,787 (16%)	7,200	0.02
Total area of United States today		2,313,678	0.13 (price per acre)			
Aggregate		2,287,772	1,804,716	33,054	175,079	

Source: Adapted from Peter Wolf, *Land in America: Its Value, Use and Control* (New York: Pantheon, 1981), 38–39.

environmental left seeking wilderness and an end to "welfare ranching" and the privatizing right seeking a Reaganite "assets management" auctioning of the public domain for development.

This disposal birthed a Western regional ethos about property and resources—the landscape is something to exploit with no limits and regulations, often with the help of federal subsidies. Among conservatives, there is often little discernment between public and private land; public land should be made private, and private lands should be off limits to interference. Among centrists and liberals, public lands such as national parks and forests, monuments, and wilderness areas are sacrosanct, communal treasures in need of guardianship and expansion. On private lands the conflict between individualism and community plays out in the arena of land use planning, where conservatives largely prevail. The land subdivision laws in much of the West are weak and function as de facto homestead acts, barely addressing how land *will be* developed, let alone whether it *should be.*[21] This circumstance is challenged by planners seeking to strengthen their regulatory grip and land trusts assembling conservation easements, land purchases, and land exchanges in order to protect key areas from development in the face of regulatory ineffectiveness. The disposal of land base continues, countered as always by the West's dualistic impulse to conserve.

Pattern

The result of all this reaping and sowing of land is an elaborate, involuted, multifarious, and bollixed-up tenure pattern, one that reflects diverse values and often contradictory intentions. The pattern is, of course, seen differently by various cultures, each with its own memory of injustices old and new, real and perceived, defensible and self-serving.

The West is a place of checkerboards, mosaics, center-pivot circles, long-lot traces, metes and bounds wanderings, and what Wilbur Zelinsky calls "relentless rectangularity"[22]—a township and range grid overlaid onto topography more suited to calculus than geometry. As a result, the survey lines are thinly etched, and beneath map colors lies dissension. Land tenure in the West is multileveled and multivariate, extending beyond the separation of mineral rights from surface rights to the very essence of fee-simple ownership itself. Westerners do not believe in map colors, and new land tenure patterns are always emerging. Land trusts cleave development rights from ranches using financial compensation;[23] the federal Conservation Reserve Program(CRP), Wetlands Reserve Program (WRP), and Payment in Kind (PIK) Program do the same on erosive soils and sensitive wetlands;[24] the BLM disposes of thousands of surplus acres around Las Vegas and completes land exchanges elsewhere;[25] conservation hybrids are configured for the expansive Baca and Gray ranches in New Mexico;[26] Hispanos challenge land grant adjudications;[27] Mormons expand an urban megalopolis onto federal lands to advance Olympic dreams;[28] and sagebrush rebels engage in jihads against the loathed federal government using bluster and threat.[29] The drive to revise tenure continues apace. However, the essential apportionment still persists like rusting, competent iron.

Conflict

Modernity is both a solvent and a reagent; it destroys and stimulates saving. This is extraordinarily true regarding the West's land tenure. The scope of topics involved ranges from mining, logging, grazing, wolf/grizzly bear reintroduction, parks, land trusts, Indian rights, subdivisions, water rights, and historic land grant claims. Moreover, vital and politically diverse regional cultures continue to exert tremendous influence on the shape of the debate. To grasp this marvelous depth and disarray, a conceptual scheme is needed.

Tables 3.2 and 3.3 are offered as a subjective starting point for dissecting the elements of land tenure conflicts. It is by no means all embracing, nor does it present the dominant or essential issue for every state. Other choices could have been made. Its aim is to evoke the complexity here and break down the subject in a somewhat systematic way for discussion.

Every land tenure conflict has a principal complainant—an aggrieved party initiating protest and/or action. The conflicts are often loudly confrontational but sometimes less so. There is always an initiating cause: a law, treaty, social trend, or historic event setting enmity in motion. Each conflict has a configuration involving varying numbers of groups.

Table 3.2 Tenure Conflicts

Configuration	Geographic Thought	Cultural Expression	Response
TRIANGULAR Ranchers Δ Env Feds	Sagebrush Rebellion	antigovernment activism	conspiracy theories and retrenchment
BIPOLAR ↔ Stewards Developers	Last Best Place	rural romanticism	land trust conservation projects
TRIANGULAR Indians Δ Feds Activists	Newe Sogobia	human rights and antinuclear activism	protest and the courts
RECTANGULAR Hispanos Indians ☐ Feds Anglos	Tierra ◯ Muerte	raza activism	*cooperativas* and the courts
BIPOLAR ↔ Gentiles Mormons	Zion	urban millennialism	consolidation of power

Table 3.3 Western Land

State	Principal Complainant	Conflict	Initiation
Arizona	Anglo ranchers	grazing vs. national park	Grand Canyon–Parashant National Monument, 2000
Montana	Conservationists	open space vs. subdivision	late twentieth-century growth
Nevada	Indians	Western Shoshones vs. federal government	Treaty of Ruby Valley, 1863
New Mexico	Hispanos	land grant heirs vs. Anglos	Treaty of Guadalupe Hidalgo, 1848
Utah	Mormons	City for God vs. Gentiles	LDS arrival, 1847

The principal complainant is empowered by a defining geographic thought that finds an activist, romanticist, millennialist, utopian, or other cultural expression. Finally, there is a response, a course of strategic or opportunistic actions across the ideological spectrum. The following examination of conflicts in five Western states illustrates this conceptual scheme and reminds us of the persistent power of land tenure in comprehending the geography of the region. Table 3.4 shows how land in five selected Western states is held at present.

Arizona

Arizona contains 20 million of the 44 million acres of Indian land in the United States—the highest acreage and percentage total of any state.[30] Regarding land tenure, Arizona is most widely known for the Navajo/Hopi land dispute dating back to 1882, when President Chester A. Arthur established a vast reservation for the Hopi "and other such Indians as the Secretary of the Interior may see fit."[31] Much has rightfully been written about this topic,[32] but the recent establishment of the Grand Canyon–Parashant National Monument is selected for review here.

President Teddy Roosevelt used the 1906 Antiquities Act to safeguard the first portions of the canyon. In 1919, Roosevelt's monument became Grand Canyon National Park. Additional monuments were added in 1932 and 1969 and melded into the whole in 1975.[33] Conservation groups such as the Grand

Canyon Trust backed the creation of the Parashant monument for decades. The issue came to a head in 1999 when Arizona Congressman Bob Stump offered a "protection" bill for the area backed by ranching and mining interests. Among its provisions were the banning of wilderness study areas, continuation of high levels of commercial air tours, requirements allowing mineral entry and development, the building of one hundred miles of roads to remote North Rim sites such as Toroweap Overlook, publicizing of antiquity sites, and the transference of vast tracts to adjacent towns and Mohave County for development.[34] These terms reflected a vocal but minority position and were not included in the final bill.

On 11 January 2000 President Clinton signed an executive order creating the 1,014,000-acre Grand Canyon–Parashant National Monument north of Grand Canyon National Park and the Lake Mead National Recreation Area. Authority for this action came from the very same 1906 Antiquities Act, meaning that no approval of Congress was needed, as is the case for national parks. The monument contains abundant geological and ecological merits as well as evidences of Anasazi, Spanish, and Mormon presence. President Clinton's action was in the tradition of Roosevelt and may result in further expansion of Grand Canyon National Park in coming years. Much of the country was thrilled with the president's action. However, ranchers continue to be alarmed about threats to grazing. Although the bill did not ban grazing, it allows changes in management that could seriously impact cattle operations.

This is a classic Western tenure standoff. Conservationists speak of "corridors, buffers, and landscape ecology."[35] Ranchers speak of "animal units, family traditions, ranching culture."[36] They portray themselves, sometimes

Table 3.4 Land Ownership in Selected Western States (%)

State	Federal	State	Indians	Private
Arizona	44.0	13.0	26.0	17.0
Montana	32.0	6.0	3.0	59.0
Nevada	88.0	0.2	2.0	9.8
New Mexico	34.0	12.0	10.0	44.0
Utah	67.0	7.0	4.0	22.0

Source: National Wilderness Institute, "State by State Government Land Ownership" (www.nwi.org/Maps/LandChart.html).

overzealously, as good stewards and are outraged by calls for the mitigation, restriction, or elimination of grazing.[37] They know they're being steam-rolled, and it enrages them. Many attack the science and philosophy behind federal policy changes and retrench into the conspiracy theories of the Sagebrush Rebellion and resort to embittered antigovernment rhetoric.[38] It is the same story across the West wherever liberal national visions collide with conservative local ones—Catron County, New Mexico, Jordan, Montana, almost anywhere in rural Nevada. Rural ranchers still perceive leased "public land" as theirs and resent environmentally green, greenhorn outsiders reminding them that it isn't.

A management plan for the Grand Canyon–Parashant National Monument will be written after the BLM and National Park Service conduct hearings and weigh the arguments of conservation groups, ranchers, recreationists, miners, and developers. From that highly charged process will emerge the true land tenure arrangements for this expanse. It will come hard.

Montana

Montana is a place of mercantile mystique. Literature and films such as *A River Runs through It* and *The Horse Whisperer* have helped make land in the state a highly marketable, mythical commodity. The anthology entitled *The Last Best Place* contains the work of scores of Montana writers.[39] Despite the difficulties of life represented in these works, they helped anoint Montana as one of the West's preferred destinations for amenity migrants.

The essential choice in Big Sky country is between land development and land conservation. Whereas 59 percent of the state is privately owned, the percentage in eight mountainous western Montana counties shrinks to 12–35 percent. These are the endangered landscapes where 90 percent of the state's population growth occurred during the 1990s—most of that from in-migration, 25 percent of the *total gain* coming from California in-migrants alone.[40] These booming valleys—the Bitterroot, the Flathead, the Gallatin, and others —also contain much of the region's big game winter range habitat, riparian and wetland ecosystems, agricultural land, historical and archeological sites and structures, day-to-day recreation opportunities (river corridors), and foreground open space. Privately owned valleys hold the landscape together. High-elevation public "islands," be they national parks or wilderness, are not sufficient to maintain the whole. What results is a spatial pressure cooker of competing landscape visions. Developers want the world to be platted and sold—for the disposal to continue. Conservationists want to save the best of what is left—for the disposal to cease or at least be transformed into a land-saving force.

In Montana, land subdivision and development have always proceeded unfettered by regulations. Montana's largest homesteading influx happened during the World War I era. The Enlarged Homestead Act and railroad companies enticed eighty-five thousand migrants to settle on dryland sections in places like the "High Line" along the state's northern tier. By 1919, demand crashed, rain ceased, and sixty-five thousand fled the state.[41] This railroading did nothing to cinch in Montanans' enthusiasm for unregulated subdivision. Let the buyer beware. As a result, state subdivision laws have consistently excluded most land splitting from planning review. Only recently did the law change to require that all splits be approved. Typically, this only involves a nominal check for road and power easements and the receipt of an easily won septic tank permit. In most places, growth spreads across the landscape with great help and little opposition from government.

This process is now being recast. The state's six nonprofit land trust groups have conserved over 550,000 acres using voluntary, financially compensating tools such as conservation easements, land acquisitions, purchases of development rights (PDRS), and land exchanges.[42] Voters have passed open space bonds in Missoula ($5 million) and Helena ($2 million) to buy land and development rights in greenbelts and create more livable cities. Great Falls has acquired a linear park along the Missouri River encompassing the route of Lewis and Clark. Land exchanges are widely used in Montana to rearrange senseless tenure patterns—the creation of the Rattlesnake Wilderness and National Recreation Area and the protection of the Missouri River Breaks being notable. The essential idea of conservation easements and PDRS is to legally and perpetually sever destructive land use rights such as subdivision, clear-cutting, and mining from the underlying fee-simple title.[43] The property stays in private hands but with the resulting protection of open space, habitat, and place. Trusts build partnerships with private landowners and otherwise create stewardship-enhancing forms of land tenure.

In the Blackfoot River Valley near Missoula, more than fifteen thousand acres of open land are now protected by conservation easements within a twenty-two-mile-long corridor. The Montana Land Reliance has saved over 300,000 acres of ecologically vital riverside ranch lands.[44] The group is now saving dozens of working ranches per year from subdivision and development. Ranching families now see land trusts as an ally in contending with immense estate tax burdens arising from the land's appreciation during the

1990s real estate boom. A conservation easement placed on a $2 million ranch can result in it being passed on to the next generation without any estate tax due. Without the easement, the tax bill could exceed $600,000, forcing the heirs to sell out for development.[45]

The conflict between open space and subdivision, stewards and developers is, on its face, structurally bipolar. However, although opposition exists to the new land tenure arrangements being forged by trusts, more and more real estate agents are now integrating tools such as conservation easements into their brokerage operations. Firms such as American Public Land Exchange in Missoula and OutLandish in Helena focus entirely on the seeming oxymoron of "conservation real estate." Whether representing a buyer or seller, these real estate agent/conservationists protect lands from inappropriate development. "Conservation buyers" are found for endangered ranches; the buyers then place perpetual conservation easements on the property prohibiting future division.

"The Last Best Place" is a typically Western dualistic refrain. It invites actions to save land but is ethnocentric and generates growth-promoting myths about Montana. The phrase has become ubiquitous in the real estate listings, as is "A River Runs through It" for every property with ten feet of frontage on an irrigation ditch. But catchphrases do not create myths, they simply name them, in this case, capturing the inherent rural romanticism and antiurban sentiments of Montanans both new and old.

The debate over the development of private land is Montana's land tenure essence. Land trusts have conserved more acreage than in any other state and continue to expand their effectiveness. Entire valleys are now being saved, indicating the ascendant practical power of the land trust response. If we are to understand land tenure in Montana we must grasp this process.

Nevada

Traditional interpretations of Nevada's historical geography sometimes describe Nevada as a leftover place, a landscape where minerals are coveted but residency is not—an unwanted "empty quarter."[46] Following the Mexican Cession in 1848, Nevada territory was expanded by carving off several pieces of Utah from expansionistic Mormons. But even with that, little of Nevada was homesteaded. It was too arid and remote. Its early history centered on mining in Austin, Eureka, and Virginia City. The vast interior lay mostly unclaimed. Ranches were established in the better-watered basins (such as the Ruby, Big Smoky, and Huntington valleys), but much of the landscape remained part of the federal domain. Today, 88 percent of Nevada is federal land administered by the Bureau of Land Management, Forest Service, and various branches of the military. Some 90 percent of its people live in anomalous Las Vegas and Reno at the very margins of the state. The interior appears empty.

This story of an unclaimed Nevada is much repeated but untrue—much of the landscape in a broad swath cutting across the central part of the state may belong to another nation, the Western Shoshones. Their name for the landscape is Newe Sogobia, and they want it back.

It is a convoluted tale.

The Treaty of Ruby Valley in 1863 initiated the dispute. The United States believed the document *ceded* much of the land in present-day Nevada; the Western Shoshones thought they were only granting *access and permission* for mineral development, fort construction, limited ranching, and the building of the transcontinental railroad—to them it was a kind of *lease*.[47]

In any case, the treaty was ignored by settlers and the federal government. In 1946, the Indian Claims Commission tried but failed to simply extinguish the entire Shoshone claim.

In 1953, U.S. nuclear testing moved from Pacific islands such as Bikini and Kwajalein to the Nevada Test Site in the heart of Newe Sogobia. Nuclearism came to the desert. Over the next forty years, 928 nuclear "tests" were conducted at the site[48]—120 were aboveground nuclear detonations that trailed lethal radiation as far away as the "down winders" of Utah.[49]

The Western Shoshones continued their struggle for Newe Sogobia. In 1966, federal courts acknowledged the unlawful taking of the land, and the federal government offered to pay the nation $1.05 per acre—the 1863 appraised value. The Western Shoshones refused the offer, and many Indian ranchers began protesting paying BLM grazing fees for land they felt was already theirs.

In 1979, President Carter proposed building the Mobile MX missile system on the contested ground. The government offered $20 million to resolve the dispute, but the tribe again refused the offer. A 1980 U.S. Air Force study again verified the legal validity of the Shoshone claim and urged making a payment to clear the way for MX construction. As payment figures grew, the tribe became split—some wanted the money, others wanted to hold out for land. In 1985, a frustrated federal judge arbitrarily "extinguished" Western Shoshone land rights based on a flawed finding of the Indian Claims Commission.[50] The government simply retreated to its initial position—the Treaty of Ruby Valley was a cession of land. However, by 1987 the issue remained sufficiently unsettled for Defense Secretary Caspar Weinberger to remove the Nevada site from M-X consideration. With the ascendance of the Strategic Defense Initiative ("Star Wars"), the issue retreated from the news.

But it did not go away. The 1985 "extinguishment" contained a puzzling offer to pay the Western Shoshones fifteen cents per acre for Newe Sogobia. Although the nation refused payment, the money was placed in a U.S. Treasury account, where it has stayed. The federal government considers the matter settled; the Western Shoshone nation does not.

This land tenure conflict has now grown dazzlingly complex. Antinuclear activists—including cancer-ravaged Mormon families and Japanese "Hibakusha," survivors of the Hiroshima and Nagasaki nuclear bombs—have joined the Indian cause. The siting of the high-level nuclear waste facility at Yucca Mountain (at the sacred center of Newe Sogobia) has broadened support for the Western Shoshone case. Activists believe the Western Shoshones would prohibit nuclear development and be more ecologically sensitive in range and timber management. Both are still unproven concepts. In fact, the revocation of BLM grazing permits from tribal members, such as the famous case of the Dann sisters, may be more about poor stewardship than a violation of social justice, as the Inter-American Commission on Human Rights contends. However, the conversion of formerly grazed lands in the Carlin Trend to cyanide heap leach gold mines under the 1972 Mining Law does add intrigue to such charges.

Today, the four thousand members of the Western Shoshone nation remain vitally concerned with the resolution of this land tenure case. In recent years, the nation has called for the return of the Newe Sogobia and an annual lease payment of $600 million, should the U.S. government wish to continue exploiting its resources. The economic and cultural future of the Western Shoshones depends on the outcome of such negotiations.

What is certain is this—the issue will not extinguish. A return of all the land appears unlikely, but ongoing efforts in Canada and Australia to turn back federal land to indigenous peoples merit watching.[51] Even if the land is not fully conveyed, it is probable that new forms of land tenure will be invented to resolve an obvious injustice. The Western Shoshones and federal agencies might share management and receipts, sacred sites could be off limits to nontribal use (including the discontinuance of Yucca Mountain as a waste repository), bicultural standards for mining could be crafted, and restoration plans could be created to reclaim the land from nuclear abuse.

New Mexico

No place in the United States has a more cryptic and divisive land tenure history than northern New Mexico. A voluminous literature explores the sometimes arcane details of the region's Indian, Spanish, Mexican, and American periods of land claiming.[52] Whereas a land ownership map can start a bar fight throughout most of the West, in New Mexico it can lead to gunplay.

The Spanish *entrada* into New Mexico focused on Rio Arriba, the upper Rio Grande country around Santa Fe. Fifty thousand Indian souls and the promising natural resources led to the partitioning of the landscape into *mercedes reales*—land grants from the king of Spain. Pueblo grants began in 1689 as small but politically vital peace offerings to the nations responsible for the temporary Spanish ouster during the Pueblo Revolt of 1680. Once back in control, the Spanish made grants to *ricos* (wealthy elites) and soldiers. Community grants were given to groups of ten families or more to develop the land, produce goods, generate taxes, and serve as border garrisons against Apache, Comanche, Ute, and Navajo raids into the Rio Grande basin. Each community land grant had a village with a defensive plaza, church, and small tracts for *parciantes* (water users often farming classic Spanish/French long lots).[53] Fields were watered using *acequias* (irrigation ditches) overseen by a *mayordomo* (ditch master).[54] The *ejido* (jointly owned common area) surrounded the village and was a place where everyone could graze livestock, cut wood, and otherwise share the resources. During the Spanish period (1539–1821), 106 pueblo, individual, and community grants were dispersed totaling eight million acres mostly within ten miles of the Rio Grande.

Following Mexican independence in 1821, land granting continued to focus more on vast *sitio* or *rancho* allocations in the valleys and plains east and north of the Sangre de Cristo Mountains. More than one hundred additional grants were made covering more than 25 million acres.

By 1846, American mercantile and military expansionism led to a brief, one-sided war with Mexico that ended in 1848 with the signing of the Treaty of Guadalupe Hidalgo, which moved the 339 million-acre Mexican Cession into U.S. hands for five cents per acre.[55]

Article 8 of the treaty stipulated that the United States would honor all land grant ownerships.[56] This stipulation has been systematically violated ever since. Whereas pueblo grants emerged relatively intact ("reservations" were a familiar idea to politicians), grants held by Hispanos were simply too immense and resource rich to let stand. Between 1854 and 1900, first the

Surveyor General's Office and then the Court of Private Land Claims refused to patent much of the land grant terrain in northern New Mexico. More than 70 percent of all claims were rejected based on inexact surveys and records, legal technicalities, and a court-permitted confiscation of *ejido* acreage based on the Sandoval decision—a convenient, ironic ruling that English common law did not allow for "the commons." In truth, *ejidos* were jointly owned private property and not *tierras realengas*—"royal lands" held by the king. In addition, even where grants were accepted they were often greatly reduced in area. Speculator cartels, such as Thomas Catron's infamous Santa Fe Ring, used various shady and illegal practices to strip away even more land. As a result, of the 33 million acres in land grants, less than 4 million acres were held on to by Hispanos and Indians.[57] The remainder fell into Anglo hands or is today mapped in the colors of the U.S. Forest Service, Bureau of Land Management, or state of New Mexico.

This land tenure pattern is fraught with continuing tensions. *La Mano Negro*—"the Black Hand" movement—has "monkey wrenched" Anglo fences, ditches, and equipment for decades.

In 1967, Reies Tijerina, head of the *Alianza Federal de Mercedes* (Federal Alliance of Land Grants) led an armed uprising in Rio Arriba County north of Santa Fe. Tijerina and twenty armed *valiantes* (militants) stormed the courthouse in Tierra Amarilla seeking to kidnap a much-hated district attorney. A deputy was wounded and two hostages taken. The governor called out the National Guard—tanks and hundreds of troops invaded the valley. Tijerina and scores of others were arrested, but no serious convictions resulted due to the sentiments of Hispano jurors at that time. John Nichols' *Milagro Beanfield War* was a loosely based, gentle version of this revolt.

Tierra o Muerte—"Land or Death"—remains the defining geographic thought of many Hispanos. Three basic responses can be seen in the state— economic development *cooperativas* (co-ops), protest, and legal action. A weaving/lamb meat co-op based near Tierra Amarilla, *Ganados del Valle*— "Livestock Growers of the Valley"—combines all three, striving for economic self-determination and fighting for a return of or access to former *ejido* lands for their flocks.[58] The Forest Trust in Santa Fe works with Hispanos on forest management and creates timber *cooperativas* for the marketing of logs, *vigas*, and *latillas* for Santa Fe chic architecture. Reies Tijerina is now a lawyer, fighting the same battle wearing a three-piece suit.

How valid are the Hispano land grant claims? Conservative New Mexico Congressman Bill Redmond supports a readjudication and states "this is simply an issue of fairness."[59] In February 2000, the dominantly Republican

New Mexico congressional delegation introduced a bill to reopen federal hearings on land grants. The heirs of the lost landscape are being asked to once again come forward and make their case. Adjustments in access to and ownership of federal land are in store. The bitter irony of the portrayal of Hispanos—the descendants of the conquistadores—as a persecuted people is not lost on the region's Indian nations, who have joined the fray to win back certain prized lands. The larger question is simply too obvious and impossible to ask.

Utah

Utah is a Mormon nation where 80 percent of the state's residents are members of the Church of Jesus Christ of Latter-day Saints. Since their arrival in 1847, the Mormon people have staked a largely uncontradicted claim to their Great Basin kingdom.[60] Brigham Young, the stern genius, marshaled both a gathering to the Wasatch Front and a diaspora throughout Utah, southern Idaho, and much of Arizona.[61] The early Mormon cultural landscape was based on Joseph Smith's agrarian, utopian vision of the plat for the City of Zion. Smith imagined clustered farming towns, reminiscent of his native upstate New York and nearby New England. After his murder on the trek west, many such towns were built in Utah where a distinctive cultural impress evolved.[62] Whereas Smith foresaw cities of no more than twenty thousand residents surrounded by open space, Brigham Young directed the settlement process, and his version of Zion was urban and industrial.[63] Young saw no limits to growth. In his view, righteousness and plain survival in an arid country depended on expansion and the vigorous exploitation of nature. This remains mostly the way things are in Utah.

In *Rocky Mountain Divide: Selling and Saving the West* (1993), I argued this point, receiving both praise and derision for doing so.[64] But the facts remain compelling: Today, 85 percent of all Utahans live in the Wasatch Front urban corridor. Utah is the least conservation-minded state in the American West (as any working conservationist can attest) and was the last state to have a Department of Natural Resources; it has the poorest record of land trust conservation projects in the region (one land trust group compared to thirty-five in adjacent Colorado), has a rambunctiously antienvironmental congressional delegation (led by Senator Orrin Hatch, a Mormon gospel doctrine instructor), is a place where President Clinton not only lost the state in the 1996 election but also finished fourth in some counties behind Dole, Perot, and separatist Bo Gritz, and is the only state in the intermountain West that would ever seek, let alone secure, the Olympic Games.

Utah is about development. Brigham Young's prime directive to "build up Zion" is still being obeyed. The surprising and much-publicized corruption exhibited by Utah's heavily Mormon Olympic Committee is testimony to the strength of this prime directive. As always, the landscape provides the final evidence—the Olympics stimulated an unprecedented construction boom in roads, businesses, and residential/recreational development. The Olympics were about building up Zion, about real estate and profit, about silk and money, not milk and honey, and were most assuredly not about feel-good sentiments such as the "international Olympic movement."

The separation of church and state is essentially nonexistent in Utah. Nothing happens by accident in this theocracy. The Beehive State is a place of aggressive capitalism but communal effort. The land tenure vision of Young, the essential prophet, is quite simple—build a city for God free from secular doubt. To seriously advocate limits in Utah is a sign of nonbelief; heresy if not apostasy. Urban millennialists with the highest birth rate in the country who await a divine advent when Christ will return to cleanse the earth and "perfect it as their paradisiacal home" tend to be little concerned with conservation.

The central land tenure conflict in Utah is between the Mormon drive for endless development and the often Gentile call for conservation, limits to growth, and diversity of thought. This may seem simplistic, but an investigation of any depth or even a brief trip to the state reveals it to be indelibly true. Given the demographic, economic, and political hold that Mormons have on the state, their main response to any challenge to development has always been the ardent consolidation of power. They continue to excel at it.

Prospect

This brief exploration reveals something deceptively plain—land tenure remains the spatial musculature of a changing region. Even as modernity advances and geographic patterns shift, the underlying question persists. Who *does* own the land?[65]

The preceding scheme (Table 3.2) reveals that much is gained by considering that question using a straightforward structural framework. A full array of cultures and ideologies jostles for position in the West, and the American ethos of winners and losers weighs heavy on the land. If new and more socially, environmentally, and economically defensible patterns are to emerge we must break the unbroken history of the American West. History must become bunk. To that end, the Darwinian struggle for dominance must shift to a zero-sum game of cooperation and collaboration. We must exhume and heal our many inconvenient pasts with an intention of equity and justice for land and people.[66] *"Real"* estate, the "royal land" concept of uncompromised control by government, individuals, churches, environmentalists, classes, or races, must be reconfigured if the American West is ever to emerge from its divisive, damaging, myth-ridden past. Some of this is already under way. But we must continue to invent new, more startling map colors. In this search, creative discernment may shift the West's central tenure question from "Who owns the land?" to "What is the most just and sensible pattern of land stewardship?"

Notes

1. The material here is voluminous. For two different treatments, see J. B. Jackson, *A Sense of Place and Sense of Time* (New Haven, Conn.: Yale University Press, 1994); William Goetzmann, *New Lands, New Men* (New York: Penguin Books, 1986).

2. The "Doctrine of First Effective Settlement" remains a useful analytical premise. See Wilbur Zelinsky's *The Cultural Geography of the United States,* rev. ed. (Englewood Cliffs, N.J.: Prentice Hall, 1992), 13.

3. Frederick Jackson Turner's 1920 book, *The Frontier in American History* (reprint; Tucson: University of Arizona Press, 1986), is arguably the most deconstructed book on the West for good reason. His simplistic demographic edicts have not proven durable in the face of keen observations of the continuity of "historic issues" in the region today, such as Philip L. Fradkin, *Sagebrush Country: Land and the American West* (New York: Knopf, 1986), and Charles Bowden, *Blue Desert* (Tucson: University of Arizona Press, 1986).

4. Patricia Nelson Limerick gave clear (but surprisingly controversial) voice to this reality in *A Legacy of Conquest: The Unbroken History of the American West* (New York: Norton, 1987). Missoula-based writer William Kittredge provided a less formal treatment of this same truth in his fine book, *Who Owns the West?* (San Francisco: Mercury House, 1996).

5. William Kittredge, *Owning It All* (St. Paul, Minn.: Greywolf Press, 1987), works this theme through the story of environmental and personal travails on his family's ranch in eastern Oregon.

6. William M. Denevan, *The Native Population of the Americas in 1492* (Madison: University of Wisconsin Press, 1992).

7. For fine coverage, see Oren Lyons, John Mohawk, Vine Deloria Jr., Laurence Hauptman, Howard Berman, Donald Grinde Jr., Curtis Berkey, and Robert Venables, *Exiled in the Land of the Free* (Santa Fe, N.M.: Clear Light, 1992).

8. The "Overkill Hypothesis" is thoroughly explored in Paul S. Martin and Richard G. Klein, eds., *Quaternary Extinctions: A Prehistoric Revolution* (Tucson: University of Arizona Press, 1984).

9. James J. Parsons was a far ranging, kind, and gifted Latin Americanist geographer at the University of California–Berkeley for fifty years. His initial exposure to ridged fields came after losing his research materials on coffee growing upon landing in Colombia. A true Sauerian, Parsons regrouped and traveled the Andes recording agricultural patterns. He

collaborated with William M. Denevan on "Pre-Columbian Ridged Fields," *Scientific American* 217 (1967): 92–101. William E. Doolittle is among those to revisit the topic in "Agriculture in North America on the Eve of Contact: A Reassessment," *Annals of the Association of American Geographers* 82 (1992): 396–401.

10. Thomas W. Whitmore and B. L. Turner II, "Landscapes of Cultivation in Mesoamerica on the Eve of Conquest," *Annals of the Association of American Geographers* 82 (1992): 402–425.

11. William M. Denevan, "The Pristine Myth: The Landscape in the Americas in 1492," *Annals of the Association of American Geographers* 82 (1992): 369–385. This important work was part of a special issue of the *Annals* entitled "The Americas before and after 1492: Current Geographical Research." Denevan's article and the entire issue remain required reading for students of pre-Columbian landscape.

12. Virginia Armstrong, *I Have Spoken: American History through the Voices of the Indians* (Chicago: Swallow Press, 1971). Armstrong provides touching translations of selected Indian speakers.

13. Jonathan Rabin, *Bad Land: An American Romance* (New York: Pantheon Books, 1996). Rabin saw some of the truth about the hard life of the Plains but resorted to ridicule. A powerful residue of anger remains in many of the ranchers who confided in him and read this book.

14. For the influence of California in-migration, see Paul F. Starrs and John B. Wright, "Great Basin Growth and the Withering of California's Pacific Idyll," *Geographical Review* 85 (1995): 417–435; Jim Robbins, *Last Refuge: The Environmental Showdown in Yellowstone and the American West* (New York: William Morrow, 1993), is a broad exploration of development issues across the region.

15. John B. Wright, *Montana Ghost Dance: Essays on Land and Life* (Austin: University of Texas Press, 1998). In particular, see the chapter "Myths," 19–56.

16. Benjamin H. Hibbard, *A History of the Public Land Policies* (Madison: University of Wisconsin Press, 1965). Hibbard offers a factually complete treatment of this history.

17. Imre Sutton, ed., *Irredeemable America: The Indians' Estate and Land Claims* (Albuquerque: University of New Mexico Press, 1985). The collection provides detailed, scholarly analysis of numerous Indian land disputes with the Indian Claims Commission.

18. Peter Wolf, *Land in America: Its Value, Use and Control* (New York: Pantheon Books, 1981), 38–39.

19. For clarity, see Charles F. Wilkinson, *Crossing the Next Meridian: Land, Water, and Future of the West* (Washington, D.C.: Island Press, 1992). For intellectual gymnastics, see Donald Worster, *The Wealth of Nature: Environmental History and the Ecological Imagination* (Oxford, U.K.: Oxford University Press, 1993).

20. Two excellent works on these topics are William Cronin, George Miles, and Jay Gitlin, *Under an Open Sky: Rethinking America's Western Past* (New York: Norton, 1992); and Richard Manning, *Grassland* (New York: Viking, 1995).

21. John B. Wright, *Rocky Mountain Divide: Selling and Saving the West* (Austin: University of Texas Press, 1993), 9–25; Wright, *Montana Ghost Dance,* 79–104.

22. Zelinsky, *The Cultural Geography of the United States,* 47.

23. John B. Wright, "Designing and Applying Conservation Easements," *Journal of the American Planning Association* 60 (1994): 380–388.

24. Frederick R. Troeh, J. Arthur Hobbs, and Roy L. Donahue, *Soil and Water Conservation: Productivity and Environmental Protection* (Upper Saddle River, N.J.: Prentice Hall, 1999).

25. Bureau of Land Management, "Southern Nevada Land Management Act of 1998, P.L. 105-203," *Field Office Newsletter* (fall 1999): 105–263. The Southern Nevada Public Land Management Act of 1998 Web site is available at www.nv.blm.gov/snplma. The sale of over $500 million of surplus BLM land to raise money for land purchases and the purchase of development rights on environmentally important sites is now under way.

26. "Bingaman Predicts Baca Ranch Purchase," *Albuquerque Tribune,* 13 August 1998, p. 12.

27. Malcolm Ebright, *Land Grants & Lawsuits in Northern New Mexico* (Albuquerque: University of New Mexico Press, 1994). This is a useful starting point in a huge literature on the subject.

28. Wright, *Rocky Mountain Divide,* 1993.

29. Paul F. Starrs, *Let the Cowboy Ride: Cattle Ranching in the American West* (Baltimore: Johns Hopkins University Press, 1998). Starrs offers an excellent analysis of the origins, adaptations, and land tenure issues involved with ranching in several study areas.

30. The National Wilderness Institute, "State by State Government Land Ownership," online at www.nwi.org/Maps/LandChart.html (a Web site with useful breakdowns of tenure).

31. Jerry Kammer, *The Second Long Walk: The Navajo-Hopi Land Dispute* (Albuquerque: University of New Mexico Press, 1980), 27.

32. Richard White, *The Roots of Dependency* (Lincoln: University of Nebraska Press, 1983); Lyons et al., *Exiled in the Land of the Free;* Sutton, *Irredeemable America: The Indians' Estate and Land Claims.*

33. Ronald A. Foresta, *America's National Parks and Their Keepers* (Washington, D.C.: Resources for the Future, 1985).

34. Grand Canyon Trust, "Grand Canyon-Parashant National Monument" (February 2000), online at www.kaibab.org/gct/cpasu98a.htm (the Web site explores the transaction details).

35. Richard T. Forman, *Land Mosaics: The Ecology of Landscapes and Regions* (Cambridge, U.K.: Cambridge University Press, 1997); Michael E. Soule and Kathryn A. Kohn, *Research Priorities for Conservation Biology* (Washington, D.C.: Island Press, 1989).

36. Terry G. Jordan, *North American Cattle Ranching Frontiers: Origins, Diffusion, and Differentiation* (Albuquerque: University of New Mexico Press, 1993); Starrs, *Let the Cowboy Ride.*

37. For an example of the rhetoric calling for cessation of Western cattle ranching, particu-

larly on public land, see Sharman Apt Russell, *Kill the Cowboy: A Battle of Mythology in the New West* (New York: Addison-Wesley, 1993).

38. Todd Wilkinson, *Science under Siege: The Politician's War on Nature and Truth* (Boulder, Colo.: Johnson Books, 1998). Wilkinson gives a factual and much needed exploration of the often brutal assault on science and reason in land management.

39. The most comprehensive collection of writing on Montana is *The Last Best Place: A Montana Anthology*, eds. William Kittredge and Annick Smith (Helena: Montana Historical Society Press, 1988).

40. Wright, *Montana Ghost Dance*, 38.

41. K. Ross Toole, *Montana: An Uncommon Land* (Norman: University of Oklahoma Press, 1959). Toole remains the most important Montana historian despite his obvious emotion and bias as a defender of the state's land and people.

42. Wright, *Montana Ghost Dance*, 79–104.

43. A growing literature exists on land conservation techniques and case studies. As good examples, see *Protecting the Land: Conservation Easements Past, Present, and Future*, eds. Julie Ann Gustanski and Roderick H. Squires (Washington, D.C.: Island Press, 2000); American Farmland Trust, *Saving American Farmland: What Works* (Washington, D.C.: American Farmland Trust, 1997); John B. Wright, "Conservation Easements: An Analysis of Donated Development Rights," *Journal of the American Planning Association* 59 (1993): 487–493; Samuel N. Stokes and A. Elizabeth Watson, *Saving America's Countryside: A Guide to Rural Conservation* (Baltimore: Johns Hopkins University Press, 1989).

44. John B. Wright, "The Power of Conservation Easements: Protecting Agricultural Land in Montana," in *Protecting the Land: Conservation Easements Past, Present, and Future*, 392–399.

45. Gregory J. Englund, *Beyond Death and Taxes: A Guide to the New Estate Planning* (Boston: Estate Planning Press, 1993). Englund provides abundant examples and tax scenarios.

46. David Thompson, *In Nevada: The Land, the People, God, and Chance* (New York: Knopf, 1999); Russell R. Elliot, *History of Nevada* (Lincoln: University of Nebraska Press, 1987); James A. Young and B. Abbott Sparks, *Cattle Ranching in the Cold Desert* (Logan: Utah State University Press, 1985); Joel Garreau, *The Nine Nations of North America* (New York: Avon Books, 1981).

47. Indian Law Resource Center spring 1996 newsletter (vol. 3, no. 1), online at www.indianlaw.org (an extremely useful Web site with abundant materials and Web links).

48. Valerie L. Kuletz, *The Tainted Desert: Environmental and Social Ruin in the American West* (New York: Routledge, 1998), 5. A field-based, passionate, activist look at the ideology of "nuclearism," a form of environmental racism.

49. Terry Tempest Williams, *Refuge* (New York: Vantage Books, 1992). This is a painful, beautiful book about family, nuclear radiation, and cancer.

50. Rebecca Solnit, *Savage Dreams* (New York: Vintage Books, 1994). *Savage Dreams* is an environmental history of the fate of the Nevada desert and the Sierra Nevada.

51. Jeffrey A. McNeely and Kenton R. Miller, *National Parks, Conservation, and Development: The Role of Protected Areas in Sustaining Society* (Washington, D.C.: Smithsonian Institution Press, 1984).

52. An exploration of the immense scholarship on northern New Mexico must include Victor Westphall, *Mercedes Reales: Hispanic Land Grants of the Upper Rio Grande Region* (Albuquerque: University of New Mexico Press, 1993); Richard L. Nostrand, *The Hispano Homeland* (Norman: University of Oklahoma Press, 1992); Alvar Carlson, *The Spanish-American Borderland* (Baltimore: Johns Hopkins University Press, 1990); Charles L. Briggs and John R. Van Ness, *Land, Water, and Culture: New Perspectives on Hispanic Land Grants* (Albuquerque: University of New Mexico Press, 1987); William deBuys, *Enchantment and Exploitation: The Life and Hard Times of a New Mexico Mountain Range* (Albuquerque: University of New Mexico Press, 1985); and Malcolm Ebright, *The Tierra Amarilla Grant: A History of Chicanery* (Santa Fe, N.M.: Center for Land Grant Studies, 1980).

53. The classic piece on the subject is Alvar Carlson, "Long Lots in the Rio Arriba," *Annals of the Association of American Geographers* 65 (1975): 48–57.

54. Essential reading is Stanley Crawford, *Mayordomo: Chronicle of an Acequia in Northern New Mexico* (Albuquerque: University of New Mexico Press, 1988).

55. Wolf, *Land in America: Its Value, Use and Control,* 38–39.

56. Richard Griswold del Castillo, *The Treaty of Guadalupe Hidalgo: A Legacy of Conflict* (Norman: University of Oklahoma Press, 1990), 189–190.

57. deBuys, *Enchantment and Exploitation,* 171–192.

58. John B. Wright, "Hispano Forestry, Land Grants, and the U.S. Forest Service in Northern New Mexico," *Focus* 44 (1994): 10–14. Highlights some of the disputes between Hispano livestock growers in the context of U.S. Forest Service management of former *ejido* lands.

59. "Delegation Eyes Land Grant Hearings," *Albuquerque Journal,* 25 March 1998, p. 1.

60. Leonard J. Arrington, *Great Basin Kingdom: Economic History of the Latter-Day Saints* (Lincoln: University of Nebraska Press, 1958).

61. Leonard J. Arrington, *Brigham Young: American Moses* (New York: Knopf, 1985).

62. For the fundamental background, see Wallace Stegner, *Mormon Country* (Lincoln: University of Nebraska Press, 1970). For detailed traits, see Richard V. Francaviglia, "The Mormon Landscape: Definition of an Image of the American West," *Proceedings of the Association of American Geographers* (1970): 59–61.

63. Leonard J. Arrington, Feramorz Y. Fox, and Dean L. May, *Building the City for God* (Salt Lake City: Deseret Books, 1976). Dan Flores provides a superb analysis of the Wasatch Front in "Zion in Eden: Phases of the Environmental History of Utah," *Environmental Review* 7 (1983): 325–344.

64. This book won the J. B. Jackson Prize and other awards but was roundly dismissed by the LDS Church as Mormon bashing. I received a two-page, single-spaced letter of scorn from a high-ranking church official castigating me for assigning blame for the obvious lack

of land conservation activity in Utah to the LDS ideologies of large families and unrepentant growth. The recent corruption scandal involving Utah's heavily Mormon Olympic Committee revealed to the world the lengths to which they will go to assure an expansion of land development and business. I stand by my book.

65. A fine recent collection exploring this question is Harvey M. Jacobs, ed., *Who Owns America? Social Conflict over Property Rights* (Madison: University of Wisconsin Press, 1998).

66. One of the most useful, fact-driven analyses extant is Thomas Michael Power, *The Economic Pursuit of Quality* (London: M. E. Sharpe, 1988).

4 | National Significance

Representation of the West in the National Park System

LARY M. DILSAVER

The national park system arose in the West. It began as an effort to preserve monumental scenery in an unfamiliar yet compelling landscape. Later the system diversified and evolved to include many types of historical, cultural, scientific, and recreational places. This diversification, plus the concomitant rise of political savvy in the new National Park Service (NPS), led the service to seek parks to represent all facets of the nation's environmental and historical legacy. Saving a "representative national park system" for public education, scientific research, and preservation of material culture became first a collateral and then the primary motive for additions to the park system. Eventually, the NPS came to realize that other governmental or private entities could relieve it of the need to cover all themes. However, thematic representation remains a critical criterion for inclusion in the national park system.[1]

Any potential addition to the system is theoretically evaluated on several criteria besides thematic representation. The most important of these is *national significance,* a vague term denoting importance to the entire nation. Other criteria include resource integrity, acquisition cost, and public support. However, Congress and other political forces have directed some of the system's expansion, not always following these criteria. This practice became increasingly common in the last quarter of the twentieth century. One park planner ruefully acknowledged that he first wrote a negative appraisal of a potential unit after an NPS study but then was ordered to write a positive one after a powerful congressman introduced legislation to establish the park. Thus, in spite of thematic planning and established criteria, the system has grown haphazardly from time to time.[2]

This chapter evaluates how well the National Park Service, through this evolving and occasionally flawed process, has succeeded in acquiring and preserving the most important examples of the natural and cultural heritage of the West, here defined as the eleven contiguous Western states. I begin with an explanation of the evolution of the national park system with particular attention to development of planning for thematic representation. Thereafter I discuss four meanings of the West and evaluate their coverage in the park system. I restrict my analysis to the III existing NPS units (Map 4.1), plus a handful of affiliated trails administered by the agency. Finally, I offer a subjective list of suggested sites to fill the most important gaps. The ultimate question is this: How well does the national park system preserve the Western story? In answering that question one must think about the character of the West as well as the purpose of the national parks.

Evolution of the National Park System

Five distinct preservation movements led to today's national park system. Each had a different motive, and each focused on a different set of places. The first sought to preserve scenic magnificence and spawned the units designated "national parks." Congress began by withdrawing Yosemite Valley from the public domain in 1864 and eight years later established Yellowstone as the world's first national park. These units define the ultimate ideal. They are large, wild places marked by a diversity of spectacular resources. Most boast monumental scenery and abundant wildlife. In the nineteenth century they engendered feelings of awe and pride in a nation smarting from snobbish European criticism of its cultural milieu. Railroad companies recognized the tourism value in these feelings and worked hard to get several early national parks established. Most of the national parks were selected individually on the basis of their superlative qualities.[3]

The second movement began with a disintegrating adobe apartment in southern Arizona. In 1889, as an afterthought to an appropriations bill, Congress authorized what became Casa Grande Ruin National Monument and allocated funds to restore it.[4] Continued entreaties from archeologists led to passage of the Antiquities Act in 1906.[5] It gave the government a second means of saving the physical wonders of the West. Although Congress primarily intended for the act to save archeological ruins, the act called for unilateral presidential withdrawal of scientific as well as prehistoric and historic sites on federal lands. Indeed, the first national monument designated under the act was Devils Tower in Wyoming. In the 1920s the young National Park Service sought to use its monuments for public education and entertainment.

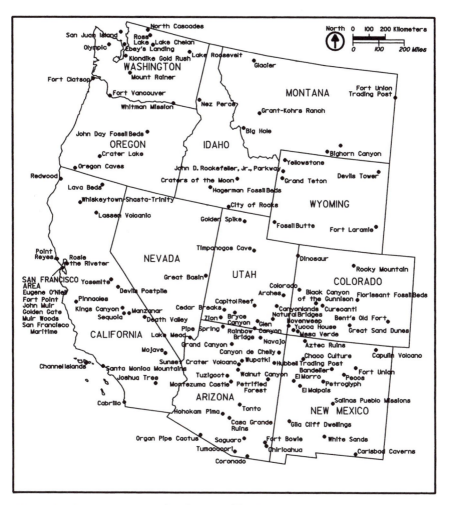

MAP 4.1. The existing national park units of the West. Map by Margarita M. Pindak.

This in turn led chief NPS field agent Roger Toll to develop a plan for representing the varied geological and ecological divisions within the United States. The first monument deliberately established to represent an environmental feature was Saguaro (now a national park) in Arizona, set aside in March 1933.[6] Three months later the federal executive branch reorganized to bring monuments from other federal land agencies under National Park Service control.[7]

A third movement arose from the ashes of the Civil War and the unhappy experience of Reconstruction. In 1890, as the twenty-fifth anniversary of the war's end approached, Congress established Chickamauga and Chattanooga

National Military Park to be administered by the War Department.[8] The importance of salving Civil War wounds was emphasized over the remainder of the decade with the establishment of similar units at Antietam, Gettysburg, Shiloh, and Vicksburg. The new century saw some attention to the American Revolution and the War of 1812, but Civil War sites continued to predominate. Eventually Congress, no doubt speculating on the financial prospects of commemorating the two thousand identified Civil War battlefields, ordered the War Department to study all battlefields for all wars in order to rank them by significance. In 1926 the department reported that two major sites, Saratoga and Yorktown, plus sixty-four other sites of national significance, remained unprotected.[9] In 1933 the federal reorganization brought twenty battlefields to the National Park Service along with their orderly system plan.

The fourth movement, preservation of historic sites, began fitfully with failed attempts to acquire Mount Vernon and Monticello during the nineteenth century. In the twentieth century two avenues opened for historic preservation. Along with its battlefields, the War Department preserved ten forts and exploration monuments. These also passed to the NPS in 1933. Meanwhile the National Park Service itself fielded nineteen monuments classed as historic areas. Most were Indian ruins and early European sites. However, two additions in 1930 became the nuclei of what is now the largest group of national park system units. A concerted campaign led by second NPS director Horace Albright convinced Congress to establish George Washington Birthplace and Colonial national monuments.[10]

During this campaign, the National Park Service's Educational Advisory Committee, specifically historian Clark Wissler, devised a framework of historic themes with which to identify necessary additions to the system. Wissler's framework would become the foundation of later system plans in 1937, 1972, and 1987.[11] In 1935 Congress passed the Historic Sites Act directing the NPS to survey historic and prehistoric places to identify those that would best illustrate the history of the United States. Those of special significance were to be nominated for national park system status.[12]

The movement for recreation areas was the last to shape the park system. It stemmed from a concern for the parks as well as for the people. The growing availability of the automobile heightened both the need for public recreation places and fears that crowds of fun seekers would damage national park resources. Beginning in 1924, a series of conferences on outdoor recreation called for a national recreation plan to cover local, state, and federal needs. From the outset the National Park Service served as the nation's lead recreation agency, a role reinforced by its direction of Civilian Conservation Corps projects. In 1936 Congress passed the Park, Parkway and Recreation Area Study Act, which charged the NPS to classify recreation opportunities and devise a nationwide plan.[13] As the five movements for parks, monuments, battlefields, historic sites, and recreation areas evolved, their motives became enshrined in the National Park Service mission. In the process another motive, political power, grew. In true messianic fashion the National Park Service has sought to acquire units in as many congressional districts as possible.

This aggregate of motives increasingly led the service to seek and justify new units on the basis of resource representation. The congressionally mandated evaluation of battlefields, the establishment of Saguaro as a monument representing a botanical community, and Wissler's framework of historic themes set the precedents. The Historic Sites Act and the Park, Parkway and Recreation Area Study Act reinforced it. When he died in 1936 Roger Toll had employed representation as a measure for at least eight years and was devising a system plan. By 1969, Secretary of the Interior Walter Hickel reminded the NPS and the public that the system should represent the "best examples" of the natural and cultural scene and that "there are serious gaps and inadequacies which must be remedied while opportunities still exist."[14]

In response to these movements and motives the national park system has grown to include 111 units in the eleven Western states. At least another 430 have been proposed by someone and evaluated by the National Park Service (Map 4.2). How well do the 111 represent the West's legacy? Would some of those 430 have filled important gaps? What is the meaning of the West in the American story?

The National Park System in the West

As research in the sciences, social sciences, and history advances, the West becomes an increasingly complex region and network of myriad processes at all scales. The body of scholarship collectively called New Western history is particularly refreshing.[15] From these data as well as traditional studies in all disciplines it is possible to discern four types of West. Each is a different theme of an interrelated confluence of processes in space and place. Each has its national park units, and each has gaps in its preservation.

The West as Environmental Challenge

To the arriving eastern American or European the West was, first and foremost, an exotic and sometimes unforgiving environment. Harsh aridity, massive mountain chains, and monumental scenery daunted yet attracted explorers and settlers. Some features—the geysers of Yellowstone, the sequoias

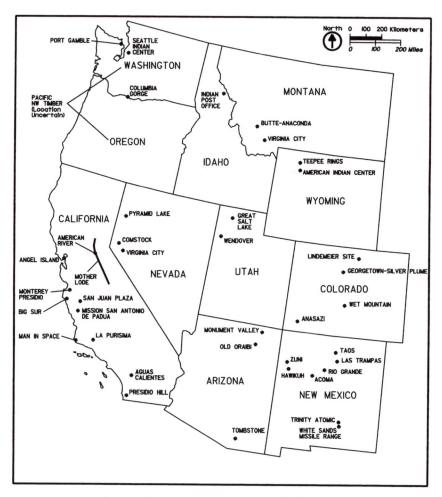

MAP 4.2. Proposed national park units mentioned in this chapter. Map by Margarita M. Pindak.

of California—excited tourism promoters, chief among them the railroads. Others remained curiosities at best, obstacles at worst. Today, half of the 111 NPS units exist primarily for their environmental features. Most of the recreation units and quite a few historic ones also preserve noteworthy landforms and biological communities.

In 1990 the service promulgated a review of natural history in the national park system to point out gaps in its coverage.[16] Park planners divided the United States and its possessions into "natural regions" based on Neville Fenneman's 1928 physiographic divisions.[17] They then applied four natural history themes—landforms of the present, geologic history, land ecosystems, and aquatic ecosystems—plus numerous subthemes appropriate to each natural region for a matrix of NPS coverage. Thirteen regions comprise the West, not including the Great Plains. Matching the four themes and assorted subthemes with these regions yields a matrix of 255 cells. Today, the national park system maintains and protects units representing 241 of them. In some cases preservation of some environmental feature may be incidental to the unit's purpose. In other cases superior examples may lie outside the system, in private, state, or other federal hands. Nevertheless, the collective preservation of environmental diversity is an impressive 95 percent. Among the most recent are City of Rocks National Reserve and Hagerman Fossil Beds National Monuments, both in Idaho. Of the fourteen missing components, half are in the Columbia Plateau and Wyoming Basin regions. Although this measure is seriously flawed from an ecological standpoint, it nonetheless suggests success in capturing the physiographic diversity of the West.[18]

The West as Multicultural Arena

When Americans pushed into the West, they met not only a forbidding yet inspiring natural scene but also peoples with whom they continued their competition for space and resources. More than two centuries of Hispanic presence and two hundred centuries of Native American life had elapsed. The imposition of the United States and its Eurocentric culture on the West disenfranchised and altered the previous groups. The degree of that Americanization varies, however, from place to place and continues to evolve with immigration. During the American conquest, African Americans and Asians also settled the region. Each generation of NPS system plans and thematic frameworks has sought to broaden representation of these peoples' experiences in the West before contact, during acculturation, and today. Despite extensive efforts in the last two decades in particular, the record in this area is, at best, uneven.

Preservation of prehistoric Indian ruins in the Southwest is the most successful effort. Eighteen units preserve the remains of Anasazi, Sinagua, Hohokam, and other desert cultures as their raisons d'être. Another eight incidentally protect such resources. Since 1986 the NPS has investigated a proposed Anasazi National Monument near Mesa Verde National Park in order to "consolidate the (interpretation of) different archaeological sites and groupings into a manageable unit." Meanwhile, at least a dozen additional sets of ruins have been proposed.[19]

Historian Hal Rothman has suggested that preservation of these ruins captured the imagination of Americans because they spoke of failure to cope with the environmental challenge of the West. This in turn celebrates the apparent success of white American settlement.[20] Another explanation may be that preservation of these sites stemmed from the ethnocentrism of conquest whereby elements of the defeated culture are trophies. Be these as they may, preservation for scientific and educational purposes has always played a part and is the principal motive today.

The more ephemeral sites outside the Colorado Plateau have not fared as well. The NPS studied one "Lindenmeier Site" near Fort Collins, Colorado, in 1947 and found its Folsom culture artifacts equal to those of the site of that name. Despite the positive recommendation, interest waned and eventually disappeared. A recurring settlement site near Cody, Wyoming, known only as Teepee Rings was proposed in 1941, deferred due to World War II, and never again pursued. Another site, called Indian Post Office, in Idaho, supposedly served as a hunters' message board. A 1955 NPS study could find no definitive evidence, however, and rejected the site.[21]

Of greater concern is the lack of units established to explain historic and modern Indian lifeways. Many NPS units treat Indian culture as a sidebar to their interpretation of natural features or American historical processes. Nevertheless, sites devoted specifically to historic or immediate prehistoric cultures are scarce. Salinas National Monument in New Mexico is one exception, with its seventeenth-century pueblo and Spanish mission church ruins. At least five occupied pueblos have been proposed, including Old Oraibi (Hopi) in 1932, Hawikuh (Fray Marcos's Cibola) in 1934 and 1947, Acoma (1939), and Taos (1945). The fifth, Zuni pueblo (Figure 4.1), was proposed in 1940, authorized by Congress in 1988, but dropped due to resistance from the Zuni in 1994. Antagonism to such proposals, bringing with them a greater federal presence on reservations, is the primary stumbling block to answering this gap in the park system. Other proposed sites have included units on the Aguas Calientes (1912) and Pyramid Lake (1933 and 1968) reservations, "native Indian centers" in Cody, Wyoming (1987), and Seattle (1991), and a Rio Grande National Historical and Cultural Park in northern New Mexico (1974).[22]

Hispanic ruins are also well represented in the border states of Arizona and New Mexico. However, interpretation of Spanish, Mexican, and Hispanic American experience is weak, especially in California. Three units exist in the Golden State: Cabrillo National Monument, Golden Gate National Recreation Area, and Juan Bautista de Anza National Historic Trail (an affiliated area). Two of these are monuments to exploration, and Golden Gate must include

FIG. 4.1. Zuni pueblo in 1929. Much of the character of the settlement remains today. Courtesy George A. Grant, National Park Service Archives.

the Hispanic story in its interpretation of the Presidio. The National Park Service has studied five other areas in California: Presidio Hill in San Diego (1935), San Juan Plaza in San Benito County (1936), the Monterey presidio (1940), La Purísima Concepción Mission (1941), and Mission San Antonio de Padua in Monterey County in 1992. The absence of a unit interpreting the era of the Californios is a significant gap.[23]

Outside California, an especially noteworthy site is the village of Las Trampas (Figure 4.2) in northern New Mexico. In 1967 the NPS Southwestern Regional Office found it to be an "exemplar of Spanish colonial architecture, village form, and culture." A 1986 revisit found it largely unchanged save for a paved road and national historic landmark designations for the village and its church. The historic landmark program was initially designed to signal areas of possible inclusion in the park system. Nevertheless, no further action has taken place.[24]

The Asian presence in the West is represented in three units: Golden Spike and Manzanar national historic sites and the multifaceted Golden Gate. The first two focus on specific episodes of complex chapters in American history. They are inadequate to the task. In 1999 the NPS entered into a partnership with California State Parks to restore and interpret the immigra-

Fɪɢ. 4.2. The village of Las Trampas, New Mexico. Both the village and its church are already historic landmarks. Courtesy Fred Mang Jr., National Park Service Archives.

tion station on Angel Island in San Francisco Bay. The island, currently a state park, served as the entry point for more than one million people, a large proportion of them Asian, between 1910 and 1940. The National Park Service has proposed a fifteen-acre enclave in the state park containing the extant immigration structures as a "bookend" to Ellis Island and a site for Asian-American history. The service has also discussed the creation of a Pacific Coast Immigration Museum in San Francisco.[25]

Finally, the story of African Americans in the West is somewhat different owing to their arrival as part of the general east-to-west migration over the last 170 years. A number of units, especially military posts, devote some attention to their role in the West. Outside the region considered in this study, Nicodemus National Historic Site, in Kansas, preserves portions of a frontier settlement by former slaves. Another chapter in the African American story may still be added. Congress established Rosie the Riveter National Historic Site in October 2000. Its five Richmond, California, sites interpret the home front during World War II. It was at that time and for those defense industries that many African Americans migrated to the urban West.[26]

Conquest as used here means the arrival and settlement of Americans in the West and the imposition of their economic and political culture. It includes exploration, migration, intercultural wars, settlement, land use, and the social system that drove those activities and was itself modified in the process. National park system coverage of these themes is very uneven. Exploration and migration are well represented in more than two dozen units plus the affiliated California, Lewis and Clark, Mormon, Oregon, Pony Express, and Santa Fe trails. A plethora of forts and battlefields memorializes Indian wars. However, park system coverage of the economic functions that Americanized the West and the societies that performed them is, at best, spotty.

The single most egregious gap in park system coverage of the West is mining, in particular, the precious metal rushes that so profoundly opened the region. Only Klondike Gold Rush National Historic Site exists west of Michigan's Upper Peninsula, and, except for a small visitor center in Seattle, it is found in Alaska. In the eleven contiguous Western states only Whiskeytown-Shasta National Recreation Area preserves structures from the early gold rush. Death Valley National Park, Mojave National Preserve, and a few others incidentally treat later mining.

The NPS has tried to redress this deficiency. Between 1915 and 1990 the service studied thirteen proposed sites, several of them more than once. Some were important mine sites, such as the American River (1934), where the first strike occurred, and Nevada's Comstock area (1931). Others were mining towns, such as Virginia City, Nevada (1950), and Tombstone, Arizona (1936). Four areas—Georgetown-Silver Plume (1986) and Wet Mountain Valley (1990) in Colorado and Virginia City (1937 and 1980) and the Butte-Anaconda copper mines (1987) in Montana—are still active files.[27]

Lumbering, too, is poorly represented. Although not as historically significant as mining, a 1999 NPS request for special study funds stated that lumbering is "critical to the nation's economy" and that "one or more sites" are significant enough for inclusion in the system. In addition to the function itself, with its attendant social organization, the concomitant story of forest conservation is also important. Concerns about Western forests crystallized into the Forest Reserve Act and the spotted owl controversy. The National Park Service lists only Redwood National Park as a Western site for interpreting the timber story. It has sought others at Port Gamble, Washington (1953), and at undesignated Pacific Northwest locations in the planned study mentioned earlier.[28]

The NPS has done better in other economic activities and their accompanying societies. The fur trade is well represented at sites like Fort Vancouver, Fort Laramie, and Bents Fort, and ranching is interpreted at Grant-Kohrs, Great Basin, and Bighorn Canyon. The national parks themselves were the most important tourism sites. Agriculture appears at Whitman Mission National Historic Site, Point Reyes National Seashore, John Muir National Historic Site, and Pipe Spring National Monument. It also is a secondary story in many other units. If there is a gap in the agricultural theme, it is in horticulture, which so dominates California and parts of Washington, Oregon, and Arizona.

The West as a Transformed Place

The West is not only a saga of conquest but also a land transformed by those actions and by more modern adaptations. There are processes and events of the twentieth century that also have national significance. By and large, the national park system contains very few examples of these resources. The transformed West has four characteristics. First, it is an altered environment. The most fundamental alteration is human manipulation of the West's water. Dams, irrigation schemes, interbasin water transfers, and the governmental and private systems to regulate them have massively transformed the region. Glen Canyon, Lake Mead, Lake Roosevelt, and Whiskeytown-Shasta National Recreation Areas address individual structures, with much of the interpretation being conducted by the Bureau of Reclamation. No national park unit explains the evolution, design, and full regional impact of water manipulation in the region. It is difficult to imagine a greater oversight.

California's twin systems, the Central Valley Project and the California Water Plan, collectively comprise the most elaborate of these schemes. Although no one has proposed a reclamation unit, Whiskeytown-Shasta, as a part of the Central Valley Project, might serve the purpose.

A second story of the New West lies in its role as a milieu for conservation. The existing parks tell much of the story, and one unit, John Muir National Historic Site, focuses exclusively on the topic. Those parks also treat other issues, such as water quality, global warming, and biological diversity. The federal hand lies heavy on the region, and each agency and each unit thereof demonstrate a part of this transformation.

The West has also served as a theater for technological innovation. Although antecedents existed, most of this change came during and after World War II. The war and the defense industries it brought to the region are poorly represented in the park system. The aforementioned Rosie the Riveter site addresses some of these concerns. However, it was the postwar years that brought tremendous growth focused on new types of industries. In 1987, the NPS released a report called "Man in Space."[29] It identified twenty-six sites across the nation to preserve the history of the space program. Six of those sites, including Vandenburg Air Force Base, are in California, and a seventh, White Sands Missile Range, is in New Mexico. In August 1945, soon after Japan surrendered, the National Park Service received a request to establish Trinity Atomic National Monument in New Mexico, site of the first atomic bomb test. Subsequent proposals followed in 1967, 1970, and 1980. In each case the location of the site on an active military bombing range quashed the plan. The National Park Service rejected a second atomic site near Wendover, Utah, in 1986, claiming it lacked national significance. Finally, Silicon Valley, the acknowledged home of computer technology, provides another opportunity to interpret the region's technology history.[30]

Major social changes have also transformed the West. The extraordinary mobility of Western Americans is one case. The National Park Service studied Route 66 as an affiliated area during the 1990s but has devoted no attention to the freeways and suburbs that reach their apogee in southern California.[31] Also, that mobility has spawned an amazing network of recreation sites throughout the region. National parks in particular fill many of the interstices on the region's destination grid. Little consideration, however, has been given to winter resorts and gambling meccas in the West. The latter take care of themselves individually, but the historical development and impact of gambling regionwide are themselves of national significance.

Recently a panel of scholars and NPS historians designed a thematic framework for history in the national park system.[32] Among the eight themes was "Creating Social Institutions and Movements," including clubs and organizations, reform movements, and religions. There is very little attention to such subjects as the free speech, peace, and civil rights movements and various utopian schemes. Even Mormonism, the most significant American-born religion, receives only desultory attention at the Pipe Spring and Golden Spike NPS units plus the affiliated Mormon Pioneer National Historic Trail.

Finally, the transformed West has become a cultural and especially a media hearth. Although Eugene O'Neill rates a historic site, John Steinbeck does not. The most glaring deficiency in this area is the movie and television industry. The history of moviemaking, its technological and cultural growth, and its regional, national and international impact are of signal importance for preservation and interpretation. To date the National Park Service has only the Paramount Ranch area, located in Santa Monica National Recreation Area, where Westerns were once filmed.

Taking Stock

Looking back over this cursory review of national park system thematic representation raises several questions. First, should the National Park Service be trying to corral the myriad topics of the Western experience into its system? Is inclusion in national forests, state parks, and private tourist sites adequate for places of national significance? This is a topic of some current debate, caught as it is in the ongoing uproar over the quality of recent NPS additions. The high-water mark for thematic representation passed in 1975, and it is now one of a portfolio of criteria. However, the service developed this rationale and has pursued new units accordingly for more than seventy years. As Congress and the public wrestle with the system's content and criteria, it remains the method the National Park Service has used. The results must be evaluated on that basis.[33]

Second, in summary how well does the national park system cover the themes and resources of the West? The answer is mixed. Most major events, peoples, and places are at least present in the system. The service is particularly strong in physical geographic diversity, archeological ruins, exploration and military conquest, and some historic economic functions. It has had very modest success with Hispanic and Asian cultures, tourism, and conservation. Few to no units deal with the gold rush, lumbering, modern society of any cultural or economic group, technological changes that have swept the West, and the concomitant social movements of the region.

If one accepts that the system should contain the nationally significant natural and historic diversity of the West, how should the service fill the gaps that remain? Local resistance has plagued both recent additions in the West and many of the studies for potential new units. The National Park Service will have to continue its innovative land acquisition and interpretive partnerships. Models exist in the system for cooperation with private, state, and local entities. In some cases, such as the new Rosie the Riveter unit, federal presence may be confined to a small visitor center and ranger-led walks.

With these thoughts in mind I offer the following suggested cultural/historical additions to the park system:

1. Mother Lode National Parkway, comprising most of California State Highway 49 in the Sierra Nevada foothills (Figure 4.3). An NPS reconnaissance team suggested a 334-mile stretch be added in 1966. It would link several existing state parks, including the American River site.[34]

2. Virginia City, Montana (Figure 4.4). First proposed in 1937, it became a

national historic landmark in 1961. The NPS proposed it again in 1979 and continues to pursue some presence in the old mining town.[35]

3. Either a vastly enhanced interpretation of water reclamation at Whiskeytown-Shasta or Lake Roosevelt or a new historic site in Arizona, California, Colorado, or Washington.

4. Angel Island Immigration Station National Historic Site.

5. Either Mission San Antonio de Padua or La Purísima Concepción (Figure 4.5).

6. Las Trampas National Cultural Park.

7. Pacific Northwest Timber Industry National Historic Site.

8. Trinity Atomic National Monument.

9. Hollywood Film Industry National Historic Site.

10. Revisit the Zuni-Cibola National Historic Site. A very limited interpretive presence both at the occupied pueblo and at Hawikuh on the Zuni Reservation would provide an integrated long-term story of a Pueblo culture.

FIG. 4.3. The Mother Lode–mining camp of Sutter Creek, California, on California Highway 49. Photo by author.

FIG. 4.4. Virginia City, Montana, the present favorite candidate for addition to the national park system. Courtesy William Wyckoff.

FIG. 4.5. Mission La Purísima Concepción near Vandenburg Air Force Base. It is currently a state historical site. Photo by author.

Although the many deficiencies in the historic record of the national park system will be difficult, controversial, and expensive to fill, the 95 percent coverage of physiographic diversity may spawn a sense of complacency. Yet another reason for natural parks in the West exists: the original one. Americans first set aside parks to preserve places that inspired awe and esthetic appreciation. Those scenic wonders still evoke such emotions, and not all are in the park system. Other federal agencies preserve some specially designated areas like the Sawtooth Mountains, Hell's Canyon, Oregon Dunes, Mount St. Helens, and Grand Staircase–Escalante. But there remain striking scenic wonders that rate national park status. Four stand out.

Monument Valley in Arizona (Figure 4.6) lies in the Navajo Reservation. The National Park Service sought its addition in 1931, 1943, 1953, and 1983. Currently the Navajo operate a tribal park there with occasional technical help from the NPS. A national preserve designation with continued primary control in the hands of the Navajo might bring further economic development to the area.[36]

FIG. 4.6. Monument Valley, Arizona. Courtesy G. Donald Bain, Geo-Images Project, Department of Geography, University of California–Berkeley. Used with permission.

The National Park Service has also pursued the Big Sur coast of California from time to time (Figure 4.7). Much of the area lies in Los Padres National Forest and Pfeiffer–Big Sur State Park. An NPS proposal for a national reserve in 1978 met stern local opposition. A few years later, Monterey County enacted the toughest landscape protection plan ever for a local government. With protection not a serious issue, perhaps another national parkway along California Highway 1 might be appropriate.[37]

The National Park Service has sought the Columbia River Gorge (Figure 4.8) under various names since 1934. Most recently, the service issued a 295-page "study of alternatives" for the management of the area in 1980. The study suggested several options, including management by a commission to include state and local governments, the U.S. Forest Service, and possibly the National Park Service.

Finally, Great Salt Lake and the vast playa to its west have drawn NPS proposals in 1948, 1960, and through the 1970s. There still remain portions of the salt flats and lakeshore where a unit could preserve the wilderness character of the area.[38]

FIG. 4.7. Big Sur coastline near Monterey, California. Photo by author.

Fɪɢ. 4.8. Gorge of the Columbia River from Crown Point. Courtesy G. Donald Bain, Geo-Images Project, Department of Geography, University of California–Berkeley. Used with permission.

Preservation in the West and in the nation is itself a topic of compelling national significance. Appraisal of the processes and results of that preservation shows that the National Park System developed its emphasis on representing the diversity of the nation from the variety of movements that gelled to create a unified system. Once under way this rationale for new units shaped system expansion through the twentieth century. Over time the service's understanding of natural and human diversity has itself changed. Measured against the modern scientific and thematic frameworks, the park system has a moderate aggregate of resources in the West to protect and interpret. As keeper of the country's natural and historical legacy, the National Park Service must continue to reevaluate the story of the West and that of the nation to remain itself nationally significant.

Notes

1. During the period 1993–2001, President Clinton used the Antiquities Act (see note 4) to create a number of new national monuments. As that act allows, many are administered by agencies other than the National Park Service. Even before the Clinton years, the U.S. For-

est Service administered several important monuments. I have chosen to exclude them from my analysis. The National Park Service has developed a particular culture and a policy framework when it comes to studying new areas. I have chosen to evaluate the system of park units that has resulted from these forces; National Park Service, "Management Policies" (Washington, D.C.: Department of the Interior, 1988).

2. Robert Newkirk, interview with author, Canaveral National Seashore, 3 March 1999.

3. Ronald F. Lee, *Family Tree of the National Park System* (Philadelphia: Eastern National Park and Monument Association, 1974); Alfred Runte, *National Parks: The American Experience*, 2d rev. ed. (Lincoln: University of Nebraska Press, 1987).

4. Hal Rothman, *Preserving Different Pasts: The American National Monuments* (Urbana: University of Illinois Press, 1989), 12–14.

5. 34 Stat. 225.

6. Rothman, *Preserving Different Pasts*, 171.

7. 5 U.S.C. §§ 124–132.

8. 26 Stat. 333.

9. H.R. 1071, 69th Congress, 1st Session.

10. Harlan D. Unrau and G. Frank Williss, *Administrative History: Expansion of the National Park System in the 1930s* (Denver: National Park Service, 1983), 161.

11. Lee, *Family Tree*, 46–47.

12. 49 Stat. 666; Barry Mackintosh, "Shaping the System" (Washington, D.C.: National Park Service, 1991); Unrau and Williss, *Administrative History*, 161–226.

13. 49 Stat. 1894; Unrau and Williss, *Administrative History*, 106–124.

14. Leo Diederich, "National Park System Planning" (statement presented to the Forty-second meeting of the Advisory Board on National Parks, Historic Sites, Buildings and Monuments, 21 March 1960) (Harpers Ferry: National Park Service Archives, wv, Box D1810); National Park Service, "Part Two of the National Park System Plan: Natural History" (Washington, D.C.: Department of the Interior, 1972), foreword.

15. William Cronon, *Nature's Metropolis: Chicago and the Great West* (Chicago: University of Chicago Press, 1991); Donald W. Meinig, *The Shaping of America*, vol. 3, *Transcontinental America, 1850–1915* (New Haven: Yale University Press, 1998); Stewart L. Udall, "The 'Wild' Old West—A Different View," *Montana: The Magazine of Western History* 49, no. 4 (1999): 64–71; Richard White, *"It's Your Misfortune and None of My Own": A History of the American West* (Norman: University of Oklahoma Press, 1991).

16. National Park Service, *Natural History in the National Park System and on the National Registry of Historic Landmarks* (Washington, D.C.: Department of the Interior, 1990).

17. Neville Fenneman, "Physiographic Divisions of the United States," *Annals of the Association of American Geographers* 18 (1928): 261–353.

18. National Park Service, *Natural History*.

19. National Park Service, "Statement of Significance, Anasazi National Monument, Resource Assessment of Alternatives" (1989), Office of Planning, proposed area files.

20. Rothman, *Preserving Different Pasts*, 143.

21. National Park Service, "New Area Study Inventory" (1988), Office of Planning, proposed area files; National Park Service, "Proposed Areas Resume" (Harpers Ferry: National Park Service Archives, wv, 158, Box 1, 1947); James Ridenour to northwest regional director, NPS, 2 December 1991, Office of Planning, proposed area files under "Seattle National Indian Center."

22. National Park Service, "New Area Study"; National Park Service, "Proposed Areas Resume"; Mark David Spence, *Dispossessing the Wilderness: Indian Removal and the Making of the National Parks* (London: Oxford University Press, 1999).

23. National Park Service, "New Area Study"; National Park Service, "Proposed Areas Resume."

24. Harry Butowski, telephone interview with author, 11 January 2000; National Park Service, "Las Trampas Historic District" (National Historic Landmark Status Report, 1979), Office of Planning, proposed areas files.

25. National Park Service, "Angel Island Immigrant Station/Immigrant Theme Study" (Special Resource Data Sheet, 1999), Office of Planning, proposed areas files.

26. 112 Stat. 3247.

27. William Everhart, *The Mining Frontier* (Washington, D.C.: National Park Service, 1959); National Park Service, "Georgetown-Silver Plume Historic District, Reconnaissance Survey" (1980), Office of Planning, proposed areas files; National Park Service, "New Area Study"; National Park Service, "Proposed Areas Resume."

28. National Park Service, "New Area Study"; National Park Service, "Pacific Northwest Timber History and Heritage" (Special Resource Study Data Sheet 1999), Office of Planning, proposed areas files.

29. National Park Service, "Man in Space: Study of Alternatives" (1987), Office of Planning, proposed areas files.

30. National Park Service, "New Area Study"; National Park Service, "Proposed Areas Resume."

31. National Park Service, "Special Resource Study Route 66" (1995), Office of Planning, proposed areas files.

32. National Park Service, "Revision of the National Park Service's Thematic Framework" (1996), Office of Planning, proposed areas files.

33. Barry Mackintosh, telephone interview with author, 2 February 2000.

34. National Park Service, "New Area Study."

35. National Park Service, "Draft Special Resource Study and Environmental Assessment,

Virginia City National Historic Landmark, Montana" (1994), Office of Planning, proposed areas files.

36. Navajo Tribe Recreation Resources Department and National Park Service, "Monument Valley Tribal Park, Master Plan" (1983), Office of Planning, proposed areas files.

37. William Duddleson, "Protecting Big Sur," *American Land Forum* 7 (1987): 28–36, 45; National Park Service, "National Reserve Feasibility Study, Big Sur, California" (1978), Office of Planning, proposed areas files.

38. National Park Service, "Columbia River Gorge: Study of Alternatives" (1980), Office of Planning, proposed areas files.

PART 2
ENDURING REGIONAL VOICES

Indians, Hispanics, Asians, blacks, Anglos, businesspeople, workers, politicians, bureaucrats, natives, and newcomers, we share the same region and its history, but we wait to be introduced. The serious exploration of the historical process that made us neighbors provides that introduction.

—PATRICIA NELSON LIMERICK

5 | Mormon Wests

The Creation and Evolution of an American Region

RICHARD H. JACKSON

Driving west from Denver or Cheyenne or north and west from Las Vegas, a traveler crosses an invisible line somewhere in the Rockies or the Great Basin that marks the boundary between the Mormon and non-Mormon West. Although not immediately obvious, a few more hours of travel will bring the visitor to farms, towns, and cities with a distinctive cultural imprint. There are few places in the United States where there is such a distinct and recognizable cultural region, a fact recognized by innumerable observers over the years. The Mormon landscape (from place names to architecture to cemeteries), the Mormon religion (from beliefs to practices to institutions and customs), and the Mormon people (from demographics to dress) have long attracted the attention of writers and travelers who have visited this region.[1] Not only is the Mormon West distinctive, but also it has persisted for over a century and a half in spite of governmental and private initiatives and the intrusion of modern American popular culture that have threatened its distinctiveness. Its persistence, however, does not signify an archaic, unchanging place, rather the term *Mormon West* is a plural designation, its plurality revealed in its changing character over time and space.

The process by which the Mormons initially tried to establish a utopian agrarian society in the arid valleys of the intermountain West and the Great Basin involved significant elements of their belief system, beliefs based on a combination of American frontier ideas of egalitarianism and cooperation combined with Puritanical interpretation of the Bible. The resultant settlement geography included remarkable elements of foresight and planning, but significant examples of ad hoc adoption of new strategies reflecting unanticipated environmental, political, and economic events. The farms and villages established by the Mormon settlers were thus a work in progress from their initial establishment, changing as the goals, knowledge, and economic goals of the Mormon leaders and their followers changed. The idealistic utopian agrocentric society envisioned by the early Mormon leaders was doomed to failure by the very American values of individualism, competition, and materialism that the Mormon faithful brought with them to the West, but Mormon struggles to remake the environment according to their vision of the stewardship conferred upon them by their God created the distinctive land and people today recognized as Mormon country.

Origin of the Mormon West

Understanding the Mormon region begins with understanding the origin (temporally and spatially) of this quintessential American religion. The Church of Jesus Christ of Latter-day Saints (nicknamed Mormon)[2] was founded by Joseph Smith Jr. on the American frontier of the early 1800s.[3] Smith's parents farmed and operated a small store in and around the town of Sharon, Windsor County, Vermont, but moved west in 1816, settling in Palmyra, New York, on the proposed route of the Erie Canal. Religious fervor in the western New York region of the time affected the young Smith, prompting his own fervent prayers, which he claimed culminated in divine revelations that led to founding of the church.[4] Smith officially organized the church on 6 April 1830, moving the church headquarters to Kirtland, Ohio, in the Western Reserve in early 1831[5] (Map 5.1). Kirtland is important in understanding the Mormon West because of important doctrines and practices introduced there by Smith, beliefs and practices that shaped the Mormon experience thereafter.

One of the important doctrines introduced by Smith was that of "gathering," the idea that converts to the new church were to join with the rest of the members to enable them to form a community of believers. Central to this community were concepts of Christian fellowship and construction of places of worship, including temples. Like other religious groups the Mormons believed that temples were holy sites where the profane secular world could intersect the higher sacred spheres, literally cosmic centers necessary for sanctification of sacred ordinances such as baptism and marriage.[6] Responding to Smith's call to "gather," Mormon converts swelled the population of Kirtland, resulting in erection of the first Mormon temple in 1836. Other principles introduced by Smith in Kirtland included the concept of a utopian city he called the City of Zion, based on his New England heritage. Smith repeatedly

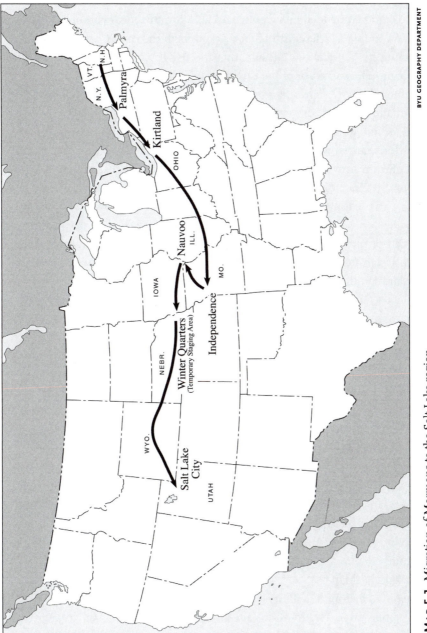

MAP 5.1. Migration of Mormons to the Salt Lake region.

preached that individuals needed to live in towns and cities rather than on scattered farms so that worship opportunities, education, and cultural advantages could be provided in a frontier milieu.[7] Smith's ideas combined the vision of a utopian society with biblical accounts of the early Christian church, including his "revelations" designating the fledgling American faith as the only legitimate successor of the early apostolic church.

Although many of the ideas promulgated by Smith were first implemented in Kirtland (schools, the temple, city planning, economic practices, and so forth), others were first experimented with in concurrent Mormon colonization efforts farther west in the Missouri frontier. Kirtland was the source from which Smith's revelations for the fledgling church were disseminated from 1831 to 1838, including one calling the faithful to "gather" to create a new City of Zion on the frontier in Missouri.[8] Smith announced in July of 1831 that Independence, Jackson County, Missouri, had been revealed as the site for a new City of Zion, and new converts began moving to the frontier settlement.[9] Smith's plan for the City of Zion specified a nucleated settlement of twenty thousand to thirty thousand inhabitants occupying small lots surrounded by farmlands. His plan anticipated that after the original city reached its maximum population it would be replicated across the fertile Midwest prairies. The Missouri saints quickly encountered hostility from other settlers, leading to their expulsion from Jackson County in 1833. Relocation to other Missouri counties coincided with renewed attempts to establish a "Zion" community, resulting in additional cycles of violence and Mormon flight from their new towns and proposed temple sites. Antipathy toward the Mormons also developed in the Kirtland community because Mormon tendencies to vote as a bloc culminated in Mormon dominance of political offices. Mob violence was substituted for the ballot, resulting in persecution and the flight in 1838 of more than sixteen hundred Mormons (including Smith) to communities established in Missouri. Ironically, the Kirtland saints and Smith arrived in Missouri only to experience more violence, including the imprisonment of Smith and other leaders. During the winter of 1838–1939 nearly twelve thousand Mormons fled Missouri, most going to Illinois under the direction of Brigham Young[10] (Map 5.1).

Rejoined by Smith in Illinois, the Mormons purchased a town site on the Mississippi River, renamed it Nauvoo and proceeded to again implement their utopian vision. Within five years the Mormons, capitalizing on their past frontier experience, were able to build a city of fifteen thousand people as converts from the eastern United States, Canada, and the British Isles joined the refugees from Missouri.[11] Continued conflicts with their neighbors during this time prompted Smith to begin looking even farther west for a homeland for his people. Under Smith's direction the Mormons acquired information about Oregon and California, and the Rocky Mountains and even considered Wisconsin and the upper Mississippi River basin as places where they might be left in peace, concluding that the Great Basin or Rocky Mountains might ultimately become their destination.[12] Growing Mormon political power, population, and related expansion combined with non-Mormon suspicion of a group that was so seemingly subservient to a small group of leaders and the Mormon penchant for publicly claiming their role as God's chosen people to foster persecution that culminated in Smith's murder by a mob in 1844.[13] Within a few weeks the Mormon membership at Nauvoo selected Brigham Young to be its new leader, a remarkably prescient choice given the number of claimants to Smith's mantle. Under Young's direction the Mormons hastened to complete the Nauvoo temple, the crowning feature of their new city on the Mississippi. Continued mob violence culminated in the evacuation of the membership during the winter of 1845–1846 just as the temple was completed.

The Great Basin Experience

Under Young's leadership the Mormons accepted Smith's earlier statements that the Rocky Mountains or Great Basin would be their new location. The Mormon flight from Nauvoo included small groups going to Texas, Wisconsin, and various areas of the Midwest, but most ultimately moved west under Young's direction to begin anew the process of establishing a city of God. The serendipitous mob violence that forced the Mormons to push far beyond the advancing frontier to the arid Great Basin marks the penultimate event requisite to understanding the characteristics of the Mormon West. Characteristics apparent to even casual observers of the Mormon region are the result of the experiences and beliefs forged in the tumultuous years of their journeying from New York to Nauvoo.

Foremost among the Mormon ideals affecting their Great Basin kingdom was acceptance of the idea that the leader of the church was a prophet and that his proclamations carried divine imprimatur. Thus, when Young stated while overlooking the Salt Lake Valley that "This is the Place," the church membership was obligated to accept his statement as a divine mandate to once again establish towns, homes, and farms and to create a new homeland. The process by which they did so was little different from that in Ohio, Missouri, Illinois, or other locales in which they had attempted to implement the revelations of their leaders, even though the arid environment was in stark contrast to their past experience. Central to the environmental transformation that created the Mormon West was a second belief: the acceptance of the necessity of creating a city of God.[14] Although Mormon efforts to implement Smith's revelations to establish a City of Zion in Independence, Missouri, and elsewhere in the Midwest had been precipitously terminated by mobocrats, his instructions concerning the nature of that city remained firmly embedded in his followers' psyches and their experience and are obvious in their Great Basin communities.[15]

Salt Lake City was the first of the Mormon settlements in the West, and it embodies many of the characteristics of Smith's City of Zion plan originally proposed for Independence, Missouri, characteristics that are evident in the other Mormon communities across the West. The key features in Salt Lake City and other Mormon communities are the use of wide blocks and wide streets oriented to the cardinal directions and designated by a simple numeric address system based on directional coordinates. Streets in Salt Lake City's initial plat are all 132 feet wide, replicating Smith's proposal for the major arterials in the City of Zion. Unlike Smith's proposal for the City of Zion plan, however, lots in Salt Lake City (and subsequent settlements in the Mormon West) are much larger.[16] Blocks remained large as in Smith's plan (ten acres in size), but the practical Young recognized the need for the frontier Mormon settlers to be self-sufficient, including producing perishable vegetables and fruits in their own gardens and maintaining barns, corrals, and chicken coops for the livestock essential to frontier life. Thus, instead of twenty one-half-acre lots per block, Young's city had only eight lots of one and one-quarter acres per block. Young required that each street include at least twenty feet for sidewalks, that houses be set back twenty feet from the property line, that houses be alternated on opposite sides of the street to prevent the image of a solid row of houses, and that all property owners plant trees, shrubs, and gardens. The combination of gardens, barns, and livestock on the lots of Salt Lake City and other Mormon settlements created a landscape of minifarms in the distinctive geographic feature known as the "Mormon village"[17] (Map 5.2).

Young's exhortations to plant trees and gardens were impossible to obey without modification of the arid environment that the Mormons had found in the Great Basin. Mormon introduction of irrigation into Mormon settlement strategy represents further evidence of Young's pragmatic approach to implementing Smith's revelations. Although Mormon folklore maintains that irrigation is further proof of Young's divine guidance, analysis of Young's and the other leaders' meetings before they were driven from Nauvoo indicate that

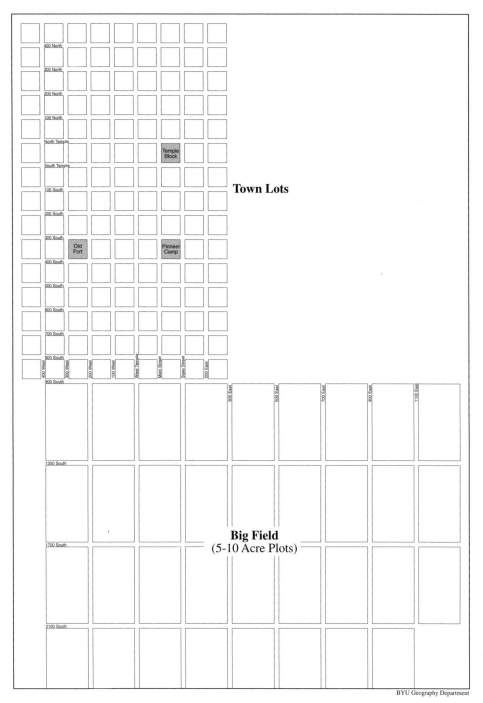

Town Lots

Big Field
(5-10 Acre Plots)

MAP 5.2. Subdivision of Salt Lake City, 1847.

they studied the Spanish settlements of Santa Fe as reported by traders and were ready to begin the practice of irrigation immediately upon arrival in the Salt Lake Valley. The cooperative nature of the Mormons, and their ecclesiastical organization that created groups through which services were provided for all their members, of course, facilitated the process of creating an irrigation system that was basically a public works project. These irrigation systems became an essential part of the Mormon landscape, initially providing both culinary and irrigation water, and remain as identifying features of the small towns of the Mormon West. The ditches and canals providing water for town lots are obvious to even casual observers. Young's admonition to initial settlers of the region also remains evident in the trees lining irrigation ditches in entirely rural areas, forming the recognizable interstices to the rectangular farm plots of the area.[18]

Salt Lake City: Capital of the Mormon West

The Mormon West is dominated by Salt Lake City. Its significance to the Mormon West is threefold.

First, it set the pattern that was used in settlements across the Mormon region. Although the actual street, lot, and block dimensions might differ, Mormon village morphology from Canada to Mexico retains the general characteristics of a regular grid survey pattern, large lots and blocks, wide streets, and use of irrigation to create miniature oases across the region.

Second, Salt Lake City illustrates the difference between Smith's utopian view—of a series of relatively small agrocentric garden communities with farmlands around them dotting the Midwest as part of a pluralistic religious environment—and Young's geopolitical view of a Mormon state, with Salt Lake City as its capital.[19] Although the Great Basin was not part of the United States when the Mormons arrived in July of 1847, on 2 February 1848 the Treaty of Guadalupe Hidalgo ending the war between Mexico and the United States added the entire Southwest to the country. By March of 1849 the Mormons had organized a provisional "State of Deseret" and petitioned Congress for admission to the Union. The proposed state covered a vast area (490,000 square miles) stretching from the Rocky Mountains to the Sierra and from Oregon Territory in the north to the Gila River with a stretch of the Pacific Coast (Map 5.3). The interregnum as the state of Deseret was brief because the territory of Utah was officially established in September of 1850. Young's vision of empire was truncated as Congress reduced its size by approximately one-half in giving the Mormons territorial status.[20] Although Young's vision of a vast Mormon state with Salt Lake City as its capital became a casualty to the political intrigue associated with the issue of slavery in the territory conquered from Mexico,[21] the modern Mormon West has become a multistate region (with international outposts as well) looking to Salt Lake for ecclesiastical direction. Centered in southern Idaho and Utah, this region stretches across the intermountain region from Canada to Mexico.

MAP 5.3. Proposed state of Deseret, territory of Utah, and state of Utah with selected settlements.

Third, Salt Lake City's importance centers on the systems of land division and resource use that the settlers adopted and that shaped the landscape of the Mormon region beyond the corporate limits of the communities themselves. The great majority of the Mormon West is not a part of any city's political limits, but rather stretches across the farm and ranch lands used by the Mormon villages' occupants. Young and the other Mormon leaders adopted a framework for land and other resource use that molded the environment of their new home. Central to the distribution system adopted in Salt Lake City were need, equality, beneficial use, and smallholdings. Adjacent to the plat of city lots the Mormons surveyed "farms" of five-acre parcels abutted by ten-acre plots, creating a "Big Field" for crops (Map 5.2). Twenty-, forty-, and eighty-acre parcels were proposed for later survey beyond this field. Each family was entitled to apply for one of the parcels, and distribution was by a simple lottery system.[22] Although the actual size of parcels might differ in subsequent communities they established, the result was to create a countryside of smallholdings, with emphasis on self-subsistence, a pattern of smallholdings that continues to reverberate through the agrarian sector of the Mormon West today.[23] Young's system for allocating nonfarmland resources was simple: "There shall be no private ownership of the streams that come out of the canyons, nor the timber that grows on the hills. These belong to the people: all the people."[24]

Under this philosophy the Mormons cooperated to construct simple irrigation systems, to fence the "Big Field" of farm plots, and to build roads to acquire timber for construction and fuel from the mountains. Young's emphasis on public ownership and development of resources was a simple continuation of the techniques that the Mormons had used in establishing towns and farms in Ohio, Missouri, Illinois, and their earlier utopian attempts. The planning for the city, the agreements on land and water division, and the communitarian development of the region distinguish the Mormon West from any other major region in the West.

The concept of community is a central element of the Mormon West but is also a fundamental part of being Mormon, whether in the Mormon West or elsewhere. The ecclesiastical organization of the Mormon Church is based on a community of believers called a ward. Each ward consists nominally of two hundred to five hundred members directed by an unpaid clergy, with a bishop as the appointed spiritual and temporal leader. When Salt Lake City was platted in 1847 and 1848, it was divided into nineteen wards of varying sizes (standardization of ward size came later), and the bishop organized the labor necessary to build the ditches, fences, and other public works in their new community. Such a communitarian approach was well suited to the practice of the Mormon irrigation-based subsistence agriculture, which required community participation and cooperation in building and maintaining diversion and distribution systems, the scheduling of length of water turns, frequency of turns, and so forth. This communitarian organization reflected the early American settlements in New England and Pennsylvania from which early Mormon leaders came. The community as the basis for development of all resources, however, is in stark contrast to the mining, logging, and ranching frontiers that prompted settlement of the balance of the American West.

The Mormons and their leaders were effectively isolated by distance and belief from the balance of the United States for over half a century. Faced with the harsh necessity of cooperating to solve the myriad problems presented in moving thousands of settlers across the Plains and establishing self-sufficient communities, the Mormon West of the nineteenth century was unique not only because of its religion, but also because the religion represented a social and economic relic of an earlier, more communitarian American age. The communitarian tendencies found in the original northeast American settlement hearth from which the Mormon leaders came was replaced across the non-Mormon West by the individualism, materialism, corporate culture, and social Darwinism that came to characterize the broader America of the last half of the nineteenth century.[25]

The settlement process that developed during the original settlement of the Salt Lake Valley became institutionalized as a system of settlement and community that is imprinted across the West in Mormon villages stretching from Mexico to Canada. The colonizing efforts of the Mormons in the last half of the nineteenth century demonstrate as well the reification of the beliefs and practices of the early formative years of the group. Under the direction of Brigham Young, settlers attempted to colonize his visionary state of Deseret. Settlers pushed outward to its boundaries, establishing nearly five hundred settlements in Idaho, Wyoming, Colorado, New Mexico, Arizona, Nevada, and Utah. Some of these settlements were at the far edges of his proposed territory, including short-lived settlements in San Bernardino, California, current Las Vegas, and Carson Valley, Nevada.[26] Later settlements extended beyond Young's original vision, extending the Mormon influence into outposts in Canada and Mexico. The imprint of the American relic communitarian pattern from New England in the American West created the widely recognized Mormon culture region in the last half of the nineteenth century[27] (Map 5.4).

The visible imprint of the Mormon settlement of the West is most obvious

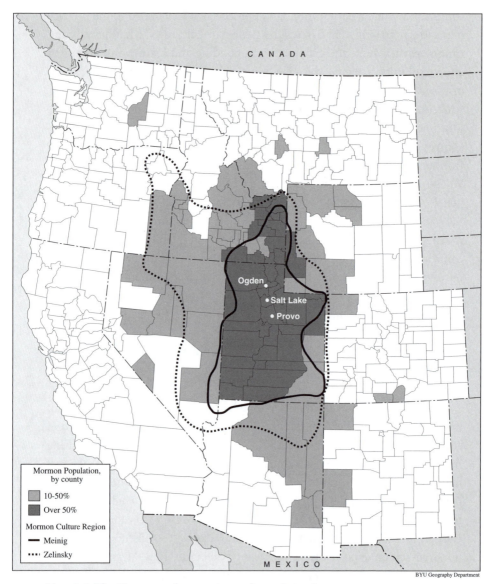

MAP 5.4. The Mormon culture region and population by county, 1990.

Within the map legend:

Mormon Population,
by county

10-50%

Over 50%

Mormon Culture Region

—— Meinig

····· Zelinsky

in the landscapes associated with the rural farm villages scattered across the region. Wherever the Mormon settlers could find adequate water they attempted to re-create the Salt Lake model of an agrarian utopia, building their signature nuclear communities surrounded by fields and pastures. As they did so the Mormon experience with the environment was transformed into a series of myths that transformed their settlement history into a sociopolitical iconography still used to demonstrate that they were indeed a chosen, heroic people. Central among these myths are widely accepted beliefs that Young had no idea of the destination of the pioneer party until his first sight of the Salt Lake Valley, that the Mormons found a "raging desert," that because of their faithfulness in trying to cultivate it the climate was "ameliorated" through divine intervention, and not only that irrigation science was developed independently but also that stream flows had been increased by God to meet settlement needs.[28] These myths strengthened the Mormons' group identity, reinforcing their belief that they were a "chosen people," and helping maintain their cohesiveness as non-Mormon forces impinged upon their settlements.

Non-Mormon Intrusions into the Mormon West

Initially welcomed by the church leaders, external forces ultimately threatened the territoriality of the Mormon West. The first external forces were associated with the discovery of gold in California and the resultant emigrant flows through the Mormon settlements. Reprovisioning these groups provided an important economic boost to the isolated Mormon settlements.[29] Subsequent contacts with the outside world varied in their impact, such as the telegraph and railroad that allowed rapid communication with members beyond the West and facilitated the gathering of converts to the new Zion but also led to growing hostility with non-Mormon merchants and federal officials. Creation of Utah Territory initially vested political leadership in Young and other church leaders, but subsequent appointment of federal officials quickly led to concerted efforts to force the Mormons to recognize the dominance of federal rather than church authorities. The fifty years of struggle that ended with the capitulation of the Mormons in 1890 (thirteen years after Young's death) coincided with their initial expansion to the margins of Deseret and their subsequent consolidation in the core of the region as San Bernardino and other settlements on the periphery of Young's empire were abandoned when federal troops were dispatched to the territory in 1857. Mormons reoccupied the scattered oases from Salt Lake to Arizona in the 1860s and 1870s, and church leaders even sent families (many of them polygamous) to Mexico and Canada in the 1880s to found settlements beyond the reach of American law.[30]

During the initial half-century of colonization and conflict across the intermountain West, Mormon experiments with boycotting non-Mormon businesses, implementation of communal economic systems, and assimilation of European converts "gathered" to Zion combined to reinforce the Mormon self-identity, creating a sense of alienation and even latent (if generally benign) hostility toward the non-Mormons within and without their Western home. It needs to be noted, however, that the Mormon self-identity masked important differences between and within individual and group acceptance of Mormon doctrine, political orientation, education, and socioeconomic status. When viewed by non-Mormon observers the internal differences among residents of the Mormon West were usually subsumed to the broader categorization of "Mormon," a categorization that depicted a uniform, monolithic Mormon culture.

By the end of the nineteenth century the outline of the space and place occupied by what was seen as an aberrant American cult was recognized by observers as the "Mormon West," a region that pundits believed was clearly defined in the landscape and life of its inhabitants.[31] Important aspects of this Mormon region were variously described, but generally included references to the industry, honesty, and religiosity of the people in general, combined with remarks on their gullible acceptance of their leaders' direction, the social aberration of polygamy, and the general ignorance of a provincial frontier populace.[32] The Mormon West's landscape was dominated by the village with its requisite irrigation system and associated gardens, farms, and relatively small and simple vernacular structures. Native materials such as adobe or rock were combined with past experience to create a colonial Federalist-style architecture, relics of which can be found in most Mormon communities even today, structures that were described with either ridicule or admiration by all observers. Less recognized by either residents of the Mormon West or diarists reporting on the exotic region were the destructive environmental changes associated with creation of the Mormon West, even though these have had an even larger spatial and temporal impact on the region. Diversion of streams for irrigation was always described with admiration, but in the nineteenth century such diversions were small scale and had limited impact on the ecology of the region's streams. Unrecognized and rarely described was the fact that growing numbers of people in the fragile semiarid and arid or mountainous environment were accompanied by even more rapid growth in herds of sheep, cattle, and horses. Lack of experience with fragile landscapes by the Mormon settlers seemingly prevented them from recognizing the overgrazing and resultant erosion of the deserts and mountains that Young had declared belonged to "all of the people," an oversight that remains today as a visible reminder of the dark side of unlimited access by "all the people" to the public lands of the region in the nineteenth century.

The Twentieth-Century Mormon West

At the dawn of the twentieth century the rural, cooperative, insular character of the Mormon people, and its geographic expression in their villages and associated landscapes, was already beginning to change to a new Mormon West, one best characterized as a bifurcated region. One part of this region was still experiencing frontier settlement as wagon trains brought Mormon settlers to places like the Big Horn Basin of Wyoming in 1900.[33] A smaller part centered on Salt Lake City and one or two other growing towns where the Mormon populace was being transformed from the nineteenth-century defensive, independent frontier farmers and villagers still smarting from real or imagined persecutions into what would become part of urban America. Utah's statehood in 1896 signaled an official end to decades of efforts by the federal government to bring the Mormons into submission, but the newly elected representatives to Congress were from the educated Mormon leaders of the urbanizing Salt Lake City, an early warning of future conflict between rural and urban residents of the region.[34]

The rural Mormon communities of the twentieth century, both inside and outside the Salt Lake Valley, remained places where the traditions and practices that created the Mormon West would continue to be dominant for nearly another century. These rural communities were the places that observers described as the Mormon West, but in reality this rural, agrarian, conservative Mormon West existed most clearly only in the most isolated portions of the intermountain West.[35] The urban Mormon region began in Salt Lake City toward the end of the colonization of the West period as population growth hastened the end of the agrocentric utopian vision of Smith and Young. Growth of the urban population effectively ended the Mormon village as a self-sufficient community of believers. Not only were the majority of Salt Lake City's inhabitants forced to find employment beyond agriculture, but also simple city size prevented development of a single cohesive community based on personal familiarity with all others in the community. Moreover, Salt Lake City was also the major location where Mormon and non-Mormon contrasts were most visible. The coming of the railroad had been followed by discovery and development of mines across Utah and neighboring states, attracting more non-Mormons to the area.[36] Although there were other communities in the Mormon West that were largely non-Mormon (especially mining towns), Salt Lake City included significant numbers of non-Mormons brought by the growing connectivity of the Mormon West to the rest of the country. By 1880 Salt Lake City had a population that was one-third non-Mormon, compared to rural Mormondom in which the percentage of Mormons generally exceeded 90 percent (and in many communities was 100 percent[37]).

Salt Lake City was no longer simply a larger version of the cohesive towns and villages that comprised the Mormon rural West, but rather was the forerunner of a new type of urban Mormon region with its attendant cultural, economic, and social diversity.[38] This urbanization was accompanied by increasing importance of ecclesiastical units (especially the ward) as vehicles to maintain religious identity and to organize to accomplish group goals, which had previously been the provenance of the entire Mormon village. Mormons in the newly emerging urban regions increasingly experienced a replacement of their unique "Mormonness" with characteristics of the broader mass culture of America. By the middle of the twentieth century residents of the urban Mormon region were identifiable as different from other Americans primarily by their geographic locale and by their own personal religious beliefs rather than by observable landscapes or behavior (Map 5.4).

Donald Meinig in his seminal article entitled "The Mormon Culture Region" discusses Salt Lake City as the center of the Mormon "core" in which are found not only concentrations of Mormons, the church headquarters, and the great temple, but also non-Mormons, industry, and productive agriculture concentrated in the valleys of the Wasatch Front.[39] Although emphasizing the numeric concentration of Mormons in the West in the 1960s, his "core" fails to adequately emphasize the urban-rural contrast within the Mormon West. Even within Meinig's "Mormon core," many of the residents still lived in small towns that were rural rather than urban at the time his article was published in 1965. Although Meinig divided the Mormon West into "core" versus "domain" based on the degree of dominance of Mormon characteristics, it is important to recognize the differences between the urban Mormon region and the rural Mormon region both within his core region and elsewhere across the West. The difference between the urban Mormon West and the rural Mormon West is a function of the transition from the agrocentric socioeconomic model of the pioneer Mormon West to the modern interconnected socioeconomic model of urban America.[40]

Forces for Change: The Rise of the Urban Mormon West

The years from 1900 to the post–World War II era witnessed a growing gulf separating the urban Mormon West from the rural Mormon West. The coming of the transcontinental railroad in 1869 had connected Ogden to the balance of the country. Under Young's direction a spur was quickly built to Salt Lake City, further consolidating its position as not only the premier settlement in Mormon country but also the largest community between Denver and San Francisco. The railroad provided the potential for hastening the "gathering" of converts from around the world to the American West and for making the newly urbanizing center more attractive to new settlers than outlying frontier communities. Within three years of arriving in the Salt Lake Valley approximately one-fifth of the church population had migrated to Utah (11,418 in Utah, 51,839 total church members).[41]

Between 1847 and 1869 Young's emphasis on "gathering" to "Zion" had markedly reduced the number of church members living outside of Utah.[42] At the same time his encouragement of colonization had led to the founding of most of the Mormon communities across the region, occupying all but the most marginal locations suitable for their simple diversion-based irrigation agriculture.[43] The result was a decline in the concentration of Mormons in the five counties comprising the Wasatch Front (an area synonymous with Meinig's core region). This five-county region accounted for 91 percent of Utah territorial population in 1850 but only 55 percent in 1870.[44] The Salt Lake Valley, however, continued to dominate the Mormon West, with Salt Lake City's population of 12,910 in 1870 eclipsing the new railroad center of Ogden's 3,200 and the next-largest city, Provo (located in the next valley south of Salt Lake) with only 2,384.[45] After the arrival of the railroad Salt Lake's dominance increased, with the city growing to 20,768 in 1880 (compared to Ogden's 5,246 and Provo's 2,432)[46] as the previous decades of dispersal of settlers to the far-flung communities of the Mormon West were replaced by migrants settling in the city and by a return flow to the center of the region from the more isolated areas to the north and south.

By the early 1900s, Salt Lake's dominance was overwhelming as it reached a population of 53,531, based on its growing political and financial role for the Mormon settlers, miners, and governmental activity in the region. The great temple had been completed in 1893 (after forty years of construction), its granite, fortresslike architecture symbolizing the permanence of the city as the center of the Mormon faithful. Increasingly, however, the Mormon faithful were not numbered among the residents of the small villages scattered across the Mormon West, but rather were found in the growing Salt Lake urban center or emerging cities of the Wasatch Front. The growth of Salt Lake City and the rest of the Wasatch Front came at the expense of the Mormon villages, the original landscape icon of the Mormon West, which experienced population loss in the latter half of the twentieth century.

The Mormon village proper was basically an ephemeral phenomenon. After ten to fifteen years of "hard pioneering" it enjoyed a "twenty- to thirty-year golden period." After that time the land and water resources for the simple Mormon agrarian culture were fully utilized, and the villages' adult offspring had to look elsewhere for cultivable land.[47] The relatively marginal nature of most of the sites for the Mormon villages outside of the Wasatch oasis ensured that the unlanded offspring of the occupants would provide the settlers for even more marginal areas (either in terms of environmental setting or presence of competing settlement groups). Thus, Mormon settlement continued to expand into Wyoming, Nevada, and Canada, and also into newly reclaimed irrigated areas financed under the terms of the Newlands Reclamation Act of 1902 into the beginnings of the twentieth century.[48] But these new iterations of Smith's dream of the garden village (modified by Young's adaptations to the realities of frontier self-sufficiency) could themselves never completely absorb the growing numbers of Mormon offspring produced by the fecund occupants of Mormondom. Church membership in 1850 was 51,839 worldwide, but only some 11,000 had been "gathered" to the Mormon West, with the balance mostly in the eastern United States and the British Isles.[49] By 1900 church membership had soared to 283,765, and Salt Lake City alone equaled the population of the entire church a half-century before (although a significant number of its residents were non-Mormons).[50]

The Future Mormon West

The Mormon West that is obvious to the road tourist who enters it from the periphery where the Mormon village still exists as a distinctive landscape feature is less apparent to the air tourist who flies into Salt Lake City with its cookie-cutter urban features of malls, fast-food chains, freeways, and sprawling suburbs. The forces that began the transformation of the Mormon West into rural versus urban regions a century earlier are far advanced as we enter the twenty-first century. The urban center of the Wasatch Front (Meinig's core) contained an estimated 40 percent of all Mormon population in the *United States* in 1964, according to Meinig, but by 2000 only slightly more than one-quarter of U.S. Mormons are found there in spite of thirty-five years of rapid population growth in the urban region.[51] At the same time, more than one-half of all Mormons in the *Mormon West* were concentrated in the urban Wasatch Front communities during the twentieth century. Utah Mormons are even more concentrated, with more than 75 percent located in this urban region and nearly 50 percent located in Salt Lake City and its contiguous suburbs alone.[52]

The concentration of Mormons in the Wasatch Front valleys represents a simple continuation of the inexorable geographic and social forces that have shaped population geography across the Mormon West since the arrival of the first pioneer party in 1847. Foremost among these forces was the simple geographic fact that the Mormons had selected the best site for settlement in the intermountain region. The fertile Salt Lake Valley is bracketed to the north and south by equally fertile Weber and Utah valleys. Well watered in an arid region, they have always been the sites most amenable to human use in the Mormon West.[53] But the physical geography was not the sole reason for the dominance of the Wasatch Front and the Salt Lake City urbanites. The great institution driving the settlement and development of the Mormon West was not just the Mormon settlers, but also the organization that controlled and directed their dogged efforts to make the desert blossom like the rose. Not only was Salt Lake the home of the prophet and other leaders of the church, it was also the designated capital of the Mormon kingdom, whether defined as Young's grandiose Deseret or as the distinct state units that comprise today's intermountain West. In either case, the Mormons within their boundaries look to Salt Lake City as their spiritual capital, creating an equally important economic capital for the region. Since the church made its peace with the American government by disavowing polygamy, non-Mormon governmental and private enterprises have had to include Salt Lake City and the Mormons in their development plans. The result has been the continued rapid growth of Salt Lake City and its suburbs as governmental and private investment anywhere within the Mormon West results in at least some impact on the economy of the Mormon spiritual and financial capital.

An important social force that affected Salt Lake City in the last half of the twentieth century will no doubt have an even greater effect in the twenty-first century: the rapid growth of the worldwide Mormon Church. The 51,165 members of 1850 represented the increase through proselytization and natural increase of twenty years. Fifty years later worldwide Mormon population totaled 283,765, most scattered across the Mormon West. The next fifty years (1950) brought a slightly slower rate of increase as the Mormon population increased to 1,111,314, with most still in the United States but beginning to move beyond the confines of the intermountain Mormon country.

The last fifty years have brought unprecedented population growth as worldwide membership reached 11 million in 2000. The majority are no longer in the Mormon West, and more than half are not even within the United States. Just over 5 million members reside in the United States (45.5 percent of world Mormon population), with Utah's 1.5 million the single largest state population, followed by California's 733,000. Ten states each have more than 100,000 Mormons, five located in the intermountain West. The percentage of the total population that is Mormon is highest in Utah and southeastern Idaho,[54] with Utah averaging 71.8 percent Mormon statewide. Across the eight states comprising the intermountain West, Mormons are either the largest or second-largest denomination, making them an important part of a region whose peoples are "largely unchurched."[55]

Outside of the United States, Mormon numbers are highest in Latin America, with 3.5 million members, with Mexico (783,000) second only to Utah in numbers.[56] A side effect of the worldwide growth in church membership, however, is concurrent growth in the church paid bureaucracy, most centered in Salt Lake City. The growth of general church bureaucracy (even though unpaid lay members staff all positions in local and regional congregations) has continued to reinforce the role of Salt Lake City as the dominant center of Mormondom. The greater Salt Lake City metropolitan area is home to the largest group of Mormons in the West (although rural communities across southern Idaho, Utah, and parts of adjacent states have a larger proportion of their total population that is Mormon). Salt Lake City remains a Mormon "mecca," as much the focus of the spiritual realm of Mormondom as at the time of Brigham Young. Today, Salt Lake City is the nucleus of an urban "heartland" stretching from Ogden to Provo, an urban enclave in the largely sparsely populated Mormon hinterland across the rest of the intermountain West. Ironically, whereas Brigham Young spent his life trying to encourage settlers to move from this heartland to the hinterland, the urbanization forces of the last half of the twentieth and first half of the twenty-first centuries continue to concentrate the western U.S. Mormon population in the urban areas of the region.

Although the urbanization of the Mormon population in the West resulted from the same forces affecting the rest of the United States in the post–World War II era, the forces signal an important change within the church itself. Until the last decades of the twentieth century, Mormon leadership was dominated by a cadre of leadership born in the pioneering era of the nineteenth century. Whether aging church leaders were born in Salt Lake City, where government-appointed officials persecuted and jailed church leaders until the 1890s, or in the rural hinterland, their views during much of the twentieth century reflected the nineteenth-century rural Mormon frontier experience, with its pioneering, hardscrabble existence. Mormon leaders in the twenty-first century from the urban heartland of Utah, the Mormon concentrations in the urban centers of the West (Los Angeles, San Diego, San Francisco, Phoenix, Las Vegas, Denver), or the far-flung growing world church will increasingly know that experience only as folklore. The experience of the majority of urban Mormons and their leaders is increasingly in contrast to that of the rural members. The rural Mormon West comprises a reservoir of nineteenth-century Mormon pioneer attitudes of self-sufficiency; isolationist cultural experience; hostility, contempt, or amusement from outsiders; and their own hostility to government agents and Mormon or non-Mormon urbanites who move to the rural settlements or use or view local resources in ways contrary to the previous century of exploitative agriculture, ranching, forestry, and mining. Ironically, the cooperative communitarian efforts required to settle Young's Mormon West now face serious challenges of reconciling the differing Mormon views of the region and its resources. Urban Mormons who see the far-flung agrarian villages and their hinterlands as playgrounds, "sacred" wilderness to be preserved, living history of the Mormon experience, or reification of the Mormon settlement myths have far different goals regarding the use of the resources upon which rural Mormondom is founded. Rural Mormons, however, still have an inordinate voice in the political arena of the Mormon West because of the representation system that granted disproportionate power to the sparsely settled rural counties, but in the next half-century no doubt church leadership will be dominated by urban and/or non-western individuals.

The Geography of Today's Mormon West

The result of the changes that have shaped or are shaping the Mormon West has distinct spatial manifestations.

First, Young's visionary Deseret is today largely populated by non-Mormons. Only in Utah, southern Idaho, and a few Mormon rural enclaves elsewhere do Mormons form a majority of the total population. Young's Deseret included a significant portion of southern California, and today California's Mormon population is second only to Utah in the United States. The Mormon population in California is nearly three times that of the entire church in 1900, yet Mormons represent less than 3 percent of the state's total population. Although the percentages vary by state, the same is true for Nevada, Wyoming, Montana, Arizona, New Mexico, and Colorado: Mormons are nearly always a small proportion of state population across the states of Young's proposed Deseret.

Second, the number of Mormons has increased dramatically across the intermountain West, but because the entire region is experiencing rapid population growth the percentage that is Mormon remains low except in Utah and neighboring counties in southern Idaho and the scattered rural Mormon enclaves of the West.[57] As in Utah, the Mormon population of the broader intermountain West is increasingly found in the large urban areas. The urban/ rural dichotomy of Mormondom creates exclaves with relatively large Mormon populations in all of the urban centers of the West, but the Mormons are generally a small fraction of the total population and do not constitute a majority in any major urban center of the West outside of Utah. At the same time, due to historic forces that caused the initial expansion of the Mormon village into even marginal locations in the intermountain West there are rural Mormon exclaves with relatively small populations that comprise either a majority or near majority in their immediate area.

Recognition of the changing spatial pattern of Mormons by the Salt Lake leadership is evident in recent location of temples. Construction of temples has been accepted as a central part of Mormon doctrine since shortly after the founding of the church. Early temples were part of the city planning process of the Mormons, and after settlement in the West temples were begun in each major population center. Four temples were completed in the nineteenth-century Mormon West: St. George, Utah, 1877; Logan, Utah, 1884; Manti, Utah, 1888; and Salt Lake City, 1893 (Map 5.3). The first half of the twentieth century brought construction of temples in the Mormon exclaves in Hawaii (1919), Canada (Cardston, Alberta, 1923), Mesa, Arizona (1927), and Idaho Falls, Idaho (1945). From 1950 to 1975 church leaders authorized temples for the urban Mormon centers of the West Coast (Los Angeles, 1956, and Oakland, 1964), in Washington, D.C. (1974), and in the growing urban core in Utah (Ogden and Provo temples, 1972). Each of these was in recognition of the growth of Mormon believers in their vicinity, but each was also a political statement signifying the church's spread from its Western refuge. The last quarter-century has brought the completion or announcement of scores of temples in response to church growth in the West and elsewhere. Five new temples were completed in Utah (three in the urban core plus two small ones that serve rural eastern and southeastern Utah), four new structures in urban areas of the intermountain West (Boise, Denver, Albuquerque, and Las Vegas), five in the Pacific Coast states (San Diego, Seattle, Portland, Spokane, and Anchorage), nineteen in major urban centers east of the Rockies, five in major Canadian cities, and forty-nine outside of the United States and Canada.[58] With the exception of a few large structures in major cities, most of these new temples are no longer massive structures designed to make a political statement about the church's presence in the area, but rather small, functional temples designed to serve only the members in the immediate area.[59]

Conclusion

Today's church leaders, no longer exclusively from the rural Mormon Western experience, indicate by their placement of these most important of Mormon structures the changing role of the Mormon West itself. Just as the rural Mormon village was the visible imprint of nineteenth-century Mormon settlement experience, temples today provide evidence of the urban diaspora of twenty-first-century Mormon population. Since 1975 the church has constructed two small temples in the more isolated rural regions of Utah (Vernal and Monticello in 1998) to serve their small but homogeneous Mormon populations, and two in sites historically important to the church (Palmyra, New York, 2000, and Nauvoo, Illinois, 2001). All others have been announced or completed in major urban areas in the United States and foreign countries. Rapid temple construction since 1975 reflects abandonment of the early doctrine of "gathering" that prompted establishment of nineteenth-century Mormon villages to house the influx of converts. Today the church is committed to providing a temple in each region of the world with sufficient local Mormon population to utilize the temple, thus, the temples become "growth poles" for the urban region in which they are found.[60]

Although not as obvious as the changes in the landscape of the Mormon West, another significant change in the region in the last twenty-five years has been the decline in direct church control of political, economic, or other activities that typified the nineteenth- and early twentieth-century Mormon settlements. Tacit acknowledgment of this is evident in a variety of church activities in the twentieth century. One example is the near abandonment of the church role in public education. The Mormons established thirty-three academies across the Mormon West to educate the children of the region, but by the end of the twentieth century all but four (Brigham Young University in Provo, Utah, with 30,000 students; Ricks College in Rexburg, Idaho, 8,000 students; Brigham Young University–Hawaii, 2,000 students; and the LDS Business College in Salt Lake City, 1,000 students) had been turned over to state educational departments.[61] The church was originally the founder and owner of numerous hospitals across the lands it settled, but in the late 1970s the church transferred ownership to a newly created private hospital corporation not affiliated with the church.[62] The church cut its final official ties to the original theocratic society of the nineteenth century when it sold its controlling interest in the chain of department stores known as ZCMI (Zion's Cooperative Mercantile Institution) to a national retail chain in 1999. ZCMI was founded under Young's direction in nineteenth-century Utah in response to non-Mormon merchants' arrival in Utah territory after completion of the transcontinental railroad in 1869. Fearing destruction of the Mormon village-based cooperative economy found in the settlements stretching from Idaho to Arizona and Nevada, Young instituted a protective campaign, including establishing Mormon boards of trade and cooperative businesses of many kinds, ranging from Mormon railroads to each local community's ZCMI. Most of the economic activities of the Mormon Church were transferred to private ownership as part of the agreement to abandon polygamy and create the state of Utah in 1896, but ZCMI remained as an institution in major communities until its recent sale. The ZCMI organization, like the Mormon village society it originally served, was a uniquely Mormon frontier institution made redundant by changes in the modern world. The demise of ZCMI signals the growing convergence of formerly distinctive Mormon economic and other non-ecclesiastical activities with the broader society of America. Smith's vision of a utopian society in which religion and day-to-day life were a seamless whole, the basis of Young's colonization of the Mormon West and its associated communitarian village life and landscape, is further replaced by the American pattern of urbanism, individualism, and social Darwinism.

A final change affecting the Mormon West revolves around the Doctrine of Prior Appropriation of water that grew out of Young's view that resources should be used beneficially based on need, equality, and small-scale agriculture. Court cases of the nineteenth century simplified Young's view into the concept of ownership of water rights based on primary rights belonging to the first to beneficially use the water. Beneficial use is defined by society. Mormon society defined irrigation as the most beneficial use because it was essential for the successful establishment of the ubiquitous Mormon village economy. The increasingly urban majority of the Mormon West has little understanding of or respect for the traditional Mormon village and its irrigation culture. Today the most beneficial use of the scarce water resources of the region is being redefined to include esthetic quality of streams, including maintaining minimum flow to protect wildlife, provide recreation use, or even to restore free-flowing streams diverted over a century ago. As governments or groups buy water rights and transfer them back to the river, there is insufficient flow to maintain the historic water turn in terms of length and volume, and that may mean that those at the end of the ditch get inadequate water. Changing views of the resources of the Mormon West magnify the marginalization of the farm village as former farmlands must be abandoned or as use of public lands beyond the borders of the Mormon village is restricted or contested by urban or non-Mormon residents.

Today's Western Mormons are overwhelmingly urbanites, wherever they are found. The Mormon West consists of a dominant urban and suburban majority who share most of the sociocultural characteristics of the larger Western urban/suburban milieu and a rural agrarian minority whose Mormon villages comprise relic landscape features in the region. The village, with its attendant features, has been repeatedly described as "typical" of the Mormon West, but it is typical only in its role as the tool by which the Mormons first occupied the region. Describing today's Mormon West, observers view a landscape that is urban or suburban and whose most typical Mormon features are the ward chapels and temples of the faith that dot an otherwise archetypical urban sprawl little different from that of many other parts of America. Even the ethnic character of the Mormon West is changing as Hispanic migrants flock into the cities and towns of the region, diluting the concentration of population with a western and northern European origin. The 2000 U.S. Census indicates that 9 percent of the state population was Hispanic (201,559), introducing new foods and holidays and strengthening the Catholic Church in the region. The Mormon West is still recognizable, but for the majority of its residents the traditional descriptions of this region represent a past iteration of the region, not the Mormon West of the twenty-first century.

Notes

1. A relatively large literature analyzes the Mormon experience. Good sources include Leonard Arrington, *Great Basin Kingdom: An Economic History of the Latter-day Saints, 1830–1900* (Cambridge: Harvard University Press, 1958); Thomas G. Alexander, *Mormonism in Transsition: A History of the Latter-day Saints, 1890–1930* (Urbana: University of Illinois Press, 1996); and Marvin S. Hill and James B. Allen, eds., *Mormonism and American Culture* (New York: Harper & Row, 1972). James B. Allen, Ronald W. Walker, and David J. Whittaker, *Studies in Mormon History, 1830–1997, an Indexed Bibliography* (Urbana: University of Illinois Press, 2000), includes 1,152 pages of references that constitute a tour de force that will be an invaluable starting point for anyone researching any topic related to Mormon history, economics, culture, politics, life, and so forth.

2. The term *Mormon* comes from the church's belief that *The Book of Mormon* is a companion volume of scripture to the Bible.

3. An in-depth discussion of the origin of the LDS Church and the American frontier is found in Richard L. Bushman, *Joseph Smith and the Beginnings of Mormonism* (Urbana: University of Illinois, 1984), or in James B. Allen and Glen M. Leonard, *The Story of the Latter-day Saints* (Salt Lake City: Deseret Book, 1976).

4. A full account of Smith's history and the events leading to the founding of the church can be found in Larry C. Porter, "A Study of the Origin of the Church of Jesus Christ of

Latter-day Saints in the States of New York and Pennsylvania" (Ph.D. diss., Brigham Young University, 1971), or Milton V. Backman Jr., *Joseph Smith's First Vision: Confirming Evidences and Contemporary Accounts* (Salt Lake City: Bookcraft, 1980).

5. A complete discussion of the church in Kirtland is found in Karl Ricks Anderson, *Joseph Smith's Kirtland: Eyewitness Accounts* (Salt Lake City: Deseret Book, 1989).

6. Joseph Smith and subsequent leaders of the Mormon Church are accepted as prophets by members of the Mormon Church. Revelations they have received that are accepted as scripture are included in the *Doctrine and Covenants*. Of the 138 sections and 2 declarations in the volume, 133 were received principally by Joseph Smith, 100 before 1834 during the formative years of the church. Some seventy-five of the total sections were received while Smith maintained his home in Kirtland. Specific sections and verses dealing with gathering are contained in *Doctrine and Covenants* 29:7–8, 51:16, 57:1–3, and 97:21. A discussion of the temples as sacred space is found in Richard H. Jackson and Roger Henrie, "Perception of Sacred Space," *Journal of Cultural Geography* 3 (spring/summer 1983): 94–107.

7. Richard H. Jackson and Robert L. Layton, "The Mormon Village: Analysis of a Settlement Type," *The Professional Geographer* 28 (May 1976): 136–141.

8. Richard H. Jackson, "The Mormon Experience: The Plains as Sinai, the Great Salt Lake as the Dead Sea, and the Great Basin as Desert-cum-Promised Land," *Journal of Historical Geography* 18, no. 1 (1992): 41.

9. Joseph Smith, *History of the Church of Jesus Christ of Latter-day Saints,* vol. 1 (Salt Lake City: Deseret News Press, 1930), 189–190.

10. The Mormon exodus from Missouri was under the direction of Brigham Young because Smith and other top Mormon leaders spent the winter in jail charged with treason, arson, and so forth, related to the mob violence that drove the Mormons from Missouri. A trial was never held, and Smith and the other leaders rejoined the saints in Illinois. The Mormon conflicts in Missouri are analyzed in Stephen C. LeSueur, *The 1838 Mormon War in Missouri* (Columbia: University of Missouri Press, 1987), and the Kirtland experience is analyzed in Milton V. Backman, *The Heaven's Resound: A History of the Latter-day Saints in Ohio 1830–1838* (Salt Lake City: Deseret Book, 1983).

11. Extended accounts of the Nauvoo experience of the Mormons are found in Brigham H. Roberts, *The Rise and Fall of Nauvoo* (Salt Lake City: Deseret News, 1900); R. B. Flanders, *Nauvoo: Kingdom on the Mississippi* (Urbana: University of Illinois Press, 1965); and D. E. Miller and D. S. Miller, *Nauvoo: The City of Joseph* (Salt Lake City: Peregrine Smith, 1974). A short account is found in Daniel H. Ludlow, ed., *Encyclopedia of Mormonism,* vol. 3 (New York: Macmillan, 1992), 987–1003.

12. Jackson, "The Mormon Experience: The Plains as Sinai, the Great Salt Lake as the Dead Sea, and the Great Basin as Desert-cum-Promised Land," 43–44.

13. Leonard Arrington, *Brigham Young: American Moses* (New York: Knopf, 1985), 111.

14. Details of the Mormon belief in the necessity of creating a City of Zion and its relationship to the Mormon communities of the West are found in Richard H. Jackson, "The Mormon Village: Genesis and Antecedents of the City of Zion Plan," *BYU Studies* 17 (summer

1977): 223–240; Lowry Nelson, *The Mormon Village: A Pattern and Technique of Land Settlement* (Salt Lake City: University of Utah Press, 1952); and Joel Ricks, *Forms and Methods of Early Mormon Settlements in Utah and Surrounding Regions, 1847–1877* (Logan: Utah State University Press, 1964).

15. Smith's original revelation was superseded by revised versions of the city plat proper, but changes were minor, affecting primarily city size and size and number of temple blocks. See R. E. Romig, "The Genesis of Zion and Kirtland and the Concept of Temples," *Restoration Studies* 3: 286–304, and Janna K. Bushman, "Prophets, Planning and Politics: Utah's Planning Heritage and Its Significance Today and Tomorrow" (master's thesis, Brigham Young University, 1997), 8–19.

16. Richard H. Jackson and Robert L. Layton, "The Mormon Village: Analysis of a Settlement Type," *Professional Geographer* 28 (May 1976): 136–141, contains an analysis of Western Mormon settlements versus non-Mormon settlements and concludes that large lot and block sizes and wide streets are the exception in non-Mormon villages but the rule in Mormon villages.

17. Richard H. Jackson, "The City of Zion Plat," in *Historical Atlas of Mormonism*, eds. S. Kent Brown, Donald Q. Cannon, and Richard H. Jackson (New York: Simon & Schuster, 1994), 44–45.

18. Richard V. Francaviglia, *The Mormon Landscape: Existence, Creation and Perception of a Unique Image in the American West* (New York: AMS, 1978).

19. It is unclear when Young's vision of a Mormon state first began, but the first report sent to the balance of the church in late 1847 recounting their new home emphasized the establishment of Great Salt Lake City, encouraged the members to emigrate there as soon as possible (bringing tools, seeds, and so forth necessary for pioneer settlement), and stated only that "We anticipate, as soon as circumstances will permit, to petition for a territorial government in the Great Basin," *Liverpool Millennial Star* 10 (1848): 85.

20. Dean L. May, "The State of Deseret," in *Historical Atlas of Mormonism*, 90–91.

21. Ray Allen Billington, *Western Expansion: A History of the American Frontier* (New York: Macmillan, 1960), 591–594.

22. Leonard J. Arrington, *Great Basin Kingdom: An Economic History of the Latter-day Saints, 1830–1900* (Cambridge: Harvard University Press, 1958), 52–53.

23. Average farm sizes and the proportion of part-time farmers are markedly higher in Utah than in any other state in the intermountain West today. Smallholdings and the self-reliance that fostered them are in return reflected in low average farm incomes, low average investment in equipment, and political views in the rural Mormon West that emphasize conservative, antifederal tendencies.

24. William Mulder, "The Mormons in American History," *Bulletin of the University of Utah* 48 (1957): 14n. 5; and Arrington, *Great Basin Kingdom*, 54, both indicate the Puritan roots of the Mormon communitarian practices. Donald W. Meinig, "The Mormon Culture Region: Strategies and Patterns in the Geography of the American West, 1847–1964," *Annals of the American Association of Geographers* 55 (1965): 195, states that the Mormon New England

heritage "is more a product of associations in lands of strong Yankee influence than directly of New England itself," illustrating the importance of the formative years of Smith, Young, and other early Mormon leaders in not only New England, but also in the New York and Ohio frontiers dominated by New England settlers.

25. A brief discussion of this idea is found in Arrington, *Great Basin Kingdom*, 62–63.

26. Lynn A. Rosenvall, "Defunct Mormon Settlements: 1830–1930," in *The Mormon Role in the Settlement of the West*, Charles Redd Monograph in Western History, no. 9, ed. Richard H. Jackson (Provo, Utah: Brigham Young University Press, 1978). Rosenvall discusses the cause for the abandonment of these and other Mormon settlements. He concludes that some 14 percent of all Mormon communities that were settled were subsequently abandoned.

27. Although a variety of articles discuss aspects of the Mormon West as a region, the following either articulate its characteristics or discuss its boundaries. Wallace Stegner, *Mormon Country*, American Folkway Series (New York: Duell, Sloan & Pearce, 1942); Meinig, "The Mormon Culture Region"; Francaviglia, *The Mormon Landscape*; Lester W. Campbell, "Perception and Land Use: The Case of the Mormon Culture Region" (master's thesis, Brigham Young University, 1974); Raymond D. Gastil, "The Mormon Region," in *Cultural Regions of the United States* (Seattle: University of Washington Press, 1975), 237–243; Dean R. Louder and Lowell C. Bennion, "Mapping Mormons across the Modern West," in *The Mormon Role in Settlement of the West*, 135–167; and Lowell C. Bennion, "Meinig's 'Mormon Culture Region' Revisited," *Historical Geography* 24, no. 1–2 (1995): 21–32.

28. Richard H. Jackson, "Mormon Perception and Settlement," *Annals of the American Association of Geographers* 68 (1978): 317–334.

29. Arrington, *Great Basin Kingdom*, 64–66, points out that the bounty received from the gold rush migrants prevented the failure or postponement of Young's dream of a Mormon empire.

30. Donald Meinig, *The Shaping of America: A Geographical Perspective on 500 Years of History*, vol. 3, *Transcontinental America, 1850–1915* (New Haven: Yale University Press, 1998), 108–113; Arrington, *Great Basin Kingdom*, 175–231.

31. Bennion, "Meinig's 'Mormon Culture Region' Revisited," 22–33. Bennion notes on p. 31 that Meinig "has perpetuated the myth of Mormon unity. The Mormon missionary net caught fish of all kinds—Yankees and Southerners, Britons and Scandinavians." Bennion concludes that "a diverse and often divided population characterized much of early Mormondom, which required a generation or two before finally achieving the unity later ascribed to it." In reality, the unity never existed across the entire region because there were always individuals and groups with different backgrounds, goals, and level of commitment to both the doctrine and practices of the group. See William Mulder, "Mother Tongue, 'Skandinavisme,' and 'The Swedish Insurrection' in Utah," *Swedish Pioneer Historical Quarterly* 7 (January 1956): 11–20; or William Mulder, "Utah's Ugly Ducklings: A Profile of the Scandinavian Immigrant," *Utah Historical Quarterly* 23 (July 1955): 233–259, for a discussion of the distinctiveness of only one subgroup within the Mormons.

32. Richard H. Jackson, "Great Salt Lake and Great Salt Lake City: American Curiosities,"

Utah Historical Quarterly 56 (spring 1988): 128–147, contains an evaluation of non-Mormon views of the Salt Lake region and its settlements in the latter half of the nineteenth century.

33. Deseret News Press, *1999–2000 Church Almanac* (Salt Lake City: Deseret News Press, 2000), 128.

34. Congressional representatives elected after Utah became a state in 1896 were from the central leadership of the Mormon Church in Salt Lake City and were initially denied their positions because of antipolygamy sentiment even though the church had officially abandoned the practice in 1890.

35. Charles S. Peterson, a historian, argued in 1976 that the *core* of the Mormon West was not the area described by Meinig as comprising the Wasatch Front communities centered on Salt Lake City but rather was found in the isolated communities of southern Utah. Charles S. Peterson, "A Mormon Town: One Man's West," *Journal of Mormon History* 3 (1976): 3–12. Leonard J. Arrington, Feramorz Y. Fox, and Dean L. May, *Building the City of God: Community and Cooperation among the Mormons* (Salt Lake City: Deseret News Press, 1976), show a photograph of a small rural Mormon village on the next-to-last page of their volume, captioning it with the statement "The social ideals of unity and order continue to knit the social fabric of settlements such as this," 363.

36. Some contemporary observers noted that without the ease that the railroad brought to transporting ores and refined products Utah would have remained entirely Mormon. Marcus E. Jones, *Report on the Internal Commerce of the United States for the Year 1890* (Washington, D.C.: Government Printing Office, 1891), 886 (quoted in Bennion, "Mormon Country a Century Ago," 17).

37. Lowell C. Bennion, "Mormon Country a Century Ago: A Geographer's View," in *The Mormon People: Their Character and Traditions*, Charles Redd Monograph in Western History, no. 10, ed. Thomas G. Alexander (Provo, Utah: Brigham Young University Press, 1980), 17.

38. Meinig, "The Mormon Culture Region," 213–214.

39. Ibid.

40. Growing connectivity to the rest of the nation in the twentieth century affected all aspects of life in the Mormon West. As only one example, not until 1908 did the church finally end the practice of issuing its own tithing "scrip" (the scrip had a face value based on the dollar) redeemable for goods at church stores, thus bowing to the irreversible fact that the U.S. currency had displaced another practice from the Mormon communitarian era (*Church Almanac, 1999–2000*, 128).

41. See ibid., 550, for total church population, and Wayne Wahlquist, "Population Growth in the Mormon Core Area: 1847–1890," in *The Mormon Role in the Settlement of the West*, 115.

42. Although the Mormon missionary effort continued at a reduced level during the pre-railroad era in the West, sheer distance from other populated regions prevented believers from simply proselytizing to neighbors or traveling through nearby non-Mormon settlements during the winter or other less busy times. Young's focus on occupying his envi-

sioned Deseret meant that church efforts were concentrated on settlement activities within the region and on moving the yearly wagon trains of migrants from the East to the inter-mountain settlements to provide the occupants for the region.

43. Meinig, "The Mormon Culture Region," 216–217, points out that Mormon settlement in the late decades of the nineteenth century was no longer an organized group movement directed by church leaders in Salt Lake City, but rather a gradual migration for economic opportunities beyond the lands originally occupied in the Mormon colonization experience of earlier decades.

44. Wahlquist, "Population Growth in the Mormon Core Area: 1847–1890," 114.

45. Ibid., 119.

46. Ibid., 125.

47. Edward A. Geary, "Mormon Country," in *After 150 Years: The Latter-day Saints in Sesqui-centennial Perspective,* Charles Redd Monograph in Western History, no. 13, eds. Thomas G. Alexander and Jessie L. Embry (Midvale, Utah: Signature Press, 1983), 89.

48. Marshall E. Bowen, *Utah People, the Nevada Desert: Homestead and Community on a Twentieth-Century Farmers' Frontier* (Logan, Utah: Utah State University Press, 1994). Bowen recounts the difficulties of settlers in eastern Nevada, contrasting the Mormons with the non-Mormons, indicating the lack of land in Utah that motivated the Mormon set-tlers in their unsuccessful attempt to re-create the Mormon village in the desert.

49. Dean L. May, "A Demographic Portrait of the Mormons, 1830–1980," in *After 150 Years: The Latter-day Saints in Sesquicentennial Perspective,* eds. Thomas G. Alexander and Jessie L. Embry, 44. The official U.S. Census figure for Utah Territory in 1850 is 11,380. Young and the Mormons thought this was too low; May argues that it was actually closer to 10,000 due to double counting of people as both residents of a place and residents of new colonies, *Church Almanac, 1999–2000,* 550. Church membership may also be overestimated due to Mormon tendency to count individuals as members after they are baptized members (at age eight or older) even if they join another church thereafter.

50. May, "A Demographic Portrait of the Mormons, 1830–1980," 51, notes that 67 percent of the residents of Utah in 1900 were Mormon, with non-Mormons concentrated in the booming mining towns of the territory, where they created distinct non-Mormon enclaves in the Mormon West.

51. Bennion, "Meinig's 'Mormon Culture Region' Revisited," 25.

52. Ibid.

53. Richard H. Jackson, "Utah's Harsh Lands: Hearth of Greatness," *Utah State Historical Quarterly* 49 (winter 1981): 4–25, discusses in detail the advantages created by the physical geography of the Wasatch Front.

54. Peter L. Halvorson and William N. Newman, *Atlas of Religious Change in America* (At-lanta: Glenmary Research Center, 1994), 174–175; and Bennion, "Meinig's 'Mormon Cul-ture Region' Revisited," 26–27.

55. Bennion, "Meinig's 'Mormon Culture Region Revisited,'" 29.

56. *Church Almanac, 1999–2000,* 545–550.

57. Bennion, "Meinig's 'Mormon Culture Region' Revisited," 28–29.

58. *Church Almanac, 1999–2000,* 441–442.

59. Ibid., 441–480 (information on temples). The Boston temple (completed in 2000) has sixty-nine thousand square feet of finished space, yet there are only twenty thousand church members in Massachusetts. The Albuquerque, New Mexico, temple (completed in 2000) has thirty-four thousand square feet, although there are fifty-six thousand members in the state. The Anchorage, Alaska, temple (completed in 2000) has only sixty-eight hundred square feet for twenty-five thousand members in the state.

60. The doctrine of gathering began to be downplayed in the early twentieth century as lack of land for expansion (or other ways to provide jobs for migrants) made assimilating migrants more difficult. During the latter decades of the twentieth century the church leaders discouraged converts from migrating to Salt Lake City and the Mormon West. Today's leaders emphasize that with the rapid diffusion of temples there is no longer a need to live in the Mormon West in order to participate in the entire gamut of church activities.

61. Leon Hartshorne, "Educational Institutions," in *Historical Atlas of Mormonism,* 142. Growing pressure on the church's university in Provo resulted in the announcement on 21 June 2000 that the school at Rexburg, Idaho, would be transformed into a four-year university beginning in 2001 to enable more members to receive a baccalaureate degree from a church school.

62. *Church Almanac, 1999–2000,* 510.

6 | Mex-America

From Margin to Mainstream

TERRENCE W. HAVERLUK

At my last Cinco de Mayo party I served chile verde, carne asada, and margaritas while listening to a Los Lobos CD, thus revealing myself as a Hispanicized Westerner. Hispanization is the process by which a person or place absorbs characteristics of Hispanic culture. Mexican American holidays, Mexican food and music, and the Spanish language have been increasingly integrated into Western society, and participation in these activities helps distinguish the West from other regions (Map 6.1).

Following the U.S. annexation of Mexico in 1848, there was little to suggest that Anglos would one day be celebrating Mexican holidays and eating Mexican food. Thousands of Anglo Americans migrated to the West and immediately set about assimilating the Mexican population; 150 years later, however, many aspects of Mexican society and culture remain. In the West, Mexican culture never "faded away" as predicted, and since the 1960s many aspects of Mexican and Hispanic[1] culture have become mainstream.

This chapter addresses Anglo-Hispanic interaction in three historical epochs: (1) preconquest northern Mexico until 1848; (2) Anglo annexation and assimilation until 1960; and (3) 1960s to present. I chronicle how the initial Anglo disdain for Hispanic culture and society has given way to the assimilation of many Hispanic cultural traits. In many respects Hispanic culture now defines what is Western.

Hispanic Settlement before 1848

The first Europeans to settle what is now the United States were from Spain, not England. In 1598, Juan de Oñate explored and eventually settled the upper

166

MAP 6.1. Cinco de Mayo festivals, 1999. After Carlson, *Journal of American Culture* 21, no. 2 (summer 1998), and local chambers of commerce.

Rio Grande Valley of Nuevo Mexico. This first *entrada*, or entry for the purpose of settlement, was followed by three others—*Tejas* in 1691, *Sonora* in 1700, and *California* in 1769 (Map 6.2). The *entradas* were part of the Spanish strategy to provide a buffer from French and Russian expansion into Spanish-claimed territory.[2]

Daily life in the four frontier regions had much in common, such as subsistence agriculture, irrigation, adobe construction, *bailes* (dances), *ranchos*, Catholicism, and the consumption of chile, maize, and beans. Material culture, however, varied greatly according to local geography.

Nuevo Mexico

Nuevo Mexicanos, called Hispanos, established several small villages near urbanized Pueblo Indian settlements. Like other Spanish frontier settlers, Hispanos grew wheat, beans, maize, and chiles in the cool, mountain climate of northern Nuevo Mexico. Unlike the rest of Spain's northern frontier, which

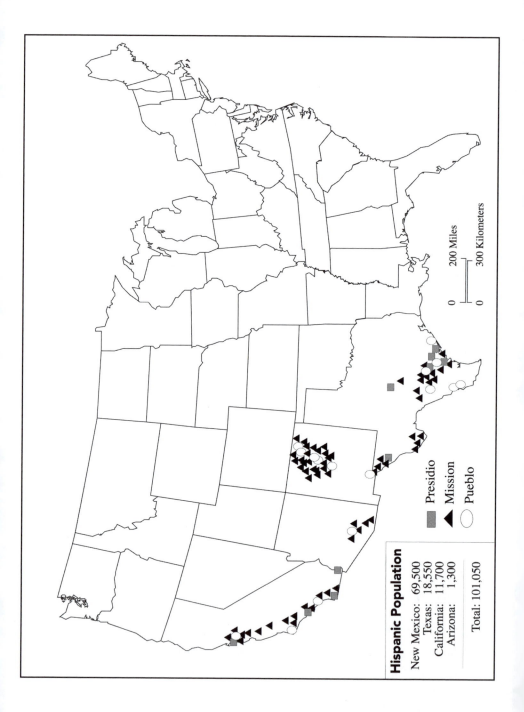

Hispanic Population

New Mexico: 69,500
Texas: 18,550
California: 11,700
Arizona: 1,300

Total: 101,050

Presidio ■
Mission ▲
Pueblo ○

0   200 Miles

0   300 Kilometers

concentrated on cattle, Hispanos concentrated on sheep, which flourished on the nutritious grama grass covering mesa uplands. Eighteenth-century trade data reveal that Hispanos annually raised one-half million sheep for wool and mutton. Hispanos and Indians used the wool to make elaborate woven patterns and coloration techniques that came to be known as the Rio Grande style. Hispanos traded textiles to Chihuahua for horses, ironware, and hoes.[3]

New Mexico also differed from other frontier regions in its widespread use of chiles, which soon became an important symbol of Hispano identification.[4] Whereas Tejanos used chiles in their bowls of chile and Californios mixed it with beans and other food, only in Nuevo Mexico did Hispanos use chiles in main dishes such as chile rellenos and chile verde. The vertical string of chiles, the *ristra,* was used as a form of currency—a first-grade *ristra* was five feet long, tightly strung, with a minimum of rotten pods, and was equal to $1 in 1930. Every village grew chiles, and several chile types, known as land races, evolved in isolated New Mexican microclimates. These included the velarde, chimayo, and dixon. Because of its value, chile was one of the few crops Hispanos grew in excess of their personal needs.[5]

Proximity to, and intermarriage with, Pueblo Indians led to several distinct material cultural characteristics such as the pueblo ladder, turquoise jewelry, outdoor ovens called *hornos,* and New Mexico–style weaving patterns.

Tejas

Unlike the mountain-dwelling Hispanos, Tejanos lived on a flat coastal plain directly in the path of expansionist French and Americans. Tejanos settled three principal regions—Nacogdoches, Bexar-Goliad, and the Rio Grande Valley.[6] The *presidio* (fort) was the most important organizing structure among Tejanos because they were constantly harassed by Comanches, the French, and eventually Americans.

Tejanos grew the standard crops—beans, chile, potatoes, and maize—but concentrated on maize because it was easier. Around San Antonio, Bexareños, as they were called, planted two crops of maize: early maize in March, which was unirrigated; and late maize in June, which was irrigated. Bexareños were often criticized by their own governor for relying too much on maize instead of devoting more time to wheat.[7]

FACING PAGE

MAP 6.2. Hispanic population, 1850. After Haverluk, *Journal of Geography* 96 (May/June 1997): 135.

Tejanos spent less time farming because they spent more time raising cattle for beef. The focus on cattle meant that Tejanos incorporated and adapted all the cattle ranching tools developed in northern Mexico—*la reata* (lariat); the *rodear* (roundup); the *rancho* (ranch); *chaparejas* (chaps); the Western saddle (with a horn for wrapping *la reata* around); cowboy boots; and the cowboy hat (*sombrero*), to name a few.

In 1794, Governor Muñoz argued that there were very few beans, peppers, or fruits in Tejas because Tejanos had given all "their attention to the capture of wild livestock of both species from the time these settlements were created." Tejanos grazed cattle and rode horses on communal property called *propios* or on private land grants called *ranchos*. Tejanos traded with Saltillo and exchanged beef, jerked meat, candle tallow, and hides for flour, chocolate, and cloth. Cattle provided much of what Tejanos needed—soap, candles, *cueras* (leather doublets), *mochilas* (saddlebags), and shields. Not surprisingly, Tejanos were among the first to establish cattle drives in what would become the United States. Between 1779 and 1786, sixty-eight confirmed drives totaling more than eighteen thousand head moved between San Antonio and Saltillo, and some into Louisiana.[8]

Sonora

Nuevo Mexico and Tejas were relatively well watered compared to the Sonoran Desert. Hispanic settlement in Sonora coalesced around the intermittent Santa Cruz River. Wherever water surfaced, Hispanics settled. Sheridan[9] described Sonoran Hispanics as "agropastoralists," that is, subsistence farmers growing primarily wheat and grazing almost equal numbers of sheep and cattle. Crop patterns were dependent on water supply. Sonorans planted wheat in December and almost always had a crop by early summer. They planted maize in the spring, but by midsummer the *acequia* (irrigation ditch) generally ran dry, and corn could rarely be brought to maturity and was generally used for fodder. Sonorans augmented their diet by incorporating local desert crops—prickly pear cactus, saguaro fruit, mesquite pods crushed into flour, and plenty of mescal—the fermented juice of the agave plant.[10]

The desert influenced other aspects of Sonoran society. Many men wore sandals, Indian-like "G-strings," and little else. Women wore short-sleeved blouses, sandals, and long unbleached skirts imported from Hermosillo—the colorful weaving patterns of New Mexico were not common in Sonora. The strong and resilient saguaro ribs were used in construction.

California

Like the Tejanos, Californios relied on cattle for subsistence. They excelled in horsemanship and raced horses almost daily.[11] Seafood was plentiful and augmented the Californio diet. Nightlong *bailes* and *corridos*—long, historical ballads accompanied by Spanish guitars—were common.[12]

Richard Henry Dana,[13] who spent a year in California participating in the hide trade, described California and Californios. He portrayed Santa Barbara as "composed of one-story houses built of sun-baked clay, or adobe, some of them white washed, with red tile roofs." He described Spanish officers as wearing broad-brimmed, dark-colored hats, short jackets, open shirts, pantaloons open at the side below the knee, and highly decorated deerskin shoes. Men of privilege always wore ponchos or serapes. Women wore gowns of various materials in the European style, "except the sleeves were short, leaving the arm bare, and they were loose around the waist, corsets not being used."[14]

The hide trade dominated the California economy during the 1830s and 1840s. Because of the trade with New England, Californios were less reliant on local production and had a wider variety of consumer goods than did other frontier regions. Boston ships sailed around Cape Horn to California loaded with spirits, teas, coffee, sugar, spices, hardware, tinware, and clothing of all kinds. New Englanders traded goods for cattle hides, which they used to make shoes, and tallow for candles.

Anglo Annexation

Following the U.S. invasion and annexation of northern Mexico in 1848, a legacy of Spanish speakers, Spanish architecture, Roman law, Roman urban morphology, and Mexican food and music remained. The majority of Anglos who encountered Hispanos, Tejanos, Sonorans, or Californios did not view this legacy as something positive but rather as an impediment to overcome. Mid-nineteenth-century Anglos were, for the most part, incapable of viewing Hispanic culture objectively. Most Anglo immigrants were Protestants who grew up imbued with the Black Legend. The legend evolved out of the long conflict between Catholic Spain and Protestant England. The English viewed Spaniards as "perfidious, cruel, wanton, sadistic and atrocious." To make matters worse in Anglo eyes, the perfidious Spaniard intermarried with the cannibalistic Aztec to create a truly depraved race of people—the mestizo.[15]

The Black Legend dovetailed nicely with the concept of manifest destiny and created a powerful ideology that justified marginalizing Mexican Americans and taking their land. After annexation, a large number of Hispanics were simply hanged and their ranchos divided among Anglos, especially in northern California, where the gold rush accelerated the process. Only two regions were able to maintain a small amount of political and economic independence—northern New Mexico and southern Texas—as Anglos rapidly controlled the rest of the Southwest.[16]

In Texas, where long-term Hispanic-Anglo interaction first began, the *San Antonio Express News* described Tejanos as "priest ridden, without schools or ambition and having little conception of Yankee progress." Almost every aspect of Hispanic society was considered inferior. Mestizos were thought to exhibit the worst characteristics of Spanish and Mexican: They gambled too much, danced and sang too much; their adobe "houses" were nothing but hovels and the *jacales* even worse; priests and the corrupt Catholic Church controlled their lives; and, of course, they were lazy.[17]

Anglos also took a dim view of Mexican food, especially chiles. Many Anglos thought chiles rotted the stomach and infected the skin and breath. The chile myth was taken to such extremes that several Texas chroniclers argued that buzzards and coyotes would not eat dead Mexicans because of the "peppery condition of their flesh." Samuel French, upon examining the dead after the Battle of Palo Duro, declared that "the flesh of the Americans was decayed and gone, or eaten by wolves and vultures; that of the Mexicans was dried and uncorrupted, which I attributed to the nature of their food, it being antiseptic."[18]

In Arizona, early Anglo ranchers called Sonoran soldiers "ragamuffins" and described Tucson as hopelessly sunk in anarchy. They described Sonoran houses as "in a state of ruin" and said that as soon as they became inhabitable "the miserable tenants" crept into another hovel. Even as invading Anglos adopted Sonoran cowboy and mining techniques, they ridiculed Sonoran technology and ranching practices.[19]

One of the first accounts of Anglo-Hispanic interaction in California comes from the journals of Jedediah Smith, who in 1826 became the first Anglo to enter California overland. Like many Anglos after him, Smith described Californios as "arbitrary, indolent, and hostile towards Protestants."[20] Dana described the men as "lazy, thriftless, proud, extravagant, and very much given to gaming" and, of course, the women as immoral. Nor did New Mexico escape Anglo scorn. New Mexican women were thought to be morally loose, and the men were described as "shabby and cowardly."[21]

Negative Anglo assessments were readily accepted during this anti-Mexican, anti-Catholic period of U.S. history. Arguing that mestizos were corrupt and racially inferior provided the United States with one of the necessary pretexts for invasion and annexation. Anglo attitudes toward Hispanics not only helped justify annexing Mexico, but also justified the creation of a two-tier wage system in which Hispanics were paid less than Anglos for the same job. Americans developed a postannexation economic system predicated on Anglo capital and Mexican labor. Chicano scholars describe the system as a "segmented labor" market or "internal colonialism."[22]

Hispanics Organize, and Anglos Discover Mexican Culture: 1900s to 1960s

In the Western labor market, certain jobs came to be associated with Mexicans and Mexican Americans. Hispanics built railroads and dams, mined copper and gold, cleared and harvested crops. From its beginning, Western capitalism relied on low-wage, seasonal Mexican and Mexican American labor, which necessitated continued emigration from Mexico. Continual emigration retarded assimilation and sowed the seeds of Hispanic political organization—and eventually Hispanization.[23]

García[24] calls the generation of Hispanics who lived through annexation the "conquered generation." The destruction of the Mexican landed and political elite left many communities devoid of leadership. Hispanics did not have the means to challenge the newly created Anglo power structure and simply focused on survival. It wasn't until after the turn of the century, and especially after World War II, that Hispanics began to challenge their second-class status.

Negative Anglo attitudes toward mestizos and the social structures associated with this view lasted well into the twentieth century (and are still not completely absent). Several events in the early 1900s led to a new political consciousness among Hispanics. During and after the Mexican Revolution from 1910 to 1930, over one million Mexicans fled to the U.S. Southwest.[25] Most of these refugees thought they would return to Mexico and were therefore generally apolitical. It was the sons and daughters of this generation— American citizens born in the United States—who actively challenged the segregated social structures of the Southwest. García calls the Hispanic cohort that organized between the 1930s and the 1950s the "Mexican American" generation. These Hispanics founded several organizations that helped end segregation in schools, theaters, and swimming pools, including the League of United Latin American Citizens (LULAC), the Community Service Organization (CSO), and the American GI forum.

The Mexican American generation was grateful to the United States for granting asylum to their parents and for the New Deal. This generation not only fought in World War II, but also was disproportionately decorated. Politically, the Mexican American generation wanted to assimilate into the American "melting pot," but structural obstacles to assimilation and continued emigration from Mexico inhibited the process. As a result of these obstacles the Mexican American generation maintained its *mejicanidad* (Mexicanness).[26] During this same period, many Anglos "discovered" Mexican culture.

The adobe missions of California, so reviled by Anglos during annexation, were viewed differently after 1900. Anglo architects and historians began to evaluate Hispanic architecture within its original context. Mission-style architecture, for example, combines several elements. The bell towers, stone arches, and Doric columns are from Gothic Spain. The interior courtyard, carved wood ceilings, and abstract geometrical design are from the Moors. The use of brilliant color and intricate ornamentation is from the Aztecs. All of these elements accompanied Hispanics as they moved northward, but lack of materials and distance from the populated core of Mexico forced priests and soldiers to borrow methods from Indians and build with local material. The result was the pueblo style in New Mexico and the Spanish mission style in the rest of the northern frontier.[27]

In the early 1900s California businessmen realized they could profit from packaging the California climate with a mythologized Spanish past based around Spanish missions. Entrepreneurs rebuilt decaying missions and constructed train stations in "Spanish style" to give the visitor a distinct California esthetic immediately upon arrival. The California "mission revival" eventually spread to New Mexico and the rest of the Southwest. In 1912 the Santa Fe city council established an ordinance forbidding any type of architecture other than pueblo style. In 1915 mission revival style achieved the Anglo architectural imprimatur at the Panama International Exposition in San Diego.[28] Today, the Spanish missions are praised for their beauty and simplicity. The *Wine Spectator,* for example, described the Sonoma mission as follows: "[its] white stucco walls and thick wood beams speak eloquently of California's early Mexican heritage . . . [it is] exquisite in its simplicity and elegance."[29] Mission style is now found throughout the United States but is most common in the arid Southwest, where it began.

In New Mexico, Anglo artists and writers such as Willa Cather, Georgia O'Keeffe, D. H. Lawrence, and Ansel Adams embraced Santa Fe's adobe architecture, blanket-clad Indians, *equipale* chairs, and chile-based cuisine. Several artists made their home in Santa Fe or Taos and adopted elements of Indian and Hispanic culture. Anglo influences combined with Hispanic and Indian to create the hybrid "Santa Fe style."

Although mission-style architecture and Santa Fe style were widespread throughout the West by 1960, residential segregation meant that most Anglos were barely aware of a Mexican population in their midst. Unsuccessful assimilation policies among the Mexican American generation gave way to the more radical, more vocal agenda of the Chicano movement.

The 1960s and Beyond: Mainstreaming Mexican American Culture

The social revolution of the 1960s and changes in immigration laws forever altered the sociopolitical dynamics of the West. The Immigration and Nationality Act of 1965 phased out the quota system imposed in 1924 and adjusted the U.S. immigrant stream from primarily European to primarily Latin and Asian.[30] The end of the poll tax in 1964 and the Voting Rights Act of 1965, combined with an increasing Hispanic population, led to greater political representation and helped strengthen the nascent Chicano movement.

The politically active Mexican American generation laid the groundwork for the Chicano movement of the 1960s. A defining moment that bridged the two generations was the election of Raymond L. Telles as the mayor of El Paso in 1957. Telles was the first Hispanic mayor of a large Western city since annexation, and he paved the way for a Hispanic political resurgence. By 1984, there were enough Hispanic elected officials (HEOs) that the National Association of Latino Elected Officials (NALEO) published its first guide to HEOs. In 1984 NALEO enumerated 2,925 HEOs in the West; by 1996 that number reached 3,489—mostly in Texas, New Mexico, and California. Hispanic political influence is more important in Texas and New Mexico, however (Map 6.3). Increased Hispanic political influence and the reduction of forced segregation led to increased social interaction between Anglos and Hispanics. Increased interaction has led to increased cultural borrowing. Data from several Southwestern cities reveal a sharp increase in intermarriage in the 1970s. Counter to traditional assimilation theory, however, not all intermarried Hispanics assimilated into Anglo culture.[31]

During the 1960s and 1970s, new Hispanic organizations, festivals, and media outlets began to emerge. The first Hispanic chamber of commerce was established in 1973, and by 1996 there were over two hundred. Contemporary U.S. Hispanics have access to a large number of sociopolitical organizations, and unlike the pre–World War II Hispanic organizations that facilitated assimilation, contemporary Hispanic organizations inhibit assimilation and help create and maintain a multicultural, multilingual West. For example, several universities have established Chicano/a and Mexican American studies programs that reinforce and even extend Hispanic/Chicano culture (Map 6.4).

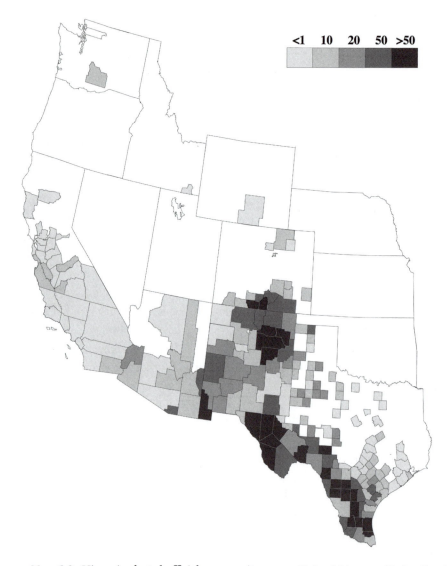

MAP 6.3. Hispanic elected officials, per capita, 1990, *National Directory of Latino Elected Officials, 1996* (Washington, D.C.: U.S. Bureau of the Census, USA Counties, 1998).

In the 1960s Chicano activists, along with African Americans and feminists, took to the streets and challenged the Anglo power structure. The term *Chicano* (pronounced chee-ka-no or shee-ka-no) is a combination of the word *mexica* (pronounced may-**shee**-ka), which is another name for Aztec, and the word *mejicano* (pronounced may-hee-**ka-no**), for Mexican, and is directly linked to, and proud of, the Aztec heritage of Western mestizos. The word

Chicano exemplifies the increased interest and acceptance not only of the Spanish/Mexican legacy in the West but also the Aztec/Indian legacy. That Aztec legacy is most evident in food.

Mexican Food

Much of the Mexican food common throughout the West is based on plants domesticated by the Aztecs—maize, tortillas, avocados, tomatoes, chiles, and chocolate. One Aztec dish, now de rigueur at many Super Bowl parties, is the Aztec blend of *ahuaca* (avocado) and *mulli* (usually a mixture of chiles and tomatoes) to create *ahuaca-mulli*. The Spanish called it guacamole.[32]

A key ingredient to guacamole, salsa, and many Mexican dishes is the chile pepper. In the 1960s, salsa consumption began to increase, and now salsa sells as well as ketchup. According to Padilla, the hippie movement led to increased chile consumption.[33] Hippies embraced salsa because it was a locally produced, low-fat, natural condiment that went well with an alternative

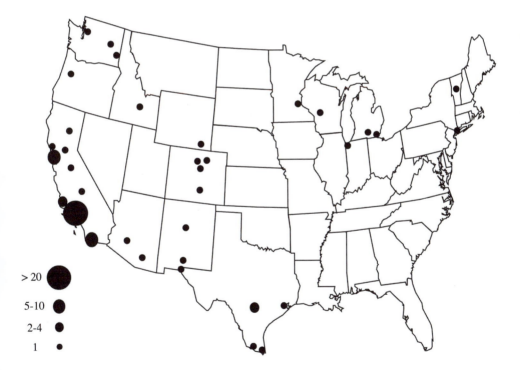

MAP 6.4. Chicano/a and Mexican American studies programs, 1997. *Hispanic Resource Directory, 1997* and university Web sites.

lifestyle. Because of increased chile consumption, regions that once provided chiles for a limited, local clientele now provide chiles for the whole United States. New Mexico produces more chile than any other state, about half of U.S. domestic consumption in 1997.[34] Other important chile-producing regions include central California, southern Colorado, and west Texas. Whereas most Americans get their chile in salsa, many Westerners are increasingly adopting the New Mexican custom of eating the chile as a main dish in rellenos or chile verde.

Chile festivals have sprung up around chile-producing areas as farmers attempt to educate consumers on how to eat chiles and to create new customs centered on chile consumption. Part of the charm of a festival is roasting chiles in large, specially designed roasters. The smell of roasted chiles wafting through the parking lots and farms of the West is a sure sign of fall. Roasted chiles are then frozen with the skins on, and when needed they are peeled and used in chile, chile verde, and salsas.

In the Arkansas River Valley east of Pueblo, Colorado, chile production doubled from 1987 to 1992.[35] The Pueblo Chamber of Commerce has worked with local farmers to make the "Pueblo pepper," or *mirasol*, one of the key images in redefining that city after the downsizing of the steel industry. The 1999 Pueblo pepper festival generated record crowds and cleaned out every chile in the valley. The Pueblo chile festival is an example of *neolocalism*, a term that describes the process by which a region incorporates real and invented historical facts from the local area to provide an "identity anchor" that distinguishes it from homogeneous, corporate America.[36] Pueblo's new motto, for example, is "Experience the Flavor." The chamber of commerce brochure goes on to state that "The same flavorful and gratifying qualities of our famous 'Pueblo' Chile Peppers can be found throughout our outstanding historical, cultural, educational, and recreation activities." Creating identity anchors is increasingly important to the Western tourist industry.

Southwestern Style and Heritage Tourism

Los Caminos del Rio Heritage project is a collaborative effort between the Texas Parks and Wildlife Department and the Mexican Secretaría de Turismo. Los Caminos attempts to entice tourists to the Rio Grande Valley by focusing on its *mejicanidad*. By concentrating its tourist pitch on its Mexican heritage, south Texas is following a tradition that started in California in the early twentieth century. Whereas California focused on its Hispanic past, Los Caminos focuses on the Mexican American present. Touting its distinct "border culture" the Caminos brochure describes the shared traditions and unique mixture of food, music, architecture, festivals, and border language—a blending of English and Spanish. Since its inception in 1990 Los Caminos has worked to create "a heritage corridor along the Lower Rio Grande to enhance the existing visitor experience and to broaden the visitor market to encompass the cultural and heritage tourist. The realization of the corridor concept will contribute to the economic development of the area and will enhance regional community pride."[37]

Similar attempts to capitalize on Hispanic culture are under way in Santa Fe, Taos, Tucson, San Juan Capistrano, and San Antonio. In the early twentieth century few Westerners—Anglo or Hispanic—could have imagined that their economic future lay in marketing "images of difference."[38] Early New Mexico boosters, for example, dreamed of making it the "next Pennsylvania" by capitalizing on its raw materials and access to the West Coast to become a manufacturing powerhouse. Today, Santa Fe bills itself as "The City Different." It took New Mexicans several decades to realize that tourism was not simply a sideshow, but also an economic powerhouse. Tourism generates more money in New Mexico than does ranching, farming, or manufacturing.

Western heritage tourism takes its esthetic clues from the geographical and cultural differences of the original Spanish and Indian settlers, hence chile festivals in New Mexico, mission revival architecture in California, Sonoran cuisine in Arizona, and the Mexican-American War in Texas. Ironically, after one hundred years of trying to hide their Spanish legacy, Western chambers of commerce are now cashing in on their failure to fully assimilate Hispanics and stamp out Hispanic material culture. Western city leaders are falling over each other restoring old mercados, creating fiestas, and touting the distinctiveness of their Mexican-based cuisine. A necessary component to Western tourism is creating an esthetic distinct from white-bread America but also distinct from other Southwestern regions. The south Texas heritage corridor, Sonoran cuisine, and the Pueblo pepper are recent forays into building distinct identities based on Hispanic heritage in hopes that it will stimulate the economy. Heritage tourism may also retard assimilation and facilitate Hispanization.

Mexican American Music

The guitar and nightlong *bailes* that were once symbols of Mexican decadence are now essential components of American music. The guitar, for example, was not used in early American music. "Old-time" and "bluegrass" music are rooted in the British Isles and rely primarily on the banjo and fiddle. After the annexation of northern Mexico, the Spanish guitar diffused from Texas to the South through slaves. Southern whites considered the guitar to be a "black" instrument and avoided it. Not until the 1920s and 1930s did Anglos begin to play the guitar—Jimmy Rodgers, Merle Travis, and Hank Williams—who learned it from African American friends. These musicians began singing about cowboys and the West, and "old-time" or "country" music got the appendage "western." Naturally, these singing cowboys outfitted themselves in vaquero attire: cowboy boots, wide-brimmed hats, silver belt buckles, and colorful shirts with Pueblo Indian or Mexican designs. Variations on this style are still common at the annual Country Music Awards.

The north-south linkages established by the Spanish continue to funnel Mexicans and Mexican cultural influences from Mexico to the U.S. Southwest. Mariachi music developed in Guadalajara and spread to California. Conjunto music, with its roots in the *corrido,* developed in Monterrey and spread to Texas, where it evolved into Tejano music.[39] The rural, working-class conjunto music of Mexico is based on the accordion, twelve-string guitar, bajo sexto, and drums. Tejano music is more urban based and uses amplification and electronic synthesizers.

Tejano music did not become mainstream until one of its rising young stars, Selena, met an untimely death in 1994. After her death, Tejano music sales went from $5 million in 1990 to $50 million in 1995.[40] Texas, especially San Antonio and Houston, is still the core of Tejano music, but it is popular throughout the West.

It's not just Tejano music that is energizing the American music scene, but other Latin genres as well. In 1997 the Recording Industry Association of America established a new Hispanic category that includes salsa, Cuban jazz, and rock en Español. To fit in the Hispanic category at least 51 percent of a song's lyrics must be in Spanish. Rock en Español consists of Spanish-language rock bands from Latin America, including Mana and Molotoy from Mexico, whose lyrics lampoon Latin social structures and have become popular in the United States. Salsa music, like the food, is a mixture of many styles but especially Caribbean. In 1998 Hispanic music accounted for $627.7 million in sales out of a total of $14.5 billion. Since 1996 Hispanic music has grown an average of 10 percent a year, whereas total music sales have remained flat. Now Latinos have several Grammy categories, and the Recording Industry Association of America recently created its first and only genre-specific award—*Los Premios de Oro y Plato.* The award is presented only to American music with lyrics more than 51 percent in Spanish.

Few scholars could have predicted such high growth for music in Spanish. The reality is that Latin musicians have influenced a wide range of artists, created new styles, and to an extent Hispanicized much of American music.

The Future

I have argued that Hispanic music, food, architecture, dress, and interior design are now mainstream in the West. Hispanics, however, still suffer from economic and political marginalization. Hispanic incomes still fall well below those of Anglos, and even though Hispanics are more politically active, Anglos still control all Western state legislatures. Although Hispanics are courted in presidential races, it seems unlikely that the United States is ready for a Hispanic president. Anglo media still often portray Hispanics as drug dealers, illegal immigrants, and criminals. The acceptance of some, but not all aspects of Hispanic society, reminds me of a line from the movie *Lone Star,* which deals with Anglo-Hispanic interaction in south Texas. During a PTA meeting, an Anglo parent noted to the effect that "I'm okay with teaching about Mexican American contributions in music, food, and art, but when you start rewriting history to fit *your* story, then you've gone too far." The line describes continued Anglo resistance at recognizing Hispanic contributions to Western society and the two-tiered wage and political system. This dialectic reveals the contested nature of Anglo-Hispanic interaction in the West. This Anglo-Hispanic dialectic has reached synthesis in some cultural aspects and has been incorporated into mainstream culture, but the process is ongoing in the political and economic realm.

Notes

1. *Hispanic* is the term created by the Census Bureau in 1978 to describe all persons living in the United States descended from Spain or from Spanish colonies. I use the term when several groups are meant to be included, such as Tejanos, Mexicans, and Spaniards.

2. Richard L. Nostrand, "The Hispanic-American Borderland: Delimitation of an American Culture Region," *Annals of the Association of American Geographers* 60 (1970): 638–661.

3. Alvar W. Carlson, *The Historical Geography of the Spanish Settlement in the Middle Rio Grande Valley, 1598–1821* (unpublished research paper, University of Minnesota, 1966), 1–47; Paul Wroth, "Hispanic Southwestern Craft Traditions and the Taylor Museum," *Journal of the West* 19 (1980): 100–116.

4. Carmella Padilla and Jack Parsons, *The Chile Chronicles: Tales of a New Mexico Harvest* (Santa Fe: Museum of New Mexico Press, 1997), 3–6.

5. Ibid., 34.

6. Jesus F. De la Teja, *San Antonio de Bexar: A Community on New Spain's Northern Frontier* (Albuquerque: University of New Mexico Press, 1995), 12.

7. Ibid., 92.

8. Ibid., 97–111.

9. Thomas E. Sheridan, *Los Tucsonenses: The Mexican Community in Tucson, 1854–1941* (Tucson: University of Arizona Press, 1986), 14.

10. English Sandal, *Fruits of the Desert* (Tucson: Arizona Daily Star, 1996), 21–36.

11. Leonard Pitt, *The Decline of the Californios: A Social History of the Spanish-Speaking Californians, 1846–1890* (Berkeley: University of California Press, 1966), 13.

12. John S. Roberts, *The Latin Tinge: The Impact of Latin American Music on the United States* (Oxford, U.K.: Oxford University Press, 1979), 18.

13. Richard H. Dana, *Two Years before the Mast Twenty-Four Years After* (New York: Dutton, 1948), 47.

14. Ibid., 62–64.

15. Arnoldo De León, *They Called Them Greasers: Anglo Attitudes toward Mexicans in Texas, 1821–1900* (Austin: University of Texas Press, 1983), 63–66.

16. Terrence W. Haverluk, "Hispanic Community Types and Assimilation in Mex-America," *Professional Geographer* 50 (1998): 465–480.

17. De León, *They Called Them Greasers*, 25–29.

18. Ibid., 67–68.

19. Sheridan, *Los Tucsonenses*, 18–31.

20. David J. Weber, *The Californios versus Jedediah Smith, 1826–1827: A New Cache of Documents* (Spokane, Wash.: A. H. Clark, 1990), 14.

21. Marc Simmons, *The Little Lion of the Southwest: A Life of Manuel Antonio Chaves* (Chicago: Sage Books, 1973), 3.

22. Mario T. García, *Mexican Americans: Leadership, Ideology, & Identity, 1930–1960* (New Haven: Yale University Press, 1989), 13.

23. Haverluk, "Hispanic Community Types," 465–480.

24. García, *Mexican Americans*, 14.

25. "Immigration: Tracking the Quest for Freedom," *USA Today*, 14 July 1993, p. 6A.

26. García, *Mexican Americans*, 21.

27. Nicholas C. Markovich, *Pueblo Style and Regional Architecture* (New York: Rhinehold Press, 1990), 13–64; Daniel D. Arreola, "Mexican American Housecapes," *Geographical Review* 78 (1988): 299–315.

28. Markovich, *Pueblo Style*, 13–64.

29. Jeff Morgan, "Pack Your Bags for California Wine Country," *Wine Spectator* (15 June 1999): 33–36.

30. Terrence W. Haverluk, "The Changing Geography of U.S. Hispanics, 1850–1990," *Journal of Geography* 96 (1997): 134–145.

31. Haverluk, "Hispanic Community Types," 465–480.

32. Sophie D. Coe, *America's First Cuisines* (Austin: University of Texas Press, 1994), 45.

33. Padilla, *Chile Chronicles*, 92.

34. Bureau of Census, "Vegetables, Sweet Corn and Melons, Table 29, Hot Peppers, Acres Harvested," *U.S. Census of Agriculture* (Washington, D.C.: U.S. Department of Commerce, 1997).

35. Ibid.

36. Barbara G. Shortridge and James R. Shortridge, *The Taste of American Place: A Reader on Regional and Ethnic Foods* (Lanham, Md.: Rowman and Littlefield, 1998), 7.

37. Mario L. Sanchez, *A Shared Experience: The History, Architecture, and Historic Design of the Lower Rio Grande Heritage Corridor* (Austin: Texas Historical Commission, 1994), 1.

38. Ken Dauber, *Tourism and the Old Pueblo Trail* (Santa Fe, N.M.: School of American Research, 1995).

39. Jose R. Reyna, "Notes on Tejano Music," *Aztlán* 13 (1982): 81–94.

40. John Morthland, "Switch Hitter: Can Tejano Heartthrob Emilio Navaira Survive the Crossover to Country Music?" *Texas Monthly* (1994): 60–65.

7 | Native America

The Indigenous West

AKIM D. REINHARDT

No group of Westerners has been the subject of as many myths, rumors, clichés, and stereotypes (and occasionally outright lies) as its indigenous peoples. Indians of the West have been celebrated as the Noble Savage, revered as the mystical medicine man, mourned as the disappearing Red Man, upheld as the harmonious environmentalist, admired as the proud and able warrior, and vilified as the conniving and treacherous barbarian, to name of few of the broad-brush themes that have proliferated in dime store novels, Hollywood Westerns, and New Age babble. The truth is, of course, much more interesting: Indians are, at the end of the day, people. And this means that the stories and lives of the aboriginal peoples of the American West are at once more universally human and more singularly unique than any myth about them.

The American West is a vast expanse that has been, and continues to be, home to a heterogeneity of aboriginal people. These many peoples have entertained a number of different perceptions of space and place and have manifested Western spaces with equal variety, be it of their own volition or through interactions with others. What follows is a survey of those many perceptions and manifestations through time: a sampling of the variance in Native American approaches and an exploration of the common themes of the human experience. As John Trudell, Santee Dakota poet/activist, wrote:

In the real world We are human being
In the Shadow world We are being human—[1]

Time Immemorial

Like all people around the world, Native Americans have traditional stories that seek to explain the origins of their existence and how they came to be where they are. And, as with all people around the world, these stories are in conflict with explanations offered by modern sciences. However, Native American creation stories are not generally accorded the same degree of respect that is shown to other traditional creation stories by mainstream society. They are frequently dismissed by Euro-Americans with labels like "myths" or "legends," whereas Judeo-Christian-Islamic stories are given the respectable title of "religion." This is unfortunate because Native American religions are equal to Western religions in the richness of their traditions and sagacity.[2] For those who believe in them, just as with other religions, they offer a firm basis for understanding the nature and origins of one's place in the universe. For those who deem them fictional, they nonetheless offer metaphorical insights and literary qualities like those found in any other religion.

The details of Native American creation stories are voluminous. However, they all assert variations on the basic theme of Native American genesis: the notion that Native American people were created in the Western Hemisphere and have been here for the whole of their existence. They are of this place. The Kiowas of the southern Great Plains, for example, believe that they came into the world one by one through an opening in a hollow log. A woman who was with child got stuck in the opening, and after that no more of their people could come through.[3]

According to the tradition of the Modocs of southwestern Oregon, all Indian people were created by Kumush, Old Man of the Ancients. Kumush went with his daughter down to the underworld of the spirits. During the night, the spirits danced and sang, but during the day they became dry bones. Kumush selected the bones of various tribes, collected them in a large basket, and brought them back up to the upper world. He then scattered the bones to various places, creating different tribes: the Klamath, Shastas, and so forth. Finally, he threw the bones of the Modocs themselves, whose name means "Southerners," ordering them to keep his place after he had gone.[4]

Osage people, who resided on the eastern edge of the central Plains before Euro-Americans removed them to Oklahoma, believe that their original ancestors lived in the sky. The Sun was their father, the Moon their mother. Mother Moon told them to go down to Earth, which was covered with water. The first elk induced the winds to blow off enough water to reveal the world. His fur then sprouted the first plants, trees, and crops.[5]

But just as modern science rejects biblical creation stories, so, too, does it challenge the creation stories of Native Americans. Although scientists have been unable to certify the origins of Native Americans, they do doubt the veracity of human genesis in the Western Hemisphere. The oldest, scientifically verified, archeological evidence of human existence in the Western Hemisphere is from a 12,800-year-old site in Chile. This seems too recent for archeologists to accept Western hemispheric genesis. Instead, they posit the Beringian crossing theory. They postulate that Native Americans are descended from Asiatic peoples, particularly Siberians, who crossed over the Bering Strait that currently separates Alaska from Siberia. These migrations, scientists assert, would have taken place during the Pleistocene Age, when the Bering Strait was covered with miles-thick ice, affording a land bridge between the hemispheres and ample opportunity for eastward migration. Most Native Americans, archeologists maintain, are descended from Asiatic migrants of the Pleistocene, although there have been some minor migrations during the modern, post-Ice Age, geological epoch of the last ten thousand years, known as the Holocene, some as recently as four thousand years ago.[6]

Regardless of the dispute between archeologists and traditional Native Americans, one thing does seem clear from a historian's point of view. The indigenous people of the Western Hemisphere have inhabited these two continents since long before the time that human beings anywhere in the world ever assembled a society that could conceivably be called a "civilization." Thus, to the extent that any people can be said to have lived in a place since time immemorial, be they European, African, or Asian, so, too, may Native Americans claim that right.

Early Spatial Relations

Homo sapiens is the only animal to inhabit every continent on the planet. This fact bespeaks its highly mobile and migratory nature. Indians in the American West have been no exception to this human trend. Many peoples have moved into, out of, and within the West over the last several millennia.

Of the many indigenous peoples in the American West, some can establish their ancestral locations earlier than others. As far back as at least thirty-two hundred years ago, farmers were planting crops in the American Southwest. By 250 B.C.E. (before the Common Era), the ancestors of the Pimas and Papagos had established permanent towns along the Gila River in what is now southern Arizona. They also constructed a three-mile-long irrigation canal about twelve hundred years ago in order to enhance their agricultural endeavors.[7]

The Mandans and Hidatsas of the northern Missouri River have been on the Plains for at least a millennium. The Pawnees and Wichitas of modern-day central Nebraska and Kansas, respectively, have been on the Plains for no less than eight and one-half centuries.[8]

People have made substantial spatial movements throughout the West more recently as well. A case in point is the Northern Shoshones. Earliest records show them inhabiting the Great Basin region in what is now northern Nevada. Life in the basin was extremely difficult given the thin margin of survival in the unforgiving environment. The Rocky Mountains proved alluring, and some of the Shoshones moved into what is now the panhandle of Idaho, where they reaped the benefits of salmon-laden rivers, big game animals, and wild fruits. Then, about the time that Christopher Columbus was stumbling upon San Salvador, the Northern Shoshones were moving onto the western edge of the northern Great Plains. Here they aligned with the Kiowas and Comanches (who themselves would eventually move to the southern Plains) and took advantage of the plentiful bison and burgeoning horse trade. After suffering at the hands of smallpox and rifle-toting Blackfeet, Crees, and Assiniboines, the Northern Shoshones retreated to the Rockies in the early 1700s. Over the next 150 years, they would continually move back and forth between the mountains and the plains while their western relatives continued to inhabit the basin.[9]

Even more recent is the Cheyennes' arrival in the West from Minnesota. The Cheyennes speak a language in the Algonquin family that is prevalent around the Great Lakes and eastward. Prior to the eighteenth century, they inhabited the prairies of southern Minnesota, where they farmed, hunted, and harvested wild rice. But by the beginning of the eighteenth century, they had begun to move westward, setting up fortified villages along the upper Missouri River in present-day North and South Dakota. By the end of the century, however, they had moved yet again, this time southwest to the Great Plains of western South Dakota and eastern Wyoming, with a southern branch in eastern Colorado.[10]

Living Spaces

Humanity has engaged in any number of settlement patterns over its history. However, for a number of centuries now, Europeans and their descendents have extolled the virtues of one particular pattern (fixed, sedentary living) and denigrated the rest. The popular, misguided stereotype of Indians in the West is that of rootless nomads, the opposite of the Euro-American archetype. But the Native American population of the American West has never advocated so uniform a prejudice on this subject in either direction. Consequently, the West has traditionally been home to peoples who have adopted every settlement pattern imaginable. One true irony is that despite the plurality of its settlement patterns and the misperceptions of outsiders, the West has been home to the true trendsetters of sedentary living in America.

More than three thousand years ago an indigenous culture, known to modern anthropologists as the Cochise, established fixed villages in what is now southern Arizona and New Mexico. The Cochise economy was based on agriculture, particularly the raising of corn. During the first millennium of the Common Era, the Cochise evolved into the Mogollon and Hohokam cultures. They developed irrigation and continually expanded the size of their settlements.[11]

The oldest continuously inhabited towns in modern America can still be found to the north of the old Cochise ruins. A pueblo is a Native American town of the American Southwest whose architecture features flat-roofed buildings constructed from adobe, an indigenous plaster made from mud. The first pueblos of northern New Mexico and Arizona and southern Colorado were built over thirteen hundred years ago. Anticipating modern, American urbanization by about a millennium was Pueblo Bonito in Chaco Canyon, whose three-acre compound was built about 900 C.E. Part of a settlement that covered eight square kilometers, the Pueblo Bonito building was initially three stories tall with 125 rooms. By 1100 it had grown to four stories, was over five hundred feet long, contained some eight hundred rooms, and housed over thirteen hundred people. Its construction had incorporated over 200,000 trees. At one time the world's largest apartment building, it was not surpassed by Euro-Americans until they built the Spanish Flats building in New York City in 1882.[12]

Today, numerous pueblos are sprawled across the Southwest on the sites where they were established many centuries ago. Pueblos like Tuie (Isleta), Ashiwi (Zuni), and Teotho (Taos) predate European arrival in the West by centuries and have been continuously inhabited since their founding. Many of today's residents continue to farm and have retained the central components of their indigenous culture, including language, religion, and government. It seems that the oldest of all is either the Hopituh (Hopi) town of Oraibi in northeastern Arizona, founded about eight and one-half centuries ago, or Akome (Acoma), just west of Albuquerque, New Mexico. Akome, also known as the Sky City for its location high atop a mesa, has been continuously inhabited for at least eight hundred years and possibly since before the Common Era.[13]

Elsewhere, there were variations on sedentary living. A number of peoples in the Pacific Northwest were sedentary, living in fixed villages but not in permanent abodes. The Chinooks—who live in the vicinity of the Columbia River, which forms today's Oregon-Washington border—are a good example. Until the mid-nineteenth century, their permanent villages on the north shore of the river were fortified with palisades. Within, their rectangular winter houses were built from wooden planks. With the onset of summer, however, these houses were deconstructed in favor of lighter, mat-roofed domiciles.[14]

Some communities combined sedentary patterns, generally based on agriculture, with more nomadic patterns, which facilitated hunting. One such example of these mixed settlement patterns is the Omaha people of northeastern Nebraska. In villages typically situated near a running stream, timber, and hills, the Omahas erected earth lodges. The lodges' walls were about eight feet tall and made of wooden poles arranged in a circle anywhere from twenty to sixty feet in diameter. The foundation was dug a foot deep, the walls were braced with willow trees, and the roof was constructed from thick, coarse grass thatch. An eastward-facing opening prevented the circle from closing, and from it sprang a hallway that protruded six to ten feet in length and served as an entrance. Complementing these were conical tipis, which were made from tent poles and bison robes and stood about fifteen feet high.[15]

For most of the year, the Omahas lived in both dwellings within the confines of their village. Once per year, however (and more than once as the nineteenth century advanced), they would strike their tipis and adopt a nomadic lifestyle. All members—save for the very old and sick and several to care for and guard them—would head out on the annual summer bison hunt. Moving ten to fifteen miles per day, the hunt was a journey of several hundred miles that lasted several weeks. The moving village would camp in different locales most every night as it set out to track, kill, and butcher a sufficient number of bison before heading back to the village.[16]

The most prominent stereotype of Indians in the West is that of the mounted nomads, brandishing eagle feather war bonnets, whooping war cries, and clashing with the U.S. cavalry. This image is rife with stereotypes and misperceptions. First, most people in the West were either completely or partially sedentary. Second, the term *nomad* is often misunderstood. A common inference is that nomads were rootless people, wandering aimlessly, who did not understand concepts of territoriality and boundaries. This is incorrect. Nomadic people around the world move to specific, known places for definite reasons. They also have a clear understanding of land usage rights and of the boundaries of territory under their control. Europeans and their descendents have traditionally glorified a sedentary, agricultural lifestyle and have denigrated those cultures that have pursued economies based on hunting and trading and/or raiding and that have frequently traversed large swaths of territory to do so. But nomads are no more aimless than a truck driver, no less cognizant of territoriality than a traveling salesman.

One such people in the West were the Comanches, who controlled much of the southern Great Plains for over 150 years until their defeat at the hands of the United States in 1875. Their nomadic lifestyle centered on bison hunting, the accumulation of massive horse herds, raiding, and trading. They lived year around in the easily transportable tipi. Successful warriors were awarded the familiar feathered war bonnet as a headdress befitting their courage. However, the otter-fur cap signaled a higher level of prestige. And the *pianu'upai* (a notched wooden club with a leather lash), not the bow and arrow, was the symbol of utmost bravery.[17]

Spatial Manipulations

With the advent of the European conquest of the Western Hemisphere, Native Americans were frequently confronted with the reality that they could no longer use space in the manner to which they were accustomed. The conquerors usually set new spatial parameters, forcing Indians from one place to another, restricting their movements, and confining their territorial claims. The first people in the American West to endure this hardship were those who came into contact with the Spanish empire. From their base in the former Aztec capital of Tenochtitlan, now known as Mexico City, the Spaniards moved northward into the present-day American Southwest, from Texas to the Pacific, and up the California coast. In the American West, their preferred stratagem for controlling the indigenous population was by controlling their living spaces.

The mission was Spain's primary institution for depriving Indians in the Southwest of their land. Spain had been using missions in Mexico since the sixteenth century and introduced the system to the Southwest in the seventeenth century. Franciscan, Dominican, and Jesuit organizers, with the coercive force of Spanish soldiers behind them, compelled entire Indian communities to leave their homes and resettle around missions: church-run, state-sponsored societies where the priests acted as pervasive rulers and strict disciplinarians. They micromanaged the Indians' new lives, which were largely devoted to supplying indentured labor in the fields and workshops and being subjected to Christian moralizing and proselytizing. Indians caught while trying to escape, or discovered practicing their own religions, faced harsh penalties up to and including death.[18]

Russian traders in Alaska also dealt with a brutal hand when interacting with the indigenous peoples of Alaska. During the last half of the eighteenth century, Russians set up fur-gathering operations along the Alaskan coast. Native Aleutian men between the ages of eighteen and fifty were virtually enslaved by the Russians, blackmailed into hunting for sea mammals while their families were held hostage. Their population was halved during this period. These horrific manipulations of Alaskan Natives continued, although with decreasing frequency, throughout the Aleutian Islands and Alaskan coast until the final Russian evacuation in 1867.[19]

As the American nation, which would come to dominate the West, grew from thirteen fledgling states to a formidable, expanding empire, Indians throughout its domain were forced to accept new homelands. The first way in which this affected the West was through the dispossession of Indians living east of the Mississippi River. These people were often forcibly relocated to the American West during the first half of the eighteenth century.

Numerous Native American nations were either conquered militarily or forced to capitulate, then subjected to the American policy known as "removal," a nineteenth-century euphemism for what is now known as ethnic cleansing. Not all removals were to the trans–Mississippi West. For example, the Oneidas of New York were removed to Wisconsin and Canada. But in the end, the majority of Indians who faced removal did find themselves relocated in the West. Even a portion of the Senecas and Cayugas, fellow members with the Oneidas in the Haudenosaunee (Iroquois) League Nations, were moved all the way from New York to the West.[20]

A number of peoples from the East were sent to what is now Kansas. Among them are the Shawnees, Potawatomis, Delawares, and Kickapoos. With the settlement of Kansas by Americans shortly thereafter, however, many of these Native American refugees would later be forced south to their ultimate destination, what is now Oklahoma, known as Indian Territory until statehood in 1907. Indian Territory, originally intended as a permanent dumping ground for Native American refugees, is also where the majority of dispossessed eastern Indian tribes were initially sent. Of the many forced west, the most notorious case is that of the Cherokees, one of the so-called Five Civilized Tribes (along with the Seminoles, Choctaws, Chickasaws, and Muskogees), so called for their willingness to adopt features of Euro-American culture such as written language, representative government, Christianity, and even a slave-based plantation economy in some cases.[21]

The Cherokees had treaties with the federal government guaranteeing their residence in the East. The U.S. Supreme Court even upheld their right to remain in the East in a trilogy of famous decisions (*Cherokee Nation v. Georgia, Worcester v. Georgia, Johnson v. McIntosh*). Nonetheless, President Andrew Jackson disregarded the precepts of checks and balances and international law and ordered the military to engage in ethnic cleansing against the Five Civilized Tribes. For the Cherokees, the result was the infamous Trail of Tears. As the U.S. Army forced the vast majority of the Cherokee nation to move westward, largely on foot, during the winter of 1838–1839, in excess of one-quarter of their nation (perhaps close to ten thousand altogether) perished from exposure, starvation, and diseases.[22]

Of course, there were already Native American people living on the lands to which the eastern Indians were relocated. The United States attempted to force these Western indigenous nations to cede land in order that the resettlements would go smoothly. However, given the rashness, disorganization, and barbarity of removal, one should not be surprised to find that conflicts did in fact arise between the Native American refugees and the aboriginal residents of the West. But the most vociferous conflicts in the region came about as a result of the United States' efforts to force the confinement of Indians who were native to the West. Indeed, most of the well-known wars between the United States and Indians took place in the West.[23]

Whereas England, and later the United States, took in excess of two centuries to solidify holdings east of the Missouri River, the American rate of conquest in the trans–Missouri River West was much more rapacious. Lewis and Clark led the first U.S. expedition across the Missouri in 1803, invading a region about which Americans knew practically nothing. But within a mere seventy-five years, every Native American nation in the West would be confined to a reservation that represented a minuscule portion of the territory they controlled before the American invasion. In one encounter after another, the United States forced Native American nations to accept treaties in which the latter ceded vast tracts of acreage. And then, one treaty after another was unilaterally abrogated by the United States, as the American nation then took even more land from the indigenous population of the West.[24]

Indeed, indigenous people were "lucky" if they merely had their lands pared down to a small core. Sometimes they were "punished" by the United States if they tried to maintain their sovereignty. Such was the case of the Bannocks of southeastern Idaho. After forcibly expelling trespassing Americans from their reservation, they fell into conflict with the U.S. Army. After killing about a hundred Bannocks, including a number who had tried to surrender,

the United States exiled them to Ft. Simcoe in Washington State before allowing them to return to their reservations two years later. Other expulsions
were more permanent.[25]

The Apaches of the Southwest have several divisions. Among them are the
Chiricahuas, who lived in what is now Arizona and to whom belonged the famous resistance leaders Naiche and Geronimo. The Chiricahuas had been
rounded up by the U.S. government after the Civil War and forced to live on a
reservation, a small patch of acreage within their ancestral homeland. Geronimo and Naiche fled the reservation with their followers in 1876, 1881, and
1885. Each time, they and their people, although enduring severe hardships,
were never captured but returned voluntarily. Naiche's and Geronimo's final
surrender came on 4 September 1886 and involved less than three dozen
people. Nonetheless, the entire Chiricahua band of nearly five hundred
people, including the same Chiricahua scouts who had helped the army track
Geronimo, were sent off as prisoners of war to Florida. After eight years' imprisonment in Florida and Alabama they, along with the rest of the Chiricahuas, were banished to the Ft. Sill Indian Reservation in what is now Oklahoma. Never again allowed to see the Southwest, Geronimo died there in
1909 at the age of eighty, still a prisoner of war. Finally, in 1913, the Chiricahuas were allowed to return to the Southwest, but then only to the Mescalero
Apache Reservation in New Mexico, the tribe's title to its Arizona homeland
permanently extinguished.[26]

Sometimes the circumstances by which Native American people lost their
land were surreal. The Poncas, who inhabited northeastern Nebraska, were
summarily deprived of their territory altogether by incompetent treaty officials they never even met. Under duress from Lakota raids from the north
and west and an influx of American settlers from the south and east, the Poncas had managed to secure a reservation for themselves. But when the Lakotas signed their own treaty with the United States in 1868, they were dealing
from a strong hand, having just defeated the United States in Red Cloud's
War (also known as the Powder River War). Consequently, when the Lakotas
claimed land that encompassed the Ponca Reservation, it was unbeknownst
to the Poncas, who were not even present at the treaty council, and no one
from the U.S. treaty commission was aware of the discrepancy. After the issues were sorted out, the United States preferred to recognize the claim of
the mighty Lakota nation as opposed to that of the small Ponca nation. In
1876 federal troops expelled the Poncas from Nebraska, marching them off to
Indian Territory. In 1878 Standing Bear led 380 Poncas back to Nebraska.
Federal authorities sought their return to Oklahoma, but a federal district

court in Nebraska ruled in favor of the Poncas. In 1879 these Northern Poncas settled on their own land, though it was no longer recognized as a reservation. Today, the nation is split between the Northern (Nebraska) and Southern (Oklahoma) Poncas.[27]

For some Native American peoples, the Americans were unwilling to afford any space at all. American actions in central and northern California during the last half of the nineteenth century were outright genocidal. A state law allowing for the indenturing of Indian labor for up to fifteen years led to a flourishing slave trade. From 1852 to 1867, between three thousand and four thousand women and children were kidnapped by Americans. Beyond this, volunteer companies were raised in various parts of the state for the sole purpose of killing Indians, no provocation required. California's Native American population in 1850 was about 300,000. By 1900, disease and murder had decimated it to about fifteen thousand, a decrease of 95 percent in only fifty years.[28]

The American government cast aside the niceties of colonial conquest in 1871 when it altogether desisted from the practice of signing treaties with Native American nations. From that period on, it used congressional legislation to justify the dispossession of Native American nations. The most effective act to do so was introduced in 1887. Henry Dawes, a liberal Massachusetts senator, actually believed he was helping Indians when he sponsored the Dawes Severalty Act, also known as the Dawes Allotment Act. The act divided up Indian reservations, which had previously been held in common by the whole of the tribe, into allotments that were portioned out to individual members. "Let us make a home for the Indian in severalty . . . ," said Dawes. "But let each one of them know that this spot is his, to be defended by him, to be protected by him, a nest to be adorned and beautified by him."[29]

Despite its intentions, the results of the Dawes Act were catastrophic. First, the government auctioned off "excess" Indian land; that which was left over after allotments were parceled out to Indians was sold to local settlers. Then, after a brief moratorium on taxes and sales, many Indians lost their allotments through fraud, tax default, sale in the face of dire poverty, and the urging of unscrupulous reservation agents. These federal patronage appointees from the Office of Indian Affairs were notorious for ineptitude and corruption. Blinded by racism and condescension, and often colluding with local white interests, they encouraged individual Indians to sell their land or sign leases that put their land under the control of white farmers and ranchers in return for minimal rental fees. Likewise, they frequently advised the entire tribe to lease huge tracts of land to large commercial interests (timber, coal, and so forth), sanctioning contracts up to ninety-nine years in duration that were grossly undervalued, all the while allegedly working for the tribe's best interest. During the turn of the century, long after the final wars had been fought and the last treaties had been signed, Indians lost more than half of their land under the auspices of the Dawes Act and the machinations of venal federal officials. By 1921, over half of the Indians affected by the Dawes Act had lost their allotments and were living in poverty.[30]

Stripping Indians of their land and, in most cases, forcibly altering their settlement patterns was odious. But perhaps no spatial manipulation was more egregious than the severing of Indian families. During the late nineteenth and early twentieth centuries, the U.S. government conscripted Indian children and shipped them off to boarding schools that were hundreds, sometimes thousands, of miles from their homes. Most Indian parents were loath to give up their children. But in a state of dependence on the government for their very survival, threats to withhold rations would oftentimes be sufficient to coerce a parent into sacrificing a child to the great American experiment in cultural genocide.[31]

To places like the Haskell Institute in Lawrence, Kansas, and the Carlisle Indian School in Carlisle, Pennsylvania, Indian children were shipped from around the country after having been torn asunder from their families. Once there, they were subjected to a program of education and manual labor and forced to completely abandon their Native cultures as school officials attempted to reshape them as Americans. Their hair was cut, their Indian clothes thrown out, and their religions replaced with Christianity. They were even punished for speaking their Native tongues.[32]

Modern Spaces

To the extent that Indians have been able to maintain title to any of their ancestral lands, it is usually in the form of reservations scattered about the West (Map 7.1). Reservations range in size from tiny rancherias in California, some less than an acre in size, to the nation's largest, the Navajo Reservation, which covers parts of three states in the Four Corners region of the Southwest. As noted, more than half of all reservation acreage was lost through the auspices of the Dawes Act and other legal sanctions from 1887 to 1934. One of the most disturbing long-term developments for the tribes in this respect has been the checkerboard phenomenon. Lands sold, seized, and leased have been lost in seemingly random lots. In addition, several generations of partible inheritance have generally fractioned the size of original parcels. As a result, many reservations, although large in size, suffer from the fact that actual

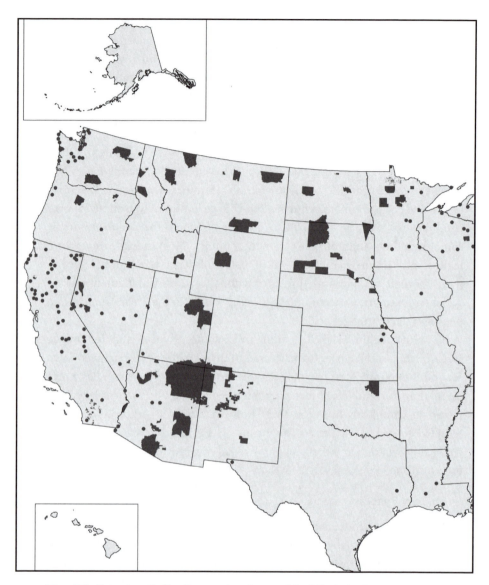

Map 7.1. "American Indian Reservations" west of the Mississippi.
Source: www.census.gov/dmd/www/pdf/512indre.pdf.

lands under the control of the tribes and their members are scattered and interspersed with lands they do not control. The resulting layout is similar to a frenetic checkerboard, severely hampering the ability of Indians to use their land base. As early as 1951, one scholar noted that economic rehabilitation efforts on the Pine Ridge Reservation in South Dakota had been crippled by this process.[33]

196 | AKIM D. REINHARDT

Although Native Americans have held on to their reservations as best they can, the post–World War II era has seen less and less of them living there. Since the start of the war, there has been a growing demographic shift as more and more Native American people are living off-reservation, particularly in large cities. This has been a national trend that applies to the West as it does to every other region of the United States. The four decades between 1930 and 1970, during which the number of Indians living in cities increased by more than a factor of ten, illustrate this movement. In 1930 less than 1 percent of all Indians lived in cities. By 1970 that figure had risen to nearly 45 percent. Today, the figure is more than 50 percent. Los Angeles, for example, had only 616 Indian residents in 1930 but nearly 24,000 by 1970. The result has been the formation of Indian ghettoes, particularly in Western cities, where Indians generally have had lower incomes and rates of home ownership than the rest of the population.[34]

There have been two primary impetuses for this development. The first is the growth of relatively high-paying jobs in the industrial sector beginning with the nation's mobilization for World War II. For the last sixty years these jobs, mostly located in cities, have attracted Indians from reservations that usually suffer from extremely high unemployment rates and other economic malaise. The second impetus was the active role of the federal government in attempting to induce Indians to leave their reservations for the cities. This role took the form of a program, inauspiciously entitled Liquidation at first and later known as Relocation. The ongoing effort to assimilate Native Americans, combined with federal desires to cut expenditures related to maintaining reservations as laid out in various treaties, led the Truman administration to adopt the policy of luring Indians to cities with the promise of good jobs and upward mobility. Lacking any significant support system, the program was largely a failure, although it persisted for nearly thirty years.[35]

The demographic information may come as a surprise to many non-Indians because common perceptions about Native America still tend to focus more on the reservation than they do on the diaspora. However, two points should be kept in mind. First, although there are higher percentages of Indians living in cities than ever before, that situation is a very fluid one. A great number of Indians leave reservations for cities only to return. Some move back and forth repeatedly. Second, non-Indian perceptions about how Indians relate to space are not always the same as Native American perceptions on the matter.

Perceptions

Traditional Native American perceptions of space are at once removed from their counterparts in the Eastern Hemisphere but at the same time evoke the universality of the human experience. Foreign to the indigenous people of the American West were some of the spatial apparatuses that are standard for Europeans and their descendents: written contracts (deeds and titles) and the courthouse registries that frame modern American land ownership. However, like all human beings, Native Americans used the land and its resources. As to specifics, different indigenous nations held various beliefs on individual land ownership. At one extreme, the Crows lived over a large swath of territory in the nineteenth century stretching from Canada to Wyoming and from the eastern slope of the Rockies to the High Plains. As with most nomadic peoples, they held their land in common, eschewing the notion of individual land ownership, yet guarding the borders of their territory from enemies. At the other extreme was the highly stratified Kwakiutl society, located on the Pacific Coast just north of the 49th parallel. With a system of land ownership reminiscent of feudal Europe, hereditary chiefs (in the name of their clan) owned and closely guarded large tracts of land and even rivers. Other Kwakiutls who poached or trespassed could be legally killed upon detection.[36]

Regardless of variance in issues of individual land ownership, every Native American nation understood the concept of international boundaries. In reality, such delineations have always been fluid throughout time. Europeans and Euro-Americans tend to insist that boundaries are hard and fast, but if this were really the case then cartographers would soon be out of business. Rather, nations and empires rise and fall, and borders shift accordingly. The historical reality of Native America was no different. For example, the Teton Lakotas (Sioux), who had once called the mouth of the Mississippi River their home, were an expanding empire on the northern Great Plains during the first two-thirds of the nineteenth century. This increasingly brought them into conflict with other Native American nations in the region, particularly the Poncas, Omahas, and Pawnees. These conflicts were often violent, and the Lakotas usually came out on top. The Lakotas were nomadic, but they had a firm understanding of which territories were under their control, which were not, and which were disputed, as is the case with any nation. Likewise, as their own empire contracted in the face of American expansion, they treated with the United States to maintain their land base. To this day, Lakotas readily differentiate between land that they legally ceded to the United States (although under duress) and land that was illegally taken from them.[37]

Other perceptions of space, however, differed greatly from those of Europeans. In Euro-American perceptions, the natural world is generally either a resource for exploitation or an abstract concept worthy of transcendental contemplations. Meanwhile, religious functions take place almost exclusively outside of the natural world and within the confines of religious structures built specifically for those purposes. Conversely, most Native American cultures in the West perceive religion and the natural world in a more holistic manner, often to the extent that certain places in the natural world are considered to be sacred sites, spiritual places of great religious importance. The discrepancy between these divergent views has made for alarming situations throughout the West.

The Hopis' reservation, by an oddity of treaty making, is completely land-locked within the Navajo Reservation. For both peoples, the peaks of Black Mesa, on the Colorado Plateau in northern Arizona, are sacred. To this day, however, the U.S. government propounds a nonexistent dispute between the two peoples as an excuse to open the region up to strip mining. Likewise, the Black Hills of southeastern Wyoming have been a sacred site for a number of northern Plains peoples, including the Shoshones, Crows, Cheyennes, and the Lakotas, who call them *He Sapa*. Illegally seized from the Lakotas by the United States in 1877, they have been mined for gold, silver, and other minerals for over a century. The ultimate insult came when the conquerors mutilated a sacred mountain with dynamite and jackhammers and then renamed it Mount Rushmore. The Lakotas, after nearly a century of legal agitation, won their case in 1980 as the U.S. Supreme Court awarded them $122 million in damages. Nonetheless, all of the Siouan tribal governments have refused the money, instead insisting that their sacred hills be returned.[38]

Beyond the meaning and usage of actual places, Native American perceptions of space itself are not identical to Euro-American perceptions. Native American places can be ephemeral, such as the junction between place and culture they refer to as "Indian country." "Indian country" is that rather existential place, existing anywhere Indians hold sway, be it on a reservation, in a city, or elsewhere. It is also the name of the widest-circulation national newspaper devoted to Native American affairs: *Indian Country Today*. Indeed, for many indigenous people in the American West, life itself is perceived in spatial terms. Life, metaphorically speaking, is a road. And the *chunka sha* ("red road"), as the Lakotas call it, is different than the white man's road. On the red road, the sanctity of life is expressed in a circle, and the four directions are sacred. Space is not just an abstract concept, but also an important component to understanding life. Places are not bereft of spiritual meaning, but rather are drenched in it.[39]

In the words of Kiowa writer N. Scott Momaday:

> Once in his life a man ought to concentrate his mind upon the remembered earth, I believe. He ought to give himself up to a particular landscape in his experience, to look at it from as many angles as he can, to wonder about it, to dwell upon it. He ought to imagine that he touches it with his hands at every season and listens to the sounds that are made upon it. He ought to imagine the creatures there and all the faintest motions of the world. He ought to recollect the glare of noon and all the colors of the dawn and dusk.[40]

This place is Native America.

Notes

1. John Trudell, *Stickman*, ed. Paola Igliori (New York: Inanout Press, 1994), pages unnumbered.

2. With respect to the sagacity of Native American religions: All religions are grounded in faith, not fact; so their sagacity is a reflection of the degree to which people believe in them. Adherents of Native American religions are every bit as devout (or not) as followers of Western religions. As for the traditions, many of these religions are just as old (sometimes older) than Christianity and Islam (of course, some are not). They are also very involved in their details and precision. In many Native American cultures, traditions play a much larger role in the overall society than in the West. For example, peoples of the northern Plains typically did not "discipline" (that is, spank or scream at) their children or even demand that they follow preferred social paths. Instead, they relied on the role of tradition; adults would conduct themselves according to traditional ways, and children would observe this. Over time, children would realize that adults deemed these things important and more likely than not would follow in that path. In other words, traditions, including religious traditions, not only served the roles that Westerners associate with them but also filled roles that Westerners frequently leave to other aspects of the social order, including behavior modification, child rearing, interpretation and execution of politics and legal matters, and so forth. It is important to stress that Native American religions deserve to be treated with the same respect as Western religions.

3. N. Scott Momaday, *The Way to Rainy Mountain* (Albuquerque: University of New Mexico Press, 1969), 3, 16.

4. Richard Erdoes and Alfonso Ortiz, eds., *American Indian Myths and Legends* (New York: Pantheon Books, 1984), 109–111, 509.

5. Ibid., 119, 512.

6. Tom D. Dillehay, *Monte Verde: A Late Pleistocene Settlement in Chile* (Washington, D.C.:

Smithsonian Institution Press, 1989). For an in-depth overview of Beringian theory posited by the leading archeologists in the field, see Tom D. Dillehay and David J. Meltzer, eds., *The First Americans: Search and Research* (Boca Raton: CRC Press, 1991). For a relevant critique of archeology see Vine Deloria Jr., *Red Earth, White Lies: Native Americans and the Myth of Scientific Fact* (New York: Scribner, 1995).

7. Alice Joseph, Rosamond B. Spicer, and Jane Cheskey, *The Desert People: A Study of the Papago Indians* (Chicago: University of Chicago Press, 1949), 14–17.

8. Alice B. Kehoe, *North American Indians: A Comprehensive Account,* 2d ed. (Englewood Cliffs, N.J.: Prentice Hall, 1991), 305; Roy W. Meyer, *The Village Indians of the Upper Missouri: The Mandans, Hidatsas, and Arikaras* (Lincoln: University of Nebraska Press, 1977), 5–17.

9. Virginia Mary Trenholm and Maurine Carley, *The Shoshonis: Sentinels of the Rockies* (Norman: University of Oklahoma Press, 1964), 3–40.

10. John H. Moore, *The Cheyenne* (Cambridge, Mass.: Blackwell, 1996), 1–29.

11. Robert Silverberg, *The Pueblo Revolt* (1970; reprint, Lincoln: University of Nebraska Press, 1994), 6–7.

12. Silverberg, *The Pueblo Revolt,* 10–12; Kehoe, *North American Indians: A Comprehensive Account,* 124.

13. Silverberg, *The Pueblo Revolt,* 14; Ward Alan Minge, *Acoma: Pueblo in the Sky,* 2d ed. (Albuquerque: University of New Mexico Press, 1991), 1–2.

14. Kehoe, *North American Indians: A Comprehensive Account,* 446; Robert H. Ruby and John A. Brown, *The Chinook Indians: Traders on the Lower Columbia* (Norman: University of Oklahoma Press, 1976), 5–8.

15. Alice C. Fletcher and Francis La Flesche, *The Omaha Tribe,* 2 vols. (1911; reprint, Lincoln: University of Nebraska Press, 1992), 1: 95–99.

16. Ibid., 1: 275–283.

17. Thomas W. Kavanagh, *Comanche Political History: An Ethnohistorical Perspective, 1706–1875* (Lincoln: University of Nebraska Press, 1996), 28–36, 435–453.

18. Woodrow W. Borah, "The California Mission," in *Ethnic Conflict in California History,* ed. Charles Wollenberg (Los Angeles: Tinnon-Brown, 1970), 1, 7–8; S. F. Cook, *The Conflict between the California Indians and White Civilization,* 4 vols. (Berkeley: University of California Press, 1943), 1: 91–100, 113–135.

19. James R. Gibson, *Imperial Russia in Frontier America: The Changing Geography of Supply of Russian America, 1784–1867* (New York: Oxford Books, 1976), 1, 8, 32–33.

20. George H. J. Abrams, *The Seneca People* (Phoenix: Indian Tribal Series, 1976), 3, 56–68; George C. Shattuck, *The Oneida Land Claims: A Legal History* (Syracuse: Syracuse University Press, 1991), xvii–xx, 9–10.

21. Arrell Morgan Gibson, *The American Indian: Prehistory to the Present* (Lexington, Mass.: D. C. Heath, 1980), 295–298.

22. Theda Perdue and Michael D. Green, eds., *The Cherokee Removal: A Brief History with Documents* (New York: Bedford Books, 1995), 1–24; Russell Thornton, "The Demography of the Trail of Tears Period: A New Estimate of Cherokee Population Losses," in *Cherokee Removal, Before and After,* ed. Wilson L. Anderson (Athens: University of Georgia Press, 1991), 83–93.

23. Gibson, *The American Indian: Prehistory to the Present,* 312–317.

24. Treaties between Native American nations and the United States may be found in Charles J. Kappler, ed., *Indian Treaties 1778–1883* (1904; reprint, New York: Interland Publishing, 1972); for a legal interpretation of the United States' propensity for ignoring its own laws and treaties with respect to U.S.-Indian relations, see Vine Deloria Jr., *Of Utmost Good Faith* (San Francisco: Straight Arrow Books, 1971).

25. Ralph K. Andrist, *The Long Death: The Last Days of the Plains Indians* (New York: Collier Books, 1964), 318–319.

26. Andrist, *The Long Death: The Last Days of the Plains Indians,* 332–333; Geronimo, *His Own Story,* ed. S. M. Barrett (London: Abacus, 1974), 33–41.

27. David J. Wishart, *An Unspeakable Sadness* (Lincoln: University of Nebraska Press, 1994), 202–216.

28. Lynwood Carranco and Estle Beard, *Genocide and Vendetta: The Round Valley Wars in Northern California* (Norman: University of Oklahoma Press, 1981), 84–97, 105–156; Sherbourne F. Cook, *The Population of California Indians, 1769–1970* (Berkeley: University of California Press, 1976), 42–43, 53, 56, 71; Cook, *The Population of California Indians, 1769–1970,* 5–25; Jack Norton, *Genocide in Northwest California* (San Francisco: Indian Historian Press, 1979), 61–63.

29. Ralph W. Goodwin, "Righting the Century of Dishonor: Indian Reform as a Reaffirmation of Conservative Values," in *Essays on the History of the American West,* ed. Stephen Salsbury (Hillsdale, Ill.: Dryden Press, 1975), 125–137; Dawes quoted in Goodwin, "Righting the Century of Dishonor," 133; John R. Wunder, *"Retained by the People": A History of American Indians and the Bill of Rights* (New York: Oxford University Press, 1994), 29–31.

30. Donald J. Berthrong, "Legacies of the Dawes Act," *Arizona and the West* 21 (winter, 1979): 335; Richard White, *"It's Your Misfortune and None of My Own": A New History of the American West* (Norman: University of Oklahoma Press, 1991), 115–116. For insight into the mind of a reservation agent, see James McLaughlin, *My Friend the Indian* (1910; reprint, Lincoln: University of Nebraska Press, 1989).

31. Clyde Ellis, *To Change Them Forever: Indian Education at the Rainy Mountain Boarding School, 1893–1920* (Norman: University of Oklahoma Press, 1996), xi–xii; K. Tsianina Lomawaima, *They Called It Prairie Light: The Story of Chilocco Indian School* (Lincoln: University of Nebraska Press, 1994), 1–8.

32. Ellis, *To Change Them Forever,* 1–27; Lomawaima, *They Called It Prairie Light,* 1–8.

33. Vine Deloria Jr., *Custer Died for Your Sins: An Indian Manifesto* (New York: Macmillan, 1969), 37–38, 46–48; Laura Thompson, *Personality and Government: Findings and Rec-*

ommendations of the Indian Administration Research (Mexico City: Ediciones del Instituto In-digenista InterAmericano, 1951), 90–92.

34. U.S. Department of Commerce, Bureau of the Census, *The Indian Population of the United Sates and Alaska* (Washington, D.C.: Government Printing Office, 1937), 8–9, 196–198; U.S. Department of Commerce, Bureau of the Census, *Subject Report: American Indians* (Washington, D.C.: Government Printing Office, 1973), 1, 138–140, pt. 1, 27, 62, 120, 129; U.S. Department of Commerce, Bureau of the Census, *General Population and Housing Statistics, 1970* (Washington, D.C.: Government Printing Office, 1970), pt. 1, 390, 398, 400, 549–551.

35. Elaine M. Neils, *Reservation to City* (Chicago: University of Chicago, 1971), 46–47; Alan L. Sorkin, *The Urban American Indian* (Lexington, Mass.: Heath, 1978), 25; U. S. Congress, American Indian Policy Review Commission, Task Force Eight, *Report on Urban and Non-Reservation Indians* (Washington, D.C.: Government Printing Office, 1976), 27–28; Larry W. Burt, "Roots of the Native American Urban Experience: Relocation Policy in the 1950s," *American Indian Quarterly* 10, no. 2 (1986): 87–89; Donald Fixico, *Termination and Reloca-tion* (Albuquerque: University of New Mexico Press, 1986), 137; Neils, *Reservation to City,* 50; U.S. Congress, *Report on Urban and Rural Non-Farm Indians,* 28.

36. Franz Boaz, *Kwakiutl Ethnography,* ed. Helen Codere (Chicago: University of Chicago Press, 1966), 35–36; Frederick E. Hoxie, *Parading through History: The Making of the Crow Nation in America* (New York: Cambridge University Press, 1995), 47–48, 57–59.

37. Richard White, "The Winning of the West: The Expansion of the Western Sioux in the Eighteenth and Nineteenth Centuries," *The Journal of American History* 65 (September 1978): 326–327; Wishart, *An Unspeakable Sadness,* 16–17, 25–29, 37, 77, 86, 91, 94, 146–147, 187, 190, 204, 276.

38. Peter Matthiessen, *Indian Country* (New York: Penguin Books, 1979), 67–102, 203–220; Edward Lazarus Jr., *Black Hills/White Justice: The Sioux Nation versus the United States, 1775–Present* (New York: HarperCollins, 1991).

39. Spatial relations and other aspects of Lakota spirituality can be found in Black Elk, *Black Elk Speaks,* ed. John G. Neihardt (1932; reprint, Lincoln: University of Nebraska Press, 1979); Floyd Looks for Buffalo Hand, *Learning Journey on the Red Road* (Toronto: Learning Journey Communications, 1998); James R. Walker, *Lakota Belief and Ritual,* eds. Raymond J. DeMallie and Elaine A. Jahner (Lincoln: University of Nebraska Press, 1980).

40. Momaday, *The Way to Rainy Mountain,* 83.

8 | Narrating Imperial Adventure

Isabella Bird's Travels in the Nineteenth-Century American West

KAREN M. MORIN

Feminist historical geographies of the American West are just beginning to come into their own.[1] Although Western women's historians have been producing feminist scholarship about the region since the 1970s,[2] only in the last decade or so have feminist historical geographers of the West begun producing a distinctive body of work. Their interests overlap those of other critical and "radical" geographies of the West, particularly in their critique of labor practices and relations,[3] as well as complement the traditional arenas of the historical geography of the region—exploration and frontier expansion, settlement patterns and sequence, environmental change, and emerging urban and economic integration. Feminist topics of interest range widely,[4] but one significant area of critique concerns tourism development in the region. Such works principally examine the ways that gendered differences situate women in feminized job categories at tourist sites and the ways that sociospatial forces position women materially and discursively as particular kinds of consumers of tourist sites and as producers of cultural knowledge about them, especially via written texts.[5]

Simply writing women's experiences into historical geography remains of primary concern to many scholars, whereas others demonstrate a more fundamental interest in the production of gender differences themselves and how they work within and through economic, political, cultural, and sexual differences in the creation of past geographies. This chapter is concerned with both of the important agendas appearing in new feminist work of the West—the need to vigilantly continue incorporating women's voices, views,

204

and activities into the past and the need to examine the ways in which gendered differences were produced within and through particular historical landscapes, places, and spatialities.[6]

To these ends, in this chapter I consider the ways in which the renowned explorer Isabella L. Bird wrote about herself and her mountaineering experiences in the Colorado Rockies in her extraordinary volume, *A Lady's Life in the Rocky Mountains* (1879).[7] My purpose is to show how Victorian gender relations and imperial geographies—both British and American—worked together to produce many "subject positions" in Bird's writing about the American West, a place with very different historical exigencies than the colonial contexts under which much nineteenth-century British women's travel literature was produced. I want to highlight the ways in which conventional as well as more transgressive discourses of Victorian womanhood worked with (but also occasionally against) imperialist, nationalist, and class discourses in Bird's text, to examine their links and interconnections. Bird negotiated place, "empire," and womanhood in a range of ways in the Rocky Mountain environs, resulting in many complex subject positionings.

Isabella L. Bird (1831–1904) (Figure 8.1) needs little introduction to historiographers of Anglophone travel writing. She was the first woman elected to the prestigious Royal Geographical Society in London, in 1892, largely on the basis of her travels to India, the Middle East, and Tibet. Later she traveled to and wrote about Korea, Japan, Malaysia, and China, producing nine travel books in the course of her career. Bird is one of the most popularized of all British Victorian women travelers, and, with two books on the subject, she is certainly among the best-known and most studied of women travelers to North America.

Born in Yorkshire to an Anglican clergyman and a clergyman's daughter, Bird had the background of a deeply religious, well-educated, and well-to-do Englishwoman.[8] She first took up travel at age twenty-three, when she came to the United States at the recommendation of her doctor for her recurring back problems. From this journey Bird produced *An Englishwoman in America* (1856). She spent most of her early adult life caring for her parents. After their deaths she took her first solo trip abroad in 1871–1873, at age forty, to Hawaii (the Sandwich Islands) via Australia. She traveled through the United States on her return home, and it was during this trip that Bird explored the Estes Park region of Colorado for four months in the autumn and early winter of 1873 and produced *A Lady's Life in the Rocky Mountains*. This volume was originally written as letters to her sister, then appeared serially as "Letters from the Rocky Mountains" in the genteel English weekly *Leisure*

Fɪɢ. 8.1. Isabella L. Bird, ca. 1881. Reproduced courtesy of the University of Hawai'i Press.

Hour in 1878. From there it flourished through eight editions by 1912.[9] Attesting to its literary quality perhaps more than anything else, in 1969 the University of Oklahoma Press reissued the volume for contemporary audiences.

A particular nexus of American and British imperialisms was evident in Colorado during the period of Bird's explorations. Coinciding with the height of British empire building and the attendant increased accumulation of wealth available for travel and investment, the Rocky Mountains became important destinations on the itineraries of many British men and women like Bird who toured the western United States in the late nineteenth century. New and improved accommodations and transportation, especially the railroad, enabled and enticed unprecedented numbers of British travelers and tourists to experience for themselves the "monumental" scenic attractions of Colorado. The healthful climate and myriad of sporting and recreational activities made the region an especially attractive destination for health seekers and foreign travelers and tourists.[10] Many transcontinental railroad travelers took side excursions from Denver to Colorado Springs and Manitou Springs, site of one of the principal tourist attractions of the region, the fourteen thousand-foot Pike's Peak. (Bird herself focused more attention on nearby Long's Peak, as discussed later.)

Colorado was also home to many wealthy British investors, titled remittance men, and retired colonels. Extensive investment opportunities, particularly in mining, cattle ranching, and railroad development, attracted British settlement and tourism.[11] Historian Robert Athearn reports that Colorado "was almost an English reserve," with one of every three ranches in Colorado in the later nineteenth century belonging to Englishmen. "Any capitalist could then come," explains Athearn, "enjoy the delightful climate, and live comfortably" off his invested income that returned 10 to 18 percent on loans.[12] British investments helped finance capitalist ventures such as the development of the Denver & Rio Grande Railroad,[13] which facilitated Colorado's deepening entry into the global economy. And clearly, such expansionism into the region depended on drastic reductions in the Native American populations by warfare, disease, near extinction of the bison, and nearly complete alienation from their former lands through the reservation and then allotment process imposed by the U.S. government.[14]

Within the context of British imperialism outside the boundaries of its "formal" empire, and corresponding to leaping-and-bounding American expansionism in the West, Isabella Bird wrote about her rugged, outdoor life of 1870s Colorado. Much of the recent literature on the multifaceted and multipositioned figure of the Victorian "Englishwoman abroad" has focused on British women's uneasy and complex relationships with colonialism and imperialism, especially in the ways in which imperial discourses on race, class, and nation combined with Victorian domestic ideologies in both the maintenance of feminine codes of behavior and contestations of that in notions of female liberation.[15] However, little recent work has focused on the complex intersections between British imperialism and gendered subjectivity for "Englishwomen abroad" in the mountainous landscapes in the late nineteenth-century American West.

In the following discussion I identify the main tropes of mountain adventure in Bird's writing, in what she wrote about both the indoor "domestic" spaces of the West as well as the outdoor, mountainous landscapes. I problematize notions of feminine codes of behavior, early "first wave" feminism, and convergences of these with imperial, national, and class discourses, as constituted within early foreign travel in the American West. In much of her *A Lady's Life,* Bird represents herself as strengthened by the outdoors, overcoming or "conquering" her own frailty through arduous hiking or horseback riding in difficult mountainous terrain. And yet Bird's narrative also exhibits contradictory or paradoxical representations of herself as a gendered individual in those same environments, such as in expressing fear of danger and fatigue. It will become clear that in many ways Isabella Bird reinscribed herself as a feminine, domestic subject in her narrative; yet she also explored and contested the powerful inscriptions of domesticity that arose out of hegemonic (masculinist) versions of Victorian femininity. In so doing she articulated with, and thereby perhaps even can be seen to have reconstituted, hegemonic ideologies about femininity, domesticity, and more contestatory versions of Victorian womanhood in the American West.

Domestic Geographies of *A Lady's Life*

A number of scholars have pointed out the extent to which British women travelers to the American West devoted considerable portions of their texts to detailing the quality of Western travel, accommodations, food, and clothing.[16] Protestations over bad food and service clearly marked them as in need of servants to enact proper (English) domesticity, with the (apparently) servantless West inhibiting that. This trope was common in aristocratic and professional-class British women's (and men's) travel writing about the American West. However, more complicated ways in which gendered subjectivity intersected with domestic class relations can be read in Isabella Bird's descriptions of establishing her own housekeeping in the mountains near Estes Park.

Early upon arrival in Colorado Bird stayed with a family named Chalmers while trying to organize an expedition to Estes Park. Holes in the roof of the cabin, unchinked logs, the absence of tables, beds, basins, towels, windows, lamps, or candles in her room and a litany of other deficiencies of the dwelling and property proved to Bird that Mr. and Mrs. Chalmers were ignorant, inept, and inefficient, even after nine years of attempted homesteading on their 160 acres.[17] The Scotsman Chalmers frequently ridiculed the English, and Bird writes that he trusted "to live to see the downfall of the British monarchy and the disintegration of the empire."[18] Their lives were "moral, hard, unloving, unlovely, unrelieved, unbeautified, [and] grinding." Bird's daily routine at their place consisted of drawing water from the river, sweeping, washing garments by hand ("taking care that there [were] no witnesses" to her inexperience, however), knitting, writing, and "various odds and ends which arise when one has to do all for oneself."[19]

Bird presents herself as equally at ease killing rattlesnakes outside the cabin as helping an emigrant who had just given birth. And in fact later in the text, at the home of her more refined neighbors, the Hugheses, she writes of

helping out by baking bread, washing dishes, and working in the fields, although preferring "field work to the scouring of greasy pans and to the wash
tub, and both to either sewing or writing."[20] In these and other excerpts, Bird
portrayed herself as enjoying the "freedom" to perform domestic tasks to
which she was unaccustomed, such as washing her own clothes. She was
pleased with the log cabin she finally moved into alone, which she illustrated
as her "home in the Rocky Mountains" (Figure 8.2). She claimed that "it is
quite comfortable—in the fashion I like" and takes only "about five minutes
to 'do,' and you could eat off the floor."[21]

A complex nexus of gendered subjectivities seems to be operating in these
passages. Bird's western displacement on one hand appears to offer her a
sense of prideful self-sufficiency in the simple circumstances of the log cabin.
Bird distances herself from the domestic realm in her descriptions of killing
rattlesnakes, performing hard physical labor in the fields, and climbing
mountains. But rather than casting off her domestic self altogether, to become a "heroic adventurer," she represents herself as embracing the domestic tasks, which presumably her own servants normally performed at home,
and becoming empowered by them. She enthused that, "I *really* need nothing
more than this log cabin offers."[22]

FIG. 8.2. This sketch of Bird's cabin near Estes Park appeared in *A Lady's Life*, 1879,
p. 103. Reproduced courtesy of University of Oklahoma Press.

Although her narrative might begin to resemble a "tour" of the working class, at other points in her text Bird represents herself as unfamiliar with and unaccustomed to unpleasant domestic work. When she offered to wash some plates, Mrs. Chalmers replied that her hands "'aint no good; never done nothing, I guess.'" Then to her awkward daughter: "'This woman says she'll wash up! Ha! ha! look at her arms and hands!'"[23] Thus, although Bird enacts domesticity she simultaneously maintains her own version of true femininity by presenting herself as ill prepared and too delicate for work other than knitting, sewing, and writing, all of which were signifying practices of the Victorian bourgeoisie. Although Bird claims that her own hands are "very brown and coarse," it is Mrs. Chalmers who frequently appears manly and with whom Bird contrasts herself: Mrs. Chalmers "is never idle for one minute, is severe and hard, and despises everything but work," she reports.[24] Mrs. Chalmers's unceasing work and heavy manual labor do not approximate the role of proper bourgeois women embedded in English Victorian patriarchal discourse: Whereas bourgeois men were judged by their success at entering and competing in the commercial sphere, the women "proved" the success of their men by their idleness and leisure-time activities—enabled through the domestic labor that servants performed—which Bird herself carefully maintained by activities such as writing.

Rhetorically distanced from the manliness and hard labor of working women, Bird asserts that class distinctions, and servants, do not inhere in uncivilized places like Colorado. She submits that "I *really* need nothing more than this log cabin offers" but also contends that "elsewhere one must have a house and servants."[25] The mountainous dwellings of the American West provide, then, a venue for testing new forms of gendered subjectivity for Bird —forms that ultimately rest on highlighting national differences in the employment of proper class relations. And it must be noted that she ignores the extent to which the class structure and labor relations of the West, particularly in regard to the domestic labor of Chicanas in the mountainous West, differed little from her "ideal."[26]

"Plucky Nell" and the Useless Guide

As Isabella Bird narrated her outdoor excursions into the mountains, by foot and horseback, she drew on the rhetorics of emergent feminist empowerment, more conventional femininity, and British nationalism and imperialism. One literary device that Bird deployed was the signifying of a local guide on a mountain excursion as incompetent, and Bird, through the prized Victorian values of resourcefulness, perseverance, and intelligence, in some way saves herself and others from indeterminate ends. This trope resonated well with the Victorian literary heroine who, as long as she retained her purity and proper manners, could be admired for her fortitude in the face of adversity.[27]

The Victorian adventure tale was a deeply gendered myth about a male hero who was courageous, strong, and persistent, who was in search of gold, land, or other "imperial dreams," and who directly or indirectly promoted British overseas investment or emigration.[28] Given the particular educational, religious, and administrative context of masculinities in Victorian Britain, colonial work itself was often constituted as an adventure for male colonial administrators, travelers, capitalist developers, or military officers. Although the identity politics of colonialism often involved adventure for men, it was not as available to colonial women, who were often discursively and materially placed within the domestic sphere and whose jobs were to articulate with and maintain proper British households in the colonies.[29]

When elite British women such as Isabella Bird traveled to the American West, however, the context was quite different. British women traveled to the West as professional writers, tourists, and/or with husbands or male relatives who were involved in capitalistic ventures with American entrepreneurs. This requires then a much different reading of the relationships between gendered subjectivities, adventure, and empire, specifically in the ways that transgressive feminist empowerment can be read as uniquely intersecting with other modalities of British imperialism.

Isabella Bird took the trope of the incompetent (male) guide to the extreme as she described a failed attempt to reach Estes Park guided by the "useless" Mr. Chalmers. An accomplished horsewoman, Bird wrote much of her text as a heroic adventure tale as she trail-blazed to mountaintops and other destinations despite blizzards, incompetent guides such as Chalmers, and logistical obstacles. In one section entitled, "Nameless Region, Rocky Mountains," Bird describes her couple of days' frustration following Chalmers through the St. Vrain Canyon in search of Estes Park. She complains that, after immediately getting lost after lunch on the first day,

> For four weary hours we searched hither and thither along every indentation of the ground which might be supposed to slope towards the Big Thompson River, which we knew had to be forded. Still, as the quest grew more tedious, Long's Peak stood before us as a landmark in purple glory . . . Chalmers, who had started confident, bumptious, blatant, was ever becoming more bewildered, and his wife's thin voice more piping and disconcerted, and my stumbling horse more insecure, and I more determined (as I am at this moment) that somehow or other I would reach that blue hollow, and even stand on Long's Peak where

the snow was glittering. Affairs were becoming serious, and Chalmers' incompetence a source of real peril.[30]

They and their horses and mules eventually fell into a gulch, mistakenly having followed a bear trail. Recovering from that, and with no remaining provisions, Chalmers, his wife, and Bird camped out the night. In the morning, to her horror, all the horses had escaped because, according to Bird, they had been improperly secured by Chalmers the night before. In resignation, Bird reported that they finally decided to return home and, dejected, wrote that "we never reached Estes Park." In what she represents as a "last resort," Bird demanded control of the doomed expedition:

> Vainly I pointed out to him that we were going north-east when we should have gone south-west, and that we were ascending instead of descending. . . . He then confessed that he was lost, and that he could not find his way back. His wife sat down on the ground and cried bitterly. We ate some dry bread, and then I said I had had much experience in traveling, and would take the control of the party, which was agreed to, and began the long descent.[31]

Bird probably did have more traveling experience at this stage of her life than Chalmers, and it might also be argued that travelers had access to some resources that local people did not, such as maps. However, Bird would not likely have depended upon Chalmers had she known the route to Estes Park. In the end she compares her own (superior) knowledge of mountaineering to that of a local (man), and by stressing the failings of others (Chalmers and his wife) in comparison to her own leadership abilities and mental toughness, she guarantees her own heroine status in the narrative.

Many scholars of British women's travel writing have noted the extent to which many women travelers represented themselves *as women* undertaking particular activities, especially transgressive ones.[32] The trope of women's heroic adventures challenged and transgressed dominant ideologies of gender roles and relations. Privileged women emphasizing attributes of courage, strength, and persistence directly challenged ideologies of self-sacrificing, duty-bound Victorian mothers and wives. In that sense they helped rewrite the terms of the Victorian adventure tale itself, and often without relinquishing their femininity to do so.[33] Isabella Bird actively created space for women outside of the domestic sphere, in this case, in the mountains of Colorado, reconstituting where bourgeois women might feel "at home." As she portrayed outdoor Rocky Mountain landscapes as a plausible destination for women, one might also read her narrative as extending British influence—a particularly progressive form of women's advancement—in Colorado. And, of course, encouraging British mountaineering in the region advanced American development as well.[34] Furthermore, because Colorado was already home to many British immigrants and investors, her additional "mappings," particularly in successful and "heroic" narratives, may have reinscribed it as an appropriate place for British assistance in American empire building, especially in mining, cattle, and railroad enterprises.[35]

The "Conquest" of Long's Peak

> Such as it is, Estes Park is mine. It is unsurveyed, "no man's land," and mine
> by right of love, appropriation, and appreciation; by the seizure of its peerless
> sunrises and sunsets, its glorious afterglow, its blazing noons, its hurricanes
> sharp and furious, its wild auroras, its glories of mountain and forest, of canyon, lake, and river, and the stereotyping them all in my memory.

Isabella Bird, writing about Estes Park for the first time in A Lady's Life,[36] often seemed concerned to defy Victorian femininity by portraying herself as strengthened by rugged mountainous environments, as an independent, adventurous woman heroically "conquering" the destinations of her travels. And yet she also, paradoxically perhaps, emphasized what some scholars have recognized as specifically feminine aspects of travel writing,[37] such as in downplaying the adventurousness of her mountaineering adventures, complaining about how emotionally or physically difficult they had become, and in representing herself as passive, weak, and in need of men's help. This ambivalence is played out most significantly in A Lady's Life within the narrative trope of "conquest" of mountain peaks.

One of the principal excursions Bird describes was her ascent of Long's Peak, the summit of which is along the North American Continental Divide. This excursion also served as the peak literary moment in the narrative overall. She was accompanied by "Rocky Mountain Jim" and two student trappers.[38] Her description of the panoramic view from the "nearly 15,000"-foot summit (Figure 8.3) contains many of the markers of heroic achievement:

> at last the Peak was won. . . . From the summit were seen in unrivaled combination all the views which had rejoiced our eyes during the ascent. It was something at last to stand upon . . . this lonely sentinel of the Rocky Range, on one
> of the mightiest of the vertebrae of the backbone of the North American continent, and to see the waters start for both oceans.[39]

This description seems to illustrate what Mary Louise Pratt[40] argues is one of the most distinguishing features of "imperialistic" Victorian travel writing," that is, what she terms the "monarch-of-all-I-survey" trope. To Pratt, this trope described peak moments at which geographical "discoveries" were "won" for England. In this "discourse of discovery," the imperial travel writer conquered the landscape and heroically claimed dominance and authority over it. Pratt characterizes the monarch-of-all-I-survey trope as deeply gendered masculine, whereby male explorers were able to render "momentously significant what is, especially from a narrative point of view, practically a non-event"—with the help of local guides "you pretend to conquer" what they already knew and thus convert local knowledge into "European national and continental knowledges—and relations of power."[41] Following Pratt, Sara Mills adds that the very act of describing a panoramic scene is also mastering or colonizing it.[42] What is actually just a passive experience of "seeing" becomes momentous when the traveler brings the information home, puts it on a map, and lectures to Sunday afternoon geographical society meetings.

Although Pratt claims that promontory descriptions are very common in romantic and Victorian writing of all kinds, women do not spend a lot of time on promontories, "nor are they entitled to,"[43] because the masculine heroic discourse of discovery is not readily available to women. Nevertheless, Isabella Bird does seem to have re-created such peak "imperial" moments in her narrative—claiming mastery and ownership of Estes Park—for home audiences in much the same way as [many] male travel writers did, and in a context very unlike the colonial settings of much British travel writing. With greater attention to the complexities of gendered subjectivity than Pratt, Mills and Alison Blunt[44] argue that peak imperial moments do occur in women's travel writing, but because particular kinds of ambivalences about gender inhere in them, ambivalence toward imperialism itself is produced in the narratives. Blunt's very different reading of Mary Kingsley's landscape descriptions of West Africa serves as a useful example.[45] Blunt reads Mary Kingsley's ascent of Mount Cameroon as marking her within the patriarchal and imperial tradition of exploration, but also outside of it. Because Kingsley could appreciate the value of a view obstructed by mist, her position in relation to the landscape ultimately . . . is esthetic, not "strategic" or resting on a relationship of domination.

That Isabella Bird's "heroic" voice could be undermined by a feminine discourse simultaneously available to her seems evident. She made her way to the top of Long's Peak guided by Jim Nugent and in fact roped to him; she describes him "dragging" her up the mountain "like a bale of goods, by sheer force of muscle." "I am only humiliated by my success," she claimed. On the way down the mountain Bird followed Jim, so that his "powerful shoulders" could help steady her.[46] In contrast to Mr. Chalmers, Jim is an intelligent and necessary guide to Bird's discoveries and achievements. Throughout the climb Bird's narrative voice was uncertain as she admitted to experiencing fear, danger, and especially fatigue and exhaustion. She wrote about *crawling* most of the way down the mountain, losing courage and strength and finally, on approach of the horses, wrote that

> With great difficulty and much assistance I recrossed the lava beds, was carried to the horse and lifted upon him, and when we reached the camping ground I was lifted off him, and laid on the ground wrapped up in blankets, a humiliating termination of a great exploit.[47]

Obviously, Bird's admissions of frailty do not fit within the heroic discourse of discovery or adventure. Or do they?

Although women writers arguably had special access to the "feminine" discursive spaces of cowardice, mistakes, and defeat in the face of danger, it must be noted that men, too, described the suffering, fatigue, danger, and even death involved in exploration and adventure.[48] Both women and men, by accentuating the difficulties connected with their achievements, in a sense improved upon them. Overcoming obstacles made the achievement that much more heroic and proved how much personal credit was due them in managing the ascent or discovery. Thus, in addition to the stock requisite features of Western travel narratives—evidence of dramatic feats of engineering and "exotic" animals and people[49]—one might include imaginings of the West itself as a place of danger for women. Thus, Bird's emphasis on danger shores up her own courage, strength, and toughness while creating points of interest in her narrative.

In addition, for women especially, mountaineering permitted a particular form of mental control over the body. Bird's collapsing on the way down Long's Peak illustrated the physical demands of the ascent, especially significant because she traveled to escape her spinal complaints (which seemed to surface only when she was at home). This type of willed control of the body to perform exceptional deeds contrasts with a more traditionally feminine way of controlling the body, through sickness, anorexia, neurasthenia, or even through wearing corsets. The medical discourses of the Victorian period, which "proved" women's weaker bodily structure and their resulting limited intellectual capacities,[50] feminized suffering itself, to the extent that overcoming suffering through arduous mountaineering might have had more discursive purchase for women climbers than men climbers.

Thus, Bird's achieving a grand view and claiming Estes Park as her "own" may be best analyzed as a mastering of the *self* rather than of Estes Park. In the context of travel in the American empire, Isabella Bird's claim that "Estes Park is mine—by love, appropriation, and appreciation" more than anything else seems to mark Bird's emotional attachment to place and conquest of her own frailty. Bird frequently located herself emotionally within Rocky Mountain landscapes. At another point in her narrative she described her horseback ride from the St. Vrain Canyon to Longmount, Colorado, through a snowstorm:

> It was simply fearful. It was twilight from the thick snow, and I faced a furious east wind loaded with fine, hard-frozen crystals, which literally made my face bleed. I could only see a very short distance anywhere; the drifts were often two feet deep. . . . I had wrapped up my face, but the sharp, hard snow beat on my eyes—the only exposed part—bringing tears into them, which froze and closed up my eyelids at once. You cannot imagine what that was, I had to take off one glove to pick one eye open, for as the other the storm beat so savagely against it that I left it frozen, and drew over it the double piece of flannel which protected my face. I could hardly keep the other open by picking the ice from it constantly with my numb fingers. . . . It was truly awful at the time.[51]

Bird's triumph over adversity seems to constitute a position of self-empowerment here, which contrasts greatly with both British imperial conquest of place and the image of the "angel in the house" Victorian matron. In this passage Bird emphasizes her pain and suffering but most of all her own endurance. It is *her* eye that she is picking open, which again calls to mind Bird's health problems and a newfound sense of self-control over her body in the Rocky Mountains.

Bird's experiences in the American West, then, might be read as signifying an emotive attachment to place and/or personal empowerment through rugged physical exercise and the overcoming of fear. Tropes of British imperial conquest may be present in her text, but they are not largely cast in the empire-building terms of "domination over" the land (or people). It seems important, then, to acknowledge that the mountainous West enabled a particular kind of relationship to the landscape for Isabella Bird, perhaps in some way complementary to those described by Annette Kolodny.[52] I have not been concerned here with landscape description per se, but it seems clear that a study of gendered subjectivity appearing in imperial discourse, through or outside of landscape description, obviously cannot proceed without close attention to geographical context.

A much different reading of the imperial tropes of adventure and empire emerges from Isabella Bird's *A Lady's Life in the Rocky Mountains*. The West appears in her narrative as a sometimes dangerous place for women and one lacking in more civilized modes of behavior, accommodation, and so forth, tropes that are nonetheless necessary for her to enact transgressive modes of gendered subjectivity. "There's nothing Western folk admire so much as pluck in a woman," she declares.[53] The West serves her as the site of expansive roles for women, usurping, perhaps, Britain's hegemonic role in advancing feminist causes,[54] while again proving its own lack of civilization in the process.

Conclusion

This chapter has illustrated the importance of the epistemic and critical context through which we frame our understandings of exploration and tourism development of the American West—enduring issues raised within the disciplinary context of historical geography. Studying the travel writings of women such as Isabella Bird places in sharp relief the patriarchal, imperial, and capitalistic incentives that worked together, albeit in very different ways, to support *both* men's and women's journeys to the region in the late nineteenth century.

In this chapter I have explored several ways in which the American West served Isabella Bird as a site for aligning herself with conventional bourgeois femininity but also more transgressive forms of gendered subjectivity. In several ways Bird collaborated in and reinforced the ideological work of British imperialism, especially in its nation- and class-based ideologies and rhetorics, and yet her expressions of self-empowerment are unlike the familiar tropes of colonial and imperial discourses.

Bird's text resonates well with late nineteenth-century female liberation and self-empowerment. She advanced into the public sphere, traveling, hiking and mountaineering, writing and publishing books, and so forth. How such modalities of self-empowerment and self-improvement worked through the impulses of empire in the American West is an important question, especially in the ways that such rhetorics articulated with class and national identity. Not surprisingly, the signifying practices of the Victorian bourgeoisie remain at the forefront of her narrative. Writing and sketching (Figure 8.1 is a portrait of Isabella Bird; Figures 8.2–8.3 are her own illustrations) and embracing and taking pleasure in domestic tasks that servants normally performed at home all helped align her with both a superior English identity and genteel femininity. And certainly her mountain excursions lend themselves to an analysis of the gendering of British adventure stories and their specific relationships to empire, especially outside of the context of more "formal" colonial settings. Bird helped rewrite the terms of the Victorian adventure tale, but on her own terms; she asserted her genteel femininity by counterpoising herself against the more active and adventurous Jim Nugent, but at the same time reconstituted where white British bourgeois women might feel at home in the American mountains—even to the extent of guiding the unlucky Mr. Chalmers out of dangerous situations. Although Bird did not explicitly position herself as a feminist, she effectively championed new social spaces for traveling bourgeois women, marking in personal ways the transformative effects of travel and mountaineering. And importantly, such narratives of adventure articulated well with a growing American tourism industry that catered to such privileged international travelers.

FIG. 8.3. Bird's sketch of her panoramic view from the Continental Divide, from *A Lady's Life*, 1879, p. 175. Reproduced courtesy of University of Oklahoma Press.

Notes

1. This chapter is substantially drawn from Karen M. Morin, "Peak Practices: English-women's 'Heroic' Adventures in the Nineteenth-Century American West," *Annals of the Association of American Geographers* 89 (1999): 489–514. Thanks to Blackwell Publishers for granting reprint permission.

2. Jeanne Kay, "Western Women's History," *Journal of Historical Geography* 15 (1989): 302–305; Jeanne Kay, "The Future of Historical Geography in the United States," *Annals of the Association of American Geographers* 80 (1990): 618–621; Jeanne Kay, "Landscapes of Women and Men: Rethinking the Regional Historical Geography of the United States and Canada," *Journal of Historical Geography* 17 (1991): 435–452.

3. For instance, Don Mitchell, *The Lie of the Land: Migrant Workers and the California Landscape* (Minneapolis: University of Minnesota Press, 1996); and *Antipode* 30, no. 2 (1998), and *Ecumene* 5, no. 1 (1998).

4. These include women's relation to landscape and nature, for example, Vera Norwood and Janice Monk, eds., *The Desert Is No Lady: Southwestern Landscapes in Women's Writing and Art* (New Haven, Conn.: Yale University Press, 1987); gendered notions of citizenship and community and the social-spatial constraints involved in the public practice of politics, for example, Meghan Cope, "She Hath Done What She Could: Community, Citizenship, and Place among Women in Late Nineteenth-Century Colorado," *Historical Geography* 26 (1998): 45–64; and Doreen Mattingly, "Gender and Politics of Scale: The Christian Right, Sex Education, and 'Community' in Vista, California, 1990–1994," *Historical Geography* 26 (1998): 65–82. Also see Silvia Lopez Estrada, "Women, Urban Life, and City Images in Tijuana, Mexico," *Historical Geography* 26 (1998): 5–25; and Heather M. Schenker, "Women's and Children's Quarters in Golden Gate Park, San Francisco," *Gender, Place and Culture* 3 (1996): 293–308.

5. See, for instance, Karen M. Morin and Jeanne Kay Guelke, "Strategies of Representation, Relationship, and Resistance: British Women Travelers and Mormon Plural Wives, ca. 1870–1890," *Annals of the Association of American Geographers* 88 (1998): 436–462.

6. For a discussion of the methodological and epistemological frameworks employed by feminist historical geographers of North America in the last decade, see Karen M. Morin and Lawrence D. Berg, "Emplacing Current Trends in Feminist Historical Geography," *Gender, Place and Culture* 6 (1999): 311–330.

7. Isabella L. Bird, *A Lady's Life in the Rocky Mountains* (1879; reprint, Norman: University of Oklahoma Press, 1969).

8. Andrew H. Clark, "Foreword," in Isabella Bird, *The Englishwoman in America* (1856; reprint, Madison: University of Wisconsin Press, 1966), x. For biographical background on Bird, see Dea Birkett, *Spinsters Abroad: Victorian Lady Explorers* (Oxford, U.K.: Basil Blackwell, 1989); Dorothy Middleton, *Victorian Lady Travellers* (1965; reprint, Chicago: Chicago Academy, 1982); Daniel Boorstin, "Introduction," in Isabella L. Bird, *A Lady's Life*, xv–xxiii; and Pat Barr, *A Curious Life for a Lady: The Story of Isabella Bird* (London: Macmillan, 1970). At age fifty Bird married Dr. John Bishop in Edinburgh, a man who had persistently courted her while caring for Bird's dying sister Henrietta. Bird was widowed just five years

later, however, and immediately returned to her traveling life. Although she produced nine popular and well-received travel books, she insisted that "health and pleasure" were her purposes in travel, as well as raising money for missionary hospitals along her routes; see Birkett, *Spinsters Abroad*, 276–277; Boorstin, "Introduction," xx; quote appears in Birkett, *Spinsters Abroad*, 31.

9. Boorstin, "Introduction," xviii–xix.

10. Anne Farrar-Hyde, *An American Vision: Far Western Landscape and National Culture, 1820–1920* (New York: New York University Press, 1990), 147–190.

11. Robert Athearn, *Westward the Briton* (Lincoln: University of Nebraska Press, 1962), 116–125; Richard White, *"It's Your Misfortune and None of My Own": A History of the American West* (Norman: University of Oklahoma Press, 1991), 260–263; Christopher Mulvey, *Anglo-American Landscapes: A Study of 19th-Century Anglo-American Travel Literature* (Cambridge, U.K.: Cambridge University Press, 1983); Christopher Mulvey, *Transatlantic Manners: Social Patterns in Nineteenth-Century Anglo-American Travel Literature* (Cambridge, U.K.: Cambridge University Press, 1990); and Monica Rico, "The Cultural Contexts of International Capital Expansion: British Ranchers in Wyoming, 1879–1889," *Antipode* 30 (1998): 119–134.

12. Athearn, *Westward the Briton*, 118, 120.

13. See, for instance, Karen M. Morin, "Surveying Britain's Informal Empire: Rose Kingsley's 1872 Reconnaissance for the Mexican National Railway," *Historical Geography* 27 (1999): 5–26; and Lucius M. Beebe and Charles M. Clegg, *Narrow Gauge in the Rockies* (Berkeley: Howell-North, 1958).

14. See, for instance, White, *"It's Your Misfortune and None of My Own"*; Patricia Limerick, *The Legacy of Conquest: The Unbroken Past of the American West* (New York: Norton, 1987); Clyde Milner II, Carol A. O'Connor, and Martha A. Sandweiss, eds., *The Oxford Dictionary of the American West* (New York: Oxford University Press, 1994); and Bruce G. Trigger and Wilcomb E. Washburn, *The Cambridge History of the Native Peoples of the Americas*, vol. 1, *North America* (pt. 2) (Cambridge, U.K.: Cambridge University Press, 1996).

15. For example, see Vron Ware, *Beyond the Pale: White Women, Racism and History* (London: Verso, 1992); Nupur Chaudhuri and Margaret Strobel, eds., *Western Women and Imperialism: Complicity and Resistance* (Bloomington: Indiana University Press, 1992); Antoinette Burton, *Burdens of History: British Feminists, Indian Women, and Imperial Culture, 1865–1915* (Chapel Hill: University of North Carolina Press, 1994); and Sara Mills, *Discourses of Difference: An Analysis of Women's Travel Writing and Colonialism* (London: Routledge, 1991).

16. See, for instance, Martha M. Allen, *Traveling West: 19th-Century Women on the Overland Routes* (El Paso: Texas Western Press, 1987); Athearn, *Westward the Briton*; and Karen M. Morin, "Trains through the Plains: The Great Plains Landscapes of Victorian Women Travelers," *Great Plains Quarterly* 18 (1998): 235–256.

17. Bird, *A Lady's Life*, 45.

18. Ibid., 46.

19. Ibid., 40–43.

20. Ibid., 69.

21. Ibid., 73, 124.

22. Ibid., 124, her italics.

23. Ibid., 44–45.

24. Ibid., 45, 47.

25. Ibid., 124.

26. See Sarah Deutsch, *No Separate Refuge: Culture, Class, and Gender on an Anglo-Hispanic Frontier in the American Southwest, 1880–1940* (New York: Oxford University Press, 1987); and Esther N. Glenn, "From Servitude to Service Work: Historical Continuities in the Racial Division of Paid Reproductive Labor," in *Unequal Sisters: A Multicultural History Reader in U.S. Women's History,* eds. Vicky L. Ruiz and Ellen C. DuBois (New York: Routledge, 1994), 405–435.

27. Patricia Thomson, *The Victorian Heroine, a Changing Ideal 1837–73* (London: Oxford University Press, 1956); Richard Phillips, *Mapping Men and Empire: A Geography of Adventure* (London: Routledge, 1997); and Kimberly Reynolds and Nicola Humble, *Victorian Heroines: Representations of Femininity in Nineteenth-Century Literature and Art* (London: Harvester Wheatsheaf, 1993).

28. Phillips, *Mapping Men and Empire,* 68–69; also see Gerry Kearns, "The Imperial Subject: Geography and Travel in the Work of Mary Kingsley and Halford Mackinder," *Transactions of the Institute of British Geographers* 22 (1997): 450–472.

29. See Margaret Strobel, *European Women and the Second British Empire* (Bloomington: Indiana University Press, 1991); Chaudhuri and Strobel, *Western Women and Imperialism;* and Helen Callaway, *Gender, Culture and Empire: European Women in Colonial Nigeria* (London: Macmillan, 1987).

30. Bird, *A Lady's Life,* 58.

31. Ibid., 60, 62.

32. See, for instance, Birkett, *Spinsters Abroad;* and Mary Russell, *The Blessings of a Good Thick Skirt* (London: Collins, 1986).

33. After Phillips, *Mapping Men and Empire,* 103.

34. The extent of this is discussed by Athearn, *Westward the Briton;* Richard L. Rapson, *Britons View America: Travel Commentary, 1860–1935* (Seattle: University of Washington Press, 1971); and Earl Pomeroy, *In Search of the Golden West: The Tourist in Western America* (1957; reprint, Lincoln: University of Nebraska Press, 1990).

35. See, for instance, White, *"It's Your Misfortune and None of My Own,"* 260–263.

36. Bird, *A Lady's Life,* 104.

37. As defined, for instance, by Mills, *Discourses of Difference.*

38. Bird, *A Lady's Life*, 83–101. Much has been made of Bird's romantic association with the "notorious" Jim Nugent. See Birkett, *Spinsters Abroad*, 55–58; Barr, *A Curious Life for a Lady*, 60–90; and Jane Robinson, *Wayward Women: A Guide to Women Travellers* (New York: Oxford University Press, 1990), 81–82.

39. Bird, *A Lady's Life*, 98.

40. Mary Louise Pratt, *Imperial Eyes: Travel Writing and Transculturation* (London: Routledge, 1992).

41. Ibid., 201–202.

42. Mills, *Discourses of Difference*, 78–79; also see Kearns, "The Imperial Subject," 457–459.

43. Pratt, *Imperial Eyes*, 213.

44. Mills, *Discourses of Difference*; Alison Blunt, "Mapping Authorship and Authority: Reading Mary Kingsley's Landscape Descriptions," in *Writing Women and Space: Colonial and Postcolonial Geographies*, eds. Alison Blunt and Gillian Rose (New York: Guilford Press, 1994), 51–72.

45. Blunt, "Mapping Authorship and Authority," 63–67.

46. Bird, *A Lady's Life*, 94, 99.

47. Ibid., 100.

48. See, for instance, Phillips, *Mapping Men and Empire*; Geoffrey J. Martin and Preston E. James, *All Possible Worlds: A History of Geographical Ideas*, 3d ed. (New York: John Wiley & Sons, 1993).

49. Farrar-Hyde, *An American Vision*, 120–130.

50. Callaway, *Gender, Culture and Empire*; Martha Vincinus, ed., *Suffer and Be Still: Women in the Victorian Age* (Bloomington: Indiana University Press, 1972).

51. Bird, *A Lady's Life*, 233–234.

52. Annette Kolodny, *The Lay of the Land: Metaphor as Experience and History in American Life and Letters* (Chapel Hill: University of North Carolina Press, 1975); and Annette Kolodny, *The Land before Her: Fantasy and Experience of the American Frontier, 1630–1860* (Chapel Hill: University of North Carolina Press, 1984).

53. Bird, *A Lady's Life*, 19.

54. Burton, *Burdens of History*.

PART 3

THE WEST AS VISIONARY PLACE

What we will see in these essays is that the myth of the West is composed of equal parts fact and fiction, and that it depends on both for its durability.

—CHRIS BRUCE

9 | The Return of the One-Armed Bandit

Gambling and the West

PAULIINA RAENTO

When the Western adventurer James Butler "Wild Bill" Hickok was shot dead at a poker table in Deadwood, South Dakota, in 1876, he became a legend. His death immortalized the combination of cards he was holding when the bullet hit him; the black pairs of aces and eights became known as the "Dead Man's Hand."[1] The legend of Wild Bill's life and death also contributed to the immortalization of the myth of the Western gambler—that of a mysterious, solitary man who took risks and lived glamorously on the edge in the rowdy frontier towns of nineteenth-century America.

Although the reality was often considerably less glamorous than the myth portrays, the gambler nevertheless came to symbolize much of the entrepreneurial, individualistic mentality that created the American West as a distinctive place. Since Wild Bill's days, both the frontier and the average gambler have been tamed, and gambling has become a multibillion-dollar leisure industry controlled by multinational corporations. Despite this transformation, gambling has not lost its essentially "Western" frontier flavor. Over the evolutionary course of American gambling from the sixteenth century to the present, this flavor has become global in a manner that is reshaping the contemporary West and its frontiers in a new, most fascinating way.

Gambling and the Frontier

American gambling was born as a frontier activity. From its onset in the sixteenth-century eastern and southern colonies to its nineteenth-century establishment in the West, gambling's fortunes oscillated from a widely accepted form of fund-raising and recreation to a morally condemned vice. During these centuries, however, gambling consolidated its ties to the values characteristic of frontier societies.

In the first colonies, gambling represented social mores that the settlers transplanted from their native lands. Following the English example, lottery soon became an institutionalized and popular—although criticized—form of collecting a "voluntary tax," of raising funds for large construction projects in colonial cities. The model of large-scale public lotteries was modified, however, to serve the requirements of the new setting. In these nascent communities, the lotteries were most often private business initiatives that supported singular, local projects. Gradually, these modifications made gambling one way to distance the colonies and their distinctive, adventurous identity from the ties to the Old World. The risk taking inherent in gambling contributed to this identity by paralleling "the chance undertaken in the larger enterprise of the movement across the Atlantic and into a new continent."[2]

An example that reflects the ties between gambling and the values associated with frontier societies and their distinctive, "new" culture and identity is quarter horse racing among the Virginian gentry in the eighteenth century. In these heated, socially exclusive and carefully regulated spectacles involving substantial economic risks, the gentlemen transformed central elements of their culture into action. The racing and its gambling relationships symbolized the local society's strongly individualistic, competitive, and materialistic values. It also helped to maintain class cohesion and erase tensions in the context of rapid social change.[3]

After the American Revolution, the nation's attention turned toward the West. In this rapidly evolving general context of risk taking and adventure, gambling gained volume and acceptance. In the early nineteenth century, however, criticism against new, commercial forms of gambling was on the rise. As new ideas swept across the increasingly heterogeneous country and as many settlements sought and gained respectability, gambling was attacked with vigor. Private betting for recreational purposes was still tolerated, but professional gamblers and organized lotteries were considered corrupted and exploitative. The increasingly loud public campaign against gambling led to the banning of lotteries in every state of the Union by 1860.[4]

The second phase of early American gambling began in the aftermath of the Civil War. In the physical and moral devastation following the war, economic necessity brought gambling back as a means to raise funds, especially in the South. A more important catalyst for the dispersion of gambling was the rapid westward movement of the frontier. In the new settlements along the rivers and, later, railroads, a new species of professional gambler emerged. His trade matched the risk-oriented, entrepreneurial atmosphere of these settlements: They were full of people who had opted for taking their chances in a virgin environment, hoping to make a quick profit with a sudden strike of luck. The movement to the West and gambling shared "high expectations, risk taking, opportunism and movement."[5] Again, gambling was a form of behavior that reflected and expressed the society's values.[6] Gambling was also a natural form of entertainment in settings where few recreational options were available (Figure 9.1).

In this process, American gambling gained new openness that gave its Western form a unique and historically influential flavor. An increasingly

FIG. 9.1. Indians gambling in Reno in the early twentieth century. Gambling was one of the few forms of entertainment available in the modest settlements of the early West. Courtesy Nevada Historical Society.

commercial and public character of gambling led to the introduction of poker, craps, faro, and other new games that soon gained popularity (Figure 9.2). They also supported the institutionalization of gambling because they were particularly suitable for casino settings, the first of which had emerged in the 1820s.[7] The gold and silver rushes throughout the West created conditions that sealed gambling's essence as a frontier activity. Refinement of the forms and settings of gambling and its wild popularity in the rowdy mining camps gave the gambler a notorious and romantic role in the popular imagery of the Wild West. Through legends, popular fiction, and, later, through the film industry, the gambler became a larger-than-life character with an independent

FIG. 9.2. Faro, craps, and roulette were among the most popular games of the early gambling halls and casinos. Courtesy Nevada Historical Society.

status among the Western fauna. The gambler thus became one of the constituents of the American West as a mythical place in the young nation's consciousness.[8]

As Western settlements became more established and sought to refine their character, the frontier's defining elements had to go. The gambler and his way of life, one that centered on making quick profit with little labor, again came to epitomize the morally detestable and to represent a threat to economic growth and hometown values. Antigambling sentiments became more vocal again, particularly in California. Despite the introduction of legal sanctions, gambling flourished in the railroad towns and mining camps throughout the West, and stiff antigambling laws were not enforced until the early 1900s. By 1910, antigambling sentiments had gained enough strength in the national context of Progressivism to outlaw gambling everywhere.[9] However, "gambling often continued in the open" in places like Nevada,[10] where many gamblers had found a liberal haven already in the nineteenth century.

The Gambler's Haven

No state's reputation in relation to gambling parallels that of Nevada. Gambling had long roots in Nevada's eighteenth-century mining and railroad towns, characterized by liberal attitudes toward drinking, gambling, and prostitution. During a prolonged mining depression in the 1880s, gambling's license fees were a welcome contribution to the local economy. Then, in the context of the Great Depression, Nevada quite naturally turned to legal gambling as a means to generate revenue. The motives behind the legalization of full-blown casino gambling in 1931 were primarily economic. The previously lucrative mining industry continued to decline, but the sparsely populated desert state had few economic alternatives. In addition, despite the predominant Progressivist ideals in the 1920s, Nevada had continued to provide the rest of the nation with services that were illegal or difficult to obtain elsewhere. Revenue and national attention were gained particularly through prizefighting and quickie divorces. This had rendered the local social climate more permissive toward gambling.[11] The state's demographic and cultural profile also played a role: A high proportion of males in the overall population, low church membership, and the strong individualism, materialism, and transient lifestyle of miners and ranchers "created a specific society that could be open to legal experimentation with social forms outlawed elsewhere."[12]

Nevada's liberal attitude soon attracted outlawed gamblers from all over the country, most notably from California and Texas. These men brought in the capital and know-how necessary for the development of Nevada gambling. The growth of gambling in Las Vegas, a modest whistle stop along the railroad in southern Nevada, was further aided by the construction of the Hoover (Boulder) Dam in the 1930s. The effort attracted growing numbers of visitors to the "Gateway to the World's Greatest Engineering Project."[13] Another boost was stimulated by federal investments and military activity in the area before and during World War II.[14] At this time, however, Las Vegans as well as other Nevadans still saw gambling as supplementary to their economy and as merely one part of their Western heritage.

The years following World War II marked a significant transformation in the recreational behavior of Americans. The improved accessibility with the construction of the interstate highways brought the West closer to the rest of the nation, which now had more money and time for leisure than ever before. The West was an attractive destination because it represented the shared, adventurous past in the national identity. Furthermore, the war effort had launched a rapid economic and demographic growth of the region known as the Sunbelt, and particularly of southern California.[15] This growth tied Las Vegas's emerging tourism economy to the Angeleno orbit. The Californian gamblers who now resided in Nevada tapped into this expanding market. Much of the necessary capital came from the Chicago underworld, which understood the economic opportunities offered by the new regional development in the West.

This development produced the new resort-casino on the Los Angeles Highway, "the Strip," that stretched from downtown Las Vegas toward California. The new resorts were tailored to attract a wealthy urban clientele who wanted to be pampered in a desert oasis equipped with casino games, swimming pools, fancy dining halls, and golf courses. The milestone was the opening of the gangster Benjamin "Bugsy" Siegel's Flamingo in 1946 (Figure 9.3).[16] It challenged the imagination with "all the new electrochemical pastels of the Florida littoral" never seen before in the desert and with neon signs that "fizzed all eight stories up into the desert sky all night long like an illuminated whisky-soda tumbler filled to the brim with pink champagne,"[17] thus drawing a highlighted "boundary between the hostile physical environment and the wonders of its man-made oases."[18] The new resort attracted a wealthy middle-class clientele who wished to rub shoulders with glamorous Hollywood celebrities and notorious underworld figures in an unimaginable set-

FIG. 9.3. An oasis in the desert. The Flamingo opened in Las Vegas in 1946 and soon transformed the concept of hotel-casino design. Courtesy Nevada Historical Society.

ting. Thus, the Flamingo triggered Las Vegas's shift away from being a local and regional intimacy toward becoming a nationally recognized gambling and entertainment destination. "The town became a distillation of postwar California culture and a combination of fun, sun, and opportunity that drove the state and eventually national popular culture."[19]

By the mid-1950s, the intended supplement to mining had become the predominant segment of Nevada's economy. Las Vegas was now the economic and political power center of the state.[20] The rapidly growing city had earned a notorious reputation as America's "Sin City," and it was frequently described as a "safe haven for organized crime" and a "hell on earth"[21]—"the final destination for those willing to drive halfway across America in search of the nation's only morality car wash."[22] This reputation added to the national attention and lure of Las Vegas at the same time when gambling was becoming an increasingly accepted form of recreation and business.

Several factors contributed to making Nevada's approach America's approach.

First, beginning in the 1940s, Nevada casinos advertised themselves all over the country. To conform to local advertising regulations, the content of the ads downplayed gambling and stressed Nevada's attractive and inexpensive recreational amenities and atmosphere. This emphasis made gambling appear more acceptable for the consuming middle classes. Gambling also became more "democratic" due to the broadening of the socioeconomic composition of the clientele.[23]

Second, the increased state and federal intervention into Nevada gambling improved gambling's image. To end organized crime's influence in Nevada, the state crafted new laws and imposed stricter control over the industry, thus drawing further attention toward the state. To further consolidate gambling as a legitimate business among others and to dilute its notorious image, the new regulatory bodies, the Nevada Gaming Control Board (1955) and the Nevada Gaming Commission (1959), replaced references to *gambling* with the term *gaming*.

Third, the passing of the federal Corporate Gaming Act in 1967 (revised in 1969) had a considerable impact on the nature of the industry. The act allowed large corporations to enter the gaming industry without having to submit each stockholder to a background check. Howard Hughes, Kirk Kerkorian, and other respectable investors entered the market, contributing to the dramatic rise of capital available in the industry. As banks began to see gaming enterprises as a safe investment and as many of the large corporations were well established and traded publicly, the industry's ownership broadened. Considerable credibility was added to gambling's image in the eyes of the more conventional business community.

Fourth, the steady growth of revenue drew attention from the media, which often portrayed gaming as any other business. The growth of the industry also created jobs and brought educational and industry interests together to guarantee a steady supply of casino workers, thus making the gaming industry a player in "normal" life. As a result, both the federal government's review committees and the general public saw Nevada gaming as an increasingly acceptable part of the American economic and recreational landscape.[24] A further improvement in accessibility, that is, the jet plane, also drew new travelers toward Nevada. Californians still formed the majority of car travelers to Las Vegas in the 1970s, but Midwesterners became the largest geographic group of Las Vegas visitors, and Californians now accounted for only one-third of the total visitation.[25] That Las Vegas's appeal "had become truly national"[26] paved the way for the return of the one-armed bandit to the national limelight—for the exportation of gambling from its Western haven back to the East and across the entire nation.

Diffusion of a Western Phenomenon

"The Americanization of Nevada gambling"[27] and the gaming industry's lucrative profits made casinos attractive in the eyes of urban developers and policymakers who searched for economic options for their communities. The first state to take its chances with the gaming industry was New Jersey, which legalized casino gambling in 1976.[28] The opening of the first casinos in Atlantic City, in 1978, marked the beginning of the gaming industry's rapid expansion across America. Lotteries and pari-mutuel betting were already available in many states, but those who wanted to gamble in casinos still had to travel to Nevada or New Jersey in 1988. Soon afterward, riverboat casinos returned to the Mississippi River, and small mining towns in the Rocky Mountains turned to gaming as a means to stimulate their tourism. At the same time, high-stakes bingos and casinos were opened on Indian reservations, especially in the Midwest and the West. By 1999, twenty-seven states had some kind of casino within their boundaries, and all forms of gambling remained illegal only in Utah and Hawaii. The nine Western states that have casinos have more gambling space (over 11 million square feet) than the rest of the country combined (over 9.3 million square feet). Nevada dominates the West, however: The gambling space in its casinos (almost 6.5 million square feet) is roughly one-third more than that in the other Western states combined (Map 9.1).[29] Naturally, much of the initial know-how and capital necessary for the new enterprises in other states was exported from Nevada, particularly from Las Vegas.

Gambling's popularity and revenue rose rapidly. By 1990, American casinos attracted 46 million visitors. In five years, the number rose to 154 million,

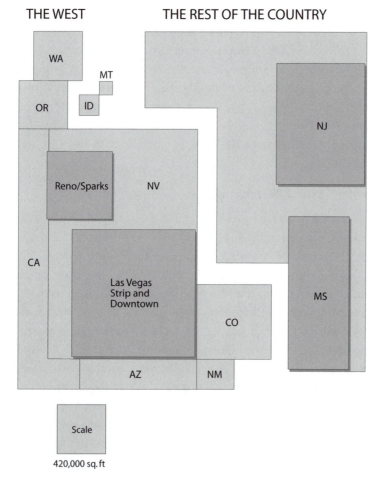

Map 9.1. The West versus the rest. Casino gambling space in the Western states and in the rest of the country in 1998. *Casino Business Directory 1999: North America* (Reno: Nevada Gaming Publishing, 1999); *Nevada Gaming Almanac 1999* (Reno: Nevada Gaming Publishing, 1999).

which was more than the visitation to major league baseball games or Broadway shows.[30] The gaming industry made a profit of roughly $54 billion in 1998, which was almost twice as much as ten years earlier (Figure 9.4).[31] According to one estimate, all residents of the coterminous United States now live within a five-hour drive from the nearest casino.[32]

In this process, what had been for almost fifty years exclusively a "Western" activity was established all over the country. Again, despite the fierce debate over moral issues,[33] gambling seemed to match the predominant value structures of postindustrial American society of the 1980s and 1990s. Gambling also went through yet another transformation of form and setting. Most importantly, it was now the one-armed bandit, the slot machine—first introduced in the 1870s—that was the most popular form of recreational gambling (Figure 9.5) and a key in making gambling a multibillion-dollar industry. In popular imagery, however, gambling still carried a flavor of individualism and materialism, and it was associated with thrilling notoriety and glamour. Having penetrated the leisure of ordinary Americans, it was now more popular and more widely accepted—and more "democratic"—than ever before. In this process of dispersion and transformation, gambling also created new frontiers—new transitional zones of political, cultural, and economic contact. In particular, it created new opportunities and dilemmas that now reshape the American West. Three cases exemplify this development.

Indian Gaming

The first shift in the course of modern Western history in relation to gambling is the case of Indian gaming. In 1979, the Seminole tribe in southern Florida opened a high-stakes bingo in its reservation and successfully defended it in a local court. A similar case that was the first to reach the Supreme Court was the legal battle between the state of California and the Cabazon Mission Indians. The landmark ruling in 1987 let the Cabazons keep their gambling enterprise on the grounds that because the state allowed other forms of gambling in its territory, any restrictions could be only regulatory in nature under the civil law. Only a year later, Congress passed the Indian Gaming Regulatory Act (IGRA) following this principle. The act made Indian gaming possible in all those states that had tribal lands and some form of legal gaming. Subsequently, gaming enterprises emerged rapidly in the reservations in the context of little competition. Indian gaming now accounts for an estimated 10–15 percent of the gaming industry's annual win.[34] It is particularly significant in the Western and the Midwestern states because 85 percent

Millions
of dollars

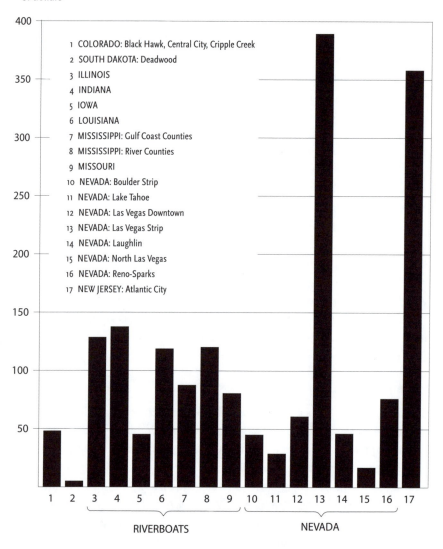

400 ─

1 COLORADO: Black Hawk, Central City, Cripple Creek
2 SOUTH DAKOTA: Deadwood
350 ─ 3 ILLINOIS
4 INDIANA
5 IOWA
6 LOUISIANA
300 ─ 7 MISSISSIPPI: Gulf Coast Counties
8 MISSISSIPPI: River Counties
9 MISSOURI
10 NEVADA: Boulder Strip
250 ─ 11 NEVADA: Lake Tahoe
12 NEVADA: Las Vegas Downtown
13 NEVADA: Las Vegas Strip
14 NEVADA: Laughlin
200 ─ 15 NEVADA: North Las Vegas
16 NEVADA: Reno-Sparks
17 NEW JERSEY: Atlantic City

150 ─

100 ─

50 ─

    1   2   3   4   5   6   7   8   9   10   11   12   13   14   15   16   17

                 └──────────────────────────┘ └────────────────────────────┘
                         RIVERBOATS   NEVADA

FIG. 9.4. Where the money is made. Monthly casino gross revenue in the United States, October 1999. The figures exclude Indian gaming enterprises because they do not usually publish their revenue. *Casino Journal* 13, no. 2 (2000): 88–89.

Fig. 9.5. "One armed bandits." The ancestor of today's slot machines and video lottery terminals (VLTS) was created in the 1870s. In the first casinos of Las Vegas, it was hidden in the corner to entertain the wives of the "serious" (that is, male) gamblers. John M. Findlay, *People of Chance: Gambling in American Society from Jamestown to Las Vegas* (New York: Oxford University Press, 1986), 149. By the 1990s, slot machines and VLTS had taken over the casinos and invaded gas stations, grocery stores, and convenience markets in many states. In the nine Western casino states, there were roughly 217,000 slot machines or VLTS in 1998. This means that the West hosts roughly one slot machine per 270 residents. *Casino Business Directory 1999; Nevada Gaming Almanac 1999; 1999 City and County Extra* (Washington, D.C.: Bernan, 1999), p. 80. Courtesy Nevada Historical Society.

of all reservations are located west of the Mississippi River, and in fourteen states in the East there are no tribal lands.[35] In 1998, over one-half of the roughly two hundred Indian casinos in the United States were located in the West.

All Western states except Utah had some form of Indian gaming by 1999 (Wyoming had only bingo) (Map 9.2). Most of these enterprises are in California, Arizona, and Washington, which also host the highest number of reservations. Particularly suitable for the opening of a gaming enterprise have been those reservations that lie close to sizeable potential markets, that is, large urban centers such as San Diego or Seattle, and whose size, demographic composition, and internal political atmosphere have supported the running of a large business.[36] Both the geographic distribution and economic success of tribal casinos are thus uneven. Gaming has brought better life to many tribes, but some lack these opportunities. This has created a new inequality among the tribes.

The successful Indian gaming enterprises have generated revenue, created jobs, and made the tribes more independent in their relationship with the federal government. New economic independence has given these tribes more political power and autonomy, thus enhancing their sovereignty within American federalism. At the same time, increased tourism in tribal lands has led to new cultural contacts with the majority population and thus renegotiated previously established cultural and social boundaries. For the tribal governments, the new economic, political, and cultural status and contacts have created new dilemmas. Fears about a loss of tribal heritage and way of life have come to the fore, and the relationship between economic interests and the impact of "cultural contamination" has led to controversy. As the establishment of new properties has intensified competition in the gaming market, tribal leaders have faced dilemmas of expansion and management. In this light, the "New Buffalo," as Indian gaming has been called, does not represent an automatic solution to Native American problems. It has nevertheless brought more visibility and independence to Native Americans. It has also created novel forms of interaction between the federal, state, and tribal authorities and among the tribes themselves. In this way, gaming has contributed to the rewriting of the "legacy of conquest."[37]

The expansion of Indian gaming in California is currently shuffling the gaming industry's layout in the West. In March of 2000, California voters approved Proposition 1A, thus putting the existing Indian gaming compacts into effect. The new legal status and the subsequent prospects of expansion

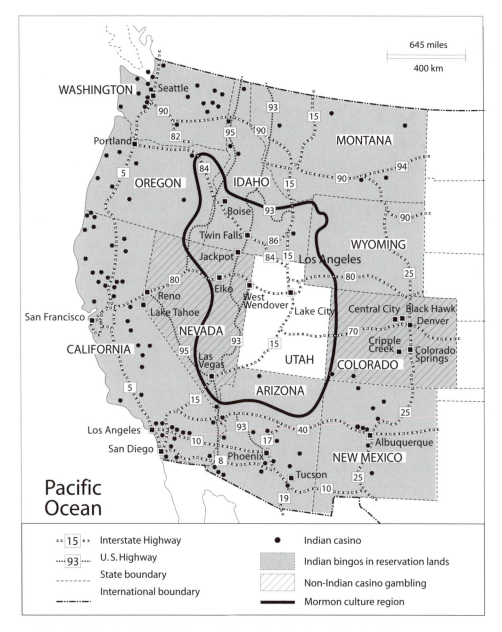

MAP 9.2. Gaming in the West, 1998. *International Gaming & Wagering Business* 20, no. 9 (1999): 42; *1999 American Casino Guide* (Dania: Casino Vacations, 1999).

attracted investors from all over the country. In addition to economic fortunes, the process enhanced Native American visibility in state politics. For example, in 1998 three tribes were among California's ten largest campaign contributors to legislators.[38] In Las Vegas and Reno, Nevada's principal gaming cities, it is expected that some of their previous customers will stay closer to home at the new or expanded Indian gaming enterprises.[39]

Gambling in Colorado

Issues of local government and community impact have also touched three small Rocky Mountain mining towns in Colorado. In the late 1980s, Black Hawk, Central City, and Cripple Creek argued that casino gaming could revitalize their declining economies. The argument focused on creating revenue for the restoration of the towns' historic buildings and on this restoration's beneficial impact on local tourism appeal. The pro-gaming lobbyists drew heavily from the example of Deadwood, South Dakota, where limited-stakes gambling had opened successfully in 1989. After a short campaign, gambling was legalized in the three Colorado towns in 1990, and the first casinos opened in October of 1991, with limited-stakes poker, blackjack, and slot machines.[40]

Crucial in the introduction of gambling in these three mining towns was their historic "gambling attitude"[41] that evolved from taking chances with nature to mining gold from the pockets of casino customers. Since the first days of the Colorado gold rushes in the nineteenth century, the mining industry conditioned the development of Black Hawk, Central City, and Cripple Creek. Its riches rapidly transformed the towns from rough camps (with prominent gambling) into more refined centers of economic, political, and cultural importance to the entire state. In addition to nature, their oscillating fortunes were determined by a larger social context—by technological changes, market trends, and governmental decisions at the state and federal levels. Regional elements, such as the early development of tourism in Colorado and the demographic growth of the nearby cities, played a significant role as well.[42] The introduction of the gaming industry thus followed a long-established pattern of thinking and matched the predominant value structures in these local communities. The willingness to take yet another chance with quick economic improvements drew heavily from the local appreciation of risk taking. Again, the towns' fortunes were influenced by larger contexts—by the spread and transformation of the gaming industry, by the novel public and governmental attitudes toward gambling, and by the rapid growth of Colorado's tourism appeal.

The material components of the Western heritage in these three towns were equally important in the adoption of gaming. The recreational resources of Black Hawk, Central City, and Cripple Creek resided exclusively in their nineteenth-century architecture, listed in the National Historic Landmark registry, and in their old cultural image, both in need of restoration. Subsequently, 28 percent of the gaming revenue was directed to historic preservation.[43] The goal was to re-create an "authentically Western" sense of place, which the towns' past and present gambling complemented as an "added attraction"[44] in an architectonically and historically sound environment. The effort was tied in with the nationally growing market of heritage tourism and with Colorado's increasingly multifaceted appeal as a recreational destination. In this context, the three towns claimed to offer an authentic and exciting trip to the nation's past, with all the necessary modern services of entertainment, food, drink, and accommodation.

Revenues and taxes generated by the Colorado casinos were much more than ever expected from the beginning. The new economic profile and the demands of the in-pouring herds of visitors upheaved the previously quiet life of the three towns (Figure 9.6). The development created pressing needs for new infrastructure, regulations, and administrative services. Real estate prices soared, quotidian services went out of business, and traffic blocked the narrow streets. In addition to economy and landscape, the character of local politics changed dramatically. Many local residents had mixed feelings about the transformation. On the one hand, they welcomed new employment opportunities and activity, but, on the other hand, they felt a profound loss of a small-town sense of place.[45]

Particularly controversial was the manipulation of history for business purposes. The "real" history vanished under "a more sophisticated, sanitized version"[46] portrayed in the marketing and public events of the three towns. The reproduction of the West in Colorado thus faced the dilemma between preservation and "commodification of the past"[47] and other problems related to the development of heritage tourism (Figure 9.7). Most paradoxically, the growth of the Colorado gaming industry put additional pressure on the preservation effort. In many cases, the industry's interests collided with those of the conservationists, creating unsatisfactory compromises and schisms that harmed both the economic development and the preservation. Ironically, "it is this very source of income for historic preservation that also destroys a larger part of the locale."[48]

Fig. 9.6. The introduction of gaming in the small Rocky Mountain mining towns in Colorado meant an enormous transformation of their previously quiet quotidian life. On Main Street in Black Hawk, the historic Lace House witnesses the continuous bus traffic to, and from, the town's largest casinos, which all emerged in the late 1990s. The signs of the town's mining booms are still visible in the surrounding slopes. Photo by author.

The Response of Las Vegas

For Las Vegas, the new competition posed a challenge even before Indian gaming spread across California. The city had to find new ways to keep attracting customers for whom gambling was now available closer to home. The initial approach in the 1980s emphasized family entertainment, but this "disneyfication"[49] of Sin City failed to meet expectations—gambling was not for kids. By the 1990s, the focus had shifted toward emphasizing luxury, exclusivity, and uniqueness for those who could afford it. A milestone comparable to the opening of Bugsy Siegel's Flamingo in the 1940s was the opening of casino developer Steve Wynn's The Mirage on the Strip in 1989 (Figure 9.8). With its emphasis on fantasy, topped with white tigers, an artificial

Fig. 9.7. Western history in the service of the tourism industry. Wild Bill Hickok's spirit lives on in Deadwood, South Dakota, the small gambling town in the Black Mountains where the famous adventurer was shot in 1876. An impersonator entertains tourists on Main Street. Photo by author.

FIG. 9.8. The Mirage launched Las Vegas's megaproperty era in 1989. Ten years later, the Venetian, a detailed replica of the best-known sights of the famous Italian city, was opened across the street. Photo by author.

volcano, and traces of a tropical paradise, The Mirage was "both reflective and transcendent of the [previous] desert theme, usher[ing] in the era of the megaproperty."⁵⁰ With its entertainment, shopping, and fine-dining ameni-ties, Wynn's casino "embodied the essence of what Las Vegas could offer a tourist: it invented a reality that only rarely required the suspension of dis-belief."⁵¹

The new development did not abandon the city's "democratic" character as an entertainment mecca for everybody, but it represented a distinctive layer of Las Vegas, targeted at conventioneers, wealthy American baby boomers, and foreign tourists. Following The Mirage's concept, convention facilities, shop-ping and gourmet-dining amenities, golf courses, and large, lavish hotel-casi-nos were built rapidly. These megaproperties (which are among the largest hotels in the world) invited their visitors "to explore emblematic world land-marks and travel in time and space"⁵²—to explore beyond conventional bor-ders, boundaries, and frontiers.⁵³ Accordingly, the new architecture and the resorts' amenities were carefully designed to resemble the wonders of the world's most powerful cities and sights, their history and culture (Figure 9.9). The strategy worked: Las Vegas became the nation's most popular convention city, and the proportion of foreign visitors of the total annual visitation of 34 million people rose from 10 to 17 percent between 1994 and 1997.⁵⁴

Las Vegas successfully outimagined its competitors, thanks to vast re-sources and its experience and reputation in the gaming and entertainment business. In the context in which gambling is a national pastime and accessi-ble to virtually every American adult, Las Vegas is the only truly national des-tination. Whereas local and regional customers form the bulk of the visitation to other American gaming destinations, Las Vegas's market area still covers the entire country. For many, it is the one and the only gambling town and the only place that offers a holistic, excitingly escapist entertainment experience.⁵⁵ Las Vegas has a unique identity, image, and reputation as the ultimate frontier in the eyes of thrill-seeking postindustrial middle-class Americans. Many of them are perhaps now more likely to take off on a gambling pilgrimage to the West because they have become more familiar with the art of gambling at home. Indeed, factors such as image and reputation are becoming increas-ingly important in distinguishing the destinations from one another in the saturating market.⁵⁶

Las Vegas has also managed to profile itself as a "positively deranged" and exciting international travel destination that offers good-quality service and a wide selection of amenities. Most importantly, Las Vegas's appeal as "the

Fig. 9.9. An exotic port of call somewhere in the Caribbean? The exterior design of the Treasure Island hotel-casino exemplifies how careful attention to detail creates a credible sense of place in the Las Vegas entertainment landscape. Photo by author.

planetary gambling capital"[57] is closely tied to the new, sophisticated prominence of the American West in international tourism. In this context, Las Vegas the entertainment mecca forms an attractive triangle with the Grand Canyon ("God's Las Vegas that displays the world's most fabulous geology"), and Los Angeles, which has recently emerged as the Western center of "high culture" and art.[58]

This global popularity points to Hollywood's (and, more generally, southern California's) continuous influence on the appeal of Las Vegas and in the making of the American West as a mythical place in the popular imagination. Throughout their evolution, and particularly since the late twentieth century, southern Californian cities have been hot spots of human interaction and innovation. Through the advancement of communication technology and the globalization of the media, the notorious, glamorous gamblers of the evolving Western frontiers have left a permanent imprint on millions and millions of

minds across the world. With the increasing ease of global travel, these mythical characters and the settings of their adventures created and re-created by
Hollywood's entertainment industry also became accessible in a new way. Las
Vegas's primary association, however, is no longer with the rowdy frontiersmen or the notorious underworld glamour. Instead, their legendary play-
ground has now brought the wonders of the world together in one place by
means of its themed architecture, dining and shopping facilities, and visitors.
By doing so, Las Vegas has once again contributed a new phase to the innovative and international frontier character of the American West. In the process,
the West has become a global place, and its example is imitated in casinos
throughout the world.

Conclusions

The advancements of communication technology have had a considerable
impact on the diffusion and image of American gambling. Gambling first
made its voyage from the Old World to North America's eastern shores. It
was adapted to the new environment, and it reached the "last frontier" in the

FIG. 9.10. The themed architecture in Las Vegas offers fantasy travel in both time and
space. The Luxor Las Vegas hotel-casino's pyramid contains 4,400 rooms. It is the
fourth-largest pyramid in the world. Photo by author.

West with the westward movement along the rivers and railroads. Gamblers found their home in the nineteenth-century gold rush settings, settling in Nevada when they were outlawed elsewhere. Gambling's evolution in Nevada sealed its role as an essential constituent of the popular imagery of the modern West, paving the way to gambling's dispersion across the country in the recent decades. The introduction of gambling enterprises in Indian reservations, urban centers, and small towns brought along a considerable change in their local economies, politics, cultures, and atmospheres. As the one-armed bandit took over the East and became uniquely popular throughout the West, and as the new gambling towns struggled with primarily local and regional issues, the birthplace of modern gambling in Nevada took the activity—and the American West—yet another step further. In the era of the jet plane and the globalization of American popular culture, the appeal and image of the last American frontier became truly global.

The historic Western flavor of many new gambling enterprises is hardly recognizable or is nonexistent. Even the most Italianate of the new Las Vegas properties, however, contributes to the reproduction of the essence of the American West. Most importantly, the new popularity of gambling and the West reproduces those values that were central in the making of modern America. Today's gambling represents the land of opportunity and the legacy of the individual entrepreneurship and opportunism of Wild Bill Hickok, Bugsy Siegel, and, later, the corporate investors such as Howard Hughes, Kirk Kerkorian, and Steve Wynn. Without this legacy, and without Hollywood's conquest of the world, the travel destinations in the American West would not be as appealing to a global audience as they now are. Again, the American West attracts people from all over the world to take their chances with luck and the prospects of prosperity. That it is now "fun" reflects the profound transformation of Western society, the frontier, and the form and appearance of gambling, but the original excitement and dream are intact. As an outcome of the extravagant return of the one-armed bandit to the national spotlight from decades from oblivion, and American popular culture's conquest of the world, the West has reemerged as a mindset and a unique global place for twisting and exploring mental frontiers in the twenty-first century.

Notes

1. Joseph G. Rosa, *Wild Bill Hickok: The Man and His Myth* (Lawrence: University Press of Kansas, 1996), 187–213.

2. John M. Findlay, *People of Chance: Gambling in American Society from Jamestown to Las Vegas* (New York: Oxford University Press, 1986), 15, see 30–33.

3. T. H. Breen, "Horses and Gentlemen: The Cultural Significance of Gambling among the Gentry of Virginia," in *Sport in America,* ed. Donald Spivey (Westport, Conn.: Greenwood, 1985).

4. Findlay, *People of Chance,* 39–42.

5. Ibid., 4.

6. Breen, "Horses and Gentlemen," 19.

7. Findlay, *People of Chance,* 61.

8. James F. Smith, "Where the Action Is: Images of the Gambler in Recent Popular Films," in *Beyond the Stars: Stock Characters in American Popular Film,* eds. Paul Loukides and Linda K. Fuller (Bowling Green: Bowling Green State University Popular Press, 1990); Anne M. Butler, "Selling the Popular Myth," in *The Oxford History of the American West,* eds. Clyde A. Milner II, Carol A. O'Connor, and Martha A. Sandweiss (New York: Oxford University Press, 1994).

9. Philip I. Earl, "Veiling the Tiger: The Crusade against Gambling, 1859–1910," *Nevada Historical Society Quarterly* 29 (1985): 175–204.

10. R. J. Roske, "Gambling in Nevada: The Yearly Years, 1861–1931," *Nevada Historical Society Quarterly* 33 (1990): 36, see 33–35.

11. Ibid., 37. See James W. Hulse, *The Silver State: Nevada's Heritage Reinterpreted,* 2d ed. (Reno: University of Nevada Press, 1998).

12. Jerome E. Edwards, "From Back Alley to Main Street: Nevada's Acceptance of Gambling," *Nevada Historical Society Quarterly* 33 (1990): 18, 19–20.

13. Hal K. Rothman, "Selling the Meaning of Place: Entrepreneurship, Tourism, and Community Transformation in the Twentieth-Century American West," *Pacific Historical Review* 65 (1996): 550.

14. Eugene P. Moehring, "Las Vegas and the Second World War," *Nevada Historical Society Quarterly* 29 (1986): 1–30; Hulse, *The Silver State,* 211–216.

15. Michael Bradshaw, *Regions and Regionalism in the United States* (Jackson: University of Mississippi Press, 1988).

16. James F. Smith, "'Bugsy's Flamingo and the Modern Casino-Hotel," in *Gambling and Public Policy: International Perspectives,* eds. William R. Eadington and Judy A. Cornelius (Reno: Institute for the Study of Gambling and Commercial Gaming, University of Nevada, Reno, 1991).

17. Tom Wolfe, *The Kandy-Kolored Tangerine-Flaked Streamlined Baby* (New York: Farrar, Straus & Giroux, 1965), 10–11.

18. Pauliina Raento and William A. Douglass, "The Naming of Gaming," *Names* 49 (2001): 1–35.

19. Rothman, "Selling the Meaning of Place," 552.

20. Eugene P. Moehring, *Resort City in the Sunbelt: Las Vegas, 1930–1970* (Reno: University of Nevada Press, 1989); James W. Hulse, *The Silver State*, 196.

21. Jerome E. Edwards, "The Americanization of Nevada Gambling," *Halcyon* 14 (1992): 202–203.

22. Nicholas Pileggi, *Casino: Love and Honor in Las Vegas* (New York: Simon & Schuster, 1995), 13.

23. Edwards, "The Americanization of Nevada Gambling," 204.

24. Ibid., 207–213. See Jerome E. Edwards, "Nevada: Gambling and the Federal-State Relationship," *Halcyon* 11 (1989): 237–254.

25. *1998 Las Vegas Visitor Profile Study* (Las Vegas: GLS Research and Las Vegas Convention and Visitors Authority, 1998), 82.

26. Rothman, "Selling the Meaning of Place," 553.

27. Edwards, "The Americanization of Nevada Gambling."

28. George Sternlieb and James W. Hughes, *The Atlantic City Gamble* (Cambridge: Harvard University Press, 1983); John Dombrink and William N. Thompson, *The Last Resort: Success and Failure in Campaigns for Casinos* (Reno: University of Nevada Press, 1990), 25–41.

29. *Casino Business Directory 1999: North America* (Reno: Nevada Gaming Publishing, 1999); *Nevada Gaming Almanac 1999* (Reno: Nevada Gaming Publishing, 1999).

30. *The Harrah's Survey of U.S. Casino Entertainment* (Memphis: Harrah's Casinos, 1994), 11; Jason N. Ader and Christine J. Lumpkins, "Atlantic City: High-Stakes Renaissance," *Bearn Stearns Gaming Industry Equity Research* (27 November 1996): 3.

31. *International Gaming & Wagering Business (IGWB)* 10, no. 8 (1989): 1, and 20, 8 (1999): 17, 25.

32. *International Gaming & Wagering Business (IGWB)* 16, no. 3 (1995): 30.

33. See William R. Eadington, "Ethical and Policy Considerations in the Spread of Commercial Gambling," in *Gambling Cultures*, ed. Jan McMillen (London: Routledge, 1996); William R. Eadington, "Casino Gaming—Origins, Trends, and Impacts," in *Casino Gambling in America*, eds. Klaus Meyer-Arendt and Rudi Hartmann (New York: Cognizant Communication, 1998); Rod L. Evans and Mark Hance, eds., *Legalized Gambling: For and Against* (Chicago: Open Court, 1998).

34. *International Gaming & Wagering Business (IGWB)* 20, no. 8 (1999): 17; cf. "Indian Gaming Facts," National Indian Gaming Library and Resource Center (2000). Online at www.indiangaming.org/library.

35. James A. Davis and Lloyd E. Hudman, "The History of Indian Gaming Law and Casino Development in the Western United States," in *Tourism and Gaming on American Indian Lands*, eds. Alan A. Lew and George A. Van Otten (New York: Cognizant Communication, 1998), 85.

36. Ibid., 85–91.

37. Patricia Nelson Limerick, *The Legacy of Conquest: The Unbroken Past of the American West* (New York: Norton, 1987). See Lew and Van Otten, *Tourism and Gaming on American Indian Lands.*

38. *Casino Journal* 12, no. 10 (1999): 12.

39. *Casino Journal* 13, no. 1 (2000): 32–33, and 13, no. 2 (2000): 50.

40. Patricia A. Stokowski, *Riches and Regrets: Betting on Gambling in Two Colorado Mountain Towns* (Niwot: University Press of Colorado, 1996); Katherine Jensen and Audie Blevins, *The Last Gamble: Betting on the Future in Four Rocky Mountain Towns* (Tucson: University of Arizona Press, 1998); Pauliina Raento, "Gambling in the Rocky Mountains," *Fennia* 179 (2001): 97–127.

41. Patricia A. Stokowski, "Community Impacts and Revisionist Images in Colorado Gaming Development," in *Casino Gambling in America,* 137.

42. Rudi Hartmann, "Booms, Busts, and Winning Streaks: Casino Development in Two Colorado Mountain Towns," in *Casino Gambling in America,* 123–124.

43. *Colorado Division of Gaming and Gaming Commission, Annual Report and Abstract* (1997): 5, 11.

44. Stokowski, in *Casino Gambling in America,* 140.

45. Stokowski, *Riches and Regrets;* Jensen and Blevins, *The Last Gamble.*

46. Stokowski, in *Casino Gambling in America,* 146.

47. Ibid., 147.

48. Hartmann, in *Casino Gambling in America,* 136; Raento, "Gambling in the Rocky Mountains."

49. Edward Relph, *Place and Placelessness* (London: Pion, 1976), 95–100, cited in Pauliina Raento and Kate A. Berry, "Geography's Spin at the Wheel of American Gambling," *Geographical Review* 89 (1999): 592.

50. Raento and Douglass, "The Naming of Gaming," 19.

51. Rothman, "Selling the Meaning of Place," 555.

52. Raento and Douglass, "The Naming of Gaming," 19.

53. John M. Findlay, "Suckers and Escapists? Interpreting Las Vegas and Post-War America," *Nevada Historical Society Quarterly* 33 (1990): 1–15.

54. Las Vegas Convention and Visitors Authority statistics, cited in *International Gaming & Wagering Business (IGWB)* 19, no. 9 (1998): 70, 73; *Casino Journal* 13, no. 2 (2000): 50; see *1998 Las Vegas Visitor Profile Study.*

55. Findlay, "Suckers and Escapists?"

56. Raento and Berry, "Geography's Spin at the Wheel."

57. William A. Douglass, anthropologist, casino entrepreneur, personal communication with the author, 11 January 1999, in Reno, Nevada; cited in Raento and Berry, "Geography's Spin at the Wheel," 592.

58. Ibid., 593.

10 | Magical Realism

The West as Spiritual Playground

PETER GOIN

I live in this place called the Great Basin. This "place" is a complex topographical basin, comprised mostly of Nevada, with added parts of Utah, Idaho, and eastern California, Wyoming, and Oregon. Death Valley is part of this enormous "basin," as is the area of the interior drainage of the Great Salt Lake, the Mojave Desert, and the Carson Sink. Those of us who travel basin and range country know well the essential geography of a "basin," yet this is a descriptive term easily and often misunderstood. The word *basin* is neither a very familiar nor an especially descriptive noun. It certainly is not a word commonly used to describe the interior West, and although the word is accurate, both topographically and descriptively, *basin* means "a depression, a sink," a phrase that somehow seems incongruous with literally hundreds of north-south-trending mountain ranges. I have not *once* heard people tell me that they, too, live in the "basin."

I am surprised at how frequently I meet people, including some neighbors and close friends, who argue that they have never been to, or "out in" the *Great Basin*. Perhaps this is because most of us, whether writers or photographers of the American West, are visitors from places with greater rainfall, walls of concrete, and masses of people. We are perhaps forever tourists with a different frame of reference and daily experience than those people whose ancestors lived within this land, hunting and gathering, for centuries. Although my birthplace is in the Midwest, I wish to argue: No longer am I "visiting" this landscape. It does depend, of course, on whom you ask. A Paiute leader once told me that all *tibo'o* (Paiute term for a person who is the color of white) are, by definition, strangers. Compared to ten thousand years of ancestral legacy, we are certainly immigrants. But we can still *belong.*

During many years of traversing these arid lands, I have noticed that birthplace is not always interpreted as birth*right.* Ancestral blood runs deep. But belonging is not always a competition of ancestry but rather a process of acceptance. Accepting the land means that we learn to live within its geography, history, character, and, perhaps most importantly, spirit. As noted poet Simon Ortiz recently told me, "I live here, in this place, and this is my home." As it is for Simon, so it is for me. I cannot share his aboriginal lineage, just as I cannot be denied the spirit within the earth. The landscape is quite as much within me as it is the stage upon which I walk. I can hear the voices of the silence, of the birds, and of the rocks. I listen patiently.

It was late afternoon, and a ferocious wind blew. Dust devils swirled and danced before dispersing their sand and alkali debris over the dry lakebed. The bellows on my camera twitched in rhythm with the wind, and minute particles of dust seeped into every crack and crevice. On the horizon, large columns of dust obscured the volcanic rock outcropping. An ephemeral rain shower drizzled onto the playa, each drop exploding in a minute cloud of alkali dust.

The process of making these photographs has become for me a journey of rediscovery. Having spent more than fifteen years traveling into this American outback, I have come to realize that this arid, often inhospitable, and unforgiving landscape possesses a character both spiritual and sublime. This is a land of contradictions that often defy description. The sound of quiet can be deafening. When the wind whistles and the dust storms grow, even the most experienced traveler can become disoriented. Distances are deceiving as human scale becomes obscured and unpredictable. The smells of sage and hot springs' sulfur are woven together. The dirt roads are laden with silken dust; combined with water, they turn into quagmires of greaselike mud. The rocks are sharp and rough, yet in the soft evening light the distant hills appear covered with velvet. At any moment, there may not be one person within ten square miles; still, every step reveals human history. Mirages are commonplace, and nothing really is what it seems. This is a landscape defined by the image and absence of water.

As the sun set on a moonless night, creating a balance between land and sky, the winds died down. I slipped into the dark, mirrorlike water of the springs and felt the hot, slippery mud ooze between my toes. The tall, green reeds at the pool's edge obscured the horizon, and time, like a photograph, froze. The stillness made it hard to imagine the violent geological forces that had shaped this range. After a few hours, my skin was wrinkled, and I surrendered to the cool night air. Gathering my lawn chair, clothes, towel, and camera gear, I prepared to leave. A coyote howled, miles away. I located the Big Dipper and the North Star and noticed the crisp, ragged, horizon line where the mountain's rim met the sky. I was beckoned.

Living means more than residing. This "Great Basin" is a land imbued with meaning for those willing to transcend looking by *seeing*. There are visitors who travel on the interstate highways through our alkali deserts, mile after mile, rarely dusting their automobiles with the fine, cream-colored silt lying in wait in the troughs on dirt roads. These visitors may be visually articulate, verbally skilled, and professionally accredited in their own right, but do they truly understand not just the sense of this "basin," but also the fundamental nature of its presence? This is, after all, a magical land with an ephemeral spirit. It is a land of mirages and miracles.

The outback of the American West is the Great Basin and range, mountain and desert, mythic geographies defined by distance, light, and isolation. These photographs are not narrative in any linear sense; they are the "visions" of this traveler, thoughts of histories unspoken and anonymous ghosts, feelings in the wind, rhythms of living within the cycle of the moon and of the sun.

These photographs are stories without plots. Perhaps it would be more appropriate to consider each image as an artifact rather than a specific, discoverable story. These photographs offer evidence of the experience of feeling the spirit of a place, of the earth, of being compelled to record in a visually technical and complex language the visceral *seeing*. The Great Basin and nearby landscapes are some of the wonderful places of encounter between familiarity and strangeness. These photographs offer a glimpse of the struggle to describe a still only part-visualized, written vastness, a hidden world with room for tremendous human imagination.

The ordinary and the extraordinary are fused into the lyrical and, occasionally, fantastic image. I know that I have in the making of these photographs accepted events contrary to the usual operating laws of the universe, that these scenes are perhaps astonishing but no less commonplace. I am not surprised, but delighted. Should you be able to suspend your disbelief and follow the path of poetic faith, I believe you might find some of the same magic in your mind's eye.

FIG. 10.1. Photographer's and tripod's shadows, Black Rock Desert, Nevada.

FIG. 10.2. Figure emerging into Santa Rosa Range, Nevada.

Fig. 10.3. Lizard petroglyph, Lagomarsino Canyon, Nevada.

Fig. 10.4. Snake near Lye Creek, Santa Rosa Range, Nevada.

Fig. 10.5. Water figure within Last Chance Ditch, Reno, Nevada.

Fig. 10.6. Figure in tent, Burnt Canyon mine site, Seven Troughs Range, Nevada.

FIG. 10.7. Mine site with campfire and burning tumbleweed, Seven Troughs Range, Nevada.

Fɪɢ. 10.8. Figure staring at sky near Gunsight Pass, Padre Canyon and Bay, Lake Powell, Utah.

Fig. 10.9. Ghost figure at Lost Horse Ranger Station–camping area, Joshua Tree National Park, California.

Fɪɢ. 10.10. Fire in water, Sevenmile Canyon, Lake Powell, Utah.

Fig. 10.11. Figure lifting airborne tent, North Gulch, Moki Canyon, Lake Powell, Utah.

Fig. 10.12. "Ground Zero," outsider art of DeWayne Williams near Gerlach, Black Rock Desert, Nevada.

Fıɢ.10.13. Healing shamanic-mud man "Buster," Burning Man, Black Rock Desert, Nevada.

Fɪɢ. 10.14. Christine C. returning from a spiritual quest walk, Burning Man, Black Rock Desert, Nevada.

Fɪɢ. 10.15. Spiral along Highway 50 southeast of Fallon, Nevada.

FIG. 10.16. Cave pictograph, Iceberg Canyon, Lake Powell, Utah.

11 | "Good, by God, We're Going to Bodie!"

Ghost Towns and the American West

DYDIA DELYSER

In the late 1870s, as legend has it, a young girl living in the California town of Truckee was told by her parents that the family would be moving to Bodie, then a booming mining camp with a growing bad reputation as a "'sea of sin,' lashed by the tempests of lust and passion."[1] Horrified at the prospect, the little girl ended her evening prayer with a farewell: "Goodbye, God, we're going to Bodie." Newspapers in the region quickly picked up the account, and the little girl's phrase spread throughout the West. Furious at this insult and not entirely pleased with their town's implied wicked reputation, Bodie's newspapers disputed the report as misquoted. What she actually wrote, they claimed, was, "Good, by God, we're going to Bodie!"

Now, over one hundred years after the first version of the story ran in a newspaper, Bodie's reputation referred to by the prayer lives on, while the town of Bodie itself continues in a new form. Intermittent large-scale mining activity ceased there only after World War II, but by the 1920s the now-isolated town had already become a tourist attraction. Beginning in the late 1950s, the state of California moved to acquire the remains of the town (some 120 buildings and their contents), lock, stock, and barrel. In 1964 Bodie was dedicated a California state historic park.[2]

Bodie, the once-successful gold-mining town, had joined the hundreds of Western settlements known popularly as "ghost towns" (Figure 11.1). And just like other ghost towns, Bodie is now often described as a "shadow of its former self." But what is significant about Western ghost towns is not that they are now smaller or less populous than they once were, but, rather it is

Fɪɢ. 11.1. Main Street, Bodie, California, ca. 1920, already called a ghost town since at least the 1910s, despite a lingering population sometimes as high as a few hundred. The dilapidated, false-fronted facades of saloons and other businesses have become the archetype of the Western ghost town. Most of these buildings burned in a disastrous fire in 1932. Courtesy Los Angeles Public Library photo collection. Used by permission.

what that *shadow* is thought to represent. Through close links to film and fiction, Western ghost towns have come to evoke images of America's mythic West. This chapter will explore these links as it attempts to chronicle the emergence of ghost towns and their place in contemporary American culture more broadly.

As it turns out, upon closer examination, little about that story of the young girl and her prayer seems to be true. Little, that is, except the fact that the story itself has become an important way of describing Bodie for its historians and those who remember the days gone by in what one of them called the "Last of the Old-Time Mining Camps."[3] Indeed, that one story has been included in nearly every book or significant article written about Bodie since 1924.[4] And yet none has ever quoted the original newspaper report, let alone the little girl herself. Although most versions of the story[5] place the young girl in Truckee, the Bodie *Standard News* of 13 February 1879 (the nearest anyone has subsequently come to the beginning of the tale) states that she was in fact from San Jose, California.[6] More important than the little girl's origin, however, is the fact that the *Standard* did *not* claim that she had been misquoted. What the writer for the *Standard* did claim was,

> we have no particular use for a God that confines himself to the limits of San Jose; and we don't wonder that even a little three year old was willing to say, "Goodbye," when she thought she had a chance to get outside of that detestable place in order to come to Bodie.

The source of the revised quote, the one so often repeated as though it were part of the original tale, is somewhat more mysterious. It seems likely, however, that it originated with another of Bodie's newspapermen, a man known by the name of "Lying Jim" Townsend. Townsend, once a pioneer Mono County journalist, published the Bodie *Miner Index* between 1895 and 1900, long after Bodie's boisterous boom had quieted and nearly twenty years after the original story about the little girl had appeared.[7] Notorious for his hyperbolic journalism, it seems to have been Townsend who was responsible for the phrase, "Good, by God, we're going to Bodie!"[8]

The truth or falsehood of the original tale aside, the story of the young girl's prayer, with its evocation of the town's wicked reputation, has become an important part of Bodie in American social memory, an important part of the way Americans have come to think about this ghost town's past: The ghost town of Bodie—*like so many other ghost towns*—is now understood, in significant part, through mythic tales like this one that are at best only loosely grounded in fact. Why then study a place like Bodie? Why should historical geographers and other scholars be interested in ghost towns? Precisely *because* of the power of the mythic, the presence of the unreal in the landscapes and histories of contemporary ghost towns.

To many historians and historical geographers, that which cannot be documented and proven to be true is of little or no interest. But for scholars interested in social memory (in how the past is made meaningful in the present), issues of truth and falsity take on new roles: As James Fentress and Chris Wickham have pointed out, "the social meaning of memory . . . is little affected by its truth" and indeed, "inaccurate memories do shed a more unmediated light on social memory than accurate ones do: they are not, so to speak, polluted by 'real' past events."[9] Or, as Marita Sturken has explained, "We need to ask not whether a memory [or a story about the past] is true but rather what its telling reveals about how the past affects the present."[10] These ideas, it seems, shed new light on Bodie and the hundreds of other Western ghost towns, making them ideal places to study for historical geographers and other scholars interested in social memory as we seek to understand the meanings of the past for the present. As this chapter will show, ghost towns are in a significant manner socially constructed: Emerging from the remains of abandoned mining camps in the twentieth century, founded both on fact as well as on tall tales, and evolving to fit particular descriptions of the perceived past, they now portray a romanticized past made to be relevant in the present.

The Mythic West

For many Americans who come to ghost towns like Bodie, even if they have never been there before, the landscape is immediately familiar: Ramshackle buildings scattered in a sagebrush-strewn valley remind them of film and television Westerns—of John Wayne and Clint Eastwood movies, of *Gunsmoke* and *Bonanza*—images so prevalent in contemporary Anglo-American culture that they are held largely in common. What these landscapes do then, is evoke intertextual connections to America's Western past as represented in such films and programs. Thus, not surprisingly, a ghost town like Bodie is a place where children will ask if the museum sells cap-gun revolvers (and are disappointed to learn that it doesn't), where teenagers will stride down the street whistling the theme song from Sergio Leone's 1967 film, *The Good, the Bad and the Ugly*, and where adults will come dressed in supposedly period Western wear. This landscape, in other words, links its viewers, through film and fiction, to the mythic American West.

The importance of these connections, however, goes far beyond their links to popular films and programs. Rather, it lies in the cultural meaning that the mythic West holds for Americans, evoking images of gunfighters and reckless bravado, but also of hard work, individualism, honor, courage, and a love for freedom[11]—ideas and images at the core of Anglo-American culture.

But the mythic West did not grow up in film or fiction alone. Rather, since the late nineteenth century, the mythic West has found its grounding, at least in part, in Western mining towns, many of which we now know as ghost towns.[12] Indeed, in significant ways, our contemporary ideas of the mythic West and the towns we now know as ghost towns grew up together in the nineteenth century: The mythic West already existed, but journalists in Western mining towns, fond of penning exaggerated tales, helped fix its location in part in booming camps like Bodie as their dramatic tales traveled eastward to reach audiences far beyond the camps themselves.[13] Thus, the mythic West and what, for lack of a better term, we might call the "real" (or historic) West have existed not separately but rather together, each one helping to create the other, "engaged in a constant conversation."[14] As places to seek the mythic West then, ghost towns may be ideal: As they grew up and grew old, the American mythic West evolved with them.

The Emergence of Ghost Towns

Whereas towns based on agriculture or manufacturing tend to live on, most of today's ghost towns began their days as mining camps.[15] Indeed, some would say that because of the boom/bust nature of extractive industry along with its attendant financial speculation and the limited resource base upon which mining towns are built, an often-terminal "ghost town phase" is a natural part of the life cycle of a mining town.[16] From the vantage point of the early twenty-first century, it may seem simple, therefore, to trace a long history of ghost towns since abandoned mining camps became a part of the Western American landscape soon after the beginnings of the California gold rush in 1848. But ghost towns themselves have not, because *ghost town* is a term and an idea that emerged much later.

By the 1850s, journalists, travelers, and residents in Western mining towns were already recording their experiences with failed mining towns, "dead camps," towns that had been largely abandoned. As early as July 1851, a leading San Francisco newspaper, the *Alta California,* was reporting that "we hear of the complete exhaustion and abandonment of many of the diggings."[17] By 1868, a federal report lamented the fate of Star City, Nevada: Organized in 1861 it had developed into a "flourishing town" with a population of some one thousand souls, but now, the report remarked, "So sudden has been its decline that—the entire population consists of a single family, the head of which is mayor, constable, postmaster, express agent, telegraph operator, and, I believe, sole and unanimous voter."[18] In 1869 traveler Samuel Bowles could declare half of California's mining towns deserted.[19] Indeed, abandoned camps had became so commonplace that by 1872 when he published *Roughing It,* renowned Western journalist Mark Twain (Samuel Clemens) could describe such towns in aggregate:

> In some such places [towns where successful gold mining had been done] . . .
> only meadows and forests are [now] visible—not a living creature, not a house,
> no stick or stone or remnant of a ruin, and not a sound, not even a whisper to
> disturb the Sabbath stillness—you will find it hard to believe that there stood at
> one time a fiercely-flourishing little city, of two thousand or three thousand
> souls, with its newspaper, fire company, volunteer militia, bank, hotels, noisy
> Fourth of July processions and speeches, gambling halls crammed with tobacco
> smoke, profanity, and rough-bearded men of all nations and colors, with tables

heaped with gold dust sufficient for the revenues of a German principality—
streets crowded and rife with business—town lots worth four hundred dollars a
front foot—labor, laughter, music, dancing, swearing, fighting, shooting, stab-
bing—a bloody inquest and a man for breakfast every morning—*everything* that
delights and adorns existence—all the appointments and appurtenances of a
thriving and prosperous and promising young city,—and *now* nothing is left of
it all but a lifeless, homeless solitude. The men are gone, the houses have vanished, even the *name* of the place is forgotten. In no other land, in modern
times, have towns so absolutely died and disappeared, as in the old mining regions of California.[20]

Evocative though his description may be (and it is echoed in many more
recent accounts of Western mining towns), Twain did not call such sites
"ghost towns." Instead, early descriptions, like Twain's, used other words for
these places, often resorting to phrases such as "deserted mining towns," as
the Cincinnati *Enquirer* did in 1875.[21] In 1908 Clifton Johnson called Virginia
City, Nevada, a "dilapidated old mining camp" but *not* a ghost town.[22] Even as
late as 1922, Will Irvin, himself a former Colorado mining town resident,
wrote for the *Saturday Evening Post* of that state's "dead camps" but not of its
ghost towns.[23]

Precisely when the term *ghost town* began to be applied to abandoned or
largely abandoned Western mining camps is not certain, but most likely the
term arose either soon after or alongside the term *ghost city*, which may first
have been used to describe what we now call ghost towns in September of
1915, when *Saturday Evening Post* author Charles Van Loan used that term to
describe Bodie.[24] By the end of 1916 *Sunset* magazine had called Hornitos,
California, a ghost town but found it necessary to put the term in quotes.[25]
Similarly, in 1917 *Sunset* ran "ghost city" in quotes in its article about a Montana town by the name of Lost Lode.[26] As late as 1922 there was still no agreement on the usage of *ghost town* over *ghost city*. Rex Burlingame, writing for
the *Illustrated World*, used both "'ghost' town" (for which he provided a definition) and "'ghost' city" as well as "dead town."[27] By the mid-1920s, however, *ghost town* was becoming the more popular term: Linguist Helen Moore,
in her 1926 article "The Lingo of the Mining Camp," found the term already
in use in various Western mining towns to describe the towns that had been
(largely) abandoned.[28] Thus, although references to ghost towns (or ghost cities) before the mid-1920s are rare, the towns themselves had existed, albeit
under different names, at least since the 1850s.

But the actual use of the term *ghost town* is critical because the widespread
adoption of the term corresponds with a shift in the meanings of the places

themselves. The earliest descriptions of abandoned mining towns were grim, full of the disappointment of failure. In 1871 writer and geologist Clarence King described a scene in one such town for the *Atlantic Monthly:* "Every deserted cabin knows a story of brave manly effort ended in bitter failure, and the lingering stranded men have a melancholy look as of faint fish the ebb has left to die."[29] Even Twain himself cast a gloomy haze over such camps, attributing to their residents not a hardy pioneer spirit, but rather an apathetic resignation to failure:

> A flourishing city of two or three thousand population had occupied this grassy dead solitude during the flush times of twelve or fifteen years before, and where our cabin stood had once been the heart of the teeming hive, the center of the city. When the mines gave out the town fell into decay, and in a few years wholly disappeared—streets, dwellings, shops, everything—and left no sign. . . . The mere handful of miners still remaining, had seen the town spring up, spread, grow and flourish in its pride; and they had seen it sicken and die, and pass away like a dream. With it their hopes had died, and their zest of life. They had long ago resigned themselves to their exile, and ceased to correspond with their distant friends or turn longing eyes toward their early homes. They had accepted banishment, forgotten the world and been forgotten of the world. They were far from telegraphs and railroads, and they stood, as it were, in a living grave, dead to the events that stirred the globe's great populations, dead to the common interests of men, isolated and outcast from brotherhood with their kind.[30]

Like Twain, writers of the early twentieth century were not apt to romanticize the abandoned camps or to glamorize their residents. In 1908 the "dilapidated old mining camp" of Virginia City, Nevada, was "indeed a strange town—a living skeleton."[31] But by the mid-1920s, when the term *ghost town* had come into common usage, the towns themselves were being described based not on their failure, but rather primarily on their ability to hearken a heroic past, based on their perceived links with the mythic West.

As in Twain's description of the first of the two deserted camps in *Roughing It,* ghost towns began to herald their rough reputations. The phrase "a man for breakfast" (which implied that shootings were so regular as to be nightly occurrences) was used to describe *the past* in any number of ghost towns—places as different as Bodie (1915), Hornitos, California (1916), and Leadville, Colorado (1922).[32] Although the "Goodbye, God" tale implies that towns like Bodie decried such reputations while they were booming camps, after such towns had drifted firmly into decline they began to boast of them (which is, of course, also demonstrated by the "Goodbye, God" tale because Townsend did not coin the rebuttal until *after* Bodie's boisterous boom had quieted). As historian Duane Smith has written, the reputations such towns now have for "wildness and lawlessness" is one of the "redoubtable misconceptions" that has arisen about Western mining towns—such rowdiness has become accepted as the norm and indeed *expected* of Western ghost towns.[33] Although violence was surely present in such towns, when historian Roger McGrath studied county courthouse, jail, and newspaper records for Bodie's boom period, he found less violent crime in legendarily rough and lawless Bodie than in eastern U.S. cities of the same period.[34] Just the same, by the 1920s, the now-quiet ghost towns began subsisting in part on their rowdy reputations.

Actually, not only on their *rowdy* reputations, because former residents were simultaneously held up as paragons of Western virtue. And this the residents regularly did *themselves* because early articles about ghost towns were often either written by residents (or former residents) of the towns or featured interviews with them. Where Twain and his contemporaries had portrayed surviving residents of "dead camps" in a less-than-flattering light, the latter-day residents of "ghost towns," once availed of their own mouthpieces, portrayed themselves, their contemporaries, and their towns in rather different terms.[35] Tales of excessive violence might be readily rendered as applications of "miner's law"; indeed, "old-timers" in Oro, Colorado, in 1922 would maintain

to their death that this is the best law. Certainly its foundation was the purest of democracy. When a crime demanded punishment, when a dispute over property arose, the miners met in convention. . . . [Advocates for each side were chosen who presented their cases, and witnesses were heard, their testimonies] unshuttered by those rules of evidence which under English common law hamper regular courts. . . . The president called for a vote. . . . From this judgement there was no appeal. If it was a capital crime and the miners had voted guilty they carried out the sentence at once.[36]

Having himself been a young child during the region's boom, the preceding article's author went on to reminisce about the past in the towns of Leadville and Oro: "Along with this wildness, dissipation, outright crime, ran counter-currents of heroism, honest effort, generosity, monumental energy."[37] And these two themes together—of crime with heroism, of the unlawful with the upstanding—came, in later days, to be characteristic of the ways that old-timers would reminisce about their towns' pasts, generally placing themselves, of course, firmly in the second camp.

In 1925 Grant H. Smith, himself a lawyer and before that a young teenage resident of Bodie during its brief nineteenth-century boom period, wrote one of the most important accounts of that town's past. Of Bodie's mining-camp men Smith wrote, "These men, as a rule, were virile, enthusiastic, and free livers; bound by few of the rules of conventional society, though with an admirable code of their own: liberal-minded, generous to a fault, square-dealing, and devoid of pretense and hypocrisy." But just the same he describes a gold-mining town "more widely known for its lawlessness than for its riches." How this is possible is outlined in his article as he describes a bifurcated society, divided between Bodie's polite society and Bodie's bad men and their company (including not only the criminal element but also gamblers and prostitutes: "The saloons and gambling houses all fronted on the main street and were 'wide-open.' Nearly everybody drank, nearly everybody gambled"). Smith placed himself squarely into that latter camp: "I neither drank nor smoked nor gambled nor frequented low places." Noting that there was often "a man for breakfast," Smith also detailed how the two elements of society remained apart: "Fortunately, the fighting was almost entirely confined to the rough element, and, so long as they killed off one another, the better citizens did not care. Every once in a while an innocent spectator would get in the way of a bullet, but that was considered partly his own fault for being there," and, "It is gratifying to recall that none of the dissolute persons with whom I came in daily contact [as a messenger boy for the telegraph office] ever tried to lead me astray." Thus, even among the badmen of this bifurcated Bodie, a code of moral conduct prevailed amid a Darwinistic struggle for survival. According to Smith, "Cold-blooded murders were uncommon. Most men were killed in open fights, where each side had at least some chance; the victory going to the men quickest in action and surest in aim," and, "Men were judged chiefly by their character and ability; not by the ordinary rules of conventional society. The mining camps had their own Ten Commandments, which included but few of those given to Moses." Articles like Smith's written version of his youthful memories of Bodie (which included not only the "man for breakfast" claim but also the "Goodbye, God" tale, told as fact) have come to set the stage for countless others as they reminisce and/or write about Western ghost towns.[38]

Such apparently contradictory claims have become standard fare. Indeed, in 1932, when T. A. Rickard, former editor of *Engineering and Mining Journal*, published his *History of American Mining*, he noted that

> The stories of the golden days leave contradictory impressions; on the one hand we read of order, generosity, honor, and high aim; on the other we see pictures of riot, bloodshed, fraud, and frenzy. Neither extreme is altogether true. . . .[39]

By the late 1920s, when the term *ghost town* came into common usage, a new mode of describing these abandoned camps and their residents had been firmly established. Memorialized in fiction and pseudohistories, the mining towns-turned-ghost towns now even more strongly took on the characteristics of the mythic West, described by adjectives like "wild," "sensual," "romantic," and "adventuresome."[40]

But the decade of the 1920s marks another transition as well: the rise of automobile tourism in the West due to the increased reliability and affordability of the automobile, as well as the proliferation of hard-surfaced roads (although admittedly most ghost towns were not on them!) and directional signs.[41] Although the expansion of railroads had made some Western mining towns accessible to tourists in the nineteenth century,[42] by the twentieth, most abandoned mining camps no longer had rail connections, and thus it was the versatility of automobile travel that enabled tourists to reach ghost towns like Bodie that lay in remote locations far from rail service.[43]

At the same time as an increased number of automobile tourists were able to reach Western ghost towns, many of these towns prepared to celebrate the fiftieth anniversaries of their booms. Some, like Tombstone, Arizona,[44] concocted elaborate celebrations. Tombstone's "Helldorado Days," first celebrated in 1929, is still celebrated annually each fall and harkens back to the days of that town's boom and what has more recently come to be called the "Shootout at the OK Corral."[45]

As tourists and article writers visited these towns in the 1920s and 1930s they could still find "old-timers" fond of remembering their now-quiet town's wild past. In Bodie, James Stuart Cain, who arrived in the town in 1879, still operated his Bank of Bodie and often spoke with reporters, telling them glamorous tales of the town's past.[46] Old-timers like Cain became nostalgic for their own pasts and, as in the case of Cain's daughter-in-law Ella Cody Cain, founder of Bodie's museum, their family's pasts. Although James Stuart Cain had not been a major player during Bodie's boom period, in its declining years he began to buy up property and businesses, eventually becoming the town's largest landholder. But beyond the acquisition of property and businesses, Cain, it seems, was also interested in acquiring a piece of the past in a different way: He frequently made himself available for interviews, and, when both his daughter-in-law and his son-in-law wrote books about Bodie's past, Cain and his family's saga were made prominent.[47]

If ghost towns were becoming places where people expected to find traces of a glamorous and exciting (if lawless) past, one relic of that past that visitors expected (and still do expect) to find is the saloon. Once the center of mining-camp life and working-class male culture in cities across the nation, the saloon is a relic that has contributed to the romanticization of ghost towns by its very presence. Before Prohibition there had been an average of one saloon for every three hundred Americans.[48] In rapidly booming Western mining towns where social institutions (such as churches, theaters, and even hotels) had had little time to develop or be built, saloons were even more numerous and served as important social centers for their towns.[49] In 1879 the bustling camp of Bodie boasted of as many as sixty-five saloons but no churches. With a population at that time probably between six thousand and ten thousand souls, 90 percent of whom were men, early Bodie experienced a saloon-to-person ratio twice as high as the national average.[50] In 1880 a Leadville, Colorado, journalist boasted that his town's 249 saloons had banked some $4 million of business—more than any of the other businesses in town except banking and mining. In 1893 a visitor to the state of Montana estimated that there was a saloon there for every eight inhabitants.[51] Thus, although saloons were once common across the country, their higher numbers in the West would help them gain a reputation in later years as a Western phenomenon.

By the late nineteenth century, such organizations as the Women's Christian Temperance Union and the Anti-Saloon League had targeted saloons as the source of many of the nation's problems.[52] With national Prohibition marking their victory, temperance organizations had even the word *saloon* banned in some places.[53] This thorough demonization of saloons helped assure that even after repeal of Prohibition, saloons, in their old form, would never be seen again.[54] But after their banishment, saloons took on a romanticized air. As saloons faded from living memory, this became still easier: By 1931, when journalist George Ade published *The Old-Time Saloon*, he lamented the saloon's passing, describing for those who could not recall it the typical saloon's "dim interior" and the bar that "always had a brass footrail in front of it." "Saw-dust on the floor," he continued, "was supposed to absorb the drippings. Behind the bar was a mirror and below the mirror a tasteful medley of lemons, assorted glasses and containers brightly labeled."[55] Such images have been imported directly into the imagery of the American mythic West. As historian Elliot West has noted,

> The swinging doors, the gilt mirror, the white-shirted barkeep, the boots on the bar rail—today, all would be recognized immediately throughout America and much of the world. The Western saloon remains an indelible part of the popular image of the American frontier [, . . . and] part of our national mythology.[56]

Today, as author West notes, for many tourists "a summer trip to western states is incomplete without a visit to a genuine saloon."[57] In the ghost town of Bodie, "Where's the saloon?" is one of the most common questions asked by visitors.

Ghost towns and saloons have become inextricably linked, thriving on this connection at least since Prohibition: When "prohi squad" raiders visited Bodie in September of 1930, they closed down fourteen saloons, exacting high fines from their proprietors. The news made the front page of the San Francisco papers, and even famed actor Will Rogers saw fit to lament the town's dry fate.[58]

World War II, almost exclusively an overseas conflict, may have had a large impact on Western ghost towns. During the war, gold mining was curtailed as not essential to the war effort.[59] In towns still clinging to life, like Bodie, this multiyear shutdown of the towns' livelihood forced many to finally leave.[60] After the war, the widespread availability of army-surplus Jeeps suddenly made even the ghost towns that had been abandoned long before the war accessible.[61]

Equally important was the 1949 one-hundredth anniversary of the California gold rush, which, as it approached, prompted the publication of books and articles about California's former gold-mining towns, many of them by then already ghost towns.[62] Beyond the realm of publishing, this renewed interest carried into preservation as well. For example, the ghost town of Columbia, California, where gold was first discovered on 27 March 1850, was declared a California State Historic Park in 1945 in order to "preserve its historic buildings and sites."[63]

By the 1950s and 1960s, as public fascination with ghost towns continued to increase,[64] the place of ghost towns in contemporary American culture had been well established. Numerous guidebooks and articles, published from this period onward, tell a remarkably similar tale—not that of disheartened failures, as Twain and others had earlier described, but rather that of hardy pioneers who labored mightily, the rewards of whose legacy we reap today. Ghost towns, then, began to be seen not as evolutionary dead ends, but rather as the haunting remnants of a past that paved the way for our present.

On the eve of the gold rush centennial, Rockwell Hunt described ghost towns as "a rich vein of memories of our unforgettable yesterdays" and therefore also as "our priceless heritage."[65] And by the 1960s, Remi Nadeau, grandson of a well-known California pioneer, wrote, "if you want to find the essence of American character, study the people who made the western mining frontier. . . . [A ghost town] is a fragment of Americana which helps to explain the whole."[66] By the 1970s another guidebook author explained to his readers that "the rollicking, individualistic spirit of the frontier has come to

seem an antidote to urban grayness. . . . and the frail ghost towns are an obvious [place to find it]."[67]

Whereas abandoned mining camps had once been derided, by the mid-
twentieth century ghost towns were being celebrated and protected. One
guidebook author wrote, "Ghost towns are fragile, they were put together
with hope as much as with nails and boards."[68] But by visiting these towns today, guidebook authors insist, contemporary observers are able to recapture
these hopes through the landscape: "the visitor can scuff through the ashes of
old dreams"[69] and "quest for dulled remnants of a lustier day."[70] Ghost towns
had gone from detritus to heritage.[71]

Today, although most guidebook authors and members of the public seem
to agree that a ghost town is any town that is now but a shadow of its former
self, a great variety exists among Western ghost towns, including towns
where virtually nothing remains, neither residents nor their traces (Aurora,
Nevada); towns where commercial life is still ongoing (Tombstone, Arizona);
and modern attractions built entirely, or almost entirely, from scratch for the
purpose of drawing tourists' dollars (Knott's Berry Farm,[72] California) (Figure
11.2). They may be big, with many structures and artifacts (as Bodie is), or
small (like Skidoo, California). Ghost towns can be publicly owned, as Bodie
is; privately owned by one owner (like Cerro Gordo, California); by numerous
owners (like Virginia City, Nevada); or seemingly unowned (like Masonic,
California) (Figure 11.3). Buildings may be abandoned and largely or completely collapsed (as in Masonic), restored (as in Columbia, California), preserved but not restored (as in Bodie), or reproduced (as in Calico, California).
Ghost towns may generate income (as in Bodie), or profit (as in Oatman, Arizona), or neither (as in Rhyolite, Nevada). And finally, those who live in or
make their living from a ghost town may be very aware of their town's ghost
town status (as in Bodie, or the artists' community of Jerome, Arizona), they
may try to deny it (as in Tombstone, Arizona), or they may attempt to fab-
ricate it (as at Knott's).[73]

Ghost Towns and the Filmic West

Because these towns now generally have few or no surviving residents, ghost
towns today are interpreted largely through their landscapes. And these landscapes, as I have described, call forth images of the mythic West familiar
from film and television. But why is it that this is so? Why should a remote
gold-mining town like Bodie resemble nearly every movie Western I have
ever seen? Or rather, why do the sets of movie Westerns so closely resemble
ghost towns like Bodie?

Fɪɢ. 11.2. The bottle house at Knott's Berry Farm, in Buena Park, California. Walter Knott assembled a ghost town from scratch beginning in the 1950s, putting together a collection of abandoned buildings and then constructing others as replicas of well-known buildings from other Western towns. Knott's bottle house was inspired by the bottle house in the ghost town of Calico, California (once also owned by Knott), which, in turn, was inspired by a house built of bottles in the ghost town of Rhyolite, Nevada. The bottle house was originally built in 1905 just as Rhyolite's boisterous boom was beginning; saloonkeeper Tom Kelly used materials readily available in a treeless desert and a thirsty mining camp: empty bottles and adobe mortar. All three bottle houses are still standing (see Murbarger, *Ghosts of the Glory Trail*). Photo by author.

Although the film *High Plains Drifter* starring Clint Eastwood was filmed nearby on the shores of Mono Lake, and *Boots and Saddles* starring Gene Autry was filmed not much farther away in the Owens Valley, no major movie Western has ever been filmed in Bodie itself. Although production designers on *High Plains Drifter* or *Boots and Saddles* may indeed have been influenced by the look of the ghost town of Bodie in their designs of their sets, the ghost town–like look of movie Westerns had already been well established.

By the time the movie Western was established as a genre, the era of the horseback West had ended, but once-booming Western towns like Bodie survived as ghost towns. Particularly for production designers in the sound era, whereas the nineteenth-century boomtown look no longer had a visitable model, the ghost town look did. By the post–World War II period when the Western films and television programs seen by the several generations of Americans alive today were made, countless ghost town guidebooks had already appeared. These reference materials, as well as the numerous ghost towns located in or near southern California, provided readily available models for production designers to turn to for inspiration and ideas. Furthermore, the look of a ghost town, with the means of production (expensive mills, for example) now vanished or dormant, the bulk of its housing stock now gone, and its business district reduced to bare minimum, provided an inexpensive model for designers who had to work on budget, building a Western town on a studio backlot or in a remote location.[74] By the mid-twentieth century, the look of ghost towns and that of movie and television Westerns had been thoroughly fused, and ghost towns themselves came to stand as readily recognizable landscape sentinels for the values and ideologies projected by the films and programs.

FIG. 11.3. Masonic, California, isolated on a rough dirt road and beset by harsh winters, teeters on the brink of collapse. Masonic enchants for its abandonment and dearth of visitors, but, with no state agency or private corporation or persons paying for its upkeep, the few buildings still partially standing in Masonic may not survive much longer. Ghost towns across the West must strike a balance between extinction from the ravages of time and vandals and overcommercialization, both of which are seen by the media and the public as threats to a town's true ghost town status. (See DeLyser, "Authenticity on the Ground.") Photo by author.

Conclusion

Abandoned mining camps have existed since not long after the California gold rush of 1848 brought large numbers of people to the American West in search of mineral wealth. But ghost towns, as I have shown, are a much newer phenomenon, arising as places that people wrote about and remembered, in the ways that we write and think about them today, really only in the twentieth century. And the imagery of these places that emerged both helped form and was formed by the mythic West, links forged even when the ghost towns were booming mining camps, links that developed and continued after the camps were proclaimed ghost towns. Movie and television Westerns have furthered this connection, relying on popularly known images of Western ghost towns for the look of the "historic" West they portrayed. Thus, since their definition in the early twentieth century, ghost towns have existed in what one could call a liminal space, in this case a precarious place in between pure fact and abject fantasy or fiction. Whereas some have been newly constructed from scratch, most are anchored at least in part in a past as mining camps. Although they may tout the details of their histories, they also rely on glamorized and heroicized tales (tales often told by local old-timers who reminisced about their towns' past) in part to draw public appeal or to fit the now well-established pattern of ghost town lore, with its mythic Western imagery. Popular as tourist attractions since the rise of the automobile, ghost towns are now visited as sites of a glorious and successful (and largely Anglo) American heritage, rather than as places of foolishness or failure (Figure 11.4).

In earlier times, harshly negative reputations kept many respectable people from mining camps. Later, ghost towns came to rely positively on those same reputations, boasting about their badness while simultaneously boosting the high morals of their populations. That many of these tales can have been only loosely based in fact is actually part of their importance in the establishment of the mythic West. In the study of social memory, as opposed to the study of history, notions of truth and falsity take on new roles because it is the social meaning of memories, and the history (and historical geography) of their emergence, that becomes most important as we seek to shed light on our contemporary culture. The way that Americans have come to think about abandoned Western mining camps has changed dramatically over the past 150 years. Today their past is recast to view them as "ghost towns," the silent reminders of America's hard-working pioneers. In many ways then, they are now seen as the very foundations of contemporary America.

Fɪɢ. 11.4. By the late twentieth century, Bodie State Historic Park was attracting 200,000 visitors annually. Despite the crowds, the park, with over one hundred structures still standing, most of them cluttered with furniture and other discarded possessions, is widely heralded as one of the best-preserved ghost towns in the United States. Bodie's buildings are never restored to their former glory but rather are maintained according to a policy of "arrested decay," which keeps them standing but looking as if they were still falling down. Photo by author.

Once, as legend has it, a little girl, terrified of moving to a rowdy and lawless mining camp, prayed, "Goodbye, God, we're going to Bodie." Now, in the twenty-first century, ghost towns are not places to fear, rather they have become increasingly popular places to visit. Today, visitors to ghost towns are much more likely to echo Lying Jim's revised version of the little girl's prayer, "Good, by God, we're going to Bodie!"

Notes

1. Reverend F. M. Warrington to Mrs. Thomas Penfield, 25 January 1881, in Russ Johnson and Anne Johnson, *The Ghost Town of Bodie as Reported in the Newspapers of the Day* (Bishop, Calif.: Chalfant Press, 1967), 101.

2. See Dydia DeLyser, "'Good, by God, We're Going to Bodie!' Landscape and Social Memory in a California Ghost Town" (Ph.D. diss., Syracuse University, 1998), hereafter referred to as DeLyser, "Landscape and Social Memory in a California Ghost Town."

3. See, for example, Ella M. Cain, *The Story of Bodie* (San Francisco: Fearon Publishers, 1956); California Department of Parks and Recreation, *Bodie State Historic Park* (Sacramento, Calif.: Department of Parks and Recreation, 1988); C. B. Glassock, "'Goodbye, God: I'm Going to Bodie'," *Pony Express Courier* 4, no. 6 (November 1937): 1–10; Warren Loose, *Bodie Bonanza: The True Story of a Flamboyant Past* (Las Vegas: Nevada Publications, 1989); C. P. Russell, "Bodie, Dead City of Mono," *Yosemite Nature Notes* 4, no. 12 (31 December 1927): 89–95; Grant H. Smith, "Bodie: Last of the Old-Time Mining Camps," *California Historical Society Quarterly* 4, no. 1 (March 1925): 64–80; Frank S. Wedertz, *Bodie 1859–1900* (Bishop, Calif.: Sierra Media, 1969); the quote is from Smith, "Bodie; Last of the Old-Time Mining Camps," 64.

4. See, for example, Cain, *The Story of Bodie;* California Department of Parks and Recreation, *Bodie State Historic Park;* Glassock, "'Goodbye, God: I'm Going to Bodie'"; Loose, *Bodie Bonanza;* Russell, "Bodie, Dead City of Mono"; Smith, "Bodie: Last of the Old-Time Mining Camps"; Wedertz, *Bodie 1859–1900.* An examination of hundreds of features in newspapers from across the United States over the last several decades reveals the story's prevalence there as well (Bodie State Historic Park, unit history files, newspaper clippings).

5. For example, Cain, *The Story of Bodie;* Glassock, "'Goodbye, God: I'm Going to Bodie'"; Russell, "Bodie, Dead City of Mono"; and Smith, "Bodie: Last of the Old-Time Mining Camps."

6. All references to this article are quoted in Loose, *Bodie Bonanza,* 85–86.

7. Cain, *The Story of Bodie;* Loose, *Bodie Bonanza;* Wedertz, *Bodie 1859–1900.*

8. Glassock, "'Goodbye, God: I'm Going to Bodie'"; Wedertz, *Bodie 1859–1900.*

9. James Fentress and Chris Wickham, *Social Memory* (Oxford, U.K.: Blackwell, 1992), xi, 91.

10. Marita Sturken, *Tangled Memories: The Vietnam War, the AIDS Epidemic, and the Politics of Remembering* (Berkeley: University of California Press, 1997), 2.

11. See Robert G. Athearn, *The Mythic West in Twentieth-Century America* (Lawrence: University Press of Kansas, 1986); Dydia DeLyser, "Authenticity on the Ground: Engaging the Past in a California Ghost Town," *Annals of the Association of American Geographers* 89, no. 4 (December 1999): 602–632; Gerald D. Nash, *Creating the West: Historical Interpretations, 1890–1990* (Albuquerque: University of New Mexico Press, 1991); Richard White, *"It's Your Misfortune and None of My Own": A New History of the American West* (Norman: University of Oklahoma Press, 1991).

12. I present a more detailed history of the connections between the mythic West and Western ghost towns in DeLyser, "Authenticity on the Ground."

13. See DeLyser, "Authenticity on the Ground"; and Marvin Lewis, ed., *The Mining Frontier: Contemporary Accounts from the American West in the Nineteenth Century* (Norman: University of Oklahoma Press, 1967); and Roger D. McGrath, *Gunfighters, Highwaymen and Vigilantes: Violence on the Frontier* (Berkeley and Los Angeles: University of California Press, 1984).

14. White, *"It's Your Misfortune,"* 615; DeLyser, "Authenticity on the Ground."

15. Western towns whose basis was agriculture have largely survived because crop raising doesn't tend to "play out" the way mineral deposits do (see Duane Allen Smith, "Mining Camps: Myth vs. Reality," *The Colorado Magazine* 44 [spring 1967]: 93–110). A good example of this is the town of Bridgeport, California, now the Mono County seat, which grew up as the breadbasket for nearby Bodie but has now long outlived its glamorized neighbor (although because the Bridgeport economy is now based on tourism, the town is still in an important way dependent on Bodie). Examples of ghost towns that did not have origins as mining centers include Shaniko, Oregon, which proclaimed itself the "wool center of the world," and Oysterville, Washington (Lambert Florin, *Ghost Towns of the West* [New York: Promontory Press, 1993], 767). Furthermore, there *are* ghost towns in the East (see, for example, Fessenden S. Blanchard, *Ghost Towns of New England, Their Ups and Downs* [New York: Dodd, Mead, 1961]), but because of the close relation of ghost towns with the mythic West, they are widely understood as a Western phenomenon. This chapter discusses only Western ghost towns.

16. Richard Maxwell Brown, "Mining Towns," in *The New Encyclopedia of the West*, ed. Howard R. Lamar (New Haven: Yale University Press, 1998), 615; Duane A. Smith, "Boomtowns," in *The New Encyclopedia of the West*, 116; and Joey Windham, *Grand Encampment Mining District: A Case Study of the Life Cycle of a Typical Western Frontier Mining District* (Ph.D. diss., Ball State University, 1981).

17. Quoted in Rodman W. Paul, *Mining Frontiers of the Far West, 1848–1880* (New York: Holt, Rinehart & Winston, 1963), 28.

18. Rossiter Raymond's report entitled *Mineral Resources 1868*, 118, quoted in Paul, *Mining Frontiers of the Far West*, 108. See also Rodman W. Paul and Duane A. Smith, "Gold and Silver Rushes," in *The New Encyclopedia of the West*, ed. Howard R. Lamar (New Haven: Yale University Press, 1998), 434.

19. Samuel Bowles, *Our New West: Records of Travel between the Mississippi River and the Pacific Ocean* (Chicago: J. A. Stoddard, 1869), cited in Randall Rohe, "The Geography and Material Culture of the Western Mining Town," *Material Culture* 16, no. 3 (1984): 99–120.

20. Mark Twain (Samuel L. Clemens), *Roughing It* (Hartford, Conn.: American Publishing, 1872 [facsimile]), 414–415.

21. *Cincinnati Enquirer* (2 July 1875), quoted in J. A. Simpson and E. S. C. Weiner, eds., *Oxford English Dictionary*, 2d ed. (Oxford: Oxford University Press, 1989), 494.

22. Clifton Johnson, "A Nevada Town with a Past," *Outing* 53 (December 1908): 283–290, 290.

23. Will Irwin, "The Camps of Yesterday," *Saturday Evening Post* 195 (4 November 1922): 8–9, 83, 86, 88–89.

24. Charles E. Van Loan, "Ghost Cities of the West: Bad, B-a-d Bodie," *Saturday Evening Post* (25 September 1915): 18–19, 55–58. Eventually *ghost city* was all but replaced by *ghost town*. One notable exception is the Arizona copper-mining town of Jerome: When residents learned, in 1952, that the Phelps-Dodge mine that their town relied upon would be closing, they promptly and proudly proclaimed their town a "ghost city" in an effort to attract tour-

ists *and* to distinguish themselves from the hundreds of ghost towns that were truly abandoned (see Ed Peplow, "Jerome—America's Only Ghost City," *Arizona Highways* [August 1955]: 18–25).

25. Elsinore Robinson Crowell, "'Little Ovens' Hornitos, a 'Ghost Town' of California," *Sunset* (November 1916): 39–40, 66, 68.

26. Gertrude A. Zerr, "The People Who Stayed: Life in a 'Ghost City' of Montana Where They Wait 'till the Railroad Comes," *Sunset* (April 1917): 22–24, 48–50.

27. Rex H. Burlingame, "The Fate of Two 'Ghost' Towns," *Illustrated World* (9 February 1922): 858–859.

28. Helen L. Moore, "The Lingo of the Mining Camp," *American Speech* 2 (November 1926): 86–88. Both the *Barnhart Dictionary of Etymology* and the *Oxford English Dictionary* cite the first use of *ghost town* at around 1931, but clearly the term was in use well before this date (Robert K. Barnhart, ed., *Barnhart Dictionary of Etymology* [New York: H. W. Wilson, 1988]; Simpson and Weiner, eds., *Oxford English Dictionary*, 494).

29. Clarence King from the *Atlantic Monthly* (1871), quoted in James E. Camp and X. J. Kennedy, *Mark Twain's Frontier: A Textbook of Primary Source Materials for Student Research and Writing* (New York: Holt, Rinehart & Winston, 1963), 158.

30. Twain, *Roughing It*, 435. Most likely, the town to which Twain here refers is Jack Ass Hill, in Tuolumne County, California, where he lived for a time with Jim Gillis (see Nigey Lennon, *Sagebrush Bohemian: Mark Twain in California* [New York: Paragon House, 1990]).

31. Johnson, "Nevada Town," 283, 290.

32. Van Loan, "Ghost Cities of the West," 56; Crowell, "'Little Ovens'," 40; Irwin, "Camps of Yesterday," 83.

33. D. Smith, "Mining Camps," 106.

34. McGrath, *Gunfighters, Highwaymen and Vigilantes*; see also DeLyser, "Authenticity on the Ground."

35. Twain, of course, was a former resident of Aurora, Nevada, now a ghost town by any standard (today, not one building is still standing), as well as of Virginia City, Nevada, a town that, although included in numerous ghost town guidebooks and articles about ghost towns, still has a booming economy and is not unanimously considered a ghost town. What is different here, in large measure, is the passage of time since the early gold rush. After the boom/bust model of Western mining towns was more accepted, and after the romanticizing term *ghost town* had been established, towns (like Rhyolite, Nevada, which boomed from 1904 to 1907 [see Nell Murbarger, *Ghosts of the Glory Trail* (Los Angeles: Westernlore Press, 1956)]) could become "ghost towns" very quickly, without a lengthy period of malaise over their decline.

36. Irwin, "Camps of Yesterday," 9.

37. Ibid., 83.

38. G. Smith, "Bodie: Last of the Old-Time Mining Camps"; the quotations, in order of oc-

currence, are from pp. 66, 67, 70, 69, 71, 69, 71, and 74. New Western historian Patricia Nelson Limerick has described how nostalgia haunts the reminiscences of those involved in Western mining, noting that their often painful and quite miserable experiences became dramatically romanticized after they left the West (see Patricia Nelson Limerick, *Something in the Soil: Legacies and Reckonings in the New West* [New York: Norton, 2000], 217).

39. T. A. Rickard, *A History of American Mining* (New York: McGraw-Hill, 1932), 35.

40. D. Smith, "Mining Camps," 96.

41. See Earl Pomeroy, *In Search of the Golden West: The Tourist in Western America* (Lincoln: University of Nebraska Press, 1990); and Alexander Wilson, "The View from the Road," in *Discovered Country: Tourism and Survival in the American West,* ed. Scott Norris (Albuquerque: Stone Ladder Press, 1994), 3–22.

42. D. Smith, "Mining Camps."

43. As early as 1922 "automobile tourists" were arriving in Colorado ghost towns, their numbers increasing with every passing year (Irwin, "The Camps of Yesterday," 91).

44. Not everyone considers Tombstone a ghost town—some of the town's residents, in fact, insist that it is not. Just the same, it is a town greatly declined from its former glory; and its strong connections to the mythic West have earned it listings in ghost town guidebooks covering Arizona (see, for example, Philip Varney, *Arizona Ghost Towns and Mining Camps, a Travel Guide to History* [Phoenix: Arizona Highways, 1994]; and Florin, *Ghost Towns of the West*).

45. See William H. Kelly, "Tombstone, Once Arizona's Wickedest Town, Will Celebrate Golden Jubilee with Re-Enactment of Historic Scenes of Early Days," *Arizona Highways* (October 1929): 6–16; and Marshal Trimble, *Roadside History of Arizona* (Missoula, Mont.: Mountain Press, 1986).

46. See, for example, Russell, "Bodie, Dead City of Mono"; "Bodie Pins Hope on Gas, Electricity and Geology in Search for 'Lost Vein'," *San Francisco Chronicle* (23 September 1930): 4; and Glassock, "Goodbye, God; I'm Going to Bodie."

47. See DeLyser, "Landscape and Social Memory in a California Ghost Town." The books are Emil W. Billeb, *Mining Camp Days* (Las Vegas: Nevada Publications, 1968); and Cain, *The Story of Bodie*. The aggrandizement of the Cain family is particularly evident, for example, in California Department of Parks and Recreation, *Bodie State Historic Park,* where the Cains receive dramatically more (and dramatically more dramatic) mention than other Bodie families. In the case of contemporary Bodie State Historic Park, this can be explained in part by the fact that when early versions of the park's tour brochure were written, few books about the history of the town were available—except Ella Cain's (first published in 1956) (see DeLyser, "Landscape and Social Memory in a California Ghost Town"; and Dydia DeLyser, "'A Walk through Old Bodie': Presenting a Ghost Town in a Tourism Map," in Stephen P. Hanna and Vincent J. Del Casino Jr., eds., *Mapping Tourism* [Minneapolis: University of Minnesota Press, forthcoming]).

48. See Edward Behr, *Prohibition: Thirteen Years That Changed America* (New York: Arcade

Publishing, 1996), 49; and Norman H. Clark, *The Dry Years: Prohibition and Social Change in Washington* (Seattle: University of Washington Press, 1988).

49. Elliott West, *The Saloon on the Rocky Mountain Mining Frontier* (Lincoln: University of Nebraska Press, 1979).

50. DeLyser, "Landscape and Social Memory in a California Ghost Town."

51. West, *The Saloon*, xv.

52. Behr, *Prohibition*.

53. Clark, *The Dry Years*.

54. David E. Kyvig, *Repealing National Prohibition* (Chicago: University of Chicago Press, 1979), 188–189.

55. George Ade, *The Old-Time Saloon: Not Wet—Not Dry, Just History* (New York: Ray Long and Richard R. Smith, 1931), 31.

56. West, *The Saloon*, 142–143.

57. Ibid., xi.

58. "Ghost Town Awakened by Dry Raiders," *San Francisco Chronicle* (17 September 1930); and Will Rogers, "Tourist's Visit to Regenerated Bodie Spoiled by Prohi Squad's Surprise Raid," *San Francisco Chronicle* (28 September 1930): 8F. I am grateful to Paul Greenstein for sharing his insights on Prohibition and the romanticization of ghost towns, encouraging me to see their connection.

59. Passed in October 1942, the Gold Limitation Order, L–280, closed all nonessential mineral mines for the duration of the war in order to free up miners and machinery for the extraction of materials critical to the war effort, like copper. See Duane A. Smith, *Colorado Mining: A Photographic History* (Albuquerque: University of New Mexico Press, 1977).

60. See DeLyser, "Landscape and Social Memory in a California Ghost Town." A number of "old Bodieites" (as old-timers there are still called) have told me that their families finally left the town in the early 1940s, when they themselves were children (in fact, the last school year in the town was 1942–1943) (on Bodie's school, see Everett V. O'Rourke, *The Highest School in California: A Story of Bodie, California* [Sacramento: Spilman Printing, 1978]).

61. See, for example, Robert L. Brown, *Jeep Trails to Colorado Ghost Towns* (Caldwell, Idaho: Caxton Printers, 1963). The increasing number of "four-wheel drivers" in the 1950s and 1960s helped make ghost towns increasingly popular as well, leading, among other things, to increasing vandalism. Duane Smith, for example, suggests that more vandalism occurred in these two decades than during the previous five, as souvenirs were "dug, ripped, or chopped out wherever they were found" (D. Smith, *Colorado Mining*, 153).

62. See, for example, W. A. Chalfant, *Gold, Guns and Ghost Towns* (Stanford: Stanford University Press, 1947); and Rockwell D. Hunt, *California Ghost Towns Live Again* (Stockton, Calif.: College of the Pacific, 1948).

63. California Department of Parks and Recreation, *California Historical Landmarks* (Sacramento: California Department of Parks and Recreation, 1990).

64. D. Smith, "Mining Camps."

65. Hunt, *California Ghost Towns*, 10–11.

66. Remi Nadeau, *Ghost Towns and Mining Camps of California* (Los Angeles: Ward Ritchie, 1965), viii.

67. William Carter, *Ghost Towns of the West: A Sunset Pictorial* (Menlo Park, Calif.: Lane Magazine and Book Co., 1971), 7.

68. S. Dallas, *Colorado Ghost Towns and Mining Camps* (Norman: University of Oklahoma Press, 1985), 4.

69. D. Miller, *Ghost Towns of Washington and Oregon* (Boulder, Colo.: Pruett Publishing, 1977), 1.

70. Lambert Florin, *Ghost Town Trails* (Seattle: Superior Publishing, 1963).

71. See David Lowenthal, *Possessed by the Past: The Heritage Crusade and the Spoils of History* (New York: Free Press, 1996).

72. The "Old West Ghost Town" that Walter Knott constructed was always part of a commercial venture, but his stated original motivation for building it was to inculcate his patrons with the hard-working individualistic spirit of the pioneers that he thought could be gleaned from such landscapes (see Helen Kooiman, *Walter Knott: Keeper of the Flame* [Fullerton, Calif.: Plycon Press, 1973]; and DeLyser, "Landscape and Social Memory in a California Ghost Town").

73. This description of types of ghost towns first appeared in almost the same form in DeLyser, "Authenticity on the Ground," 612. Numerous guidebooks describe Western ghost towns; two particularly detailed examples are Florin, *Ghost Towns of the West;* and Murbarger, *Ghosts of the Glory Trail.* Further discussions of mining landscapes and the growth and decline of mining towns (in some cases including Bodie) can be found in Homer Aschmann, "The Natural History of a Mine," *Economic Geography* 46, no. 2 (1970): 172–189; Gunther Barth, *Instant Cities: Urbanization and the Rise of San Francisco and Denver* (New York: Oxford University Press, 1975); Richard V. Francaviglia, *Hard Places: Reading the Landscape of America's Historic Mining Districts* (Iowa City: University of Iowa Press, 1991); and Paul Francis Starrs, "Esmeralda County, Nevada: Empty Land? Poor Land? Fair Land?" (master's thesis, University of California–Berkeley, Department of Geography, 1984). Although the status of ghost town does seem to bring tourism to towns such as Tombstone, with a functioning chamber of commerce and many operational businesses, some residents in such towns prefer to deny that their town is a ghost town, focusing not on the fact that their town is now much smaller than it once was, but rather on the fact that many businesses are still viable today. In this sense, the status of ghost town may be a double-edged sword: Although it brings a certain notoriety, some residents may feel it is stigmatizing as well.

74. DeLyser, "Landscape and Social Memory in a California Ghost Town." I am indebted to production designer Paul Greenstein for his insights into the film production process.

12 | Where the Cowboy Rides Away

Mythic Places for Western Film

GARY J. HAUSLADEN

In 1903 *The Great Train Robbery* transported the Western from desert dust and printed page to crisp celluloid, where it would remain an important American film genre off and on for the next seven decades. It functioned as "fantasy-folklore," reflecting "the attitudes and dreams of the West itself, and of Americans toward their West."[1] As a film genre, the Western was concerned with settlement and utopianism, with empire and territorial expansion. But primarily, the Western attempted to reassert and institutionalize male-dominated, white Anglo-Saxon society as the bedrock of American national identity. Since 1980, or so, however, the Western film has metamorphosed, continuing its reflection of our self-identity, yet in different ways. "American," only more so, the Western cries out for a geographical analysis that focuses on the role of *setting*, which a geographer might refer to as *place*, in dealing with these issues. In fact, film critics have characterized the Western as "one genre in which 'setting' functions as a living character."[2] Although perhaps a slight exaggeration, this underscores the key role of setting in the genre.

> The literature of the West is not suited to the novel. It is a genre of visual spectacle, and it found its medium—its own highest expression—in the movies.[3]

I explore, here, how film's depictions of the American West influenced and continues to influence how Americans perceive the West as a reflection of cultural and national values and how this has changed over time. A recognizable "sense of place" emerged from the genre, and it was this sense of the

296

American West that helped mold how Americans conceived of the West as a place, in and of itself, as well as part of their national cultural heritage.

The Early Years

There are numerous treatments of the history of the Western in American film that are readable and insightful.[4] Rather than repeat the wide range of discussions and arguments, this chapter offers a brief summary of key points as context for focusing on the role played by setting in this most American of genres. But there also loom a few basic questions: What made the Western so appealing? Why the love affair between the Western and cinema? How did the Western evolve into an effective conveyor of the great American myth? Why was setting such an important part of this visual mythology? And how did all this change over time, as the West itself changed?

The cultural context for understanding the rise in popularity of the Western began in the final decades of the nineteenth century. It was a time of concern and restlessness in the United States. Still living the aftermath of the Civil War, in the early stages of the Industrial Revolution, and in an economic depression surpassed only by the later Great Depression, the country was seeing a massive influx of non–Anglo-Saxon immigrants, feared by many as diluting the basic fabric of American culture. Such change added insecurity and uncertainty to our sense of who we were as a people, what we were becoming as a nation. Add to this list struggles for labor power, culminating in the Great Strike of 1877, and women's suffrage, which would eventually result in the passage of the Nineteenth Amendment in 1920.

As if these weren't enough, the feminizing effects of urbanization—ostensibly through the increasing influence of mothers on the development of young boys—was interpreted not just as bad, but as an active threat to the foundation of basic (and therefore presumably male) American values. Following in the footsteps of the YMCA, founded in 1851, to the rescue emerged the Boy Scouts of America, founded in 1910, and the Western in literature and film (1902 and 1903, respectively).

From the beginning, the Western formula included three basic components: (1) the cowboy as hero; (2) the frontier experience as storyline; and (3) the West as landscape/setting. The prototype for the cowboy was first presented by James Fenimore Cooper, between 1823 and 1850, in his Leatherstocking novels, in the guise of a frontiersman, the legendary Hawkeye, Natty Bumppo. Cooper set the stage for great Western novelists to come, including Bret Harte, Zane Grey, Louis L'Amour, and Owen Wister.[5] The *plot* was set on the frontier and included transgressions against society by Indians, Mexicans, Mormons, and flat-out bad guys, or some combination of these, generally associated with the urban East. Because they occurred beyond civilization, these transgressions had to be dealt with violently to restore law and order, by a single hero, who was generally a loner (a solitary cowboy), outside of society. And the setting for these stories was *the American West*, those "particular, picturesque American landscapes"[6] that enhance the confrontations and transformations that take place. Two of these components made this genre uniquely American and were important components of American national identity: the cowboy as hero and the American West as frontier setting (place).

Most influential in molding the vision of the West and the story of the Western into the form we know today were the novelists Owen Wister and Bret Harte, the artists Albert Bierstadt and Frederic Remington, the historian Frederick Jackson Turner, historian and later President Teddy Roosevelt, and the showman Buffalo Bill Cody.

Although James Fenimore Cooper is credited with providing the early prototype, before a popular tradition could be created, "a wider array of characters as well as a more spectacular landscape would need to be invented."[7] These were provided in the 1860s by the painter Albert Bierstadt and the novelist Bret Harte. "There is a special aptness to the fact that Bret Harte emerged at this historical moment to fictionalize a Far West being rendered in paint by Bierstadt in a style equally extravagant."[8] The particular strengths of each, however, would stay separated until after the turn of the century. In *Westerns: Making the Man in Fiction and Film,* Lee Clark Mitchell credits Owen Wister with bringing together for the first time the settings of Bierstadt and the characters of Bret Harte to create the archetypical Western as first presented in *The Virginian* (1902). John Ford would later accomplish the same feat on film with *Stagecoach* (1939).

But it was not just in literature that the formulation of the Western was taking place. In academia, politics, and entertainment, parallel transformations were under way. To this day, no one writing about the West and its role in American history can avoid paying homage to Frederick Jackson Turner and his Frontier Thesis, first presented in 1893. "The Significance of the Frontier in American History"[9] was the foundation of American historiography for most of the twentieth century, and the literary evolution of a Western genre seems to have been influenced by Turner's interpretation of the Western frontier experience. For the American public, however, Teddy Roosevelt and Buffalo Bill Cody were probably more influential. As argued in the "Introduction" to this book, the impact of Buffalo Bill's interpretation reached a much larger audience than did the academic Turner's. But even in academia, Roosevelt's *The Winning of the West*[10] was most likely the dominant model for the Western story during its formative years. Although Turner and Roosevelt agreed on many points, two aspects of Roosevelt's interpretation differ in significant ways. First, the hero of the frontier was a white Anglo-Saxon male, first a hunter, then an Indian fighter, and later a cowboy. Second, whereas Turner all but ignored Native Americans, Roosevelt made it clear that there were two barriers to Western conquest—the physical environment and the Indians. This approach was reinforced by Roosevelt's childhood friends.

> Theodore Roosevelt, Frederic Remington and Owen Wister, all, in varying degrees, subscribed to the idea of the cowboy as the last pure representative of Anglo-Saxon virility and primitive individualism.[11]

> This elite concern with personal regeneration emerged at a time when many Americans feared a decline in American morality and a rise of personal and political corruption spurred by industrialism, the new immigration, the decline of rural life, and the increasing demands of women for jobs, education, and the vote.[12]

During the first three decades of the twentieth century, filmmakers could not get enough Western scripts to satisfy their demand. It was a popular genre during the silent movie era, culminating in the Academy Award for Best Picture, which went to *Cimarron* in 1931. Just as it reached the pinnacle of popularity and critical acclaim, however, the Western faded as an important genre. Most critics blame some combination of the Great Depression and the studio system.[13] But just as the insecurity and uncertainty of turn-of-the-century America had fostered the first wave of Westerns, the need for re-establishing a clear national identity gave rise to the resurrection of the genre in the late 1930s.

The Golden Era

The resurgence of the Western in the late 1930s has been interpreted as a response to the need for America to regain faith in its patriotic myths, especially against the rising tide of German and Japanese nationalism.[14] The history of the frontier was seen as a potentially fruitful area to look for these myths. With the wagon wheels and rolling ruts of John Ford's *Stagecoach* (1939) was ushered in the "golden age" of the Western, which would last into the 1970s. During four decades the three components—the cowboy hero, the frontier plot, and the Western setting—would be stoked like enriched uranium as a mythic formula.

The Cowboy as American Hero

The cowboy hero of this era was, in his own right, a mythic figure.

> The cowboy legend is the most enduring of Western folklore . . . this man on horseback, with his boots and Stetson, has come to epitomize the West, even America itself.[15]

From the very first close-up of him in *Stagecoach*, John Wayne would epitomize this archetypical hero. He would be joined in Western deification by some of the most popular actors ever, including Robert Young, Alan Ladd, Gary Cooper, Cary Grant, Henry Fonda, James Stewart, Kirk Douglas, Clark Gable, William Holden, and Clint Eastwood. This is not to forget that Errol Flynn and Douglas Fairbanks had weathered eminently successful stints as cowboys before they rose to greater fame as swashbucklers during the silent movie era.

As we shall see, one of the criticisms of both Western history and the Western as myth is who was left out in the pantheon of heroes. Women, for example, generally served as icons of civilization and the advancement of society. Mexicans, Mormons, and Native Americans generally got thrown in with the bad guys.

> The whole history of the Western is therefore, at one level, inescapably bound up with reducing Native Americans and women to functions in a symbolic world centering on White male characters and embodying White (and particularly Anglo-Saxon) male visions of national and gender identity.[16]

This is a generalization of the genre but one that is more often true than not. It does not take into account, however, numerous movies that had strong female leads, as, for example, Joan Crawford in *Johnny Guitar* and Marlene Dietrich in *Destry Rides Again* and *Rancho Notorious,* or that were sympathetic to Native Americans, as in the case of *Devil's Doorway,* even though the lead Indian, Lance Poole, was played by Robert Taylor. In fact, Steve Neal has identified quite a stable of "pro-Indian films," made during the golden era of the classic Western.[17] As a rule, however, these kinds of movies were few and far between.

> Only the "Anglo-Saxon" (male) supposedly had "the spirit of adventure, courage, and self-sufficiency" needed for survival "in the clean cattle country" of the American West.[18]

The Frontier Plot

As for the Western plot, there are numerous categorizations for the formula. Citing Will Wright, *Six Guns and Society*, Noel Carroll lists four plot types: the classical plot, vengeance variation, transition theme, and the professional plot.[19] Jon Tuska comes up with three: the formulary Western, the historical romance, and the historical reconstruction. And Frank Gruber, a veteran writer of pulp fiction, offers seven:

> 1) The Union Pacific Story centering around the construction of a railroad, telegraph or stagecoach line or around the adventures of a wagon train; 2) The Ranch Story with its focus on conflicts between ranchers and rustlers, or cattlemen and sheepmen; 3) The Empire Story, which is an epic version of the Ranch Story; 4) The Revenge Story; 5) Custer's Last Stand, or the Cavalry and Indian Story; 6) The Outlaw Story; and 7) The Marshall Story.[20]

However categorized, the plots of the Western focused on the processes of imperialism, the antagonisms between civilization versus savagery, the ascendancy of progress and modernization, and the conquest of freedom and individualism. It was within the context of progress and conquest that the key theme of the Western was the rejuvenation of the cowboy hero, especially as icon for American society. It was the frontier experience that would allow him to renew himself and establish civility on the margins of society. And it was through violence only that law and order could be restored, the West transformed.

Mythic Locations for Western Films

The location of films became an important part of forwarding the overall mission; landscapes with wide open spaces were employed, often backdropped with mountain peaks or interrupted by buttes and rock formations—vast venues expressing the openness and danger of the frontier—fundamentally antiurban, anti-Eastern, anti-European, male.

> The one aspect of the landscape celebrated consistently in the Western is the opportunity for renewal, for self-transformation, for release from constraints associated with an urbanized East.[21]

Initially, the use of these kinds of Western places provided authenticity, unlike, for example, the New Jersey locations for *The Great Train Robbery*. A striving after authenticity was an important consideration during the early years of American cinema, partially in response to end-of-the-nineteenth-century dominance of French cinema in this country and particularly in response to the needs of the genre and the storylines.

> Part of the reason Westerns were so invested in historical authenticity . . . is paradoxically because they aspire to mythic resolution of crises.[22]

The ambiguous nature of delineating "the West," as discussed in the "Introduction," suggests that many places would be used to capture the great diversity of the American West. Nothing could be further from the truth. The key to understanding why so few places and even fewer kinds of places were selected for filming Westerns lies in the fact that the West is more psychological than geographical. Its role is to help forward mythogenesis, not to recreate history, or as Mitchell credits Harte with imagining—"the West as a dramatic (and therefore moral) terrain rather than a geographical one."[23] What and where events actually happened are not the primary focus of the myth; rather, it speaks to who we are as a people. It helps in the formulation of a national identity. This is why, even though the heroes and the storylines change over time, certain kinds of places persist as settings—because they fulfill the very same role they always have in Westerns—they are places for transformation, regeneration, rejuvenation, and resurrection. Thus, wide-open spaces, with grand vistas, often in desert lands, reflect certain of the values associated with the West in ways that mountainous regions or coastal areas, for example, do not.

> Moreover, the Western landscape is uniquely adaptable to certain powerful visual effects. The sharp contrasts of light and shadow characteristic of an arid climate together with the topographical contrasts of plain and mountain, rocky outcrops and flat deserts, steep bare canyons and forested plateaus created a uniquely effective backdrop to heroic adventure.[24]
> . . . even at their flattest [these settings] have a tendency to elevate rather commonplace plots into epic spectacles.[25]

Map 12.1 depicts where, in fact, the most popular Westerns of the twentieth century were filmed. These one hundred "major and representative Western films" are listed chronologically in Table 12.1[26] and by region in Table 12.2.

These films include Westerns identified by a number of critics as the best of the "A" Westerns. Several trends emerge; when grouped together, southern California, including Lone Pine and Death Valley; southern Utah and northern Arizona, dominated by Monument Valley; New Mexico, Old Tucson, and southern Arizona; and northern Mexico account for over 75 percent of all these major movie locations.

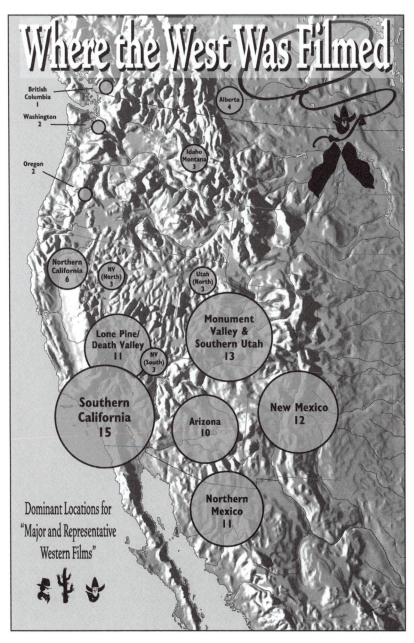

MAP 12.1. Where the West was filmed: dominant locations for "major and representative Western films." Map by Paul F. Starrs.

Table 12.1 Locations for One Hundred "Major and Representative Western Films"

The Great Train Robbery, 1903	New Jersey
Fighting Blood, 1911	San Fernando, Sierra Madre, California
The Squaw Man, 1914	San Pedro, Lake Arrowhead, California
The Outcasts of Poker Flat, 1919	Truckee, California
The Last of the Mohicans, 1920	Big Bear Lake and Yosemite, California
The Covered Wagon, 1923	Sonora, California; northern Nevada
The Iron Horse, 1924	Newhall, California
Riders of the Purple Sage, 1925	Lone Pine, California
Tumbleweeds, 1925	no location data
The Gold Rush, 1925	Truckee, California
The Vanishing American, 1926	Catalina Island, California; Monument Valley
3 Bad Men, 1926	Mojave Desert, California; Jackson Hole, Wyoming
The Virginian, 1929	no location data
Billy the Kid, 1930	Grand Canyon, Arizona; Gallup, New Mexico
Cimarron, 1931	no location data
Wells Fargo, 1937	California: Sonora, Chico, Napa Valley, Angel's Camp
Destry Rides Again, 1939	no location data
Drums along the Mohawk, 1939	Wasatch range, Utah
Stagecoach, 1939	Monument Valley
Union Pacific, 1939	Oklahoma, Utah, Iowa
Jesse James, 1939	Missouri
The Westerner, 1940	Tucson, Arizona
They Died with Their Boots On, 1941	Agoura, California
The Ox-Bow Incident, 1943	Lone Pine, California
My Darling Clementine, 1946	Monument Valley
Pursued, 1947	Gallup, New Mexico
Red River, 1948	Elgin, Arizona
Fort Apache, 1948	Monument Valley
The Treasure of the Sierra Madre, 1948	Mexico; Mojave Desert
3 Godfathers, 1948	Death Valley, Mojave Desert, Lone Pine, California
She Wore a Yellow Ribbon, 1949	Monument Valley; Death Valley, California
Broken Arrow, 1950	Lone Pine, California
Winchester '73, 1950	Tucson, Arizona
Wagonmaster, 1950	Moab, Utah
The Gunfighter, 1950	Death Valley, Lone Pine, California
The Big Sky, 1952	Grand Teton National Park, Wyoming
High Noon, 1952	Southern California

Table 12.1 (continued)

Bend of the River, 1952	Mount Hood, Oregon
Hondo, 1953	Camajo, Mexico
Shane, 1953	Jackson, Wyoming
Vera Cruz, 1954	Cuernavaca, Mexico
Johnny Guitar, 1954	Sedona, Arizona
The Far Country, 1954	Alberta, Canada
The Man from Laramie, 1955	Santa Fe, Taos, New Mexico
The Searchers, 1956	Monument Valley and southern Utah
Run of the Arrow, 1957	St. George, Utah
The Tall T, 1957	Lone Pine, California
The Left-Handed Gun, 1958	Santa Fe, New Mexico
Man of the West, 1958	Mojave Desert, California
The Horse Soldiers, 1959	Louisiana, Mississippi, Texas
Rio Bravo, 1959	Old Tucson, Arizona
The Hanging Tree, 1959	Yakima, Washington
Comanche Station, 1960	Lone Pine, California
The Magnificent Seven, 1960	no location data
One-Eyed Jacks, 1961	Big Sur, Monterey, Death Valley, California
The Misfits, 1961	Reno, Dayton, Nevada
Lonely Are the Brave, 1962	Albuquerque, New Mexico
The Man Who Shot Liberty Valance, 1962	no location data
Ride the High Country, 1962	Inyo National Forest, California
How the West Was Won, 1963	Lone Pine, California
Hud, 1963	Texas
Cheyenne Autumn, 1964	Monument Valley
The Sons of Katie Elder, 1965	Mexico
The Professionals, 1966	Death Valley, California, Las Vegas, Nevada
El Dorado, 1967	Old Tucson, Arizona
Hang 'em High, 1967	White Sands and Las Cruces, New Mexico
The Shooting, 1967	Utah
Butch Cassidy and the Sundance Kid, 1969	New Mexico, Utah
True Grit, 1969	Mexico, Colorado, Mammoth, California
The Wild Bunch, 1969	northern Mexico
The Ballad of Cable Hogue, 1970	Las Vegas, Nevada, New Mexico
Little Big Man, 1970	Montana, Alberta, Canada
A Man Called Horse, 1970	Durango, Mexico
Soldier Blue, 1970	Mexico

Table 12.1 (continued)

Two Mules for Sister Sara, 1970	Mexico
McCabe and Mrs. Miller, 1971	Vancouver, British Columbia, Canada
Jeremiah Johnson, 1972	Zion National Park, Utah
Ulzana's Raid, 1972	Nogales, Arizona, Las Vegas, Nevada
High Plains Drifter, 1973	Mono Lake, California
Pat Garrett and Billy the Kid, 1973	Durango, Mexico
Rooster Cogburn, 1975	Oregon
Buffalo Bill and the Indians:	
Or Sitting Bull's History Lesson, 1976	Alberta, Canada
Missouri Breaks, 1976	northwestern Montana
The Outlaw Josey Wales, 1976	Arizona, Oroville, California, and Utah
The Shootist, 1976	Carson City, Nevada
Heaven's Gate, 1980	Idaho, Montana
The Long Riders, 1980	Georgia
Legend of the Lone Ranger, 1981	New Mexico
Ballad of Gregorio Cortez, 1982	New Mexico
Pale Rider, 1985	Idaho, Columbia, California
Silverado, 1985	New Mexico
Three Amigos, 1986	Simi Valley, California, Old Tucson, Arizona
Young Guns, 1988	New Mexico
Dances with Wolves, 1990	South Dakota
Unforgiven, 1992	Alberta, Canada
Last of the Mohicans, 1992	North Carolina
Geronimo, 1994	Moab, Utah
Wyatt Earp, 1994	New Mexico
Dead Man, 1995	California, Nevada, Oregon, Washington
Lone Star, 1996	Texas

Source: Data from John Cawelti, *The Six-Gun Mystique Sequel* (Bowling Green, Ohio: Popular Press, 1999), 194–196.

Conspicuous by their absence, or at least minor representation, are places such as the Dakotas, Colorado, Texas, and Oklahoma, often correlated with the idea of the West but not nearly as fruitful as other locales.

What did the dominant locations have in common? Thomas Schatz "distinguishes between genres of contested and uncontested space. Those like the Western and some other action genres, in which control of the setting is largely what is at stake . . ."[27] clearly fit into any conceptualization of "contested space." They immediately solicit links to Frederick Jackson Turner's interpretation of the Western frontier as a massive void into which American frontiersmen could advance. These venues cry out to be conquered, tamed, and transformed into homelands for civilized society. That the same kinds of settings were used over and over means that for most Americans, the first glance at these settings puts us in the proper frame of mind for the transformations that are about to take place. John Cawelti puts it quite succinctly:

> These topographic features created an effective backdrop for the action of the Western because they exemplify in visual images the thematic conflict between civilization and savagery and its resolution.[28]

Special Places

Two places are most closely associated with the making of Western films—Monument Valley of southern Utah and northern Arizona and the Alabama Hills outside Lone Pine, California. Their contributions to our images of the American West cannot be overestimated. Nowhere do the necessary kinds of visual images resonate more than in these two places, where the landscape

Table 12.2 Dominant Locations for "Major and Representative Western Films," by Region

Southern California, excluding Lone Pine and Death Valley	13
Lone Pine and Death Valley	15
Northern California	6
northern Utah	3
Monument Valley and southern Utah	13
New Mexico	12
Arizona	10
northern Mexico	11
northern Nevada	3
southern Nevada	3
British Columbia	1
Washington	2
Oregon	2
Alberta, Canada	4
Idaho and Montana	3

Source: Data from table 12.1.

parallels stories of confrontation, fear, liberation, and transformation. These are landscapes that are as much a part of the Western myth as the characters and stories that inhabit them.

Monument Valley, southern Utah and northern Arizona

I imagine that many people are surprised, as I was, to discover that only twenty movies were actually made in Monument Valley, of which ten were Westerns. The power of the imagery of Monument Valley results from two factors: first, the true splendor of the landscape, which is unforgettable no matter how many times you've seen it—one time would suffice; and second, the importance of the movies that were shot there, so that most people have seen at least one of the ten films. This was John Ford's favorite location for his Westerns, which many believe are some of the most important Westerns ever produced, beginning with *Stagecoach* (Figure 12.1).

FIG. 12.1. Classic John Ford shot—stage crossing Monument Valley in *Stagecoach* (1939). Courtesy Academy of Motion Picture Arts and Sciences.

Fɪɢ. 12.2. In homage to John Ford, Sergio Leone shot much of *Once upon a Time in the West* (1968) in Monument Valley. Courtesy British Film Institute.

Ford uses the great isolated monoliths—the sandstone "teapots"—of Monument Valley in *Stagecoach* to project something richly enigmatic. Ford's panoramic long shots of the stagecoach threading its way among these massive rock formations reflected the basic uncertainty and ambiguity of human existence, and were a fitting image for a nation struggling to survive a terrible depression and on the verge of war.[29]

Stagecoach all but resurrected the Western and initiated the "golden era" of the genre. Other famous Ford Westerns include the Cavalry Trilogy—*My Darling Clementine, Fort Apache,* and *She Wore a Yellow Ribbon,* not to mention *The Searchers, Sergeant Rutledge,* and *Cheyenne Autumn.* The impact of Monument Valley is closely correlated to the grandeur of the scenery and the quality and success of the films shot there. Ironically, even Sergio Leone, in homage to John Ford, shot much of *Once upon a Time in the West* in Monument Valley (Figure 12.2).

John Ford returned to these forms for his Westerns because of their symbolic imagery and because, once established, they would continue to elicit the intended emotional responses from the audience. Interesting, however, is how Ford manipulated Monument Valley so that, although the settings were similar, they never seemed to be the same. Leutrat and Liandrat-Guigues chronicle how Ford varied his use of his favorite setting to avoid the impression of merely using the same backdrop over and over again.[30]

Although Monument Valley was not unknown as a setting for movies prior to *Stagecoach*, it is the timing of this particular film that imbued it with mythic qualities from the very start. As mentioned, America was looking for national myths to underscore our potential strength and greatness as a country in the face of economic depression and growing nationalism in Germany and Japan. In the Western and its cowboy hero we found national myths to meet these needs. That John Ford chose Monument Valley to film these early mythic tales guaranteed its contribution to American mythology and national identity.

Alabama Hills, Lone Pine, California

The Alabama Hills near Lone Pine, California, is another special place for Westerns. My first visit to this locale for myth making underscored the power of these places to elicit emotions built up over years of watching Westerns in film and on television.

July 10, 2000

Standing on the corner of Whitney Portal and Movie Road, in the Alabama Hills [Figure 12.3], for the very first time, elicits images and memories that reach back decades to a childhood filled with the Lone Ranger, Hopalong Cassidy, Roy Rogers, and Gene Autry, to name the most famous and the best remembered. For someone, especially a man in his 50s, an examination of the Western in film becomes a personal journey. Intended or not, by definition I am a participant observer.[31]

If Monument Valley's reputation was built of quality, that of the Alabama Hills was built primarily on quantity, although a number of important and successful films were shot there. The stark, forbidding images of unusual rock formations and desert vistas were fed to us over and over again (Figure 12.4). Some of the better-known Westerns shot here include *High Sierra, Riders of the Purple Sage, Bad Day at Black Rock, Comanche Station, Waterhole No. 3,* and *How the West Was Won* (Figure 12.5). In all, nearly three hundred movies were filmed there, and this does not include many of the most popular TV series, including, all or in part, *Annie Oakley, Gene Autry, Bonanza, Death Valley Days, Have Gun Will Travel, Hopalong Cassidy, The Lone Ranger, Roy Rogers, The Virginian, Wagon Train,* and *Wild Bill Hickok.*[32]

Fig. 12.3. Corner of Whitney Portal and Movie Road—entrance to the Alabama Hills, Lone Pine, California. Photo by author.

Fig. 12.4. Unusual rock formations and desert vistas typify the Alabama Hills, Lone Pine, California. Photo by author.

FIG. 12.5. With the High Sierra in the background, *How the West Was Won* (1963) was one of the more successful Westerns filmed in the Alabama Hills. Courtesy Academy of Motion Picture Arts and Sciences.

As one looks at these landscapes for Westerns, adjectives that repeat themselves include *stark, foreboding, dangerous, God-forsaken,* but at the same time *wide open, challenging, liberating.* The cowboy, as icon for an entire society, who can master and survive in such an environment must be a rugged, intelligent, inventive individualist, someone who is able to become part of this uniquely

American environment. Later, movies would extend these traits to Native Americans, Hispanics, women, and blacks. The myths and legends have changed, but the settings for the mythogenesis remain the same.

The Setting of the Western Sun

The waning of the popularity of the Western occurred in the 1970s, when the Western increasingly failed to help explain who we were as a people and was inadequate to serve as the bedrock of American national identity. Civil and women's rights movements, the war in Vietnam, and a loss of confidence in our national leadership as a result of Watergate and other scandals undermined the effectiveness of the Western to explain national identity. Several attacks on the tropes and symbols of the classic form of the genre signaled changes to come. *The Wild Bunch* (1969), which many critics chose to analyze as a commentary on American involvement in Vietnam, specifically addresses the end of the cowboy hero era and thus the end of the classic cowboy hero as American icon. Sam Peckinpah filmed *The Wild Bunch* because he believed it to be the best explanation he'd seen about what happened to the cowboy. *McCabe and Mrs. Miller* (1971) was a particularly disturbing movie, not only switching gender roles, but also setting this switch in the rainy, tree-laden Northwest. More iconoclastic was *Little Big Man* (1970), which satirized and parodied almost all the major tropes and tenets of the classic Western, and the wildly popular box office success, *Blazing Saddles* (1974). And it would be unforgivable to ignore the spate of "spaghetti Westerns" that was produced in the 1960s and 1970s—over three hundred in all, but especially the work of Sergio Leone. The *Dollars* trilogy and *Once upon a Time in the West* represent the best of a subgenre that has been attacked as trash, ignoring the moral essence of the Western, and as brilliant critiques of the history of the cinematic myth—movies about the making of Western mythology. At either extreme, or on ground somewhere in between, the spaghetti Westerns correctly fit into any discussion of the questioning of the genre that occurred in the 1960s and 1970s. Just as the theses of Turner and Roosevelt were being attacked in academia for misconstruing the nature of the American frontier experience, and just as Americans were questioning many of the tenets of American culture, the Western as myth was losing its effectiveness, and numerous films addressed this ineffectiveness.

The new Western histories and our reexamination of the Western frontier experience have called into question many of the basic tenets of the classic Western. We are now reminded that women participated in the frontiering experience and that the Western frontier was not an empty receptacle into which the United States could expand. Native Americans had been there for millennia and Hispanics for centuries. As well, we now recognize that Native Americans and Hispanics were not simply savages, barriers like the natural environment that needed to be conquered or pacified, and that white Anglo-Saxon pioneers were not always pinnacles of virtue and goodness.

But this change in cultural context did not forebode the death of the genre. It has adapted and been revised; clearly its place as one of the most important American film genres is long gone. During the past fifteen years, however, even though the numbers have diminished, there continues a string of Westerns, many of which might be referred to as revisionist in nature, but possibly reflecting simply another adaptation to the traditional formula. Westerns as parodies in the tradition of *Little Big Man* and *Blazing Saddles* include the box office flop *The Three Amigos* (1986), one of the worst Westerns ever filmed; revisionist Westerns include *Dances with Wolves* (1990), *Last of the Mohicans* (1992), and *Geronimo: An American Legend* (1994), which attempt to provide an authentic Native American discourse; *The Ballad of Little Jo* (1993), which addresses gender issues, and *Unforgiven* (1992), *Posse* (1993), which competes with *Three Amigos* for being the worst of these movies, and *Tombstone* (1993), which redefined the basic character of the cowboy hero. Several of these have been box office successes, and two, *Dances with Wolves* and *Unforgiven,* have received the highest critical acclaim possible, the Academy Award for Best Picture. The Western is a greatly revised genre.

Of these revisionist films, possibly the most intriguing is the remake of *Last of the Mohicans,* filmed in 1992. First and foremost, it returns us to the roots of the genre—James Fenimore Cooper and the prototype for the cowboy hero, Natty Bumppo—Hawkeye. But this film is more than just a nostalgic return to roots; as mentioned, it attempts to provide an authentic voice to Native Americans, which it does and which is why it is considered revisionist. But even beyond its revisionist contributions, this remake calls into question our perception of the settings for Westerns. This is a frontier Western. Set in upstate New York, west of the Hudson River, it reminds us that "the West" is not just a psychological place, it is also time specific. In the late 1700s, this was the American West, it was the frontier. And this is a story not just of the decimation of a people by the onslaught of progress, but also of the loss of the frontier as well. In the movie's waning moments, Chingachgook tells Hawkeye:

> Now, it's true. The frontier place is for people like my white son and his woman and their children. And one day there will be no more frontier. And one like you

will go too, like the Mohicans. A new people will come, work, struggle, some will make their life. But once, we were here.[33]

Somber music plays as backdrop while the three of them—Chingachgook, Hawkeye, and Cora Munro—overlook the rolling forested hills of what was then the frontier.[34] We remember from earlier in the film that Hawkeye, before he met Heyward and the Munros, was heading westward. When Major Heyward asks Hawkeye where he is headed, Hawkeye reveals a bit of frontier humor.

HAWKEYE: Heading to Kentucky.
HEYWARD: There is a war on. How is it you are heading West?
HAWKEYE: Well, we kinda face to the north and, real sudden like, turn left.[35]

For most films, however, what is curious in the first decade of the twenty-first century is that we do not necessarily find new kinds of settings for these new kinds of Westerns. The heroes have been transformed to include women, blacks, Hispanics, and Native Americans. Even the persona of the cowboy has been transformed to offer a more complex and realistic archetype. The storylines have also been modified to more closely reflect the reality of the frontier experience. Neverthless, the settings—the places for Westerns—remain the same; at least the kinds of places endure. Over the past fifteen years, of thirty major Westerns, 70 percent continue to be made in New Mexico, southern Arizona, Utah, and southern California. These *same* kinds of images serve well as settings for the *new* kinds of Westerns.

Western Legacies

Eulogies have foretold the passing of the Western as an important genre of the American cinema beginning as early as the 1910s. The 1930s saw the Western all but disappear only to be revived at the end of the decade, a revival that ushered in the "golden era" of Westerns, an era that lasted almost forty years. Most recently, 1980 has been cited as the end of the golden era of the Western, terminated by the colossal box office failure, Michael Cimino's *Heaven's Gate*. But a quick review of www.imdb.com for the past fifteen years reveals that rumors about the death of the Western are greatly exaggerated. Since 1985 (figuring that movies made in the early 1980s were already in production when *Heaven's Gate* was pummeled both in reviews and at the box office) the number of major Westerns has averaged about three a year.

The role of the Western is still to facilitate our identification of a national identity. But now, this identity does not simply rest on the shoulders of white

Anglo-Saxon men. Rather, the multiethnic nature of the evolution of our diverse and complicated society requires explanation, and part of that explanation focuses on the roles of blacks, Hispanics, Native Americans, women, Mormons, entrepreneurs, and capitalists in the settling of the frontier. The characters and the storylines change, but the setting remains the same. And it still functions as a facilitator—facilitating the transformation of all these diverse people during the frontiering experience.

> The persistence of the West in various cultural forms also attests to the central role it continues to play in conceptions of national identity.[36]

Why is it that places for Westerns remain the same? Primarily because, even though the heroes and the storylines have been modified, the role of setting remains the same—to help foster transformation, regeneration, rejuvenation, and resurrection. These are still mythic places that help us come to grips with our national identity and who we are as a people.

Notes

1. Brian Garfield, *Western Films: A Complete Guide* (New York: Da Capo Press, 1982), 3.

2. *Microsoft Cinemania 96* CD.

3. Brian Garfield, *Western Films,* 13.

4. Edward Buscombe and Roberta Pearson, eds., *Back in the Saddle Again: New Essays on the Western* (London: British Film Institute Publishing, 1998); Ian Cameron and Douglas Pye, eds., *The Book of Westerns* (New York: Continuum, 1996); John Cawelti, *The Six-Gun Mystique Sequel* (Bowling Green, Ohio: Popular Press, 1999); Michael Coyne, *The Crowded Prairie: American National Identity in the Hollywood Western* (New York: Tauris, 1998); Lee Clark Mitchell, *Westerns: Making the Man in Fiction and Film* (Chicago: University of Chicago Press, 1996); Richard Slotkin, *Gunfighter Nation: The Myth of the Frontier in Twentieth-Century America* (Norman: University of Oklahoma Press, 1998); Jon Tuska, *The American West in Film: Critical Approaches to the Western* (Westport, Conn.: Greenwood Press, 1985); Alf Walle, *The Cowboy Hero and Its Audience: Popular Culture as Market Derived Art* (Bowling Green, Ohio: Popular Press, 2000); and Will Wright, *Six Guns and Society* (Berkeley: University of California Press, 1975).

5. For an insightful and readable overview of the contribution of James Fenimore Cooper to the evolution of the quintessential American hero, see William Humphrey, *Ah, Wilderness! The Frontier in American Literature* (El Paso: Texas Western Press, 1977).

6. Richard Abel, "'Our Country'/Whose Country? The 'Americanization' Project of Early Westerns," in *Back in the Saddle Again,* 78.

7. Lee Clark Mitchell, *Westerns,* 54.

8. Ibid., 72.

9. Frederick Jackson Turner, "The Significance of the Frontier in American History," in *Annual Report of the American Historical Association for the Year 1893* (Washington, D.C.: Government Printing Office, 1894), 199–227.

10. Theodore Roosevelt, *The Winning of the West*, 7 vols. (New York: Putnam's Sons, 1907).

11. Gaylyn Studlar, "Wider Horizons: Douglas Fairbanks and Nostalgic Primitivism," in *Back in the Saddle Again*, 73 n.

12. Cawelti, *The Six-Gun Mystique Sequel*, 66.

13. Richard Slotkin, *Gunfighter Nation*, 255–277.

14. Ibid., 279–281.

15. Robert Athearn, *The Mythic West in Twentieth-Century America* (Lawrence: University Press of Kansas, 1986), 23.

16. Cameron and Pye, eds., *The Book of Westerns*, 13.

17. Steve Neal, "Vanishing Americans: Racial and Ethnic Issues in the Interpretation and Context of Post-War 'Pro-Indian' Westerns," in *Back in the Saddle Again*, 8–28.

18. Abel, "'Our Country'/Whose Country?" 82.

19. Noel Carroll, "The Professional Western: South of the Border," in *Back in the Saddle Again*, 46.

20. Cawelti, *The Six-Gun Mystique Sequel*, 19.

21. Mitchell, *Westerns*, 24.

22. Ibid., 24.

23. Ibid., 89.

24. Cawelti, *The Six-Gun Mystique Sequel*, 26.

25. Ibid., 24.

26. Ibid., 194–196. Dates and locations from www.imdb.com. Spaghetti Westerns have been excluded. Because important films were left out of Cawelti's list, additional films included Westerns included in the AFI top one hundred films, plus films from lists of other film critics, as cited in Cawelti, 194–201: Ed Buscombe, Allen Eyles, Christopher Frayling, Phil Hardy, Colin McArthur, Tom Milne, Ted Reinhart, David Thomson, and Robin Wood.

27. Cameron and Pye, eds., *The Book of Westerns*, 21.

28. Cawelti, *The Six-Gun Mystique Sequel*, 23–24.

29. Ibid., 90.

30. Jean-Louis Leutrat and Suzanne Liandrat-Guigues, "John Ford and Monument Valley," in *Back in the Saddle Again*, 160–169.

31. Author's notes.

32. Dave Holland, *On Location in Lone Pine* (Granada Hills, Calif.: Holland House, 1990).

33. *Last of the Mohicans* (Los Angeles: Twentieth Century Fox, 1992).

34. This raises a different question—one of authenticity, given that the film was actually shot in western North Carolina. Pay attention, and you would have a hard time explaining rhododendra in upstate New York!

35. *Last of the Mohicans.*

36. Buscombe and Pearson, introduction to *Back in the Saddle Again,* 3.

List of Contributors

LARY M. DILSAVER is professor of geography at the University of South Alabama. He coauthored (with William Tweed) *Challenge of the Big Trees: A Resource History of Sequoia and Kings Canyon National Parks* (Three Rivers, CA: Sequoia Natural History Association, 1994), edited *America's National Park System: The Critical Documents* (Lanham, MD: Rowman & Littlefield, 1994), and coedited (with William Wyckoff) *The Mountainous West: Explorations in Historical Geography* (Lincoln: University of Nebraska Press, 1995) and (with Craig Colten) *The American Environment: Interpretations of Past Geographies* (Lanham, MD: Rowman & Littlefield, 1992).

DYDIA DELYSER is assistant professor of geography in the Department of Geography and Anthropology at Louisiana State University. Her work on ghost towns and American social memory has been published widely, and currently she is working on a book on that topic, to be published by University of California Press.

PETER GOIN is professor of art in photography and video at the University of Nevada, Reno. He is the author of four books: *Tracing the Line: A Photographic Survey of the Mexican-American Border* (Reno: P. Goin, limited edition artist book, 1987), *Nuclear Landscapes* (Baltimore: Johns Hopkins University Press, 1991), *Stopping Time: A Rephotographic Survey of Lake Tahoe*, with essays by C. Elizabeth Raymond and Robert E. Blesse (Albuquerque: University of New Mexico Press, 1992), and *Humanature* (Austin: University of Texas Press, 1996). He coauthored (with Robert Dawson and Mary Webb) *A Doubtful River* (Reno: University of Nevada Press, 2000). He served as editor of *Arid Waters: Photographs from the Water in the West Project* (Reno: University of Nevada Press, 1992) and collaborated with members of the Center of the American West on *Atlas of the New West*. Currently, he is working with C. Elizabeth Raymond on *Changing Mines in America*, to be published by the University of Minnesota Press and the Center for American Places, and with Paul Starrs on a book about the Black Rock Desert.

GARY J. HAUSLADEN is professor of geography at the University of Nevada, Reno. He authored *Places for Dead Bodies* (Austin: University of Texas Press, 2000), which deals with sense of place in murder mysteries. He is currently working on an atlas of Western film.

TERRENCE W. (TERRY) HAVERLUK is associate professor of geography at the United States Air Force Academy. He has published on the influence of Hispanics in the American West.

RICHARD H. JACKSON is professor of geography at Brigham Young University. He edited *The Mormon Role in the Settlement of the West* (Provo: Brigham Young University Press, 1978) and (with S. Kent Brown and Donald Cannon) *Historical Atlas of Mormonism* (New York: Simon & Schuster, 1994) and authored *Land Use in America* (New York: Halsted Press, 1982). He is currently completing a book on the environmental impact of irrigation-based settlements in the intermountain West.

KAREN M. MORIN is associate professor of geography at Bucknell University. Her research on nineteenth-century British women's travel writing about the American West is widely published. Currently, she is working on a number of projects that link postcolonial studies to the historical geography of North America.

PAULIINA RAENTO is senior lecturer of human geography at the University of Helsinki, Finland. She has published articles in both English and Finnish on Basque nationalism and identities, gaming in North America, and cultural geographies in Finland. The essay in this volume is a product of her three-year project (1998–2001) on U.S. American gaming, funded by the Academy of Finland.

AKIM D. REINHARDT is assistant professor of history at Towson State University. Currently, he is working on a book about the political history of the Pine Ridge Reservation during the mid-twentieth century.

PAUL F. STARRS is associate professor of geography at the University of Nevada, Reno. He is the author of *Let the Cowboy Ride: Cattle Ranching in the American West* (Baltimore: Johns Hopkins University Press, 1998). He is currently working with Peter Goin on a book about the Black Rock Desert, and on a book about the uses of the Spanish and Portuguese oak woodlands.

JOHN B. (JACK) WRIGHT is professor of geography at New Mexico State University. He is the author of *Rocky Mountain Divide: Selling and Saving the West* (Austin: University of Texas Press, 1993), which won the prestigious J. B. Jackson Prize, *Montana Ghost Dance: Essays on Land and Life* (Austin: University of Texas Press, 1998), and *Montana Places* (Minneapolis: University of Minnesota Press, 2000). Recently, he has turned his attention to writing novels about Montana and the West.

WILLIAM (BILL) WYCKOFF is professor of geography in the Department of Earth Sciences at Montana State University. He coedited (with Lary Dilsaver) *The Mountainous West: Explorations in Historical Geography* (Lincoln: University of Nebraska Press, 1995) and is the author of *The Developer's Frontier: The Making of the Western New York Landscape* (New Haven: Yale University Press, 1988) and *Creating Colorado: The Making of a Western American Landscape* (New Haven: Yale University Press, 1999). He is currently working on *Rephotographing Montana*.

Index

Note: Italic page numbers refer to illustrations.

Britain: and historical geography, 22; imperialism of, 14, 205–7, 210, 211, 216; investors from, 206–7, 211, 212–13; and settlement of holdings, 192; travelers from, 206; treaties with, 87, 88
British Columbia, 8, 26, 37, 42
Broek, Jan, 25
Brown, J. P. S., 67
Brown, Ralph, 22, 23, 28
Bruce, Chris, 6, 223
Bureau of Land Management: and control of American West, 31; formation of, 89, 91; and Grand Canyon–Parashant National Monument, 96; and land tenure patterns, 92; and Nevada, 99; and New Mexico, 102; and ranching, 62
Bureau of Reclamation, 89, 122
Burlingame, Rex, 278
Burns, Elizabeth, 40
Burnt Canyon mine site, Seven Troughs range, Nev., 262
Butte-Anaconda copper mines, 121
Butzer, Karl, 36

Cabazon Mission Indians, 235
Cabrillo National Monument, 118
Cain, Ella Cody, 282
Cain, James Stuart, 282, 293 n. 47
California: and American West as periphery, 42; and Asians, 119–20; Chinese immigrants in, 38; and demarcating American West, 8; economic growth in, 230; environmental perception of, 34; and gambling, 229, 230, 232, 233, 235, 238, 240, 242, 246; and ghost towns, 277–78, 287; and gold rush, 147, 172, 277, 284, 288; and Hispanics, 37, 118, 171, 172, 174, 175, 178, 180; and human-environment interactions, 30; and migration to Nevada and Utah, 26; and Mormon culture region, 153, 155; and national park system, 118–19, 122–23; and Native Americans, 37, 194, 195, 240; and population density, 96; and urban geography, 40; and water manipulation, 122; and Western film, 302, 315. See also specific cities and places

California Highway 1, 128
California State Parks, 119–20
California Water Plan, 122
Canada: and environmental perception, 34; and Mormon culture region, 145, 147, 152, 156; and Native Americans, 191; and ranching, 71, 73; and return of federal land to indigenous peoples, 100
capitalism: and American West, 3; and American West as periphery, 40, 41, 42; and British investors, 207, 211; and Hispanics, 173; regional impact of, 44; and urban geography, 38, 42; in Utah, 104; and Western film, 316; and women's travel journals, 217. See also economics
Carlisle Indian School, 195
Carlson, Alvar, 37
Carroll, Noel, 301
Carson Valley, Nev., 145
Carter, George, 25
Carter, James, 99
Casa Grande Ruin National Monument, 112
casinos: in Colo., 240, 241; development of, 241, 242, 244, 245, 246, 247, 247, 248; growth of, 234–35; and introduction of new games, 228; legalization of casino gambling, 229; national advertising of, 232; and Native American reservations, 233, 235, 238, 239, 240, 248; in Nevada, 233–34, 234; and resort-casinos, 230, 232; revenues of, 235, 236
Cather, Willa, 174
Catholic Church, 159, 167, 171, 172
Catron, Thomas, 102
Cawelti, John, 307
Cayugas, 191
Central City, Colo., 30, 240–41
Central Valley Project, 122
Cerro Gordo, Calif., 285
Cherokee Nation v. Georgia, 192
Cherokees, 191–92
Cheyenne Autumn, 309
Cheyennes, 187, 199
Chicano/a and Mexican American studies programs, 175, 177
Chicano movement, 175–77

Chickamauga and Chattanooga National Military Park, 113–14

Chickasaws, 191

Chiles, 167, 169, 172, 174, 177–78, 179

Chinese immigrants, 38

Chinooks, 189

Chiricahuas, 193

Choctaws, 191

Church of Jesus Christ of Latter-day Saints: antipathy toward, 138–39, 140; and community, 142, 144–45, 150, 165 n. 60; and education, 157, 165 n. 61; external forces' effect on, 147–48; and land tenure, 110 n. 64; and leaders as prophets, 136, 160 n. 6; membership growth, 152, 153–54; origins of, 136; and Salt Lake City growth, 151, 153, 154; and temple construction, 136, 139, 150, 156, 157, 159, 165 n. 59; and tithing scrip, 163 n. 40; and urban/ rural distinctions, 155, 159. *See also* Mormon culture region

Cimarron, 299

Cimino, Michael, 315

Cinco de Mayo festivals, *167*

cities: and historical geography, 38, *39;* marginalization of, 5; ranching contrasted with, 60, 64. *See also* urban geography

City of Rocks National Reserve, 117

City of Zion, 136, 138, 140

Civilian Conservation Corps, 114–15

civil rights movement, 313

Civil War, 113–14

Clark, Andrew, 25–26

class: and American West, 4; and Bird, 208, 210; and concept of region, 2; and disposal of land base, 88; and feminism, 207; and gambling, 226, 230, 232, 235, 245; and imperial discourses, 207; and Mormon culture region, 148; and ranching, 64; and self-empowerment, 217; and women's travel journals, 205, 208

Clinton, Bill, 95, 103, 129 n. 1

Cochise, 188

Cody, Buffalo Bill, 3–4, 298–99

Cody, Wyo., 118

colonialism, 40–43, 173, 205, 207, 211, 214

colonial national monuments, 114

Colorado: American and British imperialism in, 206; British investors in, 207, 212–13; Brown on, 23; and capitalism, 42; and chiles, 178; and class, 210; and commodification of the past, 241; and demarcating American West, 8; development of, 3; and environmental perception, 34; ethnic settlement patterns in, 38; gambling in, 240–41; and gold rush, 240; and Mormon culture region, 145, 155; Native Americans of, 187, 188; and urban geography, 40; and Western film, 306. *See also specific cities*

Columbia, Calif., 284

Columbia River Gorge, 128, *129*

Columbus, Christopher, 187

Comanches, 101, 169, 187, 190

Comanche Station, 310

community: and individualism, 91; and Mormon culture region, 136, 142, 144–45, 147, 149, 151, 155, 157, 161–62 n. 24, 165 n. 60; and Mormon village, 150; and ranching, 66, 72, 79, 82 n. 10; and Young, 151, 155, 158

Community Service Organization (cso), 173

competition, 136, 226, 238, 242–47

Comstock area, 121

conservation: and cultural differences, 14; and demarcating American West, 8; and human-environment interactions, 31; and land tenure, 87, 92, 95, 96–98; and land-use planning, 92; and national park system, 112, 116, 117, 121, 122, 124, 127–28; and ranching, 67, 76, 79, 81, 97, 98; in Utah, 103, 104

Conservation Reserve Program (crp), 92

conservatives, 91, 96

Conzen, Michael, 38

Cooper, Gary, 300

Cooper, James Fenimore, 297, 298, 314

Corporate Gaming Act (1967), 232

corporations, 5, 41, 145

cowboys: as heroes of Western film, 297, 298, 299, 300, 301, 312, 313, 314, 315; and Hispanic culture, 170, 180; and ranching, 63, 65, 66, 70, 72, 73, *73*, 74; as representatives of individualism, 299 craps, 228, *228*

Crawford, Joan, 300

Crees, 187

Cripple Creek, Colo., 240–41

Crofutt, George, *65*

Cronon, William, 7

Crows, 198, 199

cultural differences: and conservation, 14; and frontiering experience, 4; and land tenure, 92, 104; and Mormon culture region, 150

cultural diversity: and Hispanics, 35, 37, 175; and historic geography, 35–38; and mineral rights, 100; and Mormon culture region, 150; and national park system, 112, 117–20; and Native Americans, 35, 36, 188; and ranching, 72; and Western film, 316. *See also* African Americans; Asians; ethnicity; Euro-Americans; Hispanics; Mormon culture region; Native Americans

cultural landscape: and cultural diversity, 36, 37; and feminist scholarship, 204; and gambling, 241, 248; and ghost towns, 276; and Great Basin, 253–55; and historical geography, 23, 24, 25, 26–27, 31–32; and national park system, 112, 117–20; and Native Americans, 238; and ranching, 32, 60, 79; and urban geography, 38, 60

Curtis, James, 37, 40

dams, 122

Dana, Richard Henry, 171, 172

Dances with Wolves, 314

Dann sisters, 100

Datel, Robin, 40

Davis, Mike, 38

Dawes, Henry, 194

Dawes Severalty Act (Dawes Allotment Act), 194–95

Deadwood, S. Dak., 240, *243*

Death Valley Days, 310

Death Valley National Park, 121, 302

Delawares, 191

DeLyser, Dydia, 5, 15, 35

Demars, Stanford, 31

democracy: and conquest of American West, 7; and frontiering experience, 3; and mining camps, 280

Denevan, William M., 30, 86

Denver, Colo., *43*

Denver & Rio Grande Railroad, 207

dependency theory, 3

Deseret, State of, 142–43, *143*, 145, 147, 153, 155, 161 n. 19, 163–64 n. 42

Desert Land Act (1877), 89

Destry Rides Again, 300

development: of casinos, 241, 242, 244, 245, 246, 247, *247*, 248; of Colorado, 3; and human-environment interactions, 31; and land tenure conflicts, 96, 97–98; and land trusts, 92, 97; and ranch landscapes, 67, 76, 81; of tourism, 217; in Utah, 104

Devil's Doorway, 300

Devils Tower, 112

De Voto, Bernard, 40, 79

Dietrich, Marlene, 300

Dilsaver, Lary: and American West as region, 2; and California, 30; and demarcating American West, 8; and national park system, 14, 31

Dingemans, Dennis, 40

divorces, 229

Dobie, J. Frank, 65

Doctrine of First Effective Settlement, 85

Doctrine of Prior Appropriation, 158

Dole, Bob, 103

Dollars trilogy, 313

domestic geographies, and Bird, 208–10

Douglas, Kirk, 300

Duncan, James, 6

East: and gambling, 233, 248; and historical geography, 22; and public lands, 44; ranching's roots in, 74; and urban geography, 40; West distinguished from, 1–2; and Western film, 298, 301

Eastwood, Clint, 276, 286, 300

economics: and American West as periphery, 40, 41–42, *41*; and cultural landscape, 32; and feminist scholarship, 204; and gambling, 15, 226, 229–30, 232–35,

236, 238, 240, 241, 248; and Hispanics, 172, 173, 179, 181; and historical geography, 22, 23, 24; and land tenure, 102; and Mormon culture region, 104, 136, 138, 145, 147, 150, 151, 153, 157–58; and national park system, 121–22, 124; of Native Americans, 188, 190, 196, 197, 238, 240; of ranching, 57, 58, 63, 66, 79–80, 81; and urban geography, 38. *See also* capitalism; imperialism

education: and Mormon culture region, 138, 148, 157, 165 n. 61; and National Park Service, 112; and Native American boarding schools, 195

Ellickson, Robert, 66, 79

Ellis Island, 120

Englishwoman in America, An (Bird), 205

Enlarged Homestead Act (1916), 89, 97

environment: and feminist scholarship, 204; and historical geography, 26; and national park system, 115–17, 124, 127. *See also* conservation; human-environment interactions

environmental determinism, 22

environmental left, 91

environmental perception: and Great Plains, 32, 34, *34*; and historical geography, 23, 32–35; of Native Americans, 14, 198–200

ethnicity: and American West, 4; and concept of region, 2; and historical geography, 36, 37–38; and ranching, 79; and urban geography, 40. *See also* cultural diversity

Etulain, Richard, 7

Euro-Americans: and annexation of northern Mexico, 171–73; and environmental perceptions, 198–99; and ethnic settlement patterns, 38; and Hispanic culture, 166, 174, 176, 181; migration of, 2; and mythic West, 314; and national park system, 117, 118; and Native Americans, 37, 187, 191, 198; and religion, 199, 200; and Western film, 300, 315–16

European conquest: and mythic West, 86; and national park system, 121–22; and Native American gambling, 238; and Native Americans, 190; and preservation of Indian ruins, 118

Evans, Simon, 69

explorers and exploration: and environmental challenges, 115; and environmental perception, 22, 32, 34; and feminist scholarship, 204; and historical geography, 23; and national park system, 118, 121, 124

Fairbanks, Douglas, 300

Fallon, Nev., *271*

Farmer's Home Administration (1950), 89

farming. *See* agriculture

faro, 228, *228*

federal government: disposal of land base by, 88–92; and gambling, 233, 240; land acquisition by, 87, 90, 91 table 3.1; and land tenure, 92; and Mormon culture region, 147, 149, 153; and Native American boarding schools, 195; and Native American gambling, 238; and Native American land tenure claims, 86, 99–100, 192, 193, 194; and Native American Relocation, 197; and Native American reservations, 199, 207; and Native American treaties, 87, 88, 99, 192, 193, 194, 195; and ranching, 72, 79, 96

fee-simple ownership, 92

feminism: and Bird, 207, 210, 217, 218; and imperialism, 207, 211; and study of West, 204–5

Fenneman, Neville, 116

Fentress, James, 275

Fernow, Bernard, 89

Fifer, Valerie, 34

Findlay, John, 38

Five Civilized Tribes, 191, 192

Flamingo, 230, 231, 232, 242

Flores, Dan, 29

Florida, 235

Flynn, Errol, 300

folk architecture: and cultural landscape, 32; and ghost towns, *286;* and mythic West, 87; and ranching, 69–70

Fonda, Henry, 300

Ford, John, 298, 299, 308–10
Ford, Larry, 40
forest conservation, 121
Forest Reserve Act, 121
forest reserves, 89
Forest Trust, 102
Fort Apache, 309
Fort Laramie, 122
Fort Vancouver, 122
Francaviglia, Richard, 30, 32, 35
freedom: and conquest of American West,
    7; and ghost towns, 276; and Western
    film, 301
French, Samuel, 172
French cinema, 302
French settlers, 167, 169
Friedman, Kinky, 65
frontiering experience: and African Ameri-
    cans, 120; and American West as excep-
    tional, 3; and feminist scholarship, 204;
    and gambling, 225–29, 246–48; and his-
    torical geography, 23, 24; and land ten-
    ure, 85; and Mormon culture region, 138,
    139, 140, 149, 154, 158; and mythic West,
    5; and national identity, 4–5; and regional
    historiography, 7; Roosevelt on, 299, 313;
    Turner on, 3–4, 6–7, 298, 307, 313; and
    Western film, 297–98, 299, 301, 314–15,
    316
fur trade, 122

Gable, Clark, 300
gambling: attacks on, 226, 229, 235; com-
    mercialization of, 227, 228; and competi-
    tion for Las Vegas, 242–47; diffusion of,
    233–47; distribution of, *239;* economic
    aspects of, 15, 229–30, 232–35, *236,* 238,
    240, 241, 248; and frontiering expe-
    rience, 225–29, 246–48; and Hispanics,
    172; and mining, 228, 229, 232, 240,
    277, 281; and national park system, 123;
    and Native Americans, 227, 233, 235,
    238–40, 248; and Nevada, 15, 229–33,
    234, 248
gaming, 232. *See also* gambling
Ganados del Valle (Livestock Growers of the
    Valley), 102

García, Mario T., 173
Gast, John, 64
Gates, Paul Wallace, 71, 75
gender: and American West, 4; and Bird,
    208, 209, 210, 214–17; and concept of
    region, 2; gendered subjectivity, 207,
    208, 209, 210, 211, 214, 216, 217; and
    place images, 35, *36;* and ranching, 72;
    and tourism, 204; and urban geography,
    297; and Victorian adventure tales, 211,
    212, 214–15, 217–18; and Victorian do-
    mestic ideologies, 207, 208, 210, 211;
    and Western film, 300, 313, 314; and
    women's travel journals, 205, 212, 214.
    See also women
Gene Autry, 310
General Land Office (1812), 89
General Preemption Act (1841), 89
Georgetown-Silver Plume, 121
George Washington Birthplace, 114
Germany, 299, 310
Geronimo (Chiricahua leader), 193
Geronimo: An American Legend, 314
Gettysburg, 114
ghost city, 278, 291–92 n. 24
ghost towns: emergence of, 277–85; and
    movie and television industry, 15, 276,
    285–87, 288; and mythic West, 15, 274,
    275, 276–77, 279, 282, 285, 288, 291 n.
    15, 293 n. 44; and place images, 35; role
    of, 15, 284–85; and saloons, 282–84; and
    social memory, 275–76; as term, 277–80,
    281, 291–92 n. 24, 292 nn. 28, 35; and
    tourism, 273, 282, 284–85, 287, 288–89,
    295 n. 73
Gibson, James, 26, 30, 42
Gilbert, Edmund, 22–23, 32
Glacier National Park, 31
Glen Canyon, 122
globalization: of American popular culture,
    248; and American West, 11; and British
    investors, 207; of capital, 3; and gam-
    bling, 246, 247; regional impact of, 44;
    and regionalism, 2; and urban geogra-
    phy, 40
Godfrey, Brian, 37, 40
Goin, Peter, 15

Golden Gate National Recreation Area, 118–19

Golden Spike National Historic Site, 119, 123

gold rush: and annexation of northern Mexico, 172; and gambling, 228, 240, 248; and ghost towns, 277, 284, 288; and Mormon culture region, 147; and national park system, 121, 124

Goldwater, Barry, 76

Good, the Bad, and the Ugly, The, 276

Graf, William L., 30, 31

Grand Canyon National Park, 31, 94, 95, 246

Grand Canyon–Parashant National Monument, 94–95, 96

Grand Canyon Trust, 94–95

Grand Staircase–Escalante, 127

Grant, Cary, 300

Grant-Kohrs, 122

grazing: and grazing fees, 99, 100; and land tenure conflicts, 92, 95–96, 101; and land use, 71, 72, 84 n. 28; and Mormon culture region, 148; and private land, 67; and public land, 70

Great Basin: and cultural landscape, 253–55; and Mormon culture region, 103, 135, 139–42; and national park system, 122; and Northern Shoshones, 187; photographs of, 255, 257–72

Great Britain. *See* Britain

Great Depression, 229, 299

Great Plains: and environmental perception, 32, 34, *34;* and ethnic settlement patterns, 38; and human-environment interactions, 29; Native Americans of, 187, 198–99; and place images, 35

Great Salt Lake, 128

Great Strike of 1877, 297

Great Train Robbery, The, 296, 301

Grey, Zane, 35, 297

Gritz, Bo, 103

Gritzner, Charles, 37

Gruber, Frank, 301

Guelke, Jeanne Kay, 35

Gunsight Pass, Padre Canyon and Bay, Lake Powell, Utah, 264

Gunsmoke, 276

Hagerman Fossil Beds National Monument, 117

Hansen, Katherine, 30

Hanson, Victor, 75

Hardwick, Susan, 38, 40

Harris, Cole, 26, 32, 37, 42

Hart, John Fraser, 67

Harte, Bret, 297, 298, 302

Haskell Institute, 195

Hatch, Orrin, 103

Haudenosaunee (Iroquois) League Nations, 191

Hausladen, Gary, 15

Have Gun Will Travel, 310

Haverluk, Terry, 14

Hawaii, 8, 87, 156, 233

Hawikuh pueblo, 118, 125

Hawkins, Bobbie Louise, 62

Heaven's Gate, 315

Hell's Canyon, 127

Henderson, Martha, 36

Henry, O., 72

Hewes, Leslie, 25

Hickel, Walter, 115

Hickok, James Butler "Wild Bill," 225, 248

Hidatsas, 187

High Plains Drifter, 286

High Sierra, 310

Hispanic culture: and Euro-Americans, 166, 174, 176, 181; and foods, 167, 169, 170, 171, 172, 174, 177–78, 179, 181; and Grand Canyon–Parashant National Monument, 95; as mainstream, 14, 166, 175–80, 181; and Mexican American music, 179–80; and tourism, 178–79

Hispanic elected officials (HEOS), 175

Hispanics: and Anglo annexation, 171–73; Anglo attitudes toward, 172–73, 181; architecture of, 174; and cultural diversity of American West, 35, 37, 175; and frontiering experience, 314; as immigrant population, 14, 173, 174, 175; and irrigation, 73, 167, 169, 170; and land grants, 92, 101–3; and land tenure conflicts, 101–2; marginalization of, 5, 171, 181; and

Mormon culture region, 159; and national park system, 117, 118–19, 124;
and politics, 172, 173–77, *176*, 181; and
ranching, 73, 170, 172; settlement patterns of, 166–71, *168*; and Western film,
313, 315, 316
Hispanization, 166, 173, 179, 180
historical geography: and cities, 38, *39;* effect of American West on, 21, 22–24,
40, 44; and feminism, 204; as field of
study, 14, 21, 22; Meinig's contributions
to, 27–29; themes of, 29–43; and University of California at Berkeley, 24–27.
See also cultural diversity; cultural landscape; environmental perception; human-environment interactions; place
images; urban geography
historic landmark program, 119
historic preservation, 76, 114, 240, 241,
284, 285. *See also* preservation of mate-
rial culture
Historic Sites Act (1935), 114, 115
Hohokams, 86, 117, 188
Holden, William, 300
Hollywood, Calif., 246–47, 248
Hollywood Film Industry National Histo-
ric Site, 125
Holtgrieve, Donald, 38
Homestead Act (1862), 89
homesteading bills, 89, 97
Hoover (Boulder) Dam, 230
Hopalong Cassidy, 310
Hopis, 37, 94, 199
Hornbeck, David, 37
Hornitos, Calif., 278, 279
Horse Whisperer, The, 96
How the West Was Won, 310, *312*
Hudson, John, 29
Hughes, Howard, 232, 248
human-environment interactions: and Eu-
ropean contact, 86; and Great Basin,
253–55; and historical geography, 25,
26, 29–31; and Las Vegas resorts, 230;
and mining, 30, *30;* and Mormon cul-
ture region, 136, 140, 146–47, 148; and
Native Americans, 184; and ranching,
58, 72

Hunt, Rockwell, 284

Iceberg Canyon, Lake Powell, *272*
Idaho: and demarcating American West, 8;
and Mormon culture region, 145, 154,
155; Native Americans of, 187, 192–93.
See also specific cities
Idaho Falls, Idaho, 156
immigrant populations: Hispanics as, 14,
173, 174, 175; and maps, 37; and mining,
38; and national park system, 117,
119–20, 125; and Western film, 297,
299
Immigration and Nationality Act of 1965,
175
imperialism: and American West as periphery, 40; and Bird, 207, 210, 214,
216; of Britain, 14, 205–7, 210, 211, 216;
and feminism, 207, 211; of United
States, 14, 205–7, 213; and Victorian adventure tales, 211, 218; and Western
film, 15, 301; and women's travel journals, 14, 205, 207, 211, 213–14, 217
Incas, 86
Independence, Mo., 138, 140
Indian Claims Commission, 99
Indian country, 199
Indian Gaming Regulatory Act (IGRA), 235
Indian Post Office, Idaho, 118
Indian Territory, 191, 193
individualism: and conquest of American
West, 7; cowboy as representative of,
299; and frontiering experience, 3; and
gambling, 225, 226, 229, 235, 248; and
ghost towns, 276, 284–85; and Mormon
culture region, 136, 145, 158; and private
land, 91; and Western film, 301, 312
information revolution, regional impact of,
44
institutions, and historical geography, *42,*
44
Inter-American Commission on Human
Rights, 100
interbasin water transfers, 122
internal colonialism, 173
irrigation: and Desert Land Act, 89; and
European contact, 86; and Hispanics,

Las Vegas, Nev.: and California gamblers, 232, 233; and competition for gambling, 242–47; and economics of gambling, 230, 232, 234, 248; and land tenure patterns, 92; and Mormon culture region, 145; mythic nature of, 15; and Native American gambling, 240; and population density, 99; resorts of, 230–31

Latin America, 154, 180

law and order: and lawlessness of mining camps, 273, 278, 279, 280–81, 282, 288; and settlement patterns, 88; and Western film, 298, 301

Lawrence, D. H., 174

Lawson, Merlin, 32

Leadville, Colo., 33, 279, 280, 283

League of United Latin American Citizens (LULAC), 173

Least-Heat Moon, William, 58

Lehr, John, 38

Leighly, John, 34

Leonard, Stephen, 38

Leone, Sergio, 276, 309, 313

Leutrat, Jean-Louis, 310

Lewis, Malcolm, 32

Lewis and Clark, 121, 192

Liandrat-Guigues, Suzanne, 310

liberals, 91, 96

Limerick, Patricia Nelson: and American West as region, 2; and capitalism, 40; and ethnicity, 14, 133; and frontiering experience, 4, 72; and land tenure, 86; and mining, 293 n. 38; and region versus process, 7

Lindenmeier Site, 118

literature: and ghost towns, 274, 276, 282; and Hispanic culture, 174; and mythic West, 15, 87, 96, 297, 298; and place images, 35; popular fiction, 35, 228, 297; and ranching, 71–72, 74, 79

Little Big Man, 313, 314

livestock: and Hispanics, 169, 170, 171; and Mormon culture region, 140, 148; and ranching, 57–58, 60, 62, 64, 66, 70–71, 72, 74, 78, 84 n. 28, 95. See also grazing

Lone Pine, Calif., 302, 307, 310–13, 311

Lone Ranger, The, 310

Lorenz, Diane, 30

Los Angeles, Calif., 246

Los Caminos del Rio Heritage project, 178–79

Los Padres National Forest, 128

Lost Lode, Mont., 278

lotteries, 226, 233

Lovell, George, 86

lumber industry, 30, 92, 102, 121, 124, 144, 145

Luxor Las Vegas, 247

Malin, James, 29

MALT (Marin Agricultural Land Trust), 78

Mandans, 187

Manzanar National Historic Site, 119

maps and mapping: and American West as exceptional, 2; and boundaries, 198; and environmental perception, 32, 34; and historical geography, 22–23; and immigrant populations, 37; and urban geography, 38

Marshall, Howard Wright, 69

Masonic, Calif., 285, 287

materialism: and gambling, 226, 229, 235; and Mormon culture region, 136, 145

May, Howard, 75

McCabe and Mrs. Miller, 313

McDonald, Jerry, 36

McGrath, Roger, 280

McIntire, Elliot, 36–37

McMurtry, Larry, 58

McQuillan, D. Aidan, 26, 38

Meinig, D. W.: and American West as periphery, 41; and American West as region, 2, 27–28; contributions to historical geography, 27–29; and demarcating American West, 8; and frontiering experience, 5; and Hispanic cultural influences, 37; and Mormon culture region, 38, 150, 151, 152; photographs of, 32; and region versus process, 6, 7; and symbol of American West, 19; and urban geography, 38

Mesa, Ariz., 156

Mesa Verde National Park, 117

Mexican Americans, 171–74, 175, 178–80.
   See also Hispanics
Mexican Cession (1848), 98, 101, 166, 171
Mexican food, 177–78
Mexican Revolution, 173
Mexicans, 5, 63, 298, 300
Mexico: annexation of northern Mexico,
   171–73, 179; and demarcating American
   West, 8; and Mormon culture region,
   145, 147, 154; treaties with, 87, 88; and
   Western film, 302
Meyer, Judith, 31
Midwest, 139, 191, 233, 235
migration: and African Americans, 120;
   and boundaries of American West, 2; of
   Californians to Nevada and Utah, 26;
   and gold rush, 147; of Mormons, *137,*
   138, 139, 145, 151; and national park system, 121; and ranching, 60. *See also* immigrant populations
Milagro Beanfield War (Nichols), 102
military conquest: and national park system, 121, 124; and Native Americans,
   191, 192
Mills, Sara, 214
mineral rights: and land tenure, 92, 96, 97;
   in Nevada, 98, 99, 100
mining: British investors in, 207, 213; cur-
   tailment of during World War II, 284,
   294 n. 59; and gambling, 228, 229, 232,
   240, 277, 281; and Hispanics, 172; and
   human-environment interactions, 30, *30;*
   and immigrant populations, 38; and lawlessness of camps, 273, 278, 279,
   280–81, 282, 288; and Mormon culture
   region, 145, 149; and national park system, 121, 124–25; and Native American
   reservations, 199; and reminiscences,
   280–81, 282, 293 n. 38; and saloons, 283.
   See also ghost towns
Mining Law (1872), 89
Mining Law (1972), 100
Minnesota, 187
Mirage, The, 242, *244,* 245
mission revival style, 174, 175, 179
Mission San Antonio de Padua, Monterey
   County, 119, 125

mission system, 190
Mississippi River, 233
Missouri River Breaks, 97
Mitchell, Don, 42
Mitchell, Lee Clark, 298, 302
Mobile mx missile system, 99, 100
modernity, and land tenure, 92, 104
Modocs, 185
Mogollons, 188
Mojave National Preserve, 121
Momaday, N. Scott, 200
Monk, Janice, 35
Montana: and American West as periphery,
   41; and demarcating American West, 8;
   eastern Montana settlement, 24, *24;* and
   land tenure conflicts, 94 table 3.3, 95 ta-
   ble 3.4, 96–98; and Mormon culture re-
   gion, 155; and place images, *36;* and
   rangeland, 71; and saloons, 283. *See also*
   specific cities
Montana Land Reliance, 97
Monterey presidio, 119
Monticello, 114
Monument Valley, Ariz., 127, *127,* 302,
   308–10, *308, 309*
Moore, Helen, 278
Moore, Tyrel, 36
Morehouse, Barbara, 31
Morin, Karen, 14, 35
Mormon culture region: and agriculture,
   103, 135, 136, 140, 144–45, 146, 148, 149,
   150, 152, 155, 158, 161 n. 23; as antinuclear activists, 100; changes in, 14,
   135–36, 150–52, 155, 157–59; and community, 136, 142, 144–45, 147, 149, 151,
   155, 157, 161–62 n. 24, 165 n. 60; "Core-
   Domain Sphere" model of, 27; and education, 138, 148, 157, 165 n. 61; future
   of, 152–55; and Grand Canyon–Parashant
   National Monument, 95; and Great Basin, 103, 135, 139–42; and land tenure,
   88, 92, 103–4, 109–10 n. 64; and land
   use, *141,* 144, 148, 152, 164 n. 48; map of,
   146; and national park system, 121, 123;
   and Nevada, 98, 145, 152, 155; non-Mormon intrusions in, 147–50, 152, 155,
   164 n. 50; origin of, 136–39, *137;* and rail-

road companies, 147, 149, 150–51, 158, 163 n. 36; and Salt Lake City, 140, 142–47, 149–51, 152, 153, 154, 156; settlement patterns in, 38, 135–36, 145–47, 148, 149, 151–52, 155, 162 n. 26, 163–64 n. 42, 164 nn. 43, 48; spatial manifestations of, 155–56; Spencer on, 25; in twentieth century, 149–50; unity of, 148, 162 n. 31; and urban geography, 138, 140, 149, 150–52, 153, 154–55, 156, 157, 158–59; urban/rural distinctions in, 149, 150, 152, 155, 156, 159; in Utah, *28*, 142, 145, 149, 152, 153, 154, 155, 158; and women, 35

Mormon Pioneer National Historic Trail, 123

Mormons, 298, 300, 316

Mormon village: and community, 150; and economics, 158; effect of growth on, 149; as ephemeral, 151–52; and land use, 144, 148, 152, 164 n. 48; and nineteenth-century Mormon settlement, 157, 159; Salt Lake City as model of, 142; and urban geography, 140, *141;* and urban/rural distinctions, 156, 163 n. 35

Morski, Jeffrey, 38

Mother Lode National Parkway, 124, *125*

mountainous West, 34, 60, 81 n. 3, 115

Mount Rushmore, 199

Mount St. Helens, 127

Mount Vernon, 114

movie and television industry: and gambling, 228; and ghost towns, 15, 276, 285–87, 288; and mythic West, 15, 87, 285; and national park system, 123, 125; and ranching, 75. *See also* Western film

Muir, John, 31

Muir Woods National Monument, 31

multiculturalism. *See* cultural diversity

Murphy, Mary, 38

music: and African Americans, 180; and Hispanic culture, 171, 179–80, 181

Muskogees, 191

My Darling Clementine, 309

mythic West: and gambling, 15, 229, 246–47; and ghost towns, 15, 274, 275, 276–77, 279, 282, 285, 288, 291 n. 15,

293 n. 44; and Hispanics, 174; historical West versus, 5–6; and land tenure, 86–87, 88, 98, 105; and literature, 15, 87, 96, 297, 298; and Mormon culture region, 146–47, 155; and national identity, 1, 5, 302; and Native Americans, 184; and place images, 32, *33;* and ranch labor, 72; and ranch landscapes, 66, *67;* and saloons, 283; Webb on, 7; and Western film, 15, 297, 299, 300, 301–7, 308, 310, 313, 316

Nadeau, Remi, 284

Naiche (Chiricahua leader), 193

Nash, Gerald, 3

Nash, Roderick, 29

National Association of Latino Elected Officials (NALEO), 175

National Forest system, 89, 91

national identity: and American West, 230; and frontiering experience, 4–5; and mythic West, 1, 5, 302; and self-empowerment, 217; and Western film, 296, 298, 299, 300, 310, 313, 315–16

nationalism: and Bird, 210; of Germany and Japan, 299, 310; and imperial discourses, 207; and women's travel journals, 205

nationalization, 2, 11

National Park Service: and battlefields, 113–14, 115; control of, 31; and Grand Canyon–Parashant National Monument, 96; and historic sites, 114, 115, 116; and monuments, 113, 114, 115; policies of, 111, 128, 129–30 n. 1; and public education and entertainment, 112; and recreation, 114–15, 116

national park system: and cultural diversity, 112, 117–20; and environment, 115–17, 124, 127; and European conquest, 121–22; evolution of, 14, 111, 112–15; and human-environment interactions, 31; and land tenure conflicts, 92; map of proposed units in West, *116;* map of units in West, *113;* and public land as sacrosanct, 91; suggested additions to, 124–29; and thematic representation, 111, 112,

117–23, 124, 129; and West as transformed place, 122–23

Native American religions, 185–86, 188, 190–91, 199, 200 n. 2

Native American reservations: and alienation from former lands, 193, 207; and casinos, 233, 235, 238, 239, 240, 248; and checkerboard phenomenon, 195–96; and Dawes Severalty Act, 194, 195; and environmental perception, 199; and Indian Territory, 191; and living off-reservation, 197; map of, 196; and national park system, 118

Native Americans: creation stories of, 185–86; and cultural diversity, 35, 36, 188; early spatial relations of, 186–87; environmental perceptions of, 14, 198–200; and frontiering experience, 314; and gambling, 227, 233, 235, 238–40, 248; and Hispanics, 167, 169, 174; images of, 15, 184; and land tenure conflicts, 86, 92, 94, 99–100, 101, 102, 103, 192, 193, 194–95; living spaces of, 187–90; marginalization of, 5; modern spaces of, 195–97; and national park system, 117–18, 121, 124, 125; as pacifist ecologists, 86; and perceptions of place and space, 14; and perceptions of space, 198–200; population density of, 86, 207; Roosevelt on, 299; spatial manipulations of, 190–95; stereotypes of, 189; and treaties with federal government, 87, 88, 99, 192, 193, 194, 195; and Western film, 298, 300, 313, 314, 315, 316. See also specific tribes

Nauvoo, Ill., 138, 139, 140

Navajos: and land tenure conflicts, 94, 101; and national park system, 127; and Navajo Reservation, 195, 199; and settlement patterns, 36

Neal, Steve, 300

Nebraska, 8

neolocalism, 178

Nevada: California migration to, 26; and demarcating American West, 8; and gambling, 15, 229–33, 234, 248; and land tenure conflicts, 94 table 3.3, 95 table 3.4, 96, 98–100; and Mormon culture region, 98, 145, 152, 155; Native Americans of, 187; and nuclear testing, 99; and ranching, 70, 98–99; and ranch space, 60. See also specific cities and places

Nevada Gaming Commission, 232

Nevada Gaming Control Board, 232

Nevada Test Site, 99

Newe Sogobia, 99–100

New Jersey, 233, 301

Newlands Reclamation Act (1902), 152

New Mexico: and chiles, 169, 178; and demarcating American West, 8; and Hispanic culture, 174, 179; and Hispanics, 167, 169, 172, 175; and land tenure, 92, 94 table 3.3, 95 table 3.4, 96, 101–3; and Mormon culture region, 145, 155; and Native Americans, 188; and Western film, 302, 315

New Western historians, 7, 8, 35, 40, 115

New York, 136, 314

Nichols, John, 102

Nicodemus National Historic Site, 120

Noel, Thomas, 38

North Dakota, 8, 187, 306

Northern Shoshones, 187

North Gulch, Moki Canyon, Lake Powell, Utah, 267

Norwood, Vera, 35

Nostrand, Richard, 37

nuclear testing, 99–100

Nuevo Mexico, 167, 169

Nugent, Jim, 214–15, 218

Nugent, Walter, 8

Oatman, Arizona, 285

O'Connor, Sandra Day, 76

Office of Indian Affairs, 194

O'Keeffe, Georgia, 174

Oklahoma, 8, 191, 306

Old Oraibi pueblo, 118

Olson, Charles, 72

Olympic Games, 92, 103, 104, 110 n. 64

Omahas, 189, 198

Oñate, Juan de, 166–67

Once upon a Time in the West, 309, 309, 313

Oneidas, 191

O'Neill, Eugene, 123
Oregon, 8, 30
Oregon Dunes, 127
organized crime, 230, 232
Oro, Colo., 280
Ortiz, Simon, 254
Osage people, 185
OutLandish, 98
Owen, Blanton, 69

Pacific Coast Immigration Museum, 120
Pacific Northwest, 34
Pacific Northwest Timber Industry National
    Historic Site, 125
Padilla, Carmen, 177
Paiutes, 253–54
Palmyra, N.Y., 136
Panama International Exposition, San
    Diego, 174
Papagos, 186
Paramount Ranch area, 123
pari-mutuel betting, 233
Park, Parkway and Recreation Area Study
    Act, 115
Parsons, James, 25, 26, 81, 105–6 n. 9
Pawnees, 187, 198
Payment in Kind (PIK) Program, 92
Peckinpah, Sam, 313
perimetropolitan bow wave, 67
Perot, Ross, 103
Peters, Gary, 38
Pfeiffer–Big Sur State Park, 128
Pike's Peak, 207
Pimas, 186
Pine Ridge Reservation, 196
Pipe Spring National Monument, 122, 123
place images: and gender, 35, *36;* and histor-
    ical geography, 21, 32–35; and mythic
    West, 32, *33;* and national identity, 298;
    and Western film, 296–98, 301–7, 316;
    and writers, 34–35
Point Reyes National Seashore, 122
poker, 228
political borders, 2
politics: and American West as periphery,
    40, 41; and feminist scholarship, 204;
    and frontiering experience, 3; and gam-

bling, 232, 235, 238, 240, 241, 248; and
    Hispanics, 172, 173–77, *176,* 181; and
    land tenure conflicts, 92–93; and Mor-
    mon culture region, 104, 136, 138, 139,
    142, 143, 146–47, 148, 151, 155, 156, 157;
    and mythic West, 298; and national
    parks system, 111, 115, 121; and Western
    film, 299
Ponca Reservation, 193
Poncas, 193–94, 198
Popper, Deborah, 8, 29
Popper, Frank, 8, 29, 69
popular fiction, 35, 228, 297
population density: and American West as
    exceptional, 1–2; and homesteading bills,
    89; in Montana, 96; and Mormon cul-
    ture region, 149–50, 151, 152, 153–56, 157;
    and mythic West, 86; of Native Ameri-
    cans, 86, 207; in Nevada, 99; and ranch
    landscape, 57–58, 59, 60, *61,* 64
Port Gamble, Wash., 121
Posse, 314
Potawatomis, 191
Powell, John Wesley, 72, 73
Pratt, Mary Louise, 213–14
preservation of material culture, 111, 112,
    113–14, 117–25, 129. *See also* historic pres-
    ervation
Presidio Hill, San Diego, 119
Preston, William, 30, 37
Price, Edward, 25
private land: and land tenure conflicts, 96,
    98; public lands discerned from, 91; and
    ranching, 14, 67, 70, 72, 76. *See also* pub-
    lic lands
prizefighting, 229
progress, and ranching, 64, *65*
Progressivism, 229
Prohibition, 283–84
property law, and ranching, 66, 82 n. 10
Protestant Church, 171, 172
public lands: and American West as excep-
    tional, 2; and demarcating American
    West, 8; evolution of, 44; and federal
    government's land acquisition, 87; and
    human-environment interactions, 31; in
    Montana, 96; and Mormon culture re-

gion, 148, 158; in Nevada, 99; private
land discerned from, 91; and ranching,
62, 67, 68, 70, 72, 76, 96. *See also* private land
Pueblo, Colo., 178
Pueblo Bonito, 188
pueblo grants, 101
Pueblo Indians, 167, 169
Pueblo Revolt of 1680, 101
purchases of development rights (PDRS), 97
Pyramid Lake, 118

quarter horse racing, 226

race and racism: and concept of region, 2;
and imperial discourses, 207; and land
tenure, 88; and Native Americans, 194
Raento, Pauliina, 15
railroad companies: British investors in,
207, 213; and British travelers, 206; and
capitalism, 42; and Mormon culture region, 147, 149, 150–51, 158, 163 n. 36; and
national park system, 112; and tourism,
34, 112, 116, 206–7, 282; and Western
film, 301
railroad grants, 89, 97
railroad towns, and gambling, 227, 229
ranching: British investors in, 207, 213; cities contrasted with, 60, 64; and community, 66, 72, 79, 82 n. 10; and conservation, 67, 76, 79, 81, 97, 98; and
cultural landscape, 32, 60, 79; and disputes, 66; economics of, 57, 58, 63, 66,
79–80, 81; evolution of, 26; and federal
government, 72, 79, 96; and Grand Canyon National Park, 95; and Hispanics, 73,
170, 172; and home ranch, 67; as iconographic, 62–63; infrastructure of, 74,
74; land requirements of, 57–58, 64; and
land tenure, 66, 75–76, 79, 92, 95–96;
and land use, 58, 60, 61–64, 63, 67, 71,
72, 75–76, 79, 80, 81; and literature,
71–72, 74, 79; and livestock, 57–58, 60,
62, 64, 66, 70–71, 72, 74, 78, 84 n. 28,
95; and Mormon culture region, 145; and
national park system, 122; opponents of,
76, 78, 80; origins of, 37; practice of,

70–81; and public lands, 62, 67, 68, 70,
72, 76, 96; and ranch space, 58, 60; and
urban/rural distinctions, 79; and Western film, 79, 301. *See also* grazing
ranch labor, 63, 65, 66, 70, 72, 73, 73, 74,
79
ranch landscapes: complexity of, 64–70;
and cultural landscape, 32; as element of
life, 14; and gateposts, 76, 77; and haystack, 75, 75; Jackson on, 61–62; and
mythic West, 66, 67; and population
density, 57–58, 59, 60, 61, 64; and ranchyard, 69, 69, 75; and subdivision of land,
64, 68, 76; subtlety of, 57, 59; value of,
78–79
Rancho Notorious, 300
rangeland: biodiversity on, 84 n. 28; definition of, 71, 74; extent of, 57; and land
tenure, 76
Rattlesnake Wilderness and National Recreation Area, 97
Raup, Hallock, 25
Reagan, Ronald, 91
Reclamation Act (1902), 89
Recording Industry Association of America,
180
recreation interests: and British travelers,
206; and environmental challenges, 116;
and gambling, 227, 230, 232, 235; and
land tenure conflicts, 96; and national
park system, 114–15
Red Cloud's War, 193
Redmond, Bill, 102
Redwood National Park, 121
Rees, Ronald, 35
regions: American West as region versus
process, 1, 6–7; and capitalism, 3; and de-
marcation of American West, 7–11; geographical study of, 2, 6, 14; and historical
geography, 22–23, 25–26, 27–28, 44; and
mythic West, 5–6; regional boundaries of
American West, 2, 28–29. *See also* American West; East; Midwest
Reinhardt, Akim, 14
religion: and national park system, 123; Native American religions, 185–86, 188,
190–91, 199, 200 n. 2; and Native Amer-

and Native Americans, 238; and Nevada, 230

Townsend, "Lying Jim," 275, 279, 289

Trail of Tears, 192

Travis, Merle, 180

Treasure Island (hotel-casino), 246

Treaty of Guadalupe Hidalgo, 101, 142

Treaty of Ruby Valley, 99

Trinity Atomic National Monument, 123, 125

Trudell, John, 184

Truman, Harry, 197

Tuan, Yi-Fu, 30

Tuie (Isleta) pueblo, 188

Turner, Eugene, 38

Turner, Frederick Jackson, 3–4, 5, 6–7, 72, 85, 298–99, 307, 313

Tuska, Jon, 301

Twain, Mark, 277–78, 279, 280, 284, 292 n. 35

Ulph, Owen, 70

Underwood, Kathleen, 38

Unforgiven, 314

United States: American West as part of, 2–3; imperialism of, 14, 205–7, 213; and land tenure, 88. *See also* federal government

University of California at Berkeley, 24–27, 31

urban geography: and American West as exceptional, 2; and American West as periphery, 42; and capitalism, 38, 42; and Colorado, 240; and cultural diversity, 37; and cultural landscape, 38, 60; and European contact, 86; and feminist scholarship, 204; and historical geography, 38–40, *39;* and land tenure, 87, 89, 92, 98; marginalization of, 5; and Mormon culture region, 138, 140, 149, 150–52, 153, 154–55, 156, 157, 158–59; and Native Americans, 188, 197; and ranching, 60, 67, 79, 80; regional impact of, 44; and Utah, 103, 104; and Western film, 298, 301. *See also* cities

urban planning, and historical geography, 38

U.S. Air Force, 99

U.S. Army, 192–93

U.S. Census Bureau, 3

U.S. Congress: and land tenure, 88; and Mormon culture region, 142, 149; and national park system, 111, 112, 113–15, 124; and Native American treaties, 88; and ranching, 60

U.S. Forest Service: and administration of monuments, 129–30 n. 1; and control of American West, 31; and national park system, 128; and Nevada, 99; and New Mexico, 102; and ranching, 62

U.S. Supreme Court, 192, 199, 235

Utah: California migration to, 26; and demarcating American West, 8; and gambling, 233, 238; and land tenure conflicts, 94 table 3.3, 95 table 3.4, 103–4, 109–10 n. 64; Mormon culture region in, *28,* 142, 145, 149, 152, 153, 154, 155, 158; and nuclear testing, 99; and public lands, *68;* and State of Deseret, 142; as territory, 142, 145, 147; and Western film, 302, 307, 308–10, 315. *See also* Salt Lake City, Utah; *and other specific cities and places*

Utes, 101

utopianism: and Mormon culture region, 103, 135, 136, 138, 142, 144, 146, 149; and mythic West, 87; and national park system, 123; and Western film, 15, 296

Vale, Geraldine, 31, 32

Vale, Thomas, 30, 31, 32

values: and frontiering experience, 226; and gambling, 226, 227, 229, 235, 240, 248; and historical geography, *42, 44;* and land tenure, 92; and ranching, 64, 72; and urban geography, 297; and Western film, 296, 302

Vance, James, 34, 42

Vandenburg Air Force Base, Calif., 123

Van Loan, Charles, 278

Veblen, Thomas, 30

Venetian, 244

Vicksburg, 114

Vietnam War, 313

and human-environment interactions, 30; and national park system, 31; photographs of, 32; and place images, 35; and urban geography, 38, 40

Wynn, Steve, 242, 245, 248

Wyoming: and demarcating American West, 8; and gambling, 238; and Mormon culture region, 145, 152, 155; Native Americans of, 187. *See also specific cities and places*

Yellowstone National Park, 31, 112

YMCA, 297

Yorktown, 114

Yosemite National Park, 31

Yosemite Valley, 112

Young, Brigham: and community, 151, 155, 158; and frontiering experience, 152; and irrigation, 140, 142; and land tenure, 103, 104; and land use, 144, 148; as leader, 138, 139, 160 n. 10; myths about, 147; and railroads, 150; and Salt Lake City, 154; and settlement patterns, 103, 154, 158; and State of Deseret, 142–43, 145, 153, 155, 161 n. 19, 163–64 n. 42; and urban geography, 103, 140; and utopianism, 149; and ZCMI, 157–58

Young, Robert, 300

Young, Terrence, 40

Yucca Mountain, 100

ZCMI (Zion's Cooperative Mercantile Institution), 157–58

Zelinsky, Wilbur, 85, 92

zero-sum game, 104

Zuni–Cibola National Historic Site, 125

Zuni pueblo, 118, *119*